CONTEMPORARY
LATIN AMERICA

A HISTORY OF THE CONTEMPORARY WORLD

General Editor: Keith Robbins

This series offers an historical perspective on the development of the contemporary world. Each of the books examines a particular region or a global theme as it has evolved in the recent past. The focus is primarily on the period since the 1980s but authors provide deeper context wherever necessary. While all the volumes offer an historical framework for analysis, the books are written for an interdisciplinary audience and assume no prior knowledge on the part of readers.

Published

Contemporary America
M. J. Heale

Contemporary Global Economy
Alfred E. Eckes, Jr.

Contemporary Japan, Second Edition
Jeff Kingston

Contemporary Latin America
Robert H. Holden & Rina Villars

In Preparation

Contemporary China
Yongnian Zheng

Contemporary South Asia
David Hall-Matthews

CONTEMPORARY
LATIN AMERICA
1970 TO THE PRESENT

ROBERT H. HOLDEN
AND RINA VILLARS

A John Wiley & Sons, Ltd., Publication

Blackwell Publishing was acquired by John Wiley & Sons in February 2007. Blackwell's publishing program has been merged with Wiley's global Scientific, Technical, and Medical business to form Wiley-Blackwell.

Registered Office
John Wiley & Sons Ltd, The Atrium, Southern Gate, Chichester, West Sussex, PO19 8SQ, UK

Editorial Offices
350 Main Street, Malden, MA 02148-5020, USA
9600 Garsington Road, Oxford, OX4 2DQ, UK
The Atrium, Southern Gate, Chichester, West Sussex, PO19 8SQ, UK

For details of our global editorial offices, for customer services, and for information about how to apply for permission to reuse the copyright material in this book please see our website at www.wiley.com/wiley-blackwell.

Library of Congress Cataloging-in-Publication Data
Holden, Robert H.
  Contemporary Latin America : 1970 to the present / Robert H. Holden, Rina Villars.
      pages cm. – (History of the contemporary world)
    ISBN 978-1-4051-3970-0 (hardback) – ISBN 978-1-4051-3971-7 (paper)   1. Latin America–History–1980–   2. Latin America–History–20th century.   I. Villars, Rina.   II. Title.
  F1414.3.H65 2013
  980–dc23

                                    2012016773

A catalog record for this book is available from the British Library.

Cover image: Bolivia's new President Evo Morales, right, and the President of Venezuela, Hugo Chavez, wave from the balcony of the presidential palace in La Paz as they watch an Oruro carnival parade, Monday, January 23, 2006. Photo © PA Photos / AP Photo / Martin Mejia.
Cover design: www.simonlevyassociated.co.uk

Set in 10 on 12.5 pt Minion by Toppan Best-set Premedia Limited
Printed in Malaysia by Ho Printing (M) Sdn Bhd
1   2013

Contents

List of Maps, Figures and Tables

Series Editor's Preface

The contemporary world frequently presents a baffling spectacle: "New world orders" come and go; "Clashes of civilizations" seem imminent if not actual; "Peace dividends" appear easily lost in the post; terrorism and "wars on terror" occupy the headlines. "Mature" states live alongside "failed" states in mutual apprehension. The "rules" of the international game, in these circumstances, are difficult to discern. What "international law" is, or is not, remains enduringly problematic. Certainly it is a world in which there are still frontiers, borders and boundaries but both metaphorically and in reality they are difficult to patrol and maintain. "Asylum" occupies the headlines as populations shift across continents, driven by fear. Other migrants simply seek a better standard of living. The organs of the "international community," though frequently invoked, look inadequate to deal with the myriad problems confronting the world. Climate change, however induced, is not susceptible to national control. Famine seems endemic in certain countries. Population pressures threaten finite resources. It is in this context that globalization, however understood, is both demonized and lauded.

Such a list of contemporary problems could be amplified in detail and almost indefinitely extended. It is a complex world, ripe for investigation in this ambitious new series of books. "Contemporary," of course, is always difficult to define. The focus in this series is on the evolution of the world since the 1980s. As time passes, and as the volumes appear, it no longer seems sensible to equate "the world since 1945" with "contemporary history." The legacy of the "Cold War" lingers on but it is emphatically "in the background." The fuzziness about "the 1980s" is deliberate. No single year ever carries the same significance across the globe. Authors are therefore establishing their own precise starting points, within the overall "contemporary" framework.

The series treats the history of particular regions, countries or continents but does so in full awareness that such histories, for all their continuing distinctiveness, can only rarely be considered apart from the history of the world as a whole. Economic, demographic, environmental and religious issues transcend state, regional or continental boundaries. Just as the world itself struggles to reconcile diversity and individuality with unity and common purpose, so do the authors of these volumes. The concept is challenging. Authors have been selected who sit loosely on their disciplinary identity – whether that be as historians, political scientists or students of international relations. The task is to integrate as many aspects of contemporary life as possible in an accessible manner.

A volume on Latin America confronts the question of identity head-on. It is a region, as this volume so amply demonstrates, which exhibits in certain aspects a unity that transcends the reality of its existence as a collection of states. That unity points to a common "Latin" heritage, one which still leaves behind a clear political, social and cultural legacy. The past still complicates political and constitutional evolution and explains turbulent patterns, regarded externally as "typically" Latin American. Yet a broad brush is inadequate. The volume brings out great, and arguably increasing, diversity – in economic performance, in political stability, in cultural vitality – as between individual states. Stock perceptions of the region as "Spanish" or "Catholic" no longer serve in a situation of increasing religious and linguistic pluralism. This volume itself ranges impressively across many subjects as it brings out Latin America's puzzling but increasingly globally significant amalgams.

Keith Robbins

Acknowledgments

We are grateful for the early encouragement and advice of a number of friends, especially Héctor Ghiretti, Pedro Gil, Ed O'Brien, Juan Fernando Segovia and Eric Zolov. Brian Loveman, ever generous with his time, read the manuscript with his customary diligence, correcting mistakes and making us rethink some of our views. We thank the anonymous referees for their good advice, and the outstanding team of editors at Wiley-Blackwell who oversaw this project. No one contributed more to this volume than the staff of the Perry Library of Old Dominion University, who promptly and cheerfully bought or borrowed whatever the library's collection lacked. Finally, we are happy to thank Matthew T. Hall, Mary K. McKnight and Christopher C. White, students in Old Dominion's Graduate Program in International Studies, for their work as research assistants.

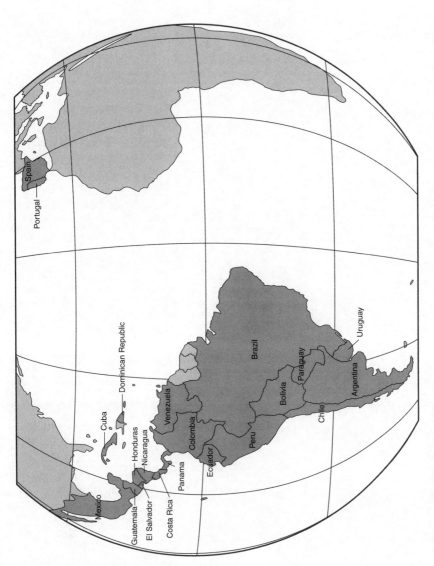

Map 0.1 The Hispanic world.

Part I

Latin America in a World Setting

Introduction

Revolts against Spanish and Portuguese rule in the Americas after 1808 produced the nineteen countries that compose Latin America today. Yet no era in
the post-independence histories of these countries can match the depth and
scope of change that swept over their peoples in the decades after about 1970.
The purpose of this book is to identify and weigh the distinctive local, national,
regional and global dimensions of those changes.

Because of the compact nature of the period covered in this book, we opted
to organize Latin America's history since about 1970 around four big themes,
each the subject of a separate "Part": Government (II), Wealth (III), Culture
(IV) and Communities (V). None outranks the others in importance, nor can
any stand alone as the ultimate "cause" of change. We have chosen them
because a *survey* of Latin America's history since 1970 should supply the broadest view of the essential aspects of the topic. We believe that these themes (plus
that of beliefs, the subject of Chapter 2) encompass what is most vital to know
about the history of any given human society. None can be plausibly analyzed
without reference to their global dimensions, which every chapter takes into
account.

Thus, change after about 1970 will be the core historical problem of each of
the chapters that follow. While in most cases the evidence for epochal change
revealed itself only in the 1980s, our account begins with the previous decade
because the multiple crises of the 1970s opened the door for the reforms that
would mark the 1980s.

Understanding change requires clarity about the subject of change. The
introductions to each of the parts that follow this one will therefore define the
theme and explain its significance in the larger context of Latin American
history.

Contemporary Latin America: 1970 to the Present, First Edition. Robert H. Holden and Rina Villars.
© 2013 Robert H. Holden and Rina Villars. Published 2013 by Blackwell Publishing Ltd.

In the first chapter, we elaborate our general interpretation of the trends of the last four decades: toward liberalization, by which we mean a loosening of restraints, a tendency toward inclusiveness, an openness to experimentation. On balance, of course, there is much more evidence of continuity than of change, as one would expect in a period of such short duration. And not every kind of change has come down on the side of liberalization.

Moreover, the movement toward liberalization in the areas that constitute the topics of Parts II to V can be expected, if carried far enough, to generate resistance and countertrends. Evidence for both is not hard to find, as we will see.

In Chapter 1, we set out to define the region, survey its more distant past, and situate it globally. We go on in Chapter 2 to characterize the array of beliefs and values that ultimately account for the distinctiveness of our nineteen countries, and thus for their status as a separate world region or civilization.

Chapter 1

What Is Latin America?

"Latin America" as the preeminent name of the lands to the south of the United States first emerged in the mid-1850s. Until then, they were normally referred to as "Spanish America" or "South America" by both English and Spanish speakers. While the origins of the term remain controversial among historians, it seems likely that two trends intersected that together gave rise to a preference for "Latin America." The first was the belief that the people of the world could be divided into separate races, each with their own distinctive temperaments and capacities. Race as the dominant explanation for the material progress of some peoples and the backwardness of others would gain currency everywhere in the nineteenth century. Second, as leading thinkers in the new republics worried increasingly about the political and cultural challenges posed by the United States, they sought to distinguish between what some considered a northern "race" of Anglo-Saxons or Yankees, on the one hand, and a contrasting "race" of Latins, on the other. At the same time, France popularized the name "Latin America" in the 1860s when it tried to justify its military invasion and occupation of Mexico by claiming a shared "Latin" racial and linguistic legacy with Mexico and the rest of the territories south of the United States. By the late nineteenth century, "Latin America" had become the preferred designation. In a nutshell, acceptance of the qualifier "Latin" seems to have represented an attempt to endow a strictly linguistic phenomenon (the strong dependence of Spanish, Portuguese and French on the Latin language) with a wholly imaginary Latin ethnicity. Even linguistically, of course, "Latin America" falls short in view of the continued vitality of hundreds of indigenous languages in most of the eighteen countries whose official language is Spanish, or in Portuguese-speaking Brazil.

Contemporary Latin America: 1970 to the Present, First Edition. Robert H. Holden and Rina Villars.
© 2013 Robert H. Holden and Rina Villars. Published 2013 by Blackwell Publishing Ltd.

"Latin America" seems even less appropriate when applied to all the lands south of the United States, a practice not uncommon among scholars of the region nor within some international organizations like the World Bank and the UN's Economic Commission for Latin America. This maximal interpretation of the region's limits would encompass thirty-three independent, self-governing states and the fourteen dependencies of three European countries (France, the Netherlands and the United Kingdom) and of the United States. While numerous, all the dependencies are clustered in the Caribbean Basin (except for the UK's Falkland Islands) and together they account for no more than 1% of the population and one-half of 1% of all the territory to the south of the United States. Of the thirty-three independent states that make up the maximal definition, half (sixteen) gained their sovereignty in the twentieth century and lie in the Caribbean Basin, but account for less than 4% of today's population and only 3% of the territory to the south of the United States. All sixteen had been British territory since at least the eighteenth century except for Cuba (a Spanish colony until 1898, then a U.S. protectorate until 1934), Panama (a province of Colombia until 1903) and Suriname (a colony of the Netherlands until 1975).

In the eighteen other countries, political independence and decolonization were a nineteenth-century affair. They are: Argentina, Bolivia, Brazil, Chile, Colombia, Costa Rica, the Dominican Republic, Ecuador, El Salvador, Guatemala, Haiti, Honduras, Mexico, Nicaragua, Paraguay, Peru, Uruguay and Venezuela. If we drop the formerly French possession of Haiti (overwhelmingly Afro-American in culture) and add Cuba and Panama to the list, we find these nineteen countries comprise 97% of the territory and 96% of the population south of the United States. They share some important characteristics that justify treating them as a cohesive entity:

- All of them except Brazil (formerly a possession of the Portuguese monarchy) were settled, colonized and governed for at least three centuries by the monarchy of Spain.
- A common process of independence (1810 to 1825) complemented the shared experience of three centuries of Spanish or Portuguese rule. The only exceptions are the island nations of Cuba and the Dominican Republic.
- During the nearly two centuries of self-rule that Brazil and most of Spain's former territories have passed through since the 1820s, turbulence and violence, including frequent disruptions of constitutional order and authoritarian rule, have defined their political histories. Writing in the late 1970s, the social scientist and future Brazilian president, Fernando Henrique Cardoso, could still compare the status of democracy in Latin America to that of an "exotic plant." Not even today would most scholars consider any

of the nineteen to be fully consolidated democracies, with the possible exceptions of Chile, Costa Rica and Uruguay.

- Spanish is the official language in eighteen of the nineteen countries, while Portuguese is spoken in Brazil; both reign over a diversity of indigenous languages. Another important cultural trait was the near-monolithic adherence, until the late twentieth century, to the Roman Catholic religion in all nineteen countries.

- Finally, the economic geography of the nineteen countries reveals important regional consistencies. The World Bank, for example, classifies all the world's economies as either developed (industrialized countries with high incomes and high standards of living) or developing economies (countries with low or mid-level incomes). All nineteen are "developing" economies, and their average level of development (as measured by life expectancy, education and purchasing power) is the highest of all the developing world regions. However, despite their *average* superiority in standard-of-living compared to other developing regions, our nineteen countries stand out in global terms as a region of extreme inequality of income. In the late 1990s, in most of the nineteen, the richest 10% of individuals were receiving 40% to 47% of total income while the poorest 20% were earning 2% to 4% of total income. Few countries in the world could match that record.

Taken together, these features indicate that in their common political history, geographical proximity, economies and basic cultural orientation, the eighteen Spanish-speaking countries and Portuguese-speaking Brazil (Table 1.1) make up a coherent and distinctive region, and thus constitute what we will refer to throughout this book as "Latin America." We exclude Puerto Rico, despite its people's success in preserving much of the culture that it inherited from its 400-year experience as a realm of the Spanish monarchy. Since its forced incorporation into the United States in 1898, followed in 1917 by the imposition of U.S. citizenship on its people, Puerto Rico has been largely isolated from the dominant patterns of social, economic and political change that will occupy us in this book.

What we have just defined as Latin America is sometimes referred to as "Iberoamerica" or "Hispanic America." "Iberia" was the ancient name for the peninsula now constituted by the modern nations of Spain and Portugal. "Hispanic" derives from the Latin *Hispania*, the name the Romans gave the Iberian peninsula when it was a province of their empire. Portugal and (by extension) Brazil can be associated with a more fanciful "Lusitanian" legacy, a name derived from *Lusitanus*, the Roman designation for the part of western Hispania out of which Portugal would one day emerge. The fact that the Romans called all of the Iberian peninsula "Hispania," of which "Lusitania" was a part, might justify calling both Brazil and the Spanish-speaking republics

Table 1.1 Latin America: basic demography, living standards and history. Based on data from *South America, Central America and the Caribbean 2006* (London: Routledge, 2006); United Nations Development Program, Human Development Report 2010; World Population Prospects, the 2010 Revision (UN Population Division, http://esa.un.org/unpd/wpp/Excel-Data/population.htm).

	Ex-metropolis[1] (after c. 1800)	Year of Independence	Population 2010 est. (UN Pop. Div.)	Area (km sq.). Includes inland water	HDI 1980	HDI 2010	Ave. annual HDI growth rate (%)
Argentina[1]	Spain	1816	40,412,000	2,780,403	0.66	0.78	0.56
Bolivia	Spain	1825	9,930,000	1,098,581	..	0.64	..
Brazil	Portugal	1822	194,946,000	8,547,404	..	0.70	0.85
Chile	Spain	1818	17,114,000	756,096	0.61	0.78	0.85
Colombia	Spain	1819	46,295,000	1,141,748	0.54	0.69	0.83
Costa Rica	Spain, Mexico, United Provinces of Central America	1821, 1823, 1838	4,659,000	51,100	0.60	0.73	0.63
Cuba	Spain, United States	1898, 1934	11,258,000	110,860	..	..	
Dominican Republic, the	Spain, Haiti, Spain	1822, 1844, 1865	9,927,000	48,734	..	0.66	0.62
Ecuador	Spain, Gran Colombia	1822, 1830	14,465,000	272,045	0.58	0.70	0.62
El Salvador	Spain, Mexico, United Provinces of Central America	1821, 1823, 1838	6,193,000	21,041	0.46	0.66	1.23

Guatemala	Spain, Mexico, United Provinces of Central America	1821, 1823, 1838	14,389,000	108,889	0.41	0.56	1.05
Honduras	Spain, Mexico, United Provinces of Central America	1821, 1823, 1838	7,601,000	112,492	0.44	0.60	1.09
Mexico	Spain	1821	113,423,000	1,964,375	0.58	0.75	0.85
Nicaragua	Spain, Mexico, United Provinces of Central America	1821, 1823, 1838	5,788,000	130,373	0.44	0.57	0.84
Panama	Colombia	1903	3,517,000	75,517	0.61	0.76	0.69
Paraguay	Spain	1811	6,455,000	406,752	0.53	0.64	0.64
Peru	Spain	1821	29,077,000	1,285,216	0.56	0.72	0.85
Uruguay	Spain	1825	3,369,000	176,215	..	0.77	0.77
Venezuela	Spain, Gran Colombia	1819, 1830	28,980,000	916,445	0.61	0.70	0.44
Totals and averages			**567,798,000**	**20,004,286**	**0.54**	**0.69**	**0.80**

¹Argentina's area includes Antarctic claim; HDI is the UN Development Program's Human Development Index.

together "Hispanic America." While contemporary usage tends to associate "Hispanic" exclusively with Spain and the Spanish language, the peninsular scope of "Hispania" in Roman times reminds us of the extremely close affinity between the cultures and languages of Spain and Portugal, and thus between Brazil today and the Spanish-speaking countries of Latin America. Along with most of the rest of Iberia, the Christian territories of the western third of the peninsula were conquered by the Islamic Umayyad Empire in 715 AD. The lands that would one day become known as Portugal thus participated in the *reconquista* or reconquest of Iberia by Christian armies, an enterprise that would continue until 1492. During the reconquest, the lands that would someday comprise the nation of Portugal came under the control of the kingdom of Castile y León, the preeminent power on the peninsula. When Portugal emerged as an independent kingdom in the twelfth century, it still lacked both a common language and a distinct tradition, for it had come into existence largely as a result of fortuitous politico-military developments arising from feudalism and the reconquest. Portuguese did not take its place as a national language distinct from Spanish (but strongly resembling it) until the early fourteenth century. Fear of reabsorption into the Spanish-speaking part of the peninsula persisted for centuries, but became a reality only once, when King Philip II of Castile seized Portugal in 1581. An armed revolt against Castile in 1640 resulted in the restoration of Portuguese independence, under the rule of the Braganza family.

Thus, although they have been politically separate for the better part of a millennium, Spain and Portugal (and their former American territories) nevertheless share a distinctive legacy of ideas, values and beliefs whose influence can be seen in literature, law, social custom, politics, religion, architecture and the arts. The Spanish monarchy in particular set out to make its New World kingdoms even more centralized, homogeneous, religiously orthodox and culturally unified than its own peninsular kingdoms. That policy was largely successful, and accounts for the remarkable sense of trans-national solidarity and shared values that has made Latin America the world's largest multinational culture zone – both more unified and more diverse than Europe, as the Mexican writer Carlos Fuentes has pointed out.[1] In places with high concentrations of indigenous and Afro-American peoples, customs and beliefs associated with those cultures continue to thrive, though invariably subordinated to an Iberian-oriented national culture.

Regardless of their identity as citizens of one country or another, or as members of particular ethnic groups or social classes, the peoples of the region habitually reflect on their experiences across national boundaries, and often seek to coordinate their responses to similar situations. In doing so, they act on the presumption that they share something larger, and more intangible, than the hard political facts of their common past.

An example in action was the university reform movement, launched by the students of a single Argentine university in 1918. Within a decade, it swept Latin America, transforming students into a potent interest group almost everywhere, while profoundly altering the political landscape. Similarly, the example of the Cuban revolution of 1959 ignited insurrectionary movements across the region, from Mexico to Argentina, in the 1960s and 1970s. Numerous other instances could be plucked from the realms of literature, music and other forms of popular entertainment. The Colombian writer Gabriel García Márquez's great novel *Cien Años de Soledad* (*One Hundred Years of Solitude*) topped the bestseller lists in every country of the region soon after it was published in 1967. Two years later, the Peruvian songwriter, Daniel Camino Díez, wrote "Los Cien Años de Macondo," celebrating the novel's main characters. Numerous singers recorded it, but the Mexican singer Oscar Chávez's version became a hit everywhere, as radio stations from rural Honduras to Santiago de Chile played the song repeatedly, inspiring many listeners to read the novel for the first time. This and countless other episodes like it cannot be explained by a common language alone, but above all by a common history and a common cultural orientation.

History

As recently as the beginning of the last quarter of the eighteenth century, most of the Americas had been part of the overseas territory of some European empire. Then, first Great Britain (between 1776 and 1783) and later Spain and Portugal (between 1810 and 1825) lost control of most of their American possessions in separate wars for independence. Haiti's African slaves wrested their land from France in 1804. Yet despite the passage of nearly two centuries (in the case of Spain and Portugal) or more (in the case of the British seaboard colonies) nothing about their past remains more consequential than the fact that they were founded, populated and ruled by one or the other of these European powers. By the middle of the sixteenth century, Spain had completed the conquest of the two main centers of American civilization, that of the Aztec empire of Mexico and the even larger Inca empire of western South America. Soon, the Spanish monarchy would effectively claim sovereignty over a contiguous territory that was among the largest of any empire in history. Stretching from the central plains of what is now the United States to the tip of South America, the bulk of Spain's America remained under its dominion until the early 1800s, except for a few Caribbean insular possessions and coastal strips acquired by Britain, France and the Netherlands in the seventeenth century. Portugal, at first confining its American claim to the Brazilian littoral, succeeded in pushing that frontier inward over the centuries. The acceleration of that process by post-colonial governments made Brazil the largest country in Latin America and the fifth-largest in the world.

But the territorial extent of these conquests is not the most significant aspect of Iberian rule in the Americas. Rather, it was both the *duration* of that rule and its relatively *unmediated* and therefore directly influential nature that mattered most in the history of Latin America. Even today, those three centuries of imperial rule (from the early 1500s to the early 1800s) exceed the period of independent status by more than a third. In other words, not until the early decades of the twenty-second century will the peoples of Latin America be able to say that their lands have been self-governing for as many years as they were governed by the monarchies of Spain and Portugal.

The Spanish and Portuguese presence in America was long-lasting, penetrating and vigorous, driven by immigration from Iberia itself and by the legal premise that the land and its resources were the property of the monarchy, and the people were its subjects, the equals of those of Iberia itself. By contrast, British rule of the Indian subcontinent exceeded a century in duration, but was mediated by native princes accountable to British colonial overseers who generally remained aloof from Indian society, while British immigration was practically nil. Of course, the great distance that separated America from Iberia and the very vastness of the overseas realms moderated the impact of Iberian control. The prohibitive cost of establishing a standing army throughout the continent to enforce every royal dictum, and the long delays in two-way communication and transportation, encouraged a certain flexibility, and even occasional defiance on the part of Spain's American bureaucrats.

Yet, to an extent unmatched anywhere else, a European settler minority implanted its language, religion, manners, morality, political institutions and economic policies across a diverse aggregation of non-European people. To be sure, the process was accompanied, especially in its early years, by the violence, intolerance and intentional cruelty altogether characteristic of European civilization in the sixteenth century. The magnitude of the native American population at the time of the conquest remains a deeply contentious subject among historians; estimates range from 7.5 million to 80 million or even more. What is not in doubt, however, is that many millions of indigenous peoples died during the first century of European rule, mainly as a result of the spread of such exclusively Eurasian diseases as smallpox and measles to which the Indians had no immunity. Other leading causes of mortality were the massive enslavement of the indigenous peoples during the first few decades of Spanish and Portuguese rule, particularly in the Caribbean zone, Central America and Brazil, and of course the many deaths resulting from direct military engagements, the forced migrations caused by military invasion, and by subsequent campaigns of pacification and forced relocation aimed at concentrating the surviving populations for administrative purposes.

Yet, of the Spanish conquest and settlement of the Americas, it is also necessary to acknowledge that no European overseas empire ever sought more conscientiously to define and protect the rights and interests of the indigenous peoples. Often, those efforts were frustrated and flouted by corrupt and disloyal Spaniards, some of whom were imprisoned or executed for their crimes. But the Spanish crown's interest in protecting the Indian peoples and their ways nevertheless worked to preserve the cultural and ethnical pluralism that characterizes much of Latin America today. Portuguese efforts to defend the Indians of Brazil were considerably less intensive, however, and as a result the Indians of Brazil continued to be enslaved on a massive scale up to the middle of the eighteenth century, when the monarchy took steps to eradicate all forms of indigenous forced labor. After independence in 1821, however, Brazil's indigenous peoples were again subjected to enslavement and other forms of forced labor.

In both empires, a totally different policy was applied to Africans and people of African descent. Unlike the Indians, whose principal claim to freedom was their status as subjects of the monarchy, Africans had been purchased from African slave traders who in turn had captured them (at least in theory) in war. As such, under prevailing European legal norms, their enslavement and that of their offspring remained licit, as long as the war in which they were captured could be considered "just." As the first European power to establish stable trade relations with the inhabitants of the West African coastal ports, Portugal began importing African slaves on a massive scale in the late sixteenth century to work on its Brazilian sugar plantations. In 1888, Brazil was the last country in the western hemisphere to emancipate its African slaves. Only two years before that, Spain freed the Africans still enslaved in its colony of Cuba. In the rest of Spanish America, where African slavery was a relatively minor feature of the national economies, all the governments had abolished slavery and emancipated African slaves by 1860.

The social, cultural and demographic consequences of this massive and long-term wave of involuntary African immigration varied considerably according to the relative weight of slavery in the local economies. By the late eighteenth century, Brazil was home to about 1 million African slaves, or one-third of all the slaves in the western hemisphere. About 1.2 million resided in the Caribbean islands, almost entirely in the ones controlled by Great Britain and France. The dependence on slavery in Brazil and the islands derived from the predominant role of plantation agriculture – above all, that of sugar – in the local economies. About 20% of the remaining African slaves in the Americas could be found in the United States and only about 9% in the mainland territories of the Spanish monarchy. During the nineteenth century, the population of African slaves continued to rise in Brazil, to some 1.5 million by 1872, and in Cuba, where the slave population jumped from about 80,000 in the late eighteenth century to about 400,000 in the mid-nineteenth century in response to rising worldwide demand for sugar and its byproducts, such as rum and molasses. Nowhere, however, had African slavery grown faster than in the plantation-agriculture sector of the U.S. economy, which employed 4 million slaves at the start of the Civil War in 1861, their numbers having leapt seven-fold (from about 575,000) since the late eighteenth century.

Despite the continuing powerful influence of the Indian and African ele-ments of Latin American culture in certain places, it is the manifold legacies of Iberian rule that continue to frame the deepest currents of contemporary Latin American life. The sixteenth-century boundaries of several *audiencias* (the principal colonial-era administrative and judicial organ) roughly defined the limits of such modern nations as Bolivia, Colombia, Ecuador and Peru. Many of today's capital cities were once the seats of *audiencias*. Since each *audiencia* was understood to be a separate realm subject to the personal rule of the monarch (rather than as a constituent element of a greater Spanish empire), it is not surprising that little serious thought was given to creating a single "Latin American" nation when Spain and Portugal lost their American lands between 1810 and 1825. Another legacy descended from the notably lax discipline of colonial administration, and its tendency to beget abundant opportunities for patronage, peculation and self-dealing – customs still characteristic of contemporary Latin American government, and regularly identified today as impediments to the consolidation of democracy. Similarly, the frequent blurring in contemporary Latin America of executive, legislative and judicial powers follows the custom of combining them in single institu-tions during the three centuries of colonial rule. Perhaps the deepest political imprint of the colonial past was not a "something" but a "nothing" – i.e., the near-absence of representative political institutions and traditions of self-government.

Spain's American realms gained their independence and adopted republican forms of government around 1821, at what seemed to be a propitious moment. A wave of political change in favor of representative government, roused by the American (1776) and then the French (1789) revolutions, swept across much of Europe and the English-speaking world, undermining or destroying absolutist and aristocratic forms of government and opening a new age in the political history of humankind. The only independent Latin American country to preserve the monarchical form of government (until 1889) was Brazil, but even it was founded on a written constitution that limited the power of the emperor.

The self-governing polities that proclaimed their independence from Spain bore the gargantuan burden of seeking a workable consensus in favor of completely novel, republican systems of government. Their frequent failures to achieve consensus during the first half-century or so of independence and beyond were accompanied by violent instability in the political sphere, and the entrenchment of habits that would give rise to certain features of Latin American politics – lawlessness, militarism, personalism and dictatorship – that thrived well into the twentieth century. As the historian Charles Gibson observed in the 1960s, Latin America's "escape from the colonial past remains much less complete than in the United States."[2] Thus, despite the auspicious timing of Latin America's independence movements, and the subsequent establishment of formally democratic procedures and institutions, the region's experience with democracy could only be described as fragile and fleeting until the 1980s, the eighteenth decade of independent rule, when Latin America entered a period of transition that compares in significance to two earlier turning points.

The first was the 1850s to the 1870s, a moment that marked the end of three to five decades of intense political disorder and economic stagnation. Authoritarian and frequently dictatorial governments oversaw a period of relative stability and growth while asserting their loyalty to the reigning ideas and values of the North Atlantic world. Chief among those ideas were the principles of economic freedom, the racial supremacy of Europeans, the need for leadership by an educated elite, and secularism in public life. Notably absent, and even explicitly rejected in some quarters, were democracy and individual rights.

The second turning point occurred in the 1920s and intensified during the 1930s and 40s. If Latin America's leadership had been characterized by an outward-looking posture before the 1920s, by the middle of the twentieth century it had become notably inward looking and nationalistic. Governments and political parties now sought to mobilize and incorporate excluded or marginalized groups. Displacing the economic leadership of both national and foreign entrepreneurs, they assumed responsibility for rapid industrialization and job-creating growth. The turn was conditioned by pressure from the rising population of urban and middle-class sectors for two kinds of changes: political equality and economic prosperity. The international political, economic and cultural dislocations provoked by Europe's Great War of 1914–1918 further contributed to the pressure for change in Latin America. The European catastrophe enhanced the appeal, well beyond the borders of Europe, of new, anti-liberal political ideologies such as communism and fascism. The worldwide economic setbacks of the Great Depression of 1929–1940 only added to the luster of these ideas and the political parties organized by their advocates, while diminishing the appeal of capitalism. Turning away from the selective liberalism of the previous era, away from one-sided economic policies that gambled on rising foreign demand for the region's agricultural and industrial commodities, Latin America gradually shifted toward a new era of populist politics, state-directed economic planning and industrialization, and increasingly politicized military forces.

But simultaneously restructuring the economy, maintaining stable growth and satisfying popular demands for genuine political participation, while checking tendencies that could lead to violent disorder, proved to be beyond the capacity of any Latin American government for more than periods measured in months, not years. Evidence of economic growth and modernization could be seen throughout the region in the 1940s, 1950s and 1960s. But it was ultimately unsustainable, and it was also clear that economic reforms alone were not the answer. A surge of violent, revolutionary political movements, led by Marxists convinced of the futility of conventional strategies for political and economic reform, seriously threatened the social order in the 1960s and 1970s. A rejoinder from the armed forces, usually with the aid of the U.S. government, in the form of military dictatorships that sought to purge their countries of ideas associated with Marxism, communism or even moderate reform, swept Latin America in those decades. In a desperate effort to sustain the strategy of state-led economic modernization, governments across the region borrowed dollars on a colossal scale in the 1970s and early 1980s. It was a disastrous decision. The foreign debt burden threatened to crush already-crippled economies just as a wave of military-directed political repression, unmatched in Latin American history, was peaking, from Guatemala to Argentina.

A new era dawned in the 1980s. In one country after another, governments took steps to liberalize national economies. Support for militaristic solutions to political conflict evaporated across the region as civilian politicians chosen in free elections took office everywhere but in Cuba. While the first trend could be interpreted as a retreat to pre-1930s market-oriented economic policies, there was no precedent in Latin American history for what, by the 1990s, seemed to be the simultaneous collapse of militarism and the rise of electoral democracy. While a new political norm – the inadmissibility of militarism and military rule – gradually began to command universal assent, coup attempts and threats did not completely disappear. Nor had some forgotten that, for a few years in the late 1950s and early 1960s, a move away from dictatorship and toward democracy in Latin America had also been declared. "The long age of dictators in Latin America is finally in its twilight," wrote *New York Times* correspondent Tad Szulc in 1959. "Indications are that democracy, so late in coming and still taking its first shaky and tentative steps forward, is here to stay in Latin America."[3] The "twilight of the dictators" instead ushered in two decades of military dictatorship.

Since the late 1970s, the central tendency of Latin America's history may be summed up in one word: "liberalization." In this respect, its history matched the general trend of world history during the same period in favor of openness and personal freedom in practically every realm of human experience. Dictatorial governments, most spectacularly those of the communist Union of Soviet Socialist Republics (USSR) and the countries of eastern and central Europe in which the USSR imposed communism after World War II, gave way to popularly elected ones that invariably pronounced themselves in favor of human rights and personal liberties. In the ex-communist bloc, centralized systems of economic planning and control surrendered a good deal of authority to the market and the principle of individual choice. In the non-communist West, beliefs and traditions governing personal conduct and social life that had been widely taken for granted before the 1970s began to shred as cultural and legislative barriers to individual freedom and personal expression fell. Of course, neither on a world scale, nor at the regional level of Latin America, nor at the level of individual countries, did liberalization proceed in a linear, consistent, orderly or predictable way. Nor can it be said that liberalization is irrevocable or inevitable; indeed, resistance to it in all its forms has been easy to find in Latin America ever since the trend emerged in the 1970s. In fact, by about 2000, signs of deep disenchantment with economic liberalization were multiplying. As a result, the trend stagnated in some places and was partially reversed in others.

Latin America and the World

Liberalization was hastened and joined by a mighty force that came to be widely known in the 1980s as globalization, a new word for a reality that has been with us since the sixteenth century, when first Portugal and then Spain linked Africa, America, Asia and Europe in worldwide networks of commerce, migration, conquest and cultural exchange that have been widening ever since. Like other regions, no period or aspect of Latin America's history can be understood apart from the global context in which it unfolded. Starting with the first encounter of Europeans and Americans in 1492, many of the most dramatic changes in the region took shape as manifestations of global trends readily apparent elsewhere. At the same time, Latin America itself passed into the stream of global social change, affecting other world regions and then coming home again, "globalized." Unbounded and diffuse, uncontrolled by any single power center, and subject to rates of acceleration determined largely by the technological imagination, globalization continues to intensify and multiply the interaction of peoples, places, ideas and institutions across regional boundaries. In that sense, globalization *expresses* liberalization. And yet, its capacity to absorb and relaunch ideas and technologies can be exploited in the service of anything at all, including de-liberalization and de-globalization.

Initially weighted heavily toward the Iberian peninsula, the global dimension of Latin American history in short order came to embrace not just Spain and Portugal but also the rest of western Europe, as well as Africa and Asia. As the Iberian monarchies expanded their commercial and territorial reach, other European powers – above all, the British, the Dutch and the French – created rival global networks that interrupted, overlapped or replaced those of the Iberian monarchies. In the nineteenth century, the rise to worldwide dominance of British commercial, maritime and financial power, and the simultaneous territorial and economic expansion of the United States of America, strongly reweighted the global dimension of Latin American history. While the Iberian and broadly European nodes of global contact retained much of their authority in the realm of ideas, beliefs and values, the two great English-speaking powers of the North Atlantic embodied the tremendous transformative capacities of the new philosophy of liberalism, in the realms of both economics (free-market capitalism) and politics (representative govern-ment and the rule of law). Powerfully attractive to some in Latin America as models to be imitated, to others Britain and the United States represented interests that might be exploited for national or individual gain as long as they were kept at arm's length. Still others saw in them serious threats to Latin America's political and economic freedom or to the region's distinctive beliefs, customs and values.

In the geography of globalization, the United States by the 1920s edged out Britain as the single most powerful source of foreign influence in Latin America, a position it has yet to cede to anyone else. That continuity is matched by the preservation of the basic three-fold response to that influence among Latin Americans. Nevertheless, the power of the United States in Latin America has more often been exaggerated than underestimated. As globalization intensified and accelerated after the 1970s, opportunities for interaction with the United States multiplied but so did those with other centers of influence, in ways that sometimes diluted or undercut the U.S. presence in Latin America. Still, unevenness remains characteristic of global interactions everywhere, and looking back over the course of the last five centuries of the region's history, it seems clear that two places, Iberia and the United States, continue to be the strongest poles of global interaction with Latin America despite the surging influence of Asia and non-Iberian Europe over the last four decades. Limiting ourselves just to the period covered in this book, we could say that some of the most dramatic changes that we will discuss in the following pages, such as liberalization in economic policy and the turn away from military to civilian rule through elections, were Latin American manifestations of global trends. So were the clamor for human rights and democracy, as well as the rise of local economic development initiatives and a stunning diversity of social move-ments. During the same period, Latin American idiosyncrasies were themselves globalized; intellectual novelties like liberation theology and dependency theory, the romanticization of guerrilla warfare, lessons learned in the ongoing debt crisis, and distinctively "Latin" music were received elsewhere and then came home, "globalized." Thus it would be wrong to think of Latin America, or any place, as a mere receptor of global trends. Latin America has also shaped those trends by exporting its own distinctive habits, institutions and values in one form or another. A core premise of this book is that Latin America constitutes a distinct civilization with its own constellations of beliefs, and coherent patterns of cultural and social life whose changes and continuities can be identified and analyzed over time, from Mexico to the Southern Cone.

It should be clear, then, that we do not define globalization as universalization, westernization or modernization; nor do we consider it limited to economic matters. The world is not marching toward a grand fusion of ideas, values or material cultures. The kinds of differences in practices and beliefs that characterize the globe's many distinct human collectivities are for the most deeply embedded rather than superficial. Their practices and beliefs change slowly, and even as they do so, they continue to distinguish themselves. In weighing the distinctive local, national, regional and global dimensions of the changes that have swept Latin America since 1970, therefore, we also hold up the continuities that still make it possible to speak of a Latin American civilization.

Notes

1   Carlos Fuentes, *El espejo enterrado* (Madrid: Taurus, 1992), 14–16, translated into English as *The Buried Mirror* (Boston: Houghton-Mifflin, 1992).
2   Charles Gibson, *Spain in America* (New York: Harper & Row, 1967), 215.
3   Tad Szulc, *Twilight of the Tyrants* (np: Henry Holt & Co., 1959), 4.

References

Fuentes, Carlos. *The Buried Mirror*. Boston: Houghton-Mifflin, 1992.
Fuentes, Carlos. *El Espejo Enterrado*. Madrid: Taurus, 1992.
Gibson, Charles. *Spain in America*. New York: Harper & Row, 1967.
Szulc, Tad. *Twilight of the Tyrants*. np: Henry Holt & Co., 1959.

Chapter 2

Beliefs

Beliefs are fundamental assumptions about life. From them spring the values and ideas that in turn shape the institutions – the political practices, the economic system, the social conventions – that govern our lives. Beliefs also frame identities – who we think we are, both as individual persons and as members of groups. Beliefs need not consist of absolute certainties, and in fact few of them probably do. But they are sufficiently stable, uniform and integrated across particular societies to warrant the proposition that underpins the logic of this chapter: namely, that the trends of the past three to four decades that await our attention cannot be understood except against the backdrop of the more consistent beliefs that characterize the history of the diverse peoples and regions of Latin America.

Besides a belief system or what we prefer to call, a little more loosely, a moral order or an ethos (from the Greek for "custom"), we will also be concerned in this chapter with preferences and values, which are expressions of beliefs. Of course, beliefs change, in part at least because material resources, institutions and interests can inspire people to revise them and the values associated with them. While both beliefs and values are subject to change, values are likely to be still more volatile, even as they preserve their link to an underlying moral order.

Identities, Cultures, Beliefs

As we have already tried to show, Latin America is much more than an economic or geopolitical expression, or a collection of separately governed countries. In the first place, Latin America is a place occupied by people who

Contemporary Latin America: 1970 to the Present, First Edition. Robert H. Holden and Rina Villars.
© 2013 Robert H. Holden and Rina Villars. Published 2013 by Blackwell Publishing Ltd.

have established, through their own creative actions over the centuries, concentric rings of *identity* that start at the level of the individual and the family, continue to the level of localities, districts, regions and nations; and finally embrace an array of communities (analyzed in Part V) that cut across those geographical units in myriad ways. The outermost ring (for our purposes) is that intangible community we refer to as "Latin America," and Chapter 17 will discuss recent attempts to turn the many intangible dimensions of an underlying Latin American cultural unity into a formal institution, a "community of nations" that might evolve into something like the European Union.

By identity we mean a set of shared beliefs about the characteristics that set one group apart from others. Identity does not mean absolute uniformity. While people who share an overarching identity can be representative of that identity, each person is also an individual with her or his own distinct, indeed unique, characteristics. In applying the concept "identity" to the people of Latin America and their history, we recall the Uruguayan philosopher Mario Sambarino's observation: "Along with that which identifies, one also finds that which diversifies."[1] Thus, it would be a mistake to let the idea of "identity" metamorphose into an argument that would attribute some eternal, essential quality to all the people of Latin America. It is true that Latin America is unique in the sense that there is nothing just like it – geographically, biologically, culturally, climatically, demographically, historically – anywhere in the world. There is only one "Latin America." But that doesn't mean that it is a unity, any more than evidence of disunity proves the absence of identity. If identity is "who you are," there are almost no limits to telling that story, beginning with your sex, family status, ethnicity, race and nationality, and branching out to all sorts of other group identities, such as economic class, social status, religion, occupation, and so on. Part IV will show how these diverse individual identities tend to cluster around certain features that can be said to constitute a "culture."

Let us now analyze the core beliefs (or ethos, or moral order) of our nineteen Latin American countries. We have already noted the affinities of history, politics and language between Portugal and Spain that were in turn carried over to the New World. Brazil's core beliefs cannot be separated from those of the Spanish-speaking countries of America, for the basic resemblances between Brazil and Spanish-speaking America outweigh the more superficial distinctions associated with language and ethnicity.

In what follows, we will first define some characteristic features of the Latin American moral order as expressed in terms of general beliefs that have been held up as broadly typical by contemporary scholars. Evidence of changes in beliefs and values since the 1970s will be presented, followed by the changing role of religion, a major component of any moral order and, some would say, the very matrix of that order. We would like to stress that what follows should not be interpreted as a list of static or unchanging characteristics of how all

Latin Americans supposedly think. Rather, they are dynamic but central tendencies that have stood out in different ways throughout the history of Latin America, over and above the weight of personal individuality, group diversity and spatial variety.

Beliefs and Values

Over the decades, many scholars of Latin American society have called attention to the persistence of a distinctive "relational ethic" that is so widely shared and so fundamental that it seems to underlie many other beliefs and values. The term was devised by Richard Morse, one of the most astute interpreters of Latin American history. "The social nucleus," he wrote, "is relationship, not the individual."[2] Another historian, Claudio Véliz, argued that Latin Americans prefer living within a "network of attachments and allegiances," as opposed to the highly individualistic ways of the United States.[3] Two prominent anthropologists of Latin America, Eric R. Wolf and Edward C. Hansen, observed that "kin, friends, patrons and clients" represent "recurring and very stable patterns of organizing people."[4] Similarly, recent research in Latin American business and government organizations emphasized the continuing strength of the core belief in a relational ethic whose main features include paternalism, fatalism, a high respect for hierarchy, the tendency to withhold trust from all but the closest friends and family members, and a strong focus on personal relationships.[5]

A range of values linked to the relational ethic was identified in 2006 by Luis Diego Herrera Amighetti, a Costa Rican psychiatrist, as being especially common in his country and widely shared by other Latin Americans. One such trait is personal avoidance of accountability; in fact, the Spanish language has no exact equivalent for the English word "accountability." To Herrera Amighetti, therefore, it is not surprising that "the rule of law in Latin America is a rare phenomenon," and that cleverness and shrewdness are considered to be higher values than honesty. A preference for indirect speech over assertiveness inhibits the capacity to learn from mistakes, Herrera argued.[6] Survey data confirmed that Latin Americans tended to repress their true feelings and intentions. Taken as a whole, these patterns lead to a weak sense of personal responsibility or "agency," and a tendency to passively accept life as it is.

We will find evidence of the relational ethic in many of the themes we present in this book. For example, Part V will highlight the centrality of the Latin American family and the tendency to place the family's interests over those of the individual. The relational character of the Latin American feminist movement has set it apart from the movement's North American branch. To be sure, one can find evidence in Latin American societies of an individualistic and aggressively competitive ethos. Perhaps it is the cohabitation of both ways of life that distinguishes the region – on the one hand, a holistic and relational tradition encompassing respect for hierarchy, and on the other, a more modern, achievement-oriented ethos centered on individual equality.

Evidence of the relational ethos can often be found in practices associated with "personalism," a term applied by scholars of Latin America to a general tendency for personal relationships and friendships to overrule and govern legal, bureaucratic, institutional or other more impersonal norms. A specific form of personalism is "patrimonialism," probably the single most frequently cited characteristic of politics and society in Latin America, and one that has been highly visible ever since the founding of the American jurisdictions of Spain and Portugal at the dawn of the sixteenth century. While the concept carries a variety of connotations, depending on the exact context in which it is applied, it basically refers to the *personalization* of political power and all the attributes of that power. Spain's monarchs received their authority and the governing apparatus that accompanied it as their "patrimony," i.e., as an inherited entitlement. By extension, a polity infused with patrimonial values is one in which a public office is understood to be the property of the person holding the office. Logically, an office that "belongs" to the holder may be exploited for personal gain. Similarly, in a patrimonial environment, the legitimacy of any given political authority – that is, his or her perceived right to rule – tends to be evaluated in highly personalistic rather than constitutional or statutory terms. Political movements build around the leader rather than a particular ideology, so that followers identify themselves as "chavistas" or as "peronistas" (adherents of Chávez, say, or of Perón).

If an office becomes so closely identified with the office holder that the office itself is understood to be his "patrimony," then the holder is evidently entitled to whatever wealth, income or other resources might be extracted from it, including the right to appoint family and friends to positions of power. Office holders sometimes assert a right to permanent tenure as well, and even the right to appoint a successor (often a family member) in the event of the holder's death or illness. The post-1970s democratic wave has done little or nothing to diminish these fundamental beliefs; typically, constitutional texts and legal statutes have been ignored, amended or repealed to accommodate them, as we will see in Chapter 5.

Another dimension of patrimonialism is the historic prominence of "clientelism" or patron–client relations. A powerful individual (the patron) distributes favors to "clients" who in return advance the cause of their patron. Such a system might operate in a variety of social contexts; the "clients" might be the armed followers of a nineteenth-century warlord, the cabinet members of an elected twentieth-century president, or the appointees of a mid-level bureaucrat. Here again, personal loyalty counts for more than professional merit. And, whenever legitimacy is closely tied to the authority of a person, rather than the office held by the person, then peculation, nepotism and self-dealing of all kinds come to seem normal and even legitimate.

The attractive force of the personal relationship finds negative expression in a tendency to withhold trust and confidence from strangers. Comparing North Americans and Mexicans, the Mexican philosopher Octavio Paz (d. 1998) wrote, "We are suspicious and they are trusting." Today, Latin Americans report higher rates of distrust toward both individuals and institutions than any other world region, confirming "what novelists and poets have long sensed and suggested," wrote Marta Lagos, a specialist in Latin American public opinion.[7]

The exceptional reliance on family members by Latin American presidents remains a prominent expression of both the patrimonial outlook and the weak sense of trust. From 1959 to 2008, President Fidel Castro of Cuba trusted just one man to command the Cuban armed forces – his younger brother Raúl. And when Fidel became too ill to govern, he arranged for Raúl to succeed him as president in 2008. The Somoza family governed Nicaragua from 1937 to 1979, but the tradition of family rule did not end with the overthrow of the last Somoza in the civil war of the late 1970s. Two of the leaders of the guerrilla army that defeated the Somozas, Daniel Ortega and his brother Humberto, became president and army chief, respectively, from 1979 to 1990. After he was reelected president in 2007, Daniel Ortega turned all the government's social welfare programs and its economic planning to his wife Rosario Murillo, who was also his administration's official spokesperson. In neighboring Costa Rica, considered a model of democracy in Latin America, President Oscar Arias in both his terms (1986–1990 and 2006–2010) made his younger brother Rodrigo his chief of staff (*ministro de la presidencia*), the most powerful post in the cabinet. After the 2010 election, Rodrigo announced his candidacy for the presidency in 2014 as a member of the Partido Liberación Nacional, which the Arias brothers continued to control.

The power of personalism and the corresponding regard, even reverence, for family ties in Argentina may be unmatched elsewhere in Latin America. As Néstor Kirchner was ending his first term as president in 2007, Argentines elected his wife Cristina Fernández to succeed him. She made it clear that her husband would share the presidency with her. Kirchner's sudden death by a heart attack in 2010 aroused a wave of sympathy for Fernández that led to a surge in her previously weak approval ratings. Winning reelection with a remarkable 54% of the vote in 2011, she insisted at her inauguration on receiving the wooden presidential baton, not from the outgoing vice president as protocol required, but from the hands of another family member – her daughter, a kind of stand-in for Néstor. Swearing allegiance to the constitution, Fernández again deviated from protocol by adding: "And if I don't, then let God, the Fatherland and he [Néstor] demand it of me."

Implying that she was somehow being guided by his mystical presence, even before her inauguration Fernández had already begun to refer to Kirchner as "he," without the mandatory noun antecedent (i.e., "Néstor") – a practice normally reserved for references to God. By mythologizing the dead president, and even turning him into a supernatural being capable of interceding for her, Fernández and the leaders of *kirchnerismo* called to mind the glorification of Eva Duarte, the second wife of President Juan Perón. Two months before her death from cancer in 1952, the Argentine Congress bestowed on her the title "Jefa Espiritual de la Nación" or "spiritual leader of the nation." The extreme reverence still evoked by the memories of both Eva and Juan Perón (president, 1946–1955 and 1973–1974) remained an essential ideological element of *peronismo* and its electoral vehicle, the Partido Justicialista, which was also the party of Kirchner and Fernández. For example, the latter's reelection campaign in 2011 circulated a poster with her deceased husband's image and the slogan, "One day the children of your children will ask about Him."

In patrimonial systems such as these, people tend to look to governing authorities not as referees or neutral dispensers of essential resources but as the society's only important provider of jobs, income and personal security. It is an attitude often thought to inhibit the full development of civil society, that part of our social world that exists apart from, and often in tension with, the apparatus of government. On this view, real democracy cannot exist without a robust civil society. Writing in the late 1980s, the historian Richard Morse observed that even at that late date, "the larger society is perceived in Latin America as composed of parts that relate through a patrimonial center rather than directly to one another."[8] Logically, members of such a society do not tend to see themselves as ones to whom the authorities in power should be held to account. Once they vote for a leader, they are likely to withdraw from active participation in government.

The patrimonial ethos may also act as an enabling condition for the outbreaks of authoritarian rule that were such a common feature of Latin American politics until the 1980s. The military junta that removed an elected civilian government in Argentina and governed from 1976 to 1983 may have been the single most brutal instance of despotic rule in Latin American history. It was responsible for the murder of at least 12,000 civilians, many of whom were subjected to unspeakable torture. But the generals could never have seized power, nor have controlled the country so completely for eight years, without the compliance of many Argentine citizens. Guillermo O'Donnell, an Argentine expatriate and one of the world's most widely quoted experts on Latin American politics, attributed the collaboration of some and the silence of many during the military dictatorship to the persistence of "extremely authoritarian" and intolerant attitudes throughout Argentine society. O'Donnell singled out blind obedience to authority as a particularly prominent value, and one that seems closely linked to personalism.[9]

Throughout Latin America, the legacies of personalism continued to frustrate full democratization well after the transition away from military rule began in the 1970s and 1980s, O'Donnell pointed out. Majorities of voters often elected office holders whom they were simply empowering to interpret the interests of the nation for them; rather than remaining active citizens, many voters became mere audiences, frustrating the principle of accountability and leaving the door open to "clientelism, patrimonialism, and corruption."[10] In a clientelistic system, those whom the patron does not consider to be clients may legitimately be regarded as "enemies," who in turn are likely to respond in a reciprocal way, making for an exceptionally polarized, bitter, winner-takes-all attitude toward political competition. The corresponding weakness of impersonal legal norms makes a patrimonial polity, even a formally democratic one, potentially unstable.

Of course, expressions of patrimonialism in Latin America have changed greatly over the centuries; considerably less violent and arbitrary than in the distant past, they also vary from place to place. Nevertheless, belief in the personal nature of legitimate authority remains strong, and evidence in the economic, legal and social realms, as well as that of government, is not hard to find. Clientelistic networks still control hiring by governments and universities; patrons (those who hire) prefer loyalty above all else, so that there is little public competition for jobs. No matter how well educated or prepared, job hunters know they need "godfathers" and personal contacts. In the selection of employees, loyalty and confidence tend to win out over efficiency and talent, reinforcing the tendency for loyalty to persons to overcome loyalty to laws, constitutions or ideologies.

Given the special force of the relational ethos in Latin American history, one would expect to find evidence of strong belief in the value of family ties even in non-political contexts. Indeed, the family remained the keystone of the Latin American social structure well into the twentieth century, owing to the belief that it was family members whose trust, loyalty and personal support could be counted on above all others. Both before and after the separation from Spain and Portugal, politics and business were largely organized and conducted through family alliances and their networks. Business deals and political choices were made to serve the family and its interests, and the system of patron–client relations mentioned above typically operated through family connections. The vitality of those connections resounded at all socio-economic levels, not just among the powerful. Between 1889 and 1937, six families directed the economic and political life of the Brazilian frontier state of Mato Grosso. Together, they expanded their power by mobilizing diverse private and public resources, including land, slaves, financial capital, government concessions, and government offices. If, by the middle of the twentieth century, complex family networks rarely dominated government as they had done earlier, they nevertheless remained highly influential, as we will see in Chapter 15.

Next to family members, friends were to be preferred as political and business associates, especially if they were also linked by birth to one's own hometown or region. Thus has the relational ethos of personalism always also included regionalism – loyalty to the place of one's birth, where the ties of family, friends, politics and business were thickest.

Finally, a belief in the special trustworthiness and loyalty that one owed to the godparent of one's child has been a common way to extend family networks and cement personal ties. Through *compadrazgo* (or *compadrio* in Brazil), a godparent not only accepted the responsibilities for the newly baptized infant as defined by the Roman Catholic Church, but in addition took on reciprocal obligations of protection or service to the parent of the child.

Paradoxically, the high value traditionally attributed to kinship and friendship is closely associated with another traditional value, *machismo*, a form of sexist behavior that often implies the father's withdrawal from responsibility for his children. The pattern of Latin American fathers who either pay little attention to their children and their family responsibilities, or who abandon the family altogether, has been widely documented. The situation is closely associated with poverty, and while this is not an unfamiliar pattern in other cultures, its frequency in Latin America has turned fatherless families into a substantial subculture, according to the Peruvian sociologist Violeta Sara-Lafosse. Distinguishing *machismo* from patriarchy, she wrote that the patriarch expressed his strong sense of fatherhood by caring for his children. But both types treat the mother of their children as an inferior whose basic function remains one of service. Among the values associated with *machismo* and patriarchy is a widespread belief (among women as well as men) in a man's duty to demonstrate his masculinity, often through aggressive, reckless or forceful behavior.[11] While there is little agreement among scholars about the origins of this belief, or in just how it is distributed either regionally or socially, its existence and its occasionally destructive results are widely acknowledged.

Changing Values

Since the 1970s, shifts in the dominant values of Latin America can be roughly identified with a general, worldwide movement in favor of personal freedom, self-expression, and social diversity. The evidence of changing values is far from definitive, owing largely to the scarcity of consistent, cross-country survey data for any period, especially before 1970. In 1993, an ambitious attempt to capture the prevailing ethos among a sample of 36,516 teenagers in eighteen of our nineteen countries (Cuba did not participate) plus Puerto Rico revealed both the persistence of traditional beliefs and values, and the effects of challenges to them that had been seeded in the 1960s and 1970s. Among the signs of overall change was the rejection, by two-thirds of the respondents, of the proposition that "it is natural that the man rules in the family and that the woman obeys him." Even more (72%) rejected the proposition that "men have no obligation to cook or clean house, which are women's work." But *machismo* and patriarchy were not so strongly questioned everywhere. About four out of ten respondents in Honduras, the Dominican Republic and Bolivia still agreed with the first statement, which drew its weakest support (only about two out of ten) in Costa Rica, Colombia and Puerto Rico.

Answers to questions about the family showed the persistence of the traditional respect, even reverence, for this institution as the primary source of fundamental values. Close to half (45%) of the teenagers said unmarried couples should abstain from sexual relations, a statement that gained the highest assent in Honduras, the Dominican Republic and El Salvador (65–70%) and the lowest in Uruguay, Argentina and Brazil (35–40%). More than half (60%) condemned abortion absolutely, with the highest levels of rejection in Guatemala, and the lowest in Uruguay. Almost half (48%) agreed that married couples should not divorce even if they don't get along, with Bolivia, Honduras and El Salvador the most opposed to divorce, and Uruguay and Brazil the least opposed. Overall, in response to eight questions dealing with sexuality and marriage, the Dominican Republic, El Salvador, Guatemala and Honduras were the least "liberal" (32–34%) and Uruguay, Brazil and Argentina were the most liberal (50–56%).

In the political realm, the survey results also suggested a distaste for traditional patrimonial attitudes toward public office. Seven out of ten youth absolutely condemned the acceptance of money for favors by a public official, a response that was strongest in Guatemala, Paraguay and Panama and weakest in Uruguay, Nicaragua and Mexico. The author of the study speculated that it showed that in today's complex and pluralistic societies, "value messages are diverse and sometimes contradictory," which itself was "radically new," forcing youth to construct their own ethical systems.[12]

Evidence of an overall trend toward a "liberal society" of the U.S. type rather than European – meaning a less intrusive state, a preference for market-oriented solutions to social problems, individualization and social mobility – is easy to find in Chile, according to one of that country's most prominent sociologists, Eugenio Tironi. The trend emerged in the 1980s, when it was associated mostly with economic liberalization during military rule. Political liberalization followed in the 1990s, and then came cultural liberalization. The traditional two-parent family diminished in prestige as single parenthood and cohabitation became more common, as we will see in Chapter 15. Political liberalization in turn reduced the tolerance of Chileans for the old patrimonial norms as they demanded more respect for legal and regulatory procedures, and more coherence between private practices and public discourses, including an end to corruption. But one of the unwanted effects of liberalization for most Chileans, Tironi argued, was an erosion of traditional communal ties. As a result, more Chileans after the 1990s longed for a more "communitarian" society – as long as the new community ties did not require any permanent obligations. Mexico, like Chile, may also be witnessing a convergence of its traditional values with those of its powerful neighbor, the United States.[13]

Religion

Among the most tenaciously held of all beliefs are religious ones. Because of their fundamental and comprehensive character, they have the capacity to shape values, attitudes and thus identity perhaps more than any other single kind of belief. And when one particular religion dominates a society for centuries, as has the Roman Catholic faith in the case of Latin America, no study of that region's beliefs can pass over its religious component. Even people who reject religion or remain indifferent to it can identify ways in which their beliefs have been shaped by the dominant faith. A survey of values carried out in forty countries in 1990–1993 found that all of the historically Roman Catholic countries of Europe and Latin America continued to display relatively similar values, as did historically Protestant societies.[14]

Since the 1970s, a religious revival has been sweeping Latin America. Mainly Christian in orientation, it can be seen in the conversion of millions to a variety of evangelical Protestant denominations, and in a remarkable rise in the number of priests in the Roman Catholic Church. More tolerance and respect for syncretic practices (those blending Christian and indigenous religious rituals) and an increase in the practice of African-based religions were also evident. In this section, we offer a brief overview of the depth and scope of these changes. The role of the Roman Catholic Church, as an institution, in the socio-political history of our period will be explored in Chapter 6. But the influence of the Church as an institution has ultimately depended on the personal beliefs of millions of adherents of the Catholic religion, even when the adherence of many could be fairly described as nominal. So it is to an examination of those beliefs that we now turn.

Catholicism

Two solidly Catholic monarchies, those of Portugal and Spain, launched the globalization of Christianity in the fifteenth century. In an age characterized throughout Europe by the alliance of Church and state, and by the fear that religious inconformity could unleash social instability, the Catholic faith of the Iberian monarchies was therefore considered the only acceptable religion in the lands that they occupied and settled. As a result, the countries of Latin America remained overwhelmingly Catholic well into the late twentieth century. By 2010, our nineteen Latin American countries were home to about one of every five Christians in the world – roughly the same proportion as in 1970. Over those four decades, Latin America's share of the world's Roman Catholics rose from 37% to 41%, the highest concentration of Catholics in any world region.[15] But in that same period, the proportion of Catholics declined from 89% of the Latin America population in 1970 to 83% in 2010, as enrollments in non-Catholic Christian denominations multiplied across the region. In Brazil – the country with the largest number of Catholics in the world – the share of people who identified themselves as Catholics declined from 89% in 1970 to 77% in 2010. Acknowledging that the trend was "true for almost all of Latin America," the archbishop of São Paulo, Cardinal Cláudio Hummes, asked, "How long will Latin America remain a Catholic continent?"[16] Other Church authorities feared that in parts of Latin America, liturgical rites were seen as nothing more than cultural expressions.[17]

At no time in the late twentieth century, however, did more than a small minority of self-identified Catholics regularly practice their faith. By the 1960s, for most people their religion was little more than a tradition. Jeffrey Klaiber, a Jesuit priest and a widely traveled historian of the Latin American church who lived in Peru since 1963, wrote in the late 1990s that "it is well known" that no more than about one of every ten Catholics in Latin America obey the Church's rule of attending Mass on Sundays. Klaiber's estimate roughly matched the results of surveys of regular Sunday Mass attendance carried out in Chile from the 1940s to the 1980s, which put the figure at 12–15% of the population.[18]

On the other hand, regular Mass attendance may not be the best measure of adherence to the Catholic faith, for many millions of Catholics – in Latin America and elsewhere – practice their faith in a variety of other, less formal ways that cannot easily be measured by opinion polls. For example, while they may attend church services sporadically or almost never, they do pray or visit shrines, participate in traditional religious festivals, decorate their homes with religious images, and pay special heed to the public admonitions of their bishop or parish priest. The annual participation of millions of Latin Americans in Catholic religious pilgrimages revealed the continuing vitality of the sacred in the lives of Latin Americans, as well as the ways in which the cults associated with the pilgrimages tend to reinforce national, regional and ethnic identities. In the first decade of the twenty-first century, the shrine of the Virgin of Guadalupe in Mexico, administered by the Archdiocese of Mexico City, was drawing up to 20 million pilgrims a year to pray at the site where the Virgin

Mary appeared to an Indian peasant in 1531. Among Mexicans, devotion to the Virgin – who was declared the patroness of all Latin America in 1910 by Pope St. Pius X – is widely interpreted as an expression of national identity, despite the fierce hostility toward religion of the one-party state that ruled Mexico from the 1920s to 2000.

While the nationalistic overtones of Mexico's devotion to the Virgin may be exceptional, similar expressions of popular Catholic religiosity can be found in most Latin American countries. Typically, they center around a particular shrine associated with Christ, the Virgin or a saint, who are in turn linked to miraculous events. By 2000, the Guatemalan town of Esquipulas was still drawing up to 1 million pilgrims a year, mostly from Central America, who came to venerate a sixteenth-century crucifix (the "Black Christ," carved of dark wood) associated with miraculous cures and housed in a basilica specially built for it in 1759. In the northern Peruvian town of Motupe, a rustic cross crafted by a nineteenth-century monk made Motupe one of the most popular pilgrimage destinations in South America, drawing thousands of pilgrims during the first two weeks of August, when the cross is carried in procession from a mountaintop cave to a church in Motupe and then returned to the cave. In the Argentine town of San Ignacio, a sanctuary for pilgrims was built in 2009 to honor Ceferino Namuncurá (1886–1905), the son of a Mapuche Indian father and a European mother. Famous for his saintly virtue, Ceferino remained the object of a cult in Chile and Argentina that began to grow after his death from tuberculosis. In 2007, the Catholic Church beatified him, thereby bestowing on him the title of "Blessed," one step short of sainthood.

Another sign of Catholic religiosity could be found in expressions of public confidence in the Catholic Church, which typically towered above that of all other institutions, including the mass media, government, and those of the private sector. In 2005, Latinobarómetro, the leading Latin American polling organization, reported that "The Catholic Church is the most credible and trusted institution in the whole region . . . Without a doubt, the role of the Catholic Church as moral leader and source of legitimacy remains as the most solid reference in every Latin American country."[19] A sign of the vitality of Catholic beliefs during this period, despite the rise of non-Catholic Christian denominations, was a 70% increase in the number of priests in Latin America between 1964 and 2004 – just the reverse of the downward trend in the United States during the same period. Mexico's priests more than doubled in that period; there, and almost everywhere else in Latin America, most of the added priests were Latin Americans rather than the foreign missionaries who in previous decades had tended to dominate in many Latin American countries. The number of seminarians studying for the priesthood in post-secondary schools increased by a factor of seven between 1972 and 2004. At the same time, the Church promoted much greater lay participation in catechesis and evangelization, areas traditionally dominated by clergy and members of religious orders.

Nevertheless, over the last four decades, strong challenges to Catholicism emerged from two very different directions: the non-Catholic wing of Christianity, and a secular culture whose dominant values seemed to be increasingly incompatible with those of the Church.

Protestantism and independent Christianity

The most remarkable religious trend in Latin America during the second half of the twentieth century was the tidal wave of desertions from the Catholic Church to communities of non-Catholic Christians (Figure 2.1). Totaling no more than 18 million in 1970, or about 7% of the population of the Latin American countries, their numbers had swelled to 104 million, or about 18% of the population in our nineteen countries, by 2010. They were strongest in Brazil, Chile, El Salvador, Guatemala and Nicaragua, where 25% to 29% of the population identified as non-Catholic Christians.[20] In 1970, only Brazil and Chile had reported a significant share of non-Catholic Christians, at about 13% and 15% respectively.

Most of the growth in non-Catholic membership appeared within the pentecostal branch of the non-Catholic denominations. Taking their name from the celebration of the feast of Pentecost reported in the second chapter of the Biblical book of Acts, pentecostalists emphasize such "spirit-filled" practices in their worship services as divine healing, speaking in tongues, and prophesying. They may belong to one of the established pentecostal denominations of the United States, such as the Assemblies of God or the Church of God in Christ, where the movement was founded, but many other groups formed independent congregations. While pentecostalists were estimated to account for no more than 5% of the U.S. population, in 2006 they made up 9% of the population of Chile, 15% of Brazil, and 20% in Guatemala. Roughly three of every four non-Catholic Christians in Latin America were thought to be pentecostalists in 2006.[21]

The Catholic Church has interpreted the challenge of non-Catholic Christianity in Latin America as an opportunity for dialogue among the different Christian communities and for fostering cooperation in support of the poor and in the promotion of justice. But why have so many Latin Americans Catholics transferred their loyalty to other Christian communities? Attempts to answer that question have spawned a sizeable scholarly literature. Most explanations highlight a rise in non-Catholic missionary activity, the growing influence of values and ideas associated with the mainly-Protestant United States, and the social disorientation brought on by the pressures of large-scale

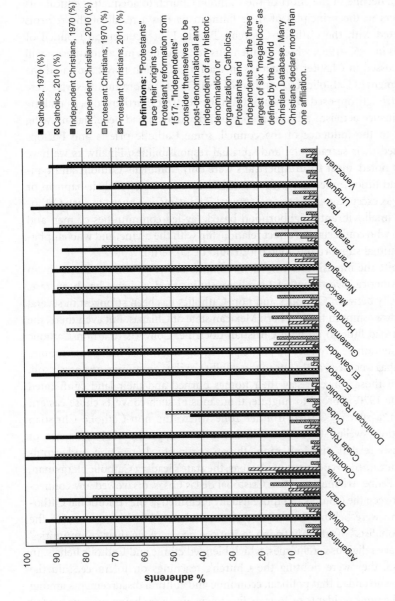

Figure 2.1 Changes in principal Christian affiliations, 1970–2010, as proportion of national population. Based on data from World Christian Database and World Religion Database. National populations for 1970 and 2010 are from United Nations, *World Population Prospects: The 2010 Revision*, medium variants.

Legend:
- Catholics, 1970 (%)
- Catholics, 2010 (%)
- Independent Christians, 1970 (%)
- Independent Christians, 2010 (%)
- Protestant Christians, 1970 (%)
- Protestant Christians, 2010 (%)

Definitions: "Protestants" trace their origins to Protestant reformation from 1517; "Independents" consider themselves to be post-denominational and independent of any historic denomination or organization. Catholics, Protestants and Independents are the three largest of six "megablocs" as defined by the World Christian Database. Many Christians declare more than one affiliation.

Chart x-axis (countries): Argentina, Bolivia, Brazil, Chile, Colombia, Costa Rica, Cuba, Dominican Republic, Ecuador, El Salvador, Guatemala, Honduras, Mexico, Nicaragua, Panama, Paraguay, Peru, Uruguay, Venezuela

Chart y-axis (% adherents): 0, 10, 20, 30, 40, 50, 60, 70, 80, 90, 100 industrialization and urban migration. Although these forces began to emerge gradually in the 1950s, their effects in religious conversions surged notably from the 1970s onward. To these explanations of protestantization is often added a decline in the effort of the Catholic Church to adequately educate its members in the principles of their faith, in part as a result of the reforms associated with the Catholic Church's Twenty-First Ecumenical Council of bishops in 1962–1965, whose momentous consequences in Latin America will be discussed in Chapter 6. Laxness in teaching the faith may have eased the recruitment of Catholics by members of rival Christian communities who were often strongly opposed to much of Catholic doctrine. Furthermore, in making social-justice activism a much higher priority than it had been, again owing largely to the influence of the council, some Catholic priests and bishops neglected their sacramental and spiritual responsibilities. Finally, as we have already noted, most Latin Americans were only nominally Catholic and typically had little connection with a Catholic community after their baptism or marriage, except for an occasional funeral. The attraction posed to such Catholics by small, vibrant neighborhood-based, lay-led communities of men and women who could claim a direct relationship with the divine, and who emphasized mutual support and solidarity, could be powerful.

Despite the intensification of denominational rivalry among Christians in Latin America, overt conflict or religiously inspired violence has been rare. Animosity between Catholics and non-Catholics has been strongest in several Indian townships in the southern Mexican state of Chiapas. But even there, the conflict had little to do with Christian doctrine. Converts to a non-Catholic denomination who refused to participate in the traditional Indian ceremonies of Chiapas were seen as threats to the stability of the community and as a result, many of those converts saw their homes burned and their land confiscated since the 1970s. Forced to migrate, thousands of such converts chose eastern Chiapas, a sparsely settled frontier zone where the non-Catholic Christian population swelled to 20–50% in some townships. In 2007, as news of religiously-related discrimination, threats, property destruction and expulsions continued to come out of Chiapas, the state's leading Catholic clergyman, Bishop Felipe Arizmendi of San Cristóbal de las Casas, disavowed any connection between the Church and those usually identified as the "traditional Catholics" who were behind the anti-Protestant violence. The bishop accused the "traditionalists" of unfairly trying to impose on everyone their communities' customary religious ceremonies, which blended ethnic and Catholic beliefs. In doing so, they were flouting the Church's teachings on tolerance, said the bishop, who added that political, economic and cultural disagreements among the indigenous residents of four or five townships were being misrepresented as religious conflict.

Syncretism and ethnoreligiosity

The events in Chiapas draw attention to the fact that, long before either Protestantism or Catholicism, the indigenous peoples of America practiced a diversity of religions associated with their own particular cultures. Some of those practices survived in forms that blended with elements of Christian doctrine and liturgy, resulting in a nominally Catholic but syncretic faith. Some indigenous beliefs survived and evolved in a sufficiently independent manner to qualify as ethnoreligions, one of the many thousands of religions whose practice is confined to the members of an ethnic group or subgroup.

In Mesoamerica (the area extending roughly from central Mexico to Honduras), indigenous beliefs have survived primarily within Catholicism. Their expression is highly localized, so that the indigenous inhabitants of any given town may consider their location to be "the literal center of the cosmos," according to Robert S. Carlsen, a specialist in contemporary Mesoamerican indigenous religious beliefs. A core feature of the syncretized Christianity in this region is what believers call *costumbre*, meaning the traditional ways of expressing their faith, ranging from a particular way of praying to the deities, to the sowing of maize. One especially important custom is the rotation among the members of the local community of certain duties associated with religious feast days and other celebrations that may be nominally Christian but fuse elements of local indigenous beliefs. Across the region, such beliefs typically include the veneration of the sun, the moon, the earth, and a variety of local deities. The organization of rituals, and the assignment of particular liturgical tasks, is carried out by a *cofradía*, a general term for the lay brotherhoods introduced into Indian communities by the Spaniards. Often merging religious with political responsibilities, the *cofradías* have contributed to the maintenance of ethnic identity as well as religious identity, and occasionally have served as points of resistance to unwanted influences from outside the community. As in Chiapas, the explosive growth of non-Catholic Christianity elsewhere in Mesoamerica, most notably in Guatemala, has undermined the authority of the cofradías and weakened the allegiance of some communities to *costumbre*.[22]

In South America, ethnoreligiosity can be analyzed according to four overarching culture zones: those of the Andes, the Northwest Amazon, the Central and Eastern Amazon, and the Gran Chaco. The most populous is that of the Andes, where the two largest groups of Indians, the Quechua and Aymara, together numbered about 7 million by 2010. Their religion divinizes the land as well as animal and plant life. *Pachamama*, a deity that refers to "mother earth" and the cycle of life, has been closely associated with Catholic veneration of the Virgin Mary. Like Mesoamerican beliefs, Andean practices are also oriented toward a particular locality, so that every Andean town imputes a sacred character to its mountain peaks, which are considered to be both the community's protectors and its ancestors. Diviners and sorcerers carry out the rituals and maintain earth shrines – small holes through which the earth is given "food" such as coca leaves. Having imported certain elements of Catholicism into their native religion, Andean Indians tend to be only nominally Catholic, but as in Mesoamerica, Protestantism posed a strong challenge to religious tradition.

A parallel religious development of both blending and independent survival can also be seen among the descendants of the 10–15 million Africans imported as slaves into the New World, especially in the two great centers of Latin American plantation slavery, Brazil and the Caribbean. Afro-Brazilian religions typically center on rituals aimed at healing and at shaping one's relations with spiritual beings and other persons. Sacred music and dance mediate these activities. Known variously as Candomblé, Umbanda, Xangô, Tambor de Mina, Tambor de Nagô, Terecô, Pajelança, Catimbó, Batuque, and Macumba, these Afro-Brazilian religions have been shaped by native American and Christian beliefs and rituals as well as African ones. In Brazil, these religions have attracted non-African Brazilians as well as Afro-Brazilians; in 2000, about 3% of the Brazilian population identified themselves to census-takers as adherents. The Brazilian novelist Jorge Amado (1912–2002), who introduced Candomblé in much of his writing, became an honorary Candomblé priest in 1959 after he turned away from communism and atheism. In Cuba, *santería* is the principal Afro-Cuban religion. Based mainly on the beliefs of the Yoruba people of Africa, and inflected with references to Christian saints, santería requires animal sacrifice to various gods, and the mediation of Yoruba music and dances.

In this chapter, we have made two key claims that we recommend readers keep in mind as they continue their journey through this book: that the people of our nineteen Latin American countries share a bundle of basic beliefs that sets Latin America apart from other world areas, and that those beliefs have decisively shaped the history of the region. A subject as intangible and capacious as beliefs is not likely to be one that generates a high level of consensus among scholars regarding their origins, content or practical effects. In the list of "Sources Consulted" for Part I, we have included works that reflect some of the contention over these matters. In keeping with our own view of the centrality of beliefs, however, the chapters that follow will extend our discusson beyond this introductory chapter by attempting to demonstrate the relevance of beliefs to the various topics of contemporary history that await us in the realms of government, wealth, culture and communities.

Notes

1 Mario Sambarino, *Identidad, Tradición, Autenticidad: Tres Problemas de América Latina* (Caracas: Centro de Estudios Latinoamericanos Rómulo Gallego, 1980), 17.
2 Richard Morse, *New World Soundings: Culture and Ideology in the Americas* (Baltimore: Johns Hopkins University, 1989), 126–7.
3 Claudio Véliz, *The New World of the Gothic Fox* (Berkeley: University of California Press, 1994), 202–5.
4 Eric R. Wolf and Edward C. Hansen, *The Human Condition in Latin America* (New York: Oxford University Press, 1972), 204, 200.
5 Joyce S. Osland, Silvio De Franco and Asbjorn Osland, "Organizational Implications of Latin American Culture: Lessons for the Expatriate Manager," *Journal of Management Inquiry* 8, no. 2 (1999): 219–34; for a comparison with other world regions, see Vipin Gupta and Paul J. Hanges, "Regional and Climate Clustering of Societal Cultures," in *Culture, Leadership, and Organizations: The GLOBE Study of 62 Societies*, ed. Robert J. House, Paul J. Hanges, Mansour Javidan, Peter W. Dorfman and Vipin Gupta (Thousand Oaks: Sage, 2004), 178–218, here 199–200.
6 Luis Diego Herrera Amighetti, "Parenting Practices and Governance in Latin America: The Case of Costa Rica," in *Developing Cultures: Essays on Cultural Change*, ed. Lawrence E. Harrison and Jerome Kagan (New York: Routledge, 2006), 21–33.
7 Marta Lagos, "Latin America's Smiling Mask," *Journal of Democracy* 8, no. 3 (1997) 3: 125–38; Corporación Latinobarómetro, "Informe – Resumen, Latinobarómetro 2004: Una Década de Mediciones," www.latinobarometro.org.
8 Morse, *New World Soundings*, 130.
9 Guillermo A. O'Donnell, "Democracia en la Argentina micro y macro," in *"Proceso", crisis y transición democrática*, ed. Oscar Oszlak (Buenos Aires: Centro Editor de América Latina, 1984), 1, 13–30.
10 Guillermo A. O'Donnell, "Delegative Democracy," *Journal of Democracy* 5, no. 1 (1994/1): 54–69, 1.
11 Violeta Sara-Lafosse, "Machismo in Latin America and the Caribbean," in *Women in the Third World: An Encyclopedia of Contemporary Issues*, ed. Nelly P. Stromquist (New York: Garland Publishing, 1998), 107–11.
12 Tomás Calvo Buezas, *Valores en los jóvenes españoles, portugueses y latinoamericanos* (Madrid: Ediciones Libertarias, 1997), chapter 4.
13 Eugenio Tironi, *El sueño chileno: Comunidad, familia y nación en el Bicentenario* (Santiago de Chile: Taurus, 2005), 23–6; Miguel Basáñez, "Mexico: The Camel and the Needle," in *Developing Cultures: Case Studies*, ed. Lawrence E. Harrison and Peter L. Berger (New York: Routledge, 2006), 287–303.
14 Ronald Inglehart, Miguel Basáñez and Alejandro Moreno, *Human Values and Beliefs: A Cross-Cultural Sourcebook* (Ann Arbor: University of Michigan Press, 1998), 19.
15 Unless otherwise stated, the source of the religious demographic data is *Religions of the World: A Comprehensive Encyclopedia of Beliefs and Practices*, ed. J. Gordon

Melton and Martin Baumann (Santa Barbara: ABC-CLIO, 2010); and World Christian Database, Center for the Study of Global Christianity, Gordon-Conwell Theological Seminary, www.worldchristiandatabase.org/wcd.

16 Holy See Press Office, *Synodus Episcoporum Bulletin*, XI Ordinary General Assembly of the Synod of Bishops, 2–23 October 2005, www.vatican.va/news_services/press.

17 Pontifical Council for Culture, *Where Is Your God? Responding to the Challenge of Unbelief and Religious Indifference Today* (Vatican City, 2004), www.vatican.va.

18 Jeffrey L. Klaiber, *The Church, Dictatorships, and Democracy in Latin America* (Maryknoll, NY: Orbis Books, 1998), 6; Paul E. Sigmund, "Revolution, Counterrevolution, and the Catholic Church in Chile," *The Annals of the American Academy of Political and Social Science* (January 1986) 483: 25–35, here 27.

19 Corporación Latinobarómetro. "El Catolicismo en América Latina al Inicio del Papado de Benedicto XVI: Latinobarómetro 1995–2004." www.latinobarometro.org.

20 Melton and Baumann, and the World Christian Database (both cited above), distinguished six Christian "megablocs": Orthodox, Roman Catholic, Anglican, Protestant, Independent and Marginal. The most numerous non-Catholics in our nineteen countries are Protestants (53.6 million) and Independents (38 million); together they account for 88% of all non-Catholic Christians. For some of the pitfalls of religious demography, see Philip Jenkins, *The Next Christendom: The Coming of Global Christianity* (Oxford: Oxford University Press, 2004), 85–9.

21 *Spirit and Power: A 10-Country Survey of Pentecostals* (Washington, DC: Pew Research Center, 2006).

22 Robert S. Carlsen, "Mesoamerican Religions: Contemporary Cultures," in *Encyclopedia of Religion*, ed. Lindsay Jones (Detroit: Thomson Gale, 2005), 5923–33.

References

Basáñez, Miguel. "Mexico: The Camel and the Needle." In *Developing Cultures: Case Studies*, ed. Lawrence E. Harrison and Peter L. Berger, 287–303. New York: Routledge, 2006.

Calvo Buezas, Tomás. *Valores en los jóvenes españoles, portugueses y latinoamericanos.* Madrid: Ediciones Libertarias, 1997.

Carlsen, Robert S. "Mesoamerican Religions: Contemporary Cultures." In *Encyclopedia of Religion*, ed. Lindsay Jones, 5923–33. Detroit: Thomson Gale, 2005.

Corporación Latinobarómetro. "El Catolicismo en América Latina al Inicio del Papado de Benedicto XVI: Latinobarómetro 1995–2004." www.latinobarometro.org.

Corporación Latinobarómetro. "Informe – Resumen, Latinobarómetro 2004: Una Década de Mediciones." www.latinobarometro.org.

Gupta, Vipin, and Paul J. Hanges. "Regional and Climate Clustering of Societal Cultures," in *Culture, Leadership, and Organizations: The GLOBE Study of 62 Societies*, ed. Robert J. House, Paul J. Hanges, Mansour Javidan, Peter W. Dorfman and Vipin Gupta, 178–218. Thousand Oaks, CA: Sage, 2004.

Herrera Amighetti, Luis Diego. "Parenting Practices and Governance in Latin America: The Case of Costa Rica." In *Developing Cultures: Essays on Cultural Change*, ed. Lawrence E. Harrison and Jerome Kagan, 21–33. New York: Routledge, 2006.

Holy See Press Office. *Synodus Episcoporum Bulletin*, XI Ordinary General Assembly of the Synod of Bishops, 2–23 October 2005, www.vatican.va/news_services/press.

Inglehart, Ronald, Miguel Basáñez and Alejandro Moreno. *Human Values and Beliefs: A Cross-Cultural Sourcebook*. Ann Arbor: University of Michigan Press, 1998.

Jenkins, Philip. *The Next Christendom: The Coming of Global Christianity*. Oxford: Oxford University Press, 2004.

Klaiber, Jeffrey L. *The Church, Dictatorships, and Democracy in Latin America*. Maryknoll, NY: Orbis Books, 1998.

Lagos, Marta. "Latin America's Smiling Mask." *Journal of Democracy* 8, no. 3 (1997): 125–38.

Melton, J. Gordon, and Martin Baumann, eds. *Religions of the World: A Comprehensive Encyclopedia of Beliefs and Practices*. Santa Barbara: ABC-CLIO, 2010.

Morse, Richard M. *New World Soundings: Culture and Ideology in the Americas*. Baltimore: Johns Hopkins University Press, 1989.

O'Donnell, Guillermo A. "Delegative Democracy." *Journal of Democracy* 5, no. 1 (1994/1): 54–69.

O'Donnell, Guillermo A. "Democracia en la Argentina Micro Y Macro." In *"Proceso", Crisis Y Transición Democrática*, ed. Oscar Oszlak, 1, 13–30. Buenos Aires: Centro Editor de América Latina, 1984.

Osland, Joyce S., Silvio De Franco and Asbjorn Osland. "Organizational Implications of Latin American Culture: Lessons for the Expatriate Manager." *Journal of Management Inquiry* 8, no. 2 (1999/6): 219–34.

Pontifical Council for Culture. *Where Is Your God? Responding to the Challenge of Unbelief and Religious Indifference Today*. Vatican City, 2004.

Sambarino, Mario. *Identidad, Tradición, Autenticidad: Tres Problemas De América Latina*. Caracas: Centro de Estudios Latinoamericanos Rómulo Gallego, 1980.

Sara-Lafosse, Violeta. "Machismo in Latin America and the Caribbean." In *Women in the Third World: An Encyclopedia of Contemporary Issues*, ed. Nelly P. Stromquist, 107–14. New York: Garland Publishing, 1998.

Sigmund, Paul E. "Revolution, Counterrevolution, and the Catholic Church in Chile." *The Annals of the American Academy of Political and Social Science* (January 1986) 483: 25–35.

Spirit and Power: A 10-Country Survey of Pentecostals. Washington, DC: Pew Research Center, 2006.

Tironi, Eugenio. *El sueño chileno: Comunidad, familia y nación en el bicentenario*. Santiago de Chile: Taurus, 2005.

Véliz, Claudio. *The New World of the Gothic Fox*. Berkeley: University of California Press, 1994.

Wolf, Eric R., and Edward C. Hansen. *The Human Condition in Latin America*. New York: Oxford University Press, 1972.

World Christian Database, Center for the Study of Global Christianity, Gordon-Conwell Theological Seminary, www.worldchristiandatabase.org/wcd.

Part II
Government

Introduction

Since the 1980s, a sustained, region-wide attempt to create stable institutions of democratic self-government has been underway everywhere in Latin America except for Cuba. But its outcome remains uncertain. For the disciples of democracy, therefore, the decades since the 1980s have been a time of hope and encouragement, tempered by frustration and disappointment at the uneven pace of change.

Before about 1980, it was widely thought that democracy simply hadn't been given a fair chance because of the intransigence of the armed forces and the overlapping interests of groups like the landed oligarchy, big business, foreign capitalists and the U.S. government. Menaced by popular aspirations for democracy, all of them seemed to require an authoritarian political order that could only be guaranteed by the armed forces. In the 1980s and 1990s, however, the power and political influence of the armed forces declined abruptly along with those of many of the groups whose interests they sheltered. The most extraordinary change has been the entrenchment of regular, competitive elections everywhere but Cuba. But in other equally important respects, democracy has clearly not taken hold, and it is now clear that the armed forces and their allies were not the only reasons why. At the dawn of the second decade of the twenty-first century, the very survival of the democratic gains of the last four decades seemed doubtful in some places.

The longstanding tension between Latin America's democratic aspirations and the failure to fully realize them has generated a huge body of scholarship. As a result, explanations of the gap between aspirations and reality, and recommendations for action, are not hard to find. To grasp the scope of the problem, and to acquire a better understanding of the victories and disappointments that have agitated the political arena over the last four decades, it would be useful to begin by clarifying three core concepts: state, government and regime.

Contemporary Latin America: 1970 to the Present, First Edition. Robert H. Holden and Rina Villars.
© 2013 Robert H. Holden and Rina Villars. Published 2013 by Blackwell Publishing Ltd.

State refers to the cluster of more or less permanent institutions – the armed forces, the presidency, the legislature and so on. They "contain" the power available for deployment by any given *government*, our second core concept. While governments come and go with some regularity, the state endures. The deepest and most intensive striving in the realm of politics, however, is not so much about the nature of the power containers (the institutions of state) or the identity of those at the levers of power (the government) but over *how* power should be distributed and exercised. The rules that define how the government and its agents relate to one another and to the larger society define our third concept: the *regime* a country operates under. How are leaders selected? What kinds of procedures govern their decisions? To whom are they accountable? How does accountability occur? A written constitution normally answers such questions in a formal, general way. But what finally determines the kind of regime is not the text of the constitution but the real relationships that prevail among the holders of power, and between the power-holders and the rest of society.

Thus, democracy is best understood as a type of regime. In its narrowest and most ancient sense, democracy is a procedure for choosing political leaders by means of popular elections. A grander, but more realistic, understanding of a democratic regime would couple it with liberalism. "Classical liberalism" (to distinguish it from the quite different liberalism of U.S. political culture) emerged in the seventeenth century before breaking out in full force as the ideological antithesis of the absolutism that the embattled monarchies of old Europe tried to defend against the democratizing movements of the late eighteenth and early nineteenth centuries. On this view, modern democracy cannot survive without liberalism, understood as a cluster of personal rights and freedoms that depend above all on respect for constitutional order and the rule of law. If the essence of democracy is rule "by the people," the essence of liberalism is freedom, especially for groups and individuals whose rights could easily be trampled if democracy were seen as nothing more than a procedure for ensuring control by the will of the majority. Understood this way, democracy is a type of regime whose time would not come in Latin America until the 1980s. Understanding the regimes that preceded democratization should clarify the reasons both for Latin America's tardiness in democratizing, and for its present difficulties in consolidating liberal democracy.

The Pattern of Regime Change in Latin America

From the 1820s until about the 1870s, individual power-holders dominated the landscape. Usually operating extra-constitutionally, they were the *caudillos* or "men on horseback" whose wealth and charisma attracted followers prepared to fight for them in exchange for protection, employment, pillage rights or other favors. Under this kind of regime, state institutions were weak and primitive. The elaborate constitutional texts that created them were practically irrelevant. In the political arena, people tended to define themselves, not so much by party labels or ideologies, but according to the individual leader to whom they professed loyalty. This period of Latin American political history thus deposited a strong legacy of *personalism* that, even as it has taken on new forms, continues to frustrate democratic aspirations even today.

The second period of Latin America's regime history saw the gradual substitution of individual strongmen or dictators by oligarchies, small groups at the top of society. From the 1870s until about the 1940s, power relations were mostly defined according to the interests of those groups. They typically included the wealthiest landowners and ranchers, mining entrepreneurs and industrialists, and sometimes foreign businesses. Oligarchical governments often took power constitutionally, by means of elections, and over time they were gradually opened to all adults, first men, and then women, who received the right to vote in the 1940s and 1950s in most countries. At the same time, oligarchical governments also depended, in varying degrees, on the intervention in political affairs of high-ranking allies in the officer corps of the armed forces.

During this period, therefore, the armed forces began to play a decisive role in Latin American politics, as coercive power was gradually displaced upward from rival *caudillo*-led bands into more centralized military organizations. Unified under a single national command, well armed and professionally trained, the armed forces increasingly saw themselves as apolitical moderators, stepping in and out of politics as circumstances required in order to defend the nation's vital interests against what their officers often considered irresponsible political parties and their civilian leaders. Instead of subordinating themselves to civilian governments, the armed forces insisted on their freedom to act independently of the constitutional government, and ultimately, even to remove governments they considered unqualified to rule. In doing so, they cited ambiguous constitutional language authorizing them to defend the nation in times of extreme emergency. Partisan political leaders often tried to manipulate the military on their own behalf, accommodating themselves to the military's moderating role. The result was the hardening of military autonomy. Both tendencies, the militarization of politics and military autonomy, would contribute to the formation of a new kind of military intervention in the 1960s and 1970s.

The third phase of regime change, from about the 1940s to the early 1960s, was notable for its proto-democratic character. Populist governments, appealing to now fully enfranchised masses of voters, nevertheless drew on traditional, non-democratic practices. Strong, charismatic leaders sought above all to secure the loyalty of the masses through the distribution of government jobs and large-scale economic development projects. In spite of their desire to associate with the masses, however, these leaders had little use for the mechanisms of democratic accountability. They resorted to demagoguery, dictatorial procedures, bribery, embezzlement and coercion, undermining their standing with the electorate and inspiring the formation of independent movements for political and social reform and even for social revolution. When the populists appeared unable to contain the popular unrest they had unleashed, the armed forces conspired to remove them from office.

At the same time, by the early 1960s, the armed forces suddenly confronted a challenge from an altogether different quarter. Guerrilla armies, animated and encouraged by the success of the revolutionaries who took power in Cuba under the leadership of Fidel Castro in 1959, went into action across the region. They operated in the cities and the countryside, taking hostages for ransom, assassinating key political figures, and assaulting government offices and military installations. Guided by Marxist ideology, their leaders aimed to undermine the legitimacy of the state and to inspire popular insurrections that would propel them into power. From there, they would replace discredited state institutions and establish socialistic regimes geared to meeting the needs of the most impoverished sectors of society.

In response to the insurgent challenge, the armed forces throughout Latin America acted independently of elected governments, removing them from office and taking power directly. They generally governed in the name of the armed forces themselves, rather than allowing a particular military strongman to lead the country, as had happened in the past. Thus began the fourth phase of regime change, one often referred to as the period of "bureaucratic authoritarianism," a label meant to convey the novel combination of both non-personal (bureaucratic) methods of government and non-democratic (authoritarian) traditions. Lasting until the 1980s, this phase witnessed the seizure of political power by the armed forces in almost every Latin American country. Only Colombia, Costa Rica, Mexico and Venezuela were spared periods of either direct military government, or rule by a nominally civilian chief executive whose tenure in office depended on the support of the armed forces.

This trend toward long-term, direct military rule in the 1960s and 1970s was of course strongly shaped by the strategic and ideological currents of the Cold War, the paramount feature of international politics from about 1947 to about 1991. That war pitted the leading capitalist and democratic countries (the United States, Canada, Japan, Australia and those of western Europe) against the self-defined "socialist bloc" of totalitarian, communist-led countries, of which the Union of Soviet Socialist Republics and China were in the forefront. While the principal contenders managed to avoid direct hostilities (hence, the "cold" war) and the calamitous exchange of nuclear weapons that such hostilities would surely have unleashed, their four-decade standoff contributed to the eruption of countless small or limited civil wars or conflicts whose combatants invariably drew on the ideological and material resources of one or the other of the two sides in the Cold War. In Latin America, the United States, acting both secretly and openly, supported governments and non-governmental organizations committed to the defeat of communism and of movements and individuals perceived as the allies of communism.

Chapters 3 and 4 analyze the nearly simultaneous abatement of two trends that peaked in the 1970s: first, that of social revolution as an instrument of change, and second, military rule as a response to the rising threat of revolution. Chapter 5 reviews the transition to democracy that began in the 1980s, and the ways that democratic aspirations were alternately fulfilled, reformulated and sometimes defied during the first decade of the twenty-first century. The influential role of religion in the political process, and the changing relations between the Roman Catholic Church and the state, are the subjects of Chapter 6. We close our study of contemporary government with a chapter on the least anticipated of all the major developments since the beginning of the current transition to democracy: the sudden rise of murderous violence that has swept Mexico and parts of Central America and South America, often with the cooperation of government agencies.

Chapter 3

The Demise of Social Revolution

In the political history of Latin America, *revolución* has been a familiar concept since the nineteenth century, when it was applied to practically any violent change in government. By the mid-twentieth century, that definition had been gradually displaced by the more ideological one of a "turning around" of the whole society and its economy through a redistribution of wealth from the rich to the poor, under the command of an exclusive, one-party state directed by the self-selected leaders of the revolution. In this more contemporary usage, "revolution" was understood to apply to society itself rather than just the government, so that mere political revolution gave way to *social revolution* as a shortcut to economic development. Because they normally aimed at the destruction of longstanding rights in privately-owned property (such as large agricultural landholdings and industrial enterprises) and the establishment of state-directed, socialist economies, the revolutionary movements invariably brought with them some degree of violence between the social classes, and sometimes civil war.

The ideology devised to justify the revolutionary movements was strongly Marxist in character, in that it depended on theories of class conflict and social change associated with Karl Marx, Friedrich Engels and Vladimir Ilich Lenin, the founders of modern communism. The paramount model of successful twentieth-century social revolution was the one led by Lenin and his Bolshevik Party (later, Communist Party) in Russia in 1917. A rival model emerged in 1949 with the seizure of power by Chinese revolutionaries under the leadership of Mao Tse-tung and his Chinese Communist Party. This one appealed to revolutionaries in less industrialized countries with a recent history of colonial overlordship by the great powers, and with economies organized mainly around the labor of rural cultivators ("peasants").

Contemporary Latin America: 1970 to the Present, First Edition. Robert H. Holden and Rina Villars.
© 2013 Robert H. Holden and Rina Villars. Published 2013 by Blackwell Publishing Ltd.

In Latin America, social-revolutionary movements and parties drawing on Marxist ideas and their application in both Russia and China would not emerge as significant political forces until the 1960s. To be sure, communist parties could be found in Latin America from the 1920s onward, but from the 1940s until the 1960s they typically shunned revolutionary violence, reasoning that Latin America was still too socially backward for revolution to be successful. Following classical Marxist theory and the Russian experience rather than the Chinese model, most theorists of Latin American revolution believed that the region first had to become fully industrialized before the poor and the working classes ("proletariat") would be capable of launching a successful revolutionary war, which would of course be directed by the leaders of the communist parties themselves. As an alternative to communism, populist parties and politicians at the time also advocated social changes to benefit the poor majority, but populists typically eschewed violence as a means of achieving power and abhorred the idea of genuine social revolution.

Hardly anyone, therefore, was prepared for the eruption of social revolutionary movements that swept nearly every country in Latin America from the late 1950s until the early 1990s. Insisting that the time for *la lucha armada* or "armed struggle" and for socialism had arrived, their leaders cited a combination of grievances. Three stood out:

- The continuing ineffectiveness of governments in reducing poverty and economic inequality, particularly in rural areas, in a time of rapid economic growth that tended to disproportionately reward the rich and the middle class.
- The harsh repression by political authorities of legal, peaceful political movements that challenged the policies of incumbent governments, leaving little alternative but rebellion.
- The dominating influence of foreign economic and political interests – above all, those of the United States – in the country's cultural, economic and political institutions, including its international relations.

The enemies of the revolutionaries could thus be identified in ideological terms as capitalism, dictatorship and imperialism, respectively. The struggle against imperialism would contribute a strong dose of nationalism to the standard logic of Marxism. Overall, the revolutionaries' goal was to eliminate economic and social inequality by liquidating state institutions and establishing new ones capable of forcibly redistributing wealth and equalizing access to healthcare, education and other goods while defending themselves against the hostile intentions of the United States (the principal "imperialist" power) that their policies were sure to provoke.

In pursuit of these goals, every Latin American country but Panama spawned at least one band of guerrilla warriors ready to take on the national armed forces in the name of social revolution.[1] The insurgents adopted the classical tactics of irregular forces when facing a powerful, well-organized, conventionally trained enemy: ambush, sabotage, hit-and-run actions to weaken and disperse enemy forces; avoidance of direct confrontation; and the cultivation of a sympathetic base of rural and urban non-combatants for food and logistical support. Revolutionary organizations also engaged in urban terrorism, including bombings, assassinations, kidnappings for ransom and bank robberies. Sometimes they created political parties and other groups that operated openly in order to compete in elections, recruit new members and drum up popular support for their objectives.

While the policies of an oppressive, authoritarian regime usually provided the immediate pretext for action, such governments were hardly a novelty in Latin America by the 1960s. Rather, certain international conditions had taken shape that encouraged the formation of armed, revolutionary movements in various world regions, and kept them in motion until the early 1990s. These global factors included the challenges to the hegemony of liberal capitalism posed by the spectacular rise of the Soviet bloc and China in the first decades of the Cold War; the prominence and prestige of the revolutionary ideology (Marxism-Leninism) that China and the countries of the Soviet bloc claimed as their own; and the simultaneous rise of a general belief in the necessity of economic development and some expansion in popular participation in government. Latin American social movements were also displaying a new self-confidence in their own ability to organize for change, rather than to accept the customary direction of populist politicians or institutions such as the military or traditional political parties.

It fell to one man, Fidel Castro of Cuba, to inspire and embolden the discontented and to convert the rising popular desire for immediate social change into a diversity of movements – some favoring the peaceful, electoral route toward reform and others violent social revolution. Without doubt the single most influential Latin American of the twentieth century, Castro owed his role as the region's chief spokesman for radical social change and violent revolution to his audacious leadership of the insurrection that placed him and his party in power in Cuba in 1959, and to the place he made for himself as the head of the communist government he established in Cuba until he resigned as president in 2006.

Leading by both example and by his captivating rhetoric, Castro contributed to Latin America's era of social revolution, and to the legacies of that era, in four ways. First, the Cuban revolt he led seemed to prove that a small band of determined guerrilla fighters, operating far from urban centers of power, could enkindle and then take command of a successful national revolt against a powerful dictator. Castro's methods were widely imitated, above all in the deployment of a rural guerrilla force dependent on peasant support and urban-terrorist tactics such as kidnappings for ransom and assassinations. Second, once in power, Castro and his followers actually began to implement the reforms (which only later were deepened enough to become "revolutionary") that his movement had promised during the insurrection. As the United States sought to soften or reverse the reforms, and then took steps to disrupt and finally overthrow the revolutionary government in 1961, Castro refused to bend. Instead, he abruptly declared himself a convinced Marxist-Leninist, rallied Cubans behind ever-deeper changes in favor of socialism, and soon converted the island into a fully socialized economy under the exclusive leader-ship of the Cuban Communist Party. What's more, he did so in alliance with the Soviet Union, the archenemy of the United States. Cubans who opposed the dictatorship were executed, imprisoned or sent into exile. Third, the fierce opposition of the United States to Castro's revolution provided Castro with the opportunity to cast the United States, rather than the more abstract "capital-ism," as Cuba's (and the hemisphere's) greatest obstacle to national dignity and social and economic equality. He thus encouraged revolutionaries elsewhere in the region to advance their own movements by means of nationalistic appeals to resist "imperialism," while fostering a renewed sense of identity as Latin Americans.

Finally, Castro and his government presented themselves as the natural leaders of Latin American social revolution. They incited revolutionaries throughout the region to overthrow the governments in power and follow the path to socialism blazed by Cuba. After declaring the irrevocably Marxist-Leninist character of the Cuban Revolution in 1961, Castro announced the following year that "The duty of every revolutionary is to make the revolution. It is known that the revolution will triumph in America and throughout the world." Cuba transferred arms, training and equipment to insurgents in Colombia and Venezuela in 1963, and to similar movements all over Latin America in subsequent years. "I want to remind you," Castro declared at an international meeting of heads of state in 1973, "that Cuba is a socialist country, Marxist-Leninist, whose final objective is communism. We are proud of this!"[2] Acting as catalysts, Castro and his government stimulated and sped up the revolutionary trend in Latin America largely by redefining the possibilities of revolution.

For a little over three decades, until about 1990, the armed, revolutionary left played a central role in Latin American domestic and international politics, even though the combined total of guerrilla combatants probably never exceeded 50,000. The era gave birth to a total of about fifty leftist military organizations dedicated to armed struggle. Seven operated in Argentina alone, six in El Salvador and five each in Guatemala, Colombia and Peru at different times. Serious internal divisions often split these groups, leading to violent struggles among rival factions for control of the organization and, ultimately, the revolutionary movement. The size, effectiveness and longevity of the guerrilla organizations varied considerably. Thus, an abundance of revolutionary *movements* operated across Latin America but only two of them – those of Cuba and Nicaragua – succeeded in seizing power. And both shared some remarkable similarities.

Though the moments in which they took power were separated by twenty years, very similar circumstances gave rise to the Cuban and Nicaraguan revolts. Dictatorial *caudillos* ruled both countries with the firm support of the U.S. government, which considered the dictators (Fulgencio Batista in Cuba, Anastasio Somoza in Nicaragua) to be valuable (if politically distasteful) allies on the hemispheric front of the worldwide battle against communism. During the first few decades of the twentieth century, both Cuba and Nicaragua had been subjected to U.S. military intervention, and their governments closely overseen by U.S. officials. Among the ruling elites of both countries, a tradition of collaboration with the United States had built up over the years. As a result, Cuba and Nicaragua would seem to have been the least likely candidates for successful social revolution. It turned out, however, that the very experience of foreign domination supplied one of the most powerful ingredients for a successful revolutionary movement: a strong sense of identity among many Cubans and Nicaraguans as a nation repressed and victimized by a powerful and greedy neighbor. The experience of unjust humiliation as a nation spurred a strong desire for dignity as a nation. Among the revolutionaries and their followers, at least, that dignity could only be acquired by an "anti-imperialist" strategy: annihilation of the state and the political class that for decades had collaborated in their humiliation.

Another similarity in the Cuban and Nicaraguan revolutionary movements could be found in the ways that those movements unfolded over time. Only four years before they seized power, the guerrilla armies in both countries had appeared to be broken by the armed forces of the dictators. The Cuban guerrillas numbered no more than twenty in December 1956. The Nicaraguans, just a few dozen at most in late 1975, had dwindled to eleven by the end of 1977. But at their weakest moments, both guerrilla organizations gradually began to draw popular support and recruit combatants in ever-larger numbers, aided largely by the dictatorships' increasingly corrupt, repressive and arbitrary policies. Batista in Cuba and Somoza in Nicaragua not only alienated the downtrodden majority in the cities and the countryside, but large groups of erstwhile backers in the middle class and upper class. At the same time, both dictatorships became so closely associated with the interests of the U.S. government, and so dependent on Washington's military and economic support, that they greatly facilitated guerrilla appeals to the patriotic and nationalistic sensibilities of potential recruits. Under conditions like these, demands for social reform and political democracy were, by definition, anti-United States, even though in both cases Washington eventually abandoned Batista and Somoza alike in a futile search for a "third force" that would stave off a guerrilla victory.

In both countries, the Cuban and Nicaraguan dictatorships relied on old-fashioned, personalistic *caudillo* armies, rather than the more professionalized and autonomous military institutions common elsewhere in Latin America. Having staffed their respective armies with trusted cronies, who in return for personal loyalty to the dictator had been allowed to exploit their power to enrich themselves freely, the dictators in effect tied their own fates to that ever-doubtful virtue in a patron–client system: the personal loyalty of their own generals. Batista and Somoza did not really command *national* armies, loyal to the nation and its constitution, but a gang of bodyguards hired to protect the despot, his extended family, their collaborators and their property. As the dictators' chances of survival dimmed, and even the U.S. government began to back away from them in a desperate search for a "third force," the dictators' armies scattered. Lacking popular legitimacy, they were nothing without their patrons, who in turn were nothing without U.S. support.

Deserted by their armies, the dictators deserted their countries, opening the door for the immediate seizure of power by the insurgents. In Cuba, the directing force in the rebellion was the 26th of July Movement, led by Fidel Castro, which took power on 1 January 1959. In Nicaragua, the Frente Sandinista de Liberación Nacional (FSLN) and its leader, Daniel Ortega, took over on 19 July 1979. Once in power, the same prodigious obstacle to their plans confronted both revolutionary governments, and shaped the course of change in both countries more forcefully than any other single factor: the permanent and unappeasable hostility of the U.S. government. As we will see in the separate analyses that follow of the revolutions in power, a strategic move by the Sandinistas to escape Cuba's fate by adjusting their domestic policies proved unavailing.

Cuba

Cuba's passage through communism fused the Soviet-inspired apparatuses of totalitarian rule with the customary *caudillismo* of Hispanic political culture. A more resounding characteristic of Cuban communism was a particular discourse that came of age in the 1960s with the decolonization of Asia and Africa. Its principal themes were liberation, anti-imperialism and "solidarity-in-struggle" – all inventively exploited by Fidel Castro in his ceaseless, and largely successful, efforts to draw support for his revolution from around the globe.

By the late 1970s – bearded, clad in green combat fatigues and waving a big cigar – Castro had positioned himself as the most popular and articulate spokesman for the emancipation of the downtrodden masses of what was then called the "Third World" – the poor countries, mainly of the southern hemisphere, that fit neither in the "first world" of the advanced capitalist countries nor the "second world" of the communist bloc. Their liberation from capitalism, racism and other maladies of colonial and neo-colonial oppression awaited the formation of a vanguard party, unafraid of the United States and its allies, and prepared for armed struggle. That message would find a receptive audience in Latin America.

Leading by example, Castro went to work immediately upon taking power in 1959 to carry out the fiercely nationalistic program of radical reforms that Castro's 26th of July Movement had promised during the insurrection. The centerpiece was the seizure of privately owned sugar plantations and other agricultural estates, and their conversion into state-owned farms and, less commonly, their redistribution to landless families. Further state-ordered expropriations of private property followed, along with increasingly friendly relations with the Soviet-led bloc of self-declared socialist countries controlled exclusively by communist parties. From their governments Castro found the material and ideological resources to successfully resist the increasing hostility to his program of social revolution both within Cuba and outside of it.

In Cuba, opposition by Cubans themselves to the Castro regime intensified as the regime imprisoned thousands for political crimes. More than 200,000 Cubans, or nearly 3% of the population, had abandoned the island by mid-1962 and over the decades, roughly 1.4 million Cubans – between 10% and 20% of the island's population – would flee in serial waves of both authorized and unauthorized immigration, mostly to the United States.

U.S. government hostility to the revolution consistently provoked results exactly opposite to those intended by Washington. Instead of surrendering, or even proposing concessions, Castro responded with carefully calibrated acts of willful defiance that extended the reach of his revolutionary program, enhanced his own popularity on the island and elsewhere in the world, and gave him an excuse to jail his opponents and to close ranks with Washington's greatest enemy, the Soviet Union. On 16 April 1961, as U.S.-trained Cuban exiles flying U.S. B-26 bombers fired on Cuban airfields in an attempt by the U.S. government to incite a rebellion against the revolutionary government, Castro exulted: "We have brought about a socialist revolution right under the nose of the United States!" The next day, the U.S-organized invasion of the island by 1,300 Cuban exiles was easily turned back by the Cuban army at the Bay of Pigs. Having humiliated the United States more spectacularly than any enemy in its history, Castro seized on the failed invasion to justify even closer ties with the Soviet Union, and ever-more forceful declarations of his faith in communism.

"I am a Marxist-Leninist and I shall be a Marxist-Leninist until the day I die," he announced on 1 December.

Gradually, the entire economy came under state control. Ordinary Cubans welcomed a variety of basic social and economic goods that remained beyond the reach of the poor majority almost anywhere else in Latin America. With a state-controlled economy came nearly full employment. Access by all to the benefits of healthcare and education, and a minimally adequate diet, were among the first fruits of the revolution and a key source of the regime's continuing legitimacy. Massive financial subsidies from the Soviet Union enabled much of this generosity. Despite the grave limits on personal freedom and the totalitarian regime's lack of respect for traditional political and civil rights, most Cubans saw themselves as materially better off in comparison both to the majority of their counterparts in the rest of Latin America, and to their own pre-revolutionary living standards. By the mid-1980s, most of the Cubans who had elected to stay on the island also took a certain national pride in having humbled the world's greatest power even as they had defeated a particularly squalid dictatorship, liquidated the old political and socio-economic arrangements that had sustained it, consolidated a social revolution, achieved stability and maturity as a socialist state (at least by Soviet standards), defeated extreme poverty, diversified the economy and acquired immense global prestige.

That prestige derived not only from the Castro revolution's domestic achievements but from Cuba's outsized influence, for such a small, poor country, on the course of the Cold War. We have already noted Cuba's staunch support for revolution in Latin America even in the face of intense U.S. hostility, and its status as a model of social change in the eyes of millions of Latin Americans. To those challenges the United States responded with a Latin American policy aimed above all at preventing "another Cuba." It did so by vastly increasing its spending on economic development and military assistance programs for friendly Latin American governments, while undermining the governments and economies of countries deemed unfriendly to U.S. interests. But the scene of Cuba's most overt interventions was not Latin America but Africa. There, U.S. interests were comparably slight and its presence negligible. As early as the mid-1960s, the Castro government was bolstering African rebel movements with Cuban soldiers, military instructors and medical personnel. Between November 1975 and April 1976, Cuba shipped 36,000 soldiers to Angola to support one of the three guerrilla armies then fighting each other for control of the country, and by 1988 the Cuban force had grown to 55,000. In 1978, Ethiopia's socialist government welcomed 12,000 Cuban soldiers to help it defeat an invasion force of Somalians.

Firmly integrated into the worldwide economic and political networks of the socialist bloc, Cuba by the 1970s saw itself – and was largely seen elsewhere in the world – as a model of revolutionary politics and equitable development.

Liberal democratic procedures like competitive elections, freedom of speech and association, and the rule of law were, to Castro's many admirers, trivialities in comparison to the material gains of the revolution.

Perhaps the most dramatic demonstration of the Cuban revolution's potency was its ability to survive the worldwide decomposition of the communist bloc, despite Cuba's heavy material dependence on it for both aid and trade. In an extraordinarily abrupt and unforeseen reversal of the status quo, all eight of the eastern and central European countries that had become dependencies of the Soviet Union after World War II declared their independence of Moscow and renounced communism between 1989 and 1991. The Soviet Union itself collapsed into fifteen separate republics in December of 1991, replacing totalitarian, one-party rule with pluralist political systems and ditching socialism for capitalism. It was clear, in hindsight, that popular pressures for economic and political freedom had become irresistible, effectively terminating the grand experiment in Communist Party-led state socialism.

Only four communist-ruled countries besides Cuba survived the great counterrevolutions of 1989–1991: China, Laos, North Korea and Vietnam. But even that list is misleadingly long, for even as China and Vietnam preserved one-party rule they replaced their monolithically state-controlled economies with mixed ones, encouraging privately owned enterprises to take the lead. In all five countries (Cuba and the above four), though, monopoly rule by the communist party survived for roughly the same reason: the party leaderships had succeeded in fusing communism as an ideology with a strong sense of national identity. "Patriotic" and "communist" became practically synonymous. All five countries had long been surrounded by neighbors who could also be identified as powerful enemies, and it was not difficult to inspire popular support for the incumbent regimes by pronouncing the names of their historic enemies and the injustices associated with them.

Fidel Castro perfected the technique and applied it to the United States with consummate rhetorical skill. U.S. leaders, in turn, cooperated flawlessly by seizing every opportunity to punish Cuba for its insolence. None of Washington's policies played into Castro's hands more conveniently than its habitual renewal, and occasional enhancement, of the partial trade embargo that became nearly total by the mid-1960s. In the military and political realm, the United States maintained a decades-long program of sabotage, subversion and espionage that did little to weaken the regime but much to discredit Washington among patriotic Cubans. All in all, the U.S. response made it easy for Castro to blame the United States for the island's economic misfortunes, and to rally support for further repression of Castro's political enemies and for the extension of state controls over the economy.

Castro's faith in communism as the island's best ideological defense against the United States remained undaunted. Three days after the collapse of the

Soviet Union under a wave of popular demands for democratic freedoms, Castro declared that he still believed strongly "in the tremendous convenience of the single party system . . . because the multiparty system is an instrument of imperialism to keep societies fragmented and divided . . . I am firmly convinced that one party is and must be – for a long historical period, no one can predict how long – the form of political organization in our society." Once again linking patriotism and communism, he called on Cubans to defend the revolution with their lives: "We are not a lineage that surrenders, we are another type of people . . . They can occupy the whole country [but] they would have to fight against millions of people . . . We should never give up ground in ideology . . . Socialism or death, fatherland or death, we will win. . . ."[3]

The loss of Soviet trade and aid devastated an economy that had already been stumbling badly since the mid-1980s. Among average Cubans, living standards fell sharply amid multiplying signs of popular cynicism and discontent with the regime. In the United States, predictions of the Castro regime's imminent collapse surged forth once again on TV screens and the covers of news magazines. Yet once again Castro defied seemingly insuperable odds. He declared "a special period in time of peace" that included some minor, and carefully regulated, market-oriented reforms – including the expansion of opportunities for much-needed foreign investment. They helped the island increase food production and employment. But private entrepreneurship on the scale of that being carried out in communist-ruled China and Vietnam was not yet seriously considered, and the economy remained closely controlled by the state until further pro-market reforms were introduced in 2010, a topic discussed in Chapter 10.

As if sensing the potential for popular uprisings of the kind that ended socialism in the Soviet bloc, the Cuban government moved cautiously toward more popular participation during the "special period." In 1991, Cubans were allowed to vote directly for delegates to provincial legislatures and the national assembly. But in a system that still allowed only a single, officially approved nominee for each seat, the reform did nothing to satisfy democracy-minded Cubans. In 1998, a group of dissidents sought to implement Article 88 of the Cuban constitution of 1976, which permitted citizens to initiate legislation by gathering the signatures of at least 10,000 voters. The organizers of the Varela Project (named after Félix Varela, a nineteenth-century Cuban patriot) gathered more than 11,000 signatures on a petition that would have legislated freedom of speech and association, amnesty for political prisoners, a free-enterprise economy, and competitive elections. Submitted in 2002, the petition was rejected by the government on the grounds that the petition drive itself was a subversive act, "conceived, financed and directed" by the U.S. government. The Varela Project collected an additional 13,000 signatures between 2002 and 2004, but in the midst of that campaign the government arrested seventy-five people linked with political reform initiatives, charged them with collaborating with foreign enemies, and sentenced them to prison terms ranging from six to twenty-eight years.

Large public protests against government repression continued to be a rare sight in Cuba. Public opposition more often took the form of campaigns carried out by individuals – journalists, human rights activists and hunger strikers – and small groups such as the *Damas de Blanco* or Ladies in White. They were female relatives of political prisoners who began peacefully marching every Sunday, starting in 2003, to demand the release of their kin. In 2010, following negotiations initiated by the Catholic Church and the government of Spain, Cuba released fifty-two "prisoners of conscience" but only on condition that they leave the island for good.

Cuba's record of political despotism, unmatched in the history of Latin America, was imposed by reformers who had promised, in the words of Castro's "Program Manifesto" of 1956, to implement "the ideal of a democratic republic, inspired in the credo of freedom and founded in the character and capacity of its citizens." Cubans last voted in a competitive election in 1948, thus preserving intact Gen. Batista's interruption of the constitutional order in his *golpe de estado* of 1952 for more than another half-century.

Nicaragua

The Nicaraguans who founded the FSLN in the early 1960s did so in conscious imitation of Castro's success and his embrace of Marxism as the revolution's guiding ideology. Like nearly all the Latin American insurrectionary groups of the time, the FSLN declared war on imperialism and capitalism, while promising a socialist revolution. But after taking power in 1979, the FSLN softened its public stance. The Sandinistas seized the plantations, banks and factories most closely associated with the Somoza family but they ruled Nicaragua with a much lighter hand than Castro did in Cuba. The economy combined free enterprise and state ownership, and opposition parties were legally allowed to contest FSLN rule in regular elections, albeit under sometimes harshly repressive conditions.

The FSLN decided in favor of a more open and pluralistic society in part to avoid antagonizing the United States. But Washington remained unappeased. The FSLN's long-term plans for a socialist economy; its growing dependence on Cuba, the Soviet Union, and other communist countries for military and economic assistance; and its commitment to exporting its revolution beyond its borders (most notably to neighboring El Salvador), earned it the implacable hostility of the U.S. government. Within weeks of the Sandinista victory, President Jimmy Carter signed a series of secret directives, at first authorizing the

Central Intelligence Agency to covertly aid non-Sandinista political groups in Nicaragua, then escalating to covert action against Nicaragua in 1980. To officials of the Reagan administration (1981–1991), the Sandinistas were the long arm of communist subversion, manipulated from Moscow and Havana. "Central America is . . . our doorstep," President Ronald Reagan declared in 1984, "and it's become the stage for a bold attempt by the Soviet Union, Cuba, and Nicaragua to install communism by force throughout the hemisphere." By then, Reagan had vastly expanded Carter's program of covert action. The U.S. Central Intelligence Agency organized up to 10,000 anti-FSLN Nicaraguan exiles into guerrilla armies known as *contras* ("against" in Spanish) that attacked Nicaragua from safe havens in neighboring Honduras and Costa Rica. The U.S. strategy provoked unpopular defensive measures in Nicaragua – a military draft, heavier defense spending and the repression of some political foes – that contributed to a gradual decline in popular support for the FSLN. As a result, Nicaraguans voted the revolutionaries out of office in 1990, replacing them with a government led by a political party that had been richly subsidized by the U.S. government, and that shared Washington's ideological preference for liberal democratic rule and a more traditional, free-enterprise economy.

Revolutionary Movements that Fell Short of Victory

During the 1980s, the FSLN government of Nicaragua struggled in vain to defend its revolution not only against the military aggression of the United States and its *contra* army, but also against rising political opposition among Nicaraguans. At the same time, revolutionary movements in two other countries in Central America approached their denouement. The fighting in El Salvador (1980–1992) and Guatemala (1962–1994) did not end in victory for the insurgents, but neither were the revolutionaries defeated, despite prodigious transfers of military and economic assistance to both governments by the United States. As the insurgents and the governments in both countries concluded that neither could decisively defeat the other, negotiations to end the conflicts commenced. The various Salvadoran insurgent groups – united under the banner of the Frente Farabundo Martí de Liberación Nacional (FMLN, founded in 1980) – gained considerably more at the peace talks than the Guatemalan rebels. By the time the fighting ended in late 1992, the Salvadoran rebels had acquired governmental commitments to major judicial and electoral reforms, large reductions in the size and influence of the armed forces, and the establishment of a police force that would include guerrilla veterans. The FMLN, having given up its goal of state socialism through armed insurrection, went on to become a major political party, winning the presidency in 2009.

In Guatemala, on the other hand, even though the army clearly had the upper hand over the guerrilla alliance (the Unidad Revolucionaria Nacional Guatemalteca or URNG, founded in 1982), both the insurgents and the Guatemalan army resisted the idea of peace talks, making the Guatemalan guerrilla war the longest and bloodiest in Latin America.[4] Having started in 1962, it ultimately claimed more than 200,000 victims, some 93% of whom were killed by government forces. In the end, after a fitful series of negotiating sessions between 1991 and 1996, the government and the URNG signed a peace accord on 29 December 1996. One immediate result was a massive reduction in the size of the Guatemalan army and the hastening of its very gradual depoliticization. The treaty created a new national police force, and established procedures for monitoring human rights. But intense conflicts within the URNG crippled it as a postwar political force, weakening the ability of the ex-revolutionaries to effectively press for the political and social transformations that they had envisioned after their disarmament, as their counterparts in El Salvador had managed to do.

In the revolutionary civil wars that devastated Guatemala, Nicaragua and El Salvador during the Cold War, the United States consistently defended the status quo, while supporting the incumbent governments against the insurgents with transfers of military and economic assistance that vastly exceeded the assistance flowing to the rebels and the Sandinista government from Cuba, the Soviet Union and other socialist bloc countries. Eventually, U.S. policy preferences prevailed in all three countries: in Guatemala and El Salvador, democratic reforms replaced guerrilla victories; in Nicaragua, military pressure by means of the *contra* army contributed decisively to the Sandinistas' electoral defeat.

Oscar Arias, the president of Costa Rica (1986–1990; 2006–2010) played a decisive role in starting the peace process by convening a series of meetings among the presidents of the five Central American countries in 1986 and 1987. The dialogues terminated in the signing of the peace plan known as "Esquipulas II" (after the Guatemalan town where the presidents held one of their meetings) on 7 August 1987. The agreement paved the way for the individual country settlements by committing all five countries to respect the legitimacy of each other's government, eject foreign military forces and open the way toward democratization and demilitarization.

Arias, who for his efforts won the Nobel Peace Prize in 1987 at the age of 46, believed that the basic causes of the wars in Guatemala, El Salvador and Nicaragua were not to be found in their external relationships but internally. Therefore, peace without a process of national reconciliation, dialogue and free elections would be impossible, and agreement on that key point established the context for the national-level negotiations that followed. As a result of Esquipulas II, the UN Security Council sent emissaries and observers whose presence helped to build a climate of confidence and trust in all three countries. Initially, the United States opposed the Arias initiative and sought to derail it on the grounds that it would legitimize the revolutionary government of Nicaragua. That stance changed with the inauguration in 1989 of President George H. W. Bush, who recognized the futility of maintaining military pressure on the Sandinistas. By backing away from support for the *contras* and joining the peace process, Bush removed the last major hurdle to reconciliation in the region.

In the Marxist-guided insurgencies of Latin America from the 1960s to the 1980s, the fighting was nowhere more intense and destructive, and the results more favorable to the revolutionaries, than in the cases we have just discussed in Cuba and Central America. That leaves South America, where the outcomes were different. There, the national armed forces annihilated most of the revolutionary organizations. Others melted away, or tried to convert themselves into regular political parties. Only a very few guerrilla armies, notably in Colombia and Peru, survived into the twenty-first century, and then only after turning away from social revolution and toward organized crime.

Peru recorded the most distinctive – and most nearly successful – case of revolutionary insurgency warfare in South America. A cult-like group calling itself the "Partido Comunista del Perú por el Sendero Luminoso del Pensamiento de José Carlos Mariátegui," but commonly known as Sendero Luminoso ("Shining Path"), seemed poised to seize power during the peak of the fighting between 1989 and 1992. The war killed about 69,000 people. But unlike all the rest of Latin America's insurgencies, in this one most (about 54%) died at the hands of the guerrillas rather than the armed forces. Conspicuous for its brutality, idiosyncratic beliefs and numerical strength, Sendero Luminoso was founded in 1970 by Abimael Guzmán (b. 1934), a philosophy professor at the Universidad Nacional San Cristóbal de Huamanga in the southern Andean highlands town of Ayacucho. Exploiting his influence as a teacher and administrator, Guzmán concentrated on building the group's core membership from among his university's students. His heterodox ideology combined the doctrines of Mao Tse-tung, the leader of the Communist Party-led revolution in China in 1949, and those of José Carlos Mariátegui (d. 1930), the Peruvian essayist who sought to link Marxism with the values he associated with Peru's indigenous peoples. Like Mao, Mariátegui revised Marx in ways that Guzmán found useful in a country with a large indigenous population and a peasant-based rural economy. Guzmán believed a socialist revolution could succeed in Peru, just as it had in China, under the leadership of the peasant class rather than an industrial proletariat, as Marx and Lenin had insisted.

In the late 1970s, Sendero Luminoso activists carried this message to the peasant population around Ayacucho as well as to other Peruvian universities.

After initiating military operations in 1980, Sendero's fulltime fighting forces rose within a decade from about 200 to as many as 10,000, plus tens of thousands of unarmed collaborators throughout Peru. Seizing political and military control of much of rural Peru, the group targeted rival guerrilla organizations and revolutionary parties, as well as government officials and uncooperative peasants. Its tactical use of kidnapping, massacre, assassination and bombing was matched by a government counterinsurgency campaign of massacre, torture and assassination. Both sides victimized the innocent as well as the guilty, and the main victims were the highland peasantry in whose name Sendero had launched its war against what it called "semi-feudalism and imperialist domination." Sendero's strategy of gradually encircling the major cities from its rural strongholds appeared to be succeeding until 1992, when the police arrested Guzmán and other high-level party officials in a raid on their Lima hideout. The insurgency's momentum faltered, then diminished considerably as the authoritarian (but elected) government of President Alberto Fujimori (1990–2000) responded with a revised combination of tactics aimed at strengthening the national economy and bolstering national security.

After 2000, Sendero Luminoso survived by exploiting its intimate knowledge of the country's major coca-growing zones, selling "protection" to drug traffickers and then gradually seeking to take control of the cultivation and distribution of coca and the production of cocaine. Thus Sendero's battle against the authorities – and anyone who collaborated with them – continued, but largely on the terrain of organized crime rather than revolutionary politics. During 2008 alone, Peru's government lost twenty-two soldiers and police officers to Sendero attacks as it vainly sought to crush the group. From the prison cell where he was still serving a life sentence, Guzmán published his memoirs, *De puño y letra* (*In My Own Hand*) in September 2009 at the age of 74. Unrepentant, he called himself a "communist, marxist-leninist-maoist, a soldier of the proletariat, ready to face prison, exile and death," and acknowledged that his was the "principal political responsibility" for the insurgency that began in 1980.

Sendero Luminoso's shift, from a guerrilla army dedicated primarily to social revolution, to a criminal organization dedicated primarily to enriching itself in the drug trade, followed the experience of the two main Colombian insurgent groups, the Ejército de Liberación Nacional (ELN) and the Fuerzas Armadas Revolucionarias de Colombia (FARC) in the 1990s and after. Like other guerrilla armies, those of Colombia initiated their insurgencies in the mid-1960s with the goal of leading a popular insurrection that would result in the destruction of the Colombian state and a Cuban-style socialist regime. But until the early 1980s, neither group could claim more than a few hundred members; clashes between the guerrillas and state forces were rare, and consequently the "armed struggle" had little impact on Colombia's political life.

That began to change when the new opportunities to participate in the illegal drug trade coincided with Colombia's rise as the world's leading producer of cocaine.

The FARC and the ELN, from about 1980 onward, began collaborating with the crime syndicates (or "cartels") that controlled the production and export of illegal narcotics. In addition to organizing the cultivation and processing of coca (into cocaine) and poppies (into heroin), the guerrilla groups also increased their incomes by kidnappings, bank robberies and extorting protection money from business firms. Colombians witnessed a tremendous rise in violence and lawlessness. Massacres, kidnappings and assassinations multiplied, while conflicts over access to the immensely profitable trade in narcotics intensified. Colombia's homicide remained among the highest of any country in Latin America, jumping from about 16 per 100,000 persons in the early 1970s to more than 80 in the early 1990s. Numerous armed groups – not just the guerrilla armies, but also anti-guerrilla vigilante gangs or so-called "paramilitaries" (secretly backed by the state), the crime syndicates, and of course the national armed forces – operated as if the traditionally weak state itself were irrelevant. In fact, the Colombian state had scarcely penetrated large parts of the national territory, leaving many remote settled areas to fend for themselves. Outside its big cities, Colombia by the 1990s was controlled not by a unified state but by a congeries of guerrilla groups, anti-guerrilla vigilante armies, networks of large landowners, drug dealers, and operatives of the two traditional political parties (Liberals and Conservatives).

In a desperate move to reassert the authority of the government, President Andrés Pastrana in 1998 formally yielded control of a territory the size of Switzerland to the FARC as an incentive to encourage the group to negotiate. Instead, the FARC used it as a safe haven for its operations. After a series of fruitless negotiating sessions between Pastrana and the FARC's leader, the Colombian army was ordered to retake the territory in 2002. By then, public support for the guerrillas had almost completely disappeared.

The combination of massive U.S. financial and military collaboration beginning in 2000 under the bilateral "Plan Colombia" program, and the election in 2002 of a hardline president, Alvaro Uribe, led to the first significant setbacks for the guerrilla armies and other non-state armed groups. "Sometimes," Uribe said a year after taking office, "I close my eyes and ask myself where my country is going. And I see that the country is tearing itself apart, everyone pulling on a little piece, stealing a shred. Anyone who has two guns, three coca plants, and four kilograms of explosives sets up a feudal state, changing Colombia into a collection of rags, something that cannot be allowed."[5] Uribe put the FARC and the ELN on the defensive, forcing them to cede territory even as they continued to lash out with acts of urban terrorism and attacks on the country's infrastructure.

Uribe's popularity surged well beyond that of any recent president. Colombians reelected him in 2006 with the largest margin (64%) ever recorded by a presidential candidate, thanks largely to sharp declines in the rates of murder, kidnapping and massacre, and the highest economic growth rate in nearly thirty years. Even though the homicide rate had fallen to about 38 per 100,000 in 2005, it was still the highest in Latin America, and Colombia remained the only Latin American country still engaged in a major guerrilla war. Both the FARC and the ELN continued to show considerable military strength while still benefiting financially from the government's inability to stop the cultivation of the coca and poppy plants that sustained the illegal drug trade.

Social revolution through armed struggle had practically disappeared by the 1990s. The momentum in favor of social revolution in Latin America was already declining when the sturdiest descendant of the Cuban revolution, Nicaragua's FSLN, was voted out of power in 1990. Why? For one thing, Nicaragua's experience showed that revolutionary triumphs could be reversed when counter-revolutionaries joined forces with the perpetually anti-revolutionary government of the United States. At the same time, the refusal of the original Cuban insurgents – above all, Fidel Castro and his brother Raúl – to yield control of the Cuban revolutionary government after four decades in power showed how revolutionary social change could preserve some of the very conditions – dictatorship and the suppression of human rights – that inspired revolutionary movements in the first place. Across Latin America in the late 1980s, the wave of democratization, the rising expectations in favor of individual freedom and respect for human rights, signs of economic growth after years of debt-induced stagnation, and the breakdown of deeply discredited military dictatorships, made social revolution both less attractive and less urgent than it had been in the 1960s. Finally, the hundreds of millions of people who had lived for decades under communist rule in the Soviet Union and eastern Europe openly expressed their revulsion for it by rising up against it in the late 1980s, administering a spectacular blow to revolutionary politics and the passion for socialism.

Post-Cold War Socialism and the New Populism

Despite these serial setbacks, the socialist ideal not only persisted but enjoyed a revival in the first decade of the new century. The versatility of its doctrine made it an ideal vehicle for a new generation of populists that emerged after 2000. To them, "el socialismo" seemed just the right tool for popular appeals for electoral support. In confronting the region's continuing poverty and extreme inequality, socialism seemed to be the only sure answer to the failures of the regnant system of free enterprise. Against the individualistic striving of capitalism, socialism could be presented as the highest form of democracy, offering the warmth of collectivism and nationalistic solidarity in contrast to the calculated scheming of an entrepreneurial class easily portrayed as the enemy of the nation. Socialistic solutions stood to foment governmentally imposed welfare schemes, and thus to revive the flow of political and welfare dividends historically associated with Latin American patrimonialism and corporatism. In addition, socialism invariably implied hostility to the United States – the apotheosis of liberal capitalism and the historic foe of socialism. Of all the varieties of nationalism, none was easier to inspire and sustain than that animated by resentment of the United States.

The leading voice in the socialist revival was that of the populist president of Venezuela, Hugo Chávez. In 2005 he announced that his country would follow a program of "twenty-first century socialism" and two years later renamed his electoral vehicle the Partido Socialista Unido de Venezuela (United Socialist Party of Venezuela). Chávez accelerated moves in favor of political centralization, the concentration of power in the presidency, the nationalization of privately owned enterprises, and limits on the freedom of speech. "We are moving to full democratization which we have called Bolivarian socialism whose primary objective is to give power to the people," Chávez declared on 11 July 2010. "Just like Christ, the Revolution supports the poor and exploited and seeks their liberation through social justice." Five months later, the Venezuelan congress bowed to the country's rich legacy of presidentialism by granting Chávez his request to rule by decree until 2012.

Like Chávez, populists elsewhere took advantage of socialism's ideological versatility while exploiting its appeal to national solidarity. Evo Morales won the presidency of Bolivia in 2006 as the candidate of the Movimiento al Socialismo or Movement Toward Socialism whose aim, according to Vice President Alvaro García Linera, was the construction of "an Andean-Amazonian Socialism, which does not imitate anything or anyone, which does not adopt as its model either Venezuela or Cuba, either Russia or China." In Ecuador, President Rafael Correa endorsed Chávez's vision of socialism, while insisting on its adaptability to different national realities.

Despite the announcement in 2010 by the Communist government of Cuba that it planned to dismantle the island's fifty-year-old socialist economy and encourage private enterprise, the populists' appeals to socialism continued. While the content of their socialist vision was far from clear, "twenty-first century socialism" undermined political and economic freedoms and thus posed new obstacles to the consolidation of liberal democracy. Unlike the summons to socialism that had resounded across Latin America decades earlier, however, these failed to arouse the indignation of the region's armed forces. Much had changed over the intervening years. Perhaps the most notable was the gradual submission of the armed forces to civilian government, a stunning turnaround in the political culture of the region, and the subject of the next chapter.

Notes

1   Costa Rica was no exception. "La Familia" engaged in assaults and bombings from 1981 until police arrested its leaders in 1983. From 1986 to 1988, the Organización Patriótica Santamaria/Ejército de la Democracia y la Soberanía (OPS) carried out bombings and bank robberies.
2   H. Michael Erisman, *Cuba's International Relations: The Anatomy of a Nationalistic Foreign Policy* (Boulder, CO: Westview Press, 1985), 20, 61.
3   Fidel Castro, "Cuba–Castro Holds Out," in *A Documentary History of Communism and the World from Revolution to Collapse*, ed. Robert V. Daniels (Hanover: University Press of New England, 1994), 377–82.
4   Although Colombia's Fuerzas Armadas Revolucionarias de Colombia (FARC) guerrilla army initiated operations in 1966 and was still active in 2012, its social-revolutionary aims had been overshadowed for at least two decades by its lucrative drug-trafficking and kidnapping activities. It had evolved from a politico-military group to a criminal organization.
5   Harvey F. Kline, *Showing Teeth to the Dragons: State-Building by Colombian President Álvaro Uribe Vélez, 2002–2006* (Tuscaloosa: University of Alabama Press, 2009), 5.

References

Castro, Fidel. "Cuba–Castro Holds Out." In *A Documentary History of Communism and the World from Revolution to Collapse*, ed. Robert V. Daniels, 377–82. Hanover: University Press of New England, 1994.
Erisman, H. Michael. *Cuba's International Relations: The Anatomy of a Nationalistic Foreign Policy*. Boulder, CO: Westview Press, 1985.
Kline, Harvey F. *Showing Teeth to the Dragons: State-Building by Colombian President Álvaro Uribe Vélez, 2002–2006*. Tuscaloosa: University of Alabama Press, 2009.

Chapter 4

The Armed Forces Bow to Civilian Rule

In the public mind, no world region has been more closely associated with militarism than Latin America. The image of the haughty officer, chest heaped with medals and gold braid, was a staple caricature of the region for decades. One of its most enduring versions is the self-styled general and tyrannical megalomaniac who "governed as if he knew he was predestined never to die," in the 1975 novel *El otoño del patriarca* (*The Autumn of the Patriarch*) by Gabriel García Márquez, the Colombian writer who won the Nobel Prize for Literature in 1982. The novel owed its popularity throughout Latin America in large part to García Márquez's ability to depict a military despot whose characteristics could be recognized by people in many countries of the region. Militarism was a deeply embedded feature of Latin American political life and lore, and part of everyone's experience. Between 1920 and 1960 at least seventy-eight military revolts resulted in the seizure of power by the armed forces in every country but Mexico and Uruguay, and nearly all of the regimes they established were known by the name of the general at their head. The old pattern continued in 1961, 1962 and 1963 as the armed forces seized power in eight countries – from Central America (Guatemala, Honduras and El Salvador) to the Caribbean (the Dominican Republic) and South America (Argentina, Ecuador and Peru).

In a political culture long characterized by weak or inept civilian governments, indifference to the rule of law, military engagement in politics, and the use of violence to settle political disputes, it was not difficult in any given political or economic crisis for the military to justify a *golpe de estado* and to gain popular support, at least at the outset. Moreover, the Cold War invariably magnified the ideological implications of almost any national crisis. As a result, civilian politicians, political parties and large sectors of the population often

Contemporary Latin America: 1970 to the Present, First Edition. Robert H. Holden and Rina Villars.
© 2013 Robert H. Holden and Rina Villars. Published 2013 by Blackwell Publishing Ltd.

summoned the military and welcomed its direct rule. The armed forces in turn could usually justify the seizure of power by citing customary statutes and constitutional provisions allowing for a "state of siege" or a "state of exception" during periods of extreme public emergency, when normal government procedures and even the basic rights of citizens could be legally suspended. Some constitutions actually required the armed forces to act to defend the country's laws and constitution, and to keep the peace. The ambiguous language of these stipulations opened the door to abuse by civilian and military regimes alike as they took advantage of the opportunity to repress law-abiding political opponents as well as seditious or lawless rebel movements and insurgencies.

The Brazilian coup of 1964 shared with the Guatemalan coup of 1963 the distinction of inaugurating the regime phase we identified in the introduction of Part II as "bureaucratic authoritarianism." As the Brazilian coup unfolded on 31 March to 1 April, the military leadership announced its twin purposes: to defeat "the communist plan for seizing power," and to "reestablish order so that legal reforms [could] be carried out."[1] Variations on these two themes would come to dominate the justifications proffered by the armed forces elsewhere in Latin America over the next decade or so. But it was the Brazilians' second grand objective – that of restoring a certain kind of order – that emerged as perhaps the most characteristic feature of the bureaucratic-authoritarian regimes. No longer content with merely rearranging the civilian administration of government, as it had traditionally done, the armed forces now prepared to reorganize and "purge" society itself of an enemy depicted variously as agents of disorder, communism, panic and anarchy. Military leaders predicted an imminent takeover by radical, subversive elements inspired by the success of the Cuban revolution of 1959.

"Subversive" could be expanded to embrace individuals and groups who merely sympathized with armed rebels, or those whom the authorities only suspected of such sympathy, or simply dissenting from the military's policies. Within the leadership of the military and among its civilian supporters, the most deeply rooted values of the West were held to be at stake in the battle between the two Cold War blocs. Seeing itself as the ultimate defender of those values and thus of the security of the nation, the Latin American military establishments explicitly rejected their customary role of "moderator." Instead, they saw themselves as duty-bound to rid the nation of the parties, ideologies and individuals (usually those associated with the political left, but not always) responsible for the political convulsions of the 1960s and 1970s. Those convulsions were often interpreted by military leaders as the partial result of one of the great challenges of the Cold War era in Latin America: the need to find ways to develop and modernize economies capable of quickly raising the living standards of the millions of people bowed down by chronic poverty and unemployment. Here too, military officers saw themselves as uniquely capable of directing a process that, they argued, had been bungled by incompetent, self-seeking civilian politicians.

This goal of achieving both socio-political and economic reconstruction helps explain why the armed forces adopted an institutional or bureaucratic style of military rule. The goal also helps explain two other novel aspects of this period of military rule. The first was its durability. Because remaking society, purging the political system and developing the economy would require many years, even decades, in power, these coups were not intended to be the temporary interventions typical of previous military takeovers. Military regimes aimed to stay in power much longer than they had ever done before. The second novel aspect was the exceptionally cruel and barbarous conduct of some of the military governments and the sweeping character of the repression – particularly in Argentina, Brazil, Chile and Guatemala. To the leadership of the armed forces in those places, thoroughgoing reform required *la mano dura*, a "firm hand" that typically included torture and murder, often on a massive scale. As a result, the human costs of military rule during the 1960s and 1970s were so great that they inflicted wounds that would take many decades to heal. Routinely and systematically, military authorities tortured, murdered and illegally detained individuals suspected of opposing the regimes. Constitutional or statutory norms under which the accused might have sought protection were often repealed or flouted by the authorities. Apart from violations of basic human rights, the regimes repealed or trimmed longstanding political rights, including those of association and expression, and terminated the practice of free elections.

We turn now to a comparison of the experiences of Chile, Guatemala and Argentina under military rule. They illustrate both the diversity in the form that militarism took in Latin America, and the harshness of the bureaucratic-authoritarian model of rule.

Chile

Throughout Latin America, sizeable elements, even majorities, of the population often welcomed military takeovers of constitutionally elected civilian governments, despite the threat the military posed to civil liberties. On 22 August 1973, three weeks before the Chilean armed forces overthrew the socialist-communist coalition government of Salvador Allende, that country's Chamber of Deputies adopted 81–47, a resolution widely interpreted as an invitation to the military to take power. Blaming Allende for the collapse of the rule of law, and for the imminent imposition of a "totalitarian dictatorship," the deputies specifically called on the government, the armed forces and the national police to "poner inmediato término" – "to end immediately" – the state of violence and constitutional disorder. Among the parties that welcomed the coup of 11 September 1973 was the Christian Democratic Party, the main opponent of the Allende government.

That so much public support for military intervention could arise in Chile was itself remarkable, for the Chilean armed forces were widely thought to be among the least likely in all of Latin America to carry out a coup. Famed for its relatively intense devotion to the rule of law and the constitution, Chile had not seen a military coup since 1932, but even it was more Chilean than Latin American. Masterminded by a civilian politician-journalist whose self-styled "revolutionaries" proclaimed a "República Socialista de Chile," it lasted about three months before it was terminated by an opposing faction of the armed forces, which yielded power two months later to elected leaders. Conspiracies within the military, aimed at moving against certain elected governments, surfaced in 1939, 1946, 1948, 1951 and 1955 but failed to eventuate in coups.

In 1969, in a conspiracy organized by Gen. Roberto Viaux, rebel officers seized control of the Tacna army barracks in Santiago. It was the first open act of military subordination since 1939. The revolt was snuffed out within a day, and upon surrendering, Viaux declared that he had only sought to protest the low pay and poor working conditions of his soldiers. In response, the Chilean congress immediately approved a large pay increase for the armed forces, though Viaux was forced to retire from the military. True to popular beliefs about Chile's tradition of respect for constitutional order, the coup attempt not only generated an outpouring of public support for civilian rule and against the would-be usurpers, but inspired the army commander in chief, Gen. René Schneider, to publicly declare that the armed forces would support whomever was elected president in 1970.

Ideologically, however, Chile found itself more and more divided between a restive and well-organized working class, and a middle and upper class fearful of radical change. As a result, the military's devotion to constitutionalism would be tested again – and fail. Less than a year after declaring the armed forces' political neutrality, Gen. Schneider himself would lose his life defending his stance. In the election of 4 September 1970 Allende won a plurality of the votes, narrowly defeating his two rivals. In response, Gen. Viaux and a few other officers organized a plot, with the knowledge and support of the U.S. Central Intelligence Agency, to kidnap Gen. Schneider in hopes of provoking the armed forces into seizing power and preventing Allende's inauguration on 3 November. Gen. Schneider unexpectedly resisted his would-be kidnappers by drawing a handgun. He was shot in the gun battle that followed and died as a martyr for constitutional rule the day after the Chilean congress affirmed Allende's victory. The plotters not only failed to provoke the military into rebelling, but once again generated a wave of support for constitutional rule and thus for Allende, who, having been elected with just 36.5% of the vote, desperately needed to expand his base. Gen. Schneider's successor as commander in chief, Gen. Carlos Prats, eulogized Schneider as a "hero of peace and martyr of democracy." As we will see, Prats himself would follow Schneider as a martyr for constitutionalism.

Allende identified himself as a Marxist. The two principal parties in his multiparty governing coalition, Unidad Popular (Popular Unity; UP), were the Communist Party and the Socialist Party. After taking office, Allende began to implement the program of sweeping change promised by the UP in its published platform: "To bring to an end the rule of the imperialists, the monopolists, and the landed oligarchy and to initiate the construction of socialism in Chile." The UP program included the nationalization of privately owned firms (including two giant U.S.-owned copper-mining companies) and the acceleration of Chile's slow-moving program to redistribute agricultural land to the rural poor. In early 1971, in his first message to the Chilean congress, Allende compared the situation in Chile to that of Russia and China on the eve of their respective communist revolutions, and announced the guiding principle of his administration: "the transference of political and economic power to the workers and to the people as a whole," which in turn required "the socialization of the basic means of production."[2]

Allende tried to impose this agenda in the face of political obstacles that turned out to be insuperable. Not only had the majority of the Chilean electorate voted against the Unidad Popular, but the coalition itself was sharply divided between militants who accused Allende of selling out, insisting that he accelerate the socialization of the economy, and others who counseled a slower pace in order to avoid provoking a military coup. The intensely hostile U.S. administration of President Richard Nixon had secretly schemed with anti-Allende Chileans to keep Allende from taking office, and then took action to destabilize the Chilean economy while secretly funding anti-Allende political parties and newspapers, and increasing U.S. aid to the Chilean military.

Though the United States would welcome the removal of the Allende government by the Chilean military, none can reasonably doubt that the coup was an entirely Chilean operation, inspired above all by the Allende government's calamitous policy judgments and its extreme ideological commitments. By mid-1973, the productivity of the newly "socialized" sectors of the national economy had declined sharply. Political life was so adversarial, chaotic and violent that the country appeared to be on the verge of civil war. In a little less than three years, the tide of political and economic disorder had deeply eroded the Chilean public's stout disposition in favor of constitutional rule.

Support within the armed forces for a coup took months to build but came to a head in August 1973 when the high command forced Allende's highest-ranking constitutionalist officers, including Gen. Prats, to resign. Meeting on 9 September 1973, the newly installed high command, led by Gen. Augusto

Pinochet (whom Allende had appointed to replace Prats) decided to move two days later. On 11 September, the armed forces quickly overcame what little resistance it encountered, including that of the president. Cornered in his office with an assault rifle, Allende broadcast a defiant radio message. In response to his refusal to surrender, the air force bombed the presidential palace, setting it afire. At about 2 p.m. Allende turned the weapon on himself and died.

For the next seventeen years, with Gen. Pinochet at the helm, the armed forces ruled Chile. The military government shut down the congress, banned all political parties, and closed "subversive" publications and broadcasting stations. Tens of thousands of Chileans were arrested; within a few years the number of exiles exceeded 100,000. Political activists associated with the Unidad Popular government were tortured, murdered and made to "disappear," a technique of infusing terror by kidnapping and killing the victim, and then secretly disposing of the body. Nothing would be publicly recorded because the military itself would identify suspected subversives, apprehend them, torture them to identify more subversives, and then kill them. Without a public record of their death, nothing could be said with certainty about their fate. The dictatorship even extended the repression outside Chile. In September 1974, Gen. Prats and his wife, living in exile in Buenos Aires, were killed by a car bomb planted by agents of the Pinochet government; two years later, they struck again, killing Orlando Letelier, Allende's ambassador to the United States, and an aide, in Washington, DC.

The Pinochet government abruptly reversed the socialist direction of the economy, aiming it in a robustly free-enterprise direction. Political life revived very slowly. In 1977 Pinochet announced his plan for a gradual transition toward democracy, "protected" by a constitution that was approved by a three-to-one margin in a plebiscite held on 11 September 1980, though only groups favoring a "yes" vote were fully allowed to campaign. The new constitution created a weak congress, gave the military a relatively free hand, made Pinochet the president until 1990, and provided for a plebiscite in 1988 at which voters would be allowed to approve or reject the military's candidate for a second term of eight years (1990–1998). As the 1980s unfolded, public protests against the dictatorship multiplied. The regime permitted the organization of some political parties in preparation for the 1988 plebiscite. A fifteen-party coalition campaigned for a "No" against another eight-year term for Pinochet, and in favor of competitive elections. On 5 October 1988, some 97% of the country's registered voters turned out, voting "No" by 54% to 43%. Astonished and angered by the result, Pinochet nevertheless followed the procedure established by his own constitution and announced elections for president and congress in December 1989. Rejecting both the extreme left and the right, Chileans gave 55% of their vote to a seventeen-party, center-left coalition headed by 72-year-old Patricio Aylwin, a founding member of the Christian Democratic Party.

Aylwin took office on 11 March 1990 while Pinochet, in compliance with the constitution, remained as army commander until 1998.

Guatemala

Chile, despite its status as the Latin American country with one of the strongest traditions of constitutional rule and electoral democracy, had succumbed to one of the longest and most repressive military regimes in Latin American history. Guatemala, situated at the opposite end of Latin America, likewise yielded at about the same time to a long period of harshly repressive military rule. The immediate causes of the military takeovers in both countries were identical – the fear of an impending takeover by Marxist revolutionaries. While the outcome (repressive military rule) and the motivation (fear of communism) were thus alike, the conditions that gave rise to the coups were fundamentally different, as was the corresponding role played by the U.S. government.

Guatemala, unlike Chile, had seen very little constitutional government, and its experience with free elections was also limited. Tyrannical regimes headed by *caudillos*, whose authority rested on little more than armed might, followed one another in dreary succession until 1944–1954, when Guatemalans elected two civilian governments in the freest elections in the country's history. Beginning in 1954, after a coup secretly organized by the U.S. Central Intelligence Agency had removed the constitutional president, Jacobo Arbenz, the Guatemalan armed forces gradually asserted control over the political process. A guerrilla army's declaration of war on the Guatemalan state in 1962, and the prospect of victory by a leftwing presidential candidate, led to another military coup in 1963.

This one was different from the many that had preceded it. The armed forces took power as an institution, rather than under the authority of a leading military personality, and did so for the explicit purpose of reordering society and purging it of "subversives," thus anticipating the justification for the Brazilian coup the following year. All three of the political parties that welcomed the Guatelaman coup received permission to compete in the carefully supervised 1966 presidential elections, held against the background of an intensifying guerrilla offensive that pitted urban and rural insurgents against the U.S.-backed armed forces. The armed forces allowed the winning candidate, Julio César Méndez Montenegro, to take office only after he secretly signed a pledge that his government would neither seek a negotiated settlement with the insurgents nor interfere with the military's conduct of the war. The army, the agreement stated, would "maintain complete autonomy in its membership, organization and administration."

Not until 1973 did the army and the government publicly confirm the existence of the pact, which essentially authorized a system of military rule masked by regular elections. By then, the armed forces had fully consolidated its control over the state, and presidential elections had degenerated into vehicles for favored generals to fraudulently ascend to the presidency. As the armed forces repressed what little political opposition had survived, the highest-ranking officers exploited their near-total freedom to act with absolute impunity. They paid themselves immense salaries and accumulated huge fortunes by simply using their control over state institutions to seize income-producing properties of all kinds for personal use.

Accompanying the rise in corruption was an intensification of military-directed violence against the armed forces' political enemies – a category now stretched well beyond the guerrilla bands. Guatemala joined Chile as Latin America's most notorious human-rights outcasts, a title that Argentina would procure in the late 1970s. To the handbook of state-terrorism strategies, a work in progress of the Latin American military regimes of the 1960s and '70s, Guatemala contributed three notable techniques: the "death squad," the "disappearance" and the mass murder. The first was the generic name for any number of shadowy organizations (e.g., "La Mano Blanca" or the White Hand) specializing in kidnapping, torture and assassination. The basic innovation here was to provide the military government with deniability for the crimes committed against their enemies, though in most cases the death squads either operated under the protection of the armed forces (from which they often received training, financing and intelligence) or were actually made up of "off duty" military or police personnel. Death squads became a more or less permanent part of the social landscape in Guatemala; as late as 2008, they were thought to have killed about 130 people that year.

The second technique, the disappearance, was defined above in our discussion of the Chilean case. The third, mass murder, became the key tactic in the Guatemalan armed forces' rural counter-insurgency strategy. Brigades of soldiers swept through villages suspected of harboring or otherwise aiding the guerrillas, burning them to the ground and massacring everyone in sight – women, men and children. The principal victims (83%) were Mayan Indians suspected of cooperating with the guerrillas; hundreds of their villages were razed, and tens of thousands of their inhabitants cruelly murdered, according to the 1999 UN-sponsored Guatemalan "truth commission" report (see below). The victims were burned alive, chopped to death with machete blows, decapitated, slowly dismembered while still alive, beaten to death and suffocated as well as being simply shot. Over the course of the 1962–1996 civil war, the worst years were 1981–1983, when four-fifths of the principal outrages (disappearances, arbitrary execution, privation of liberty, torture and rape) studied by the commission were committed. Government agents would later be found responsible for 93% of all human rights crimes and the guerrilla 3%; the rest could not be accounted for.

Two successive military coups, one in 1982 and another in 1983, revealed longstanding tensions within the armed forces over economic development policy, counterinsurgency strategy, the use of death squads and the self-enrichment schemes of its officers. A carefully controlled transition to civilian rule, though one in which the military would preserve much of its autonomy, was increasingly seen by military leaders as the path to overcoming Guatemala's international isolation and to reviving its economy. Elections for a constitutional convention in 1984 set in motion a process that culminated in the election of Marco Cerezo, a Christian Democrat, as president in 1985.

It was the first free election in Guatemala since 1950. But Guatemala's transition to democracy remained a joint military-civilian endeavor in which the military would decide the precise limits of civilian rule. By turns antagonistic and collaborative, it was a relationship that left considerable doubt about whether Guatemala could ever demilitarize to the extent that Chile and Argentina had. The arrangement's appeal to the armed forces was not hard to discern, for it gave them a strong voice in government without public accountability or responsibility. Attempted coups in 1988 and 1989 once again revealed serious divisions inside the military over counterinsurgency strategy and the limits of democratic change. Though human rights outrages were less frequent, death-squad style political assassinations and army massacres of rural noncombatants persisted into the 1990s and beyond, long after the military had ceded its direct control of government.

Argentina

Like Guatemala, Argentina too could look back on a long history of collaboration between military leaders and civilian politicians, and of authoritarian tendencies deeply rooted in the country's society and culture. In few Latin American countries had the military established itself so firmly as a political force. In 1973, Argentina's fifth military government since 1930 was facing another surge of political and economic instability, including a Marxist-led guerrilla insurgency that specialized in urban terrorism. A desperate armed forces responded by allowing the former president, Gen. Juan Perón, whom the army had removed from power in 1955, to return from exile in Spain. At the age of 77 and in ill-health, Perón remained immensely popular, and on 20 June 1973 Argentines welcomed him back as the messiah fated to save the country from imminent chaos. In October they would give him and his vice presidential running mate, his wife Isabel (a former nightclub dancer), 62% of the vote.

When Perón died in 1974, Isabel inherited the presidency but proved unable to cope with rising terrorist violence, labor unrest and soaring inflation. The armed forces removed her from office on 24 March 1976, and established a junta of generals that took control of almost all levels of government, promising to sweep the country clean of subversives. Unlike Perón or his widow, the military had a plan – the Proceso de Reorganización Nacional (National Reorganization Process). The new leader of the governing military junta, Gen. Jorge Videla, summarized it by saying that this coup represented more than just the overthrow of a government; it would also mark "the final closing of a historical cycle and the opening of a new one."[3] Videla and his military colleagues, who had planned the coup for months, were about to carry out what they regarded as the final solution to the problem of revolutionary Marxism and guerrilla war: they would simply kill as many subversives as they could find, and do so without the judicial formalities of arrests, investigations, trials and sentencing. Like the victims of state terror in Guatemala and Chile, the enemies of military rule would be "disappeared."

The guerrilla threat was indeed real, but it provoked a grossly disproportionate reaction from the military. Between 1969 and 1975 deaths caused by insurgents escalated steadily, reaching a total of 179 in 1975. That was also the first year that the total of individuals "disappeared" by the military (359) began to outnumber deaths caused by the guerrillas. Before the coup, the military concentrated on killing armed guerrillas; after the coup, it broadened the target to "subversives" – anyone suspected of opposing military rule, whether or not they were associated with revolutionary combatants. Having declared that nothing less than the survival of Western civilization and Christian morality was at stake, the armed forces accepted no limits to its power to eliminate the threat. In substituting the terrorism of revolutionary insurgents with the terrorism of the state, the junta launched what became known as "la guerra sucia" or the dirty war, and established a Latin American record of human rights crimes exceeded only by Guatemala. By 2001, a team of forensic anthropologists had confirmed the deaths of about 9,150 persons, and the Argentine government estimated the total at 15,000. Others placed the number as high as 30,000.

Kidnapped by security forces, the victims were taken to one of more than 300 secret detention centers where torture was so common, "sadistic" and "horrendous," according to the post-coup investigating commission, that some methods seemed to be without precedent anywhere else in the world. Military personnel executed prisoners by firing squad or at close range by pistol. Their bodies were buried in mass graves, incinerated, dynamited or dropped in the Atlantic Ocean. Others were executed by throwing them out of airplanes into the Atlantic. Pregnant prisoners were allowed to deliver their babies but after birth the children were placed with favored couples while the mothers were either returned to prison or executed.

Argentina's experience with military rule in the 1970s and 1980s showed how initial popular approval for a coup typically withered as the repression widened and intensified. As a defensive measure, some military regimes adopted strongly populistic and nationalistic discourses, and as a result could often count on a base of unwavering support despite their contempt for fair elections and freedom of expression. By 1980, after four years in power, the military government of Argentina was being forced to confront the question of a transition to civilian government. Isolated and scorned at home and abroad for its bestiality, corruption and failure to manage an economic crisis, the regime under the leadership of its president, Gen. Roberto Viola, opened an informal dialogue with some elements of the opposition.

Alarmed by Viola's flexibility, the armed forces replaced him with a hardliner, Gen. Leopoldo Galtieri, on 29 December 1981. Galtieri had a plan to win back public support for military rule that almost succeeded. He secretly ordered the armed forces to seize and occupy the Falkland Islands (or Islas Malvinas in the Hispanic world). Held since 1833 by Great Britain over the vociferous objections of Argentines who asserted a rival claim to possession, the islands were quickly taken in a surprise invasion by Argentina on 2 April 1982. The angry protest marches and strike threats that had bedeviled the military regime for months instantly gave way to ecstatic demonstrations of support for the military. People even donated money and property to help pay for the invasion. Observed the Argentine historian Luis Alberto Romero:

> The military government had obtained a complete political victory on identifying itself with a deeply felt popular demand nourished by the country's nationalist anti-imperialist political culture . . . Indeed, it was surprising that virtually no one questioned the legality of the takeover, which revealed the disintegration of political convictions that had once been deeper and more solid. The country that had celebrated the Argentine victory in the World Cup soccer tournament [1978] now rejoiced in having won a battle. With the same ingenuousness, it was preparing to proceed, if necessary, to war.[4]

War with Great Britain did indeed follow the occupation, which ended on 14 June with the surrender of Argentina. The war had cost the lives of 746 Argentines and 252 Britons. President Galtieri, confident that he could count on the people even in defeat, convoked a rally the next day at the presidential palace. But before he could speak from the same balcony at which he had received the exuberant embrace of tens of thousands of Argentines only ten weeks earlier, an enraged crowd rushed the building, breaking windows and setting fire to parked vehicles while fending off a violent counterattack by the police. Galtieri, forced to address the nation from a television studio instead of the presidential balcony, was removed from office three days later by his military colleagues.

Engaged in a real war against enemy troops rather than unarmed students, the Argentine armed forces' crude attempt to earn legitimacy ended in disgrace and humiliation. They had no choice but to negotiate their own departure from power. Except for their success in liquidating the guerrilla threat, largely by terroristic means, the military's last try at governing Argentina ended in failure. The Proceso de Reorganización Nacional wrecked the economy, corrupted the armed forces, led to its total defeat in an unprovoked war of aggression, and produced a Latin American record of barbarity in a military's treatment of their own countrymen matched only by Guatemala.

The United States and Military Rule

During the Cold War, the transfer of weapons from one government to another became an essential tool of diplomacy. In order to attract and keep allies in the global struggle between communism and liberal capitalist democracy, the major powers used their superior wealth to provide arms to the military forces of governments in the developing world. By the mid-1950s, the United States was supplying weapons, military equipment and military training services to governments seeking to protect their borders from Soviet and Chinese-inspired aggression. That strategy soon gave way to one focused on internal security, particularly after Cuba's 1959 revolution quickened the formation of insurgent armies across Latin America. Now, the enemy was redefined as groups and individuals already present in the target country who were loyal to communism, or at least adhered to ideas about social change that the authorities judged to be "subversive." Their status as presumed threats to the national security of friendly governments in Latin America, and therefore as possible threats to U.S. security, justified the transfer of military and police equipment and training services to those governments. But even when such threats were slight, the transfers were regularly justified on a variety of other grounds – that they gave Washington leverage and influence over military-dominated regimes, or pro-tected and promoted U.S. investment and trade, or that they kept the recipient from establishing military supply relations with a U.S. rival. From 1950 to 1990, when the Cold War ended, the U.S. government conveyed military goods and services worth about $16.2 billion (in constant 1990 dollars) to Latin American governments. Of that, 43% was in the form of gift aid and the rest in sales. Another $2.8 billion in military goods and services were sold directly to Latin American governments by U.S. manufacturers, with U.S. government approval.

Compared to total worldwide U.S. military transfers during the Cold War, Latin America's share was a pittance – no more than 7% of total gift aid, and no more than 4% of total government sales. Nevertheless, it significantly bolstered the strength of the armed forces in many cases, and thus their political influence as well. For small, poor countries with relatively primitive military and police organizations, like those of Central America, even small amounts of aid could substantially enhance the capacities of the police and the armed forces in intelligence gathering and analysis, communications, the quality of training and of course firepower. In addition, military and police transfers intended for a particular function often liberated existing military and police resources for other purposes, effectively expanding the potential scope of military action.

In the 1970s, as military rulers tightened their grip on power across the region, people in both Latin America and the United States increasingly accused the U.S. government of complicity in the *golpes* that removed elected civilian governments from power, and in the appalling record of crimes against human rights committed by the military regimes after they seized power. By providing arms, equipment and training to the Latin American armed forces, Washington not only appeared to contradict its own stated interest in promoting democracy, but indirectly cooperated in the suppression of democracy and basic human rights. The administrations of presidents Richard M. Nixon (1969–1974) and Gerald Ford (1974–1977) seemed almost indifferent to the problem, a response congruent with the policy recommendations of Nelson A. Rockefeller, the governor of New York (1959–1973) and a major investor in the region. After consulting with Latin American leaders on four trips in 1969, Rockefeller had advised President Nixon to accept, in a spirit of pragmatism, Latin America's "authoritarian and hierarchical tradition," and to put aside "philosophical disagreements . . . with the nature of particular regimes." Rockefeller continued:

> Many of our neighbors find it incomprehensible that the United States will not sell them military equipment which they feel is required to deal with internal subversion. They have been puzzled by the reduction in U.S. military assistance grants in view of the growing intensity of the subversive activities they face . . . In many cases, it will be more useful for the United States to try to work with them in these efforts, rather than to abandon or insult them because we are conditioned by arbitrary ideological stereotypes. . . .

As criticism of Nixon and Ford administration policies mounted on human rights grounds, the U.S. Congress responded with legislation aimed at restricting U.S. military and police collaboration with repressive governments. In 1973 and 1974, Congress terminated all U.S. government assistance to train and equip foreign police forces because in some countries the United States had assisted police forces that repressed the political opposition and regularly tortured suspects. In Uruguay and Brazil, U.S. police advisers were variously accused of either teaching the police to torture suspects, or of having been present at torture sessions, a belief further popularized by the 1972 film directed by Constantinos Gavras, "État de siège" ("State of Siege"), based on the true story of the kidnapping and murder of a U.S. police adviser by leftist guerrillas in Uruguay in 1970.

Legal restrictions adopted in 1973 on U.S. economic (or "development") aid to repressive governments were strengthened by Congress in 1975 with the Harkin Amendment (after Representative Tom Harkin, Democrat of Iowa) to the Foreign Assistance Act. The next year Congress banned military and police assistance "to any government which engages in a consistent pattern of gross violations of internationally recognized human rights." In response, the military regimes governing Argentina, Brazil, El Salvador, Guatemala and Uruguay announced they would no longer accept any U.S. military aid. All five denounced the human-rights law as an intolerable interference in their internal affairs. They had little to lose, however, considering that a good deal of aid was already "in the pipeline" and thus unaffected by the congressional restrictions. Nor did the ban apply to commercial arms sales by U.S. manufacturers. Besides, other countries (such as Israel in the case of Guatemala) eagerly stepped in to replace the United States.

On taking office in 1977, President Jimmy Carter proposed a sharp reduction in U.S. arms transfers, not only suggesting that they would become an exceptional instrument of foreign policy in his administration but that he would weigh the human rights records of foreign governments in considering the distribution of military and economic aid. Encouraged by President Carter's announcement that human rights would be "the soul of our foreign policy," Congress in 1978 toughened the restrictions on military assistance that it had passed in 1976. Despite the limitations imposed by both the executive branch and the Congress, however, arms exports remained an important tool of U.S. foreign policy during the Carter administration and beyond.

After his inauguration in 1981, President Reagan sought to dismantle the human rights policies that had been institutionalized during the Carter years. In seeking to improve relations with Latin America's ruling military juntas, the Reagan administration often downplayed or denied, as exaggeration or rumor, well-documented records of massive human rights violations. In 1981 and 1982, the period of the most murderous repression in Guatemala's history, the U.S. State Department went out of its way to defend the governing military junta against incontestable evidence that its principal counterinsurgency strategy was the massacre of unarmed rural villagers. During a tour of Latin America in December 1982, President Reagan met with the president of Guatemala, Gen. Efraín Ríos Montt, in Honduras and told reporters afterward that

Ríos Montt, who had seized power in a coup only nine months before, was "a man of great personal integrity and commitment" who was "totally dedicated to democracy." Guatemala, Reagan added, was getting a "bum rap" about its human rights record.

But Reagan himself would soon find that public opinion refused to allow human rights records to be separated from foreign policy, and his administration began to emphasize the promotion of democracy in its dealings with Latin America's authoritarian regimes. A month after his reelection, Reagan commemorated Human Rights Day on 10 December 1984 by attributing to the United States "a special responsibility to advance the claims of the oppressed . . . We strongly object to the lack of progress toward democratic government in Chile and Paraguay," among other "affronts to the human conscience." Delivering on his pledge, Reagan's emissaries privately told Chile's Gen. Pinochet in 1985 that the United States would oppose World Bank loans to Chile unless he lifted the state of siege. He did, and the United States voted for the loans. The new U.S. ambassador to Chile, Harry Barnes, reached out to the Chilean opposition, even including human rights groups and members of the Socialist Party. The United States also publicized its support for a "No" vote in the 1988 plebiscite on whether Pinochet should stay in office until 1997.[5]

Washington's overall record of Cold War cordiality with Latin American despots, and in particular its lavish disbursement of funds for training, weapons and equipment for the region's security forces, would in later years become the occasion for expressions of remorse. In separate announcements in 1996 and 1997, the U.S. Department of Defense disclosed that from 1965 to 1991, its intelligence-training curriculum for military students in Latin America and elsewhere included instructions in how to infiltrate and suppress opposition groups, including political parties, labor unions, and religious organizations. As part of a program the Pentagon called "Project X," U.S. instructors also taught trainees how to recruit and control collaborators by means of "fear, payment of bounties for enemy dead, beatings, false imprisonment, executions and the use of truth serum," in the words of a 1992 Pentagon investigative report.[6] Such "objectionable" techniques "did not represent U.S. government policy," and their use had been discontinued in 1991, according to a 1996 Defense Department statement.[7]

While the triumphalism in Washington that accompanied the collapse of communism between 1989 and 1991 never disappeared, it eventually allowed for small doses of introspection. In a visit to Guatemala in 1999, U.S. President Bill Clinton declared: "For the United States, it is important that I state clearly that support for military forces or intelligence units which engage in violent and widespread repression . . . was wrong, and the United States must not repeat that mistake."[8] But expressions of remorse for Cold War excesses were not limited to Washington. As we will see below and in Chapter 6, apologies would be issued by such diverse participants in the Cold War as the Chilean army and the Catholic Church of Argentina. In 2011, the government of Guatemala apologized to the descendants of President Arbenz, who had been forcibly removed from office in the 1954 military *golpe* mentioned above. In a public ceremony attended by Arbenz's son Jacobo Arbenz Vilanova, President Alvaro Colom declared that Guatemala had yet to recover from the "great crime" of Arbenz's overthrow. The family in turn expressed hope for a similar apology from the U.S. government, which had organized the coup.

The Reckoning: Truth Commissions and Criminal Prosecution of Military Officers

When the armed forces held political power in the 1960s, 1970s and 1980s, they typically acted in secret, scorning what little tradition might be found in most countries in favor of constitutional procedures and norms of accountability. For that reason, a complete and accurate reckoning of their crimes will probably never be made. Nevertheless, most of the countries afflicted by repressive military rule went on to create commissions of inquiry, often referred to as "truth commissions," to ascertain as precisely as possible the methods of repression and to identify and quantify both the perpetrators and the victims. The purpose was not so much to amass the kind of evidence necessary for a judicial prosecution; in fact, most of the commissions were specifically prohibited from doing so, and the officials who carried out the crimes had invariably arranged amnesties upon leaving office to protect themselves from prosecution.

The aim of the truth commissions, therefore, was to seek justice by exposing the scope of the repression and its effects, tearing away the veil of secrecy that had protected the bureaucracies that organized the illegal persecutions, tortures, killings and disappearances. It was hoped that future episodes of military repression might thus be avoided, a goal reflected in the identical titles (*Never Again*) of the government-created truth commission reports issued in Argentina and Brazil, and in that sponsored by the Catholic Church in Guatemala.

In all, thirteen Latin American countries established truth commissions between 1979 and 2007 for the purpose of investigating human rights violations committed by agents of the state (or, in a few cases, by both state agents and insurgent groups) from the 1960s to the 1990s. Taken together, their published reports reveal patterns of abuse that were remarkably similar from country to country. Across Latin America, tens of thousands of individuals suspected of being political enemies of the authoritarian regimes in power were arrested, many illegally in what amounted to kidnappings by agents who refused to identify themselves. Working in secret detention centers, they commonly applied horrifying methods of torture in their search for information. Thousands of their victims died – under torture, massacred in groups, or individually executed, sometimes under the authority of a military court but more often completely outside any formal system of justice. Their battered bodies might be dumped in a public place as a warning to others. Many thousands were innocent of any wrongdoing, and their killers in the armed forces knew it, for their goal was to instill terror and thus obedience. The most frequent cases of public mass murder took place in Guatemala and El Salvador, where the military faced a rural insurgency that depended for its survival on the cooperation of noncombatants.

As we have already seen in our three case studies, thousands of victims were also made to "disappear" – their bodies secretly burned, buried, or dropped in the ocean. The Spanish term *desaparecido* first came into use in Guatemala in 1966, when the paramilitary groups known as "death squads" kidnapped and "disappeared" individuals suspected of supporting Marxist insurgents. The term gained wider currency following the 1973 military coup in Chile, but not until the practice was applied on a massive scale against thousands of Argentines after the 1976 military takeover there did *desaparecido* gain notoriety. Although the Latin American armed forces popularized the practice, they could not claim to have invented it. German dictator Adolf Hitler's *Nacht und Nebel* ("night and fog") degree of 1941 authorized the German armed forces to secretly transfer to Germany under "cover of night" anyone suspected of resisting the German occupations of France and other European countries. The measure was justified by the chief of the German High Command, Field Marshal Wilhelm Keitel, in a way that would be precisely fulfilled by the high commands of Argentina, Chile and Guatemala in the Cold War. In a 1942 directive, Keitel wrote that the secret transportation of the suspects to Germany "will have a deterrent effect because (a) the prisoners will vanish without leaving a trace, (b) no information may be given as to their whereabouts or their fate."[9]

The truth commissions drew their estimates of the dead, the disappeared, the tortured and the illegally detained from a diverse combination of sources: personal testimony by the kin or acquaintances of the victims and even by the perpetrators themselves; press reports; informed guesses by human rights investigators; records maintained during the repression by the Catholic Church and other religious institutions: and any surviving government documentation. Their findings are summarized in Table 4.1. The nature of the violations, the likely sources of information, and the investigative methods of the commissions were shaped by the nature of the confrontation between the state and its enemies. In El Salvador, Guatemala, Nicaragua and Peru, at different moments during the 1960s, 1970s and 1980s, militarized governments confronted highly organized and well-supplied insurgencies numbering thousands

Table 4.1 Truth Commission mandates and findings. Source: author.

Country and Period Investigated	Name of Commission	Origin	Date of Investigation	Year of Publication of Report	Mandate	Findings
Argentina 1976–1983	National Commission on the Disappeared (Comisión Nacional sobre la Desaparición de Personas, CONADEP)	S	1983–1984	1984	Investigate disappearances	Between 10,000 and 30,000 persons were "disappeared" after having been kidnapped by security forces and taken to one of more than 300 secret detention centers; torture was common and so "sadistic" and "horrendous" that some methods were without precedent anywhere else in the world.
Bolivia 1964–1982	National Commission for Investigation of the Disappeared (Comisión Nacional de Investigación de Desaparecidos)	S	1982–1984	Commission disbanded by government before it could finish, in 1984	Investigate disappearances	

Brazil 1964–1979	Brasil: Nunca Mais	C	1979–1982	1986	Investigate human rights violations	Thousands of suspected enemies of the regime were routinely and systematically tortured at more than 200 secret torture centers; nearly 300 were killed (some under torture) or "disappeared" (about 125).
Chile 1973–1990	National Commission for Truth and Reconciliation (Comisión Nacional de Verdad y Reconciliación or the "Rettig Commission")	S	1990–1991	1991	Investigate the most serious violations of human rights	Of 3,400 cases presented for investigation, state agents were found responsible for the murder of 2,025 persons including an unspecified number under torture; in another 641 cases, further investigation was necessary.

(*Continued*)

Table 4.1 (*Continued*)

Country and Period Investigated	Name of Commission	Origin	Date of Investigation	Year of Publication of Report	Mandate	Findings
Chile 1973–1990	National Commission on Political Imprisonment and Torture (Comisión Nacional Sobre Prisión Política y Tortura, "Valech Commission")	S	2003–2005	2004 and 2005	Investigate abuses of civil rights or politically motivated torture	Found that 28,461 persons were jailed for political reasons and tortured, showing that torture was routine and massive and carried out in numerous secret detention centers
Ecuador 1979–1996	Truth and Justice Commission (Comisión de Verdad y Justicia)	S	1996–1997	Commission disbanded; report never issued	Investigate human rights abuses	
Ecuador 1984–1988 and other periods	Truth Commission to Impede Impunity (Comisión de la Verdad para Impedir la Impunidad)	S	2007–2009	Pending	Investigate human rights abuses	

El Salvador 1980–1991	Commission on the Truth for El Salvador (Comisión de la Verdad Para El Salvador)	T	1992–1993	1993	Investigate "serious acts of violence" and their effects	Commission received accusations that the state and death squads allied with it were guilty of 18,700 acts of extra-judicial executions, forced disappearance or torture; the FMLN was accused of 1,100 of such acts. Only about 30 cases were investigated. Extrajudicial executions totaled 13,200; disappearances, 5,500; torture, 4,400.
Guatemala 1960–1996	Commission for Historical Clarification (Comisión para el Esclarecimiento Histórico)	T	1997–1999	1999	Investigate human rights violations	Commission estimated 160,000 extrajudicial executions and 40,000 disappearances; 93% of total carried out by state agents.

(Continued)

Table 4.1 (Continued)

Country and Period Investigated	Name of Commission	Origin	Date of Investigation	Year of Publication of Report	Mandate	Findings
Guatemala 1960–1996	Proyecto Interdiocesano de Recuperación de la Memoria Histórica.	C	1994–1998	1998	Investigate human rights violations	Received testimony of mass murder and individual murder (25,123 victims), torture (4,219 victims) and disappearances (3,893 victims).
Haiti 1991–1994	National Truth and Justice Commission (Commission Nationale de Vérité et de Justice): 1994–1996	S	1995–1996	1996	investigate human rights violations	Received 5,500 testimonies and identified 8,667 victims of various human rights violations
Mexico 1970s–1980s	National Human Rights Commission (Comisión Nacional de los Derechos Humanos)	S	1990–2001	2001	Investigate fate of disappeared.	Of 532 complaints filed regarding disappearances in the 1970s and early 1980s, the commission verified that 275 were disappeared by state agents; in 160 other cases, evidence was insufficient but merited further investigation. Torture was routine and systematic.

Country	Commission		Dates		Mandate	Findings
Mexico 1960s–1970s	Special Prosecutor for Past Social and Political Movements (Fiscalía Especial para Movimientos Sociales y Políticos del Pasado)	S	2002–2006	2006	Investigate crimes committed by federal government in connection with social and political movements.	In combating political and social movements, the government committed massacres, disappearances, systematic torture, and genocide.
Panama 1968–1989	Panama Truth Commission (Comisión de la Verdad de Panamá)	S	2001–2002	2002	Investigate human rights violations	Of 148 cases of reported human rights abuses including torture and extrajudicial execution, 110 were documented. The commission found 24 gravesites and excavated 36 graves, many of which were located in military buildings and prisons.
Paraguay 1954–1989	Truth and Justice Commission (Comisión Verdad y Justicia, CVJ)	S	2004–2008	2008	investigate human rights violations	Commission found 18,772 cases of torture, at least 59 victims of summary executions, and 336 disappearances.

(Continued)

Table 4.1 (*Continued*)

Country and Period Investigated	Name of Commission	Origin	Date of Investigation	Year of Publication of Report	Mandate	Findings
Peru 18–19 June 1986	Commission of Inquiry to Investigate the Massacre of Prisoners (Comisión investigadora de las masacres en los Penales)	S	1986–1988	1988	Investigate government massacre of rebellious prison inmates	Commission divided; minority report said state was directly responsible for the death of 246 prisoners but majority denied this.
Peru 1980–2000	Truth and Reconciliation Commission (Comisión de la Verdad y Reconciliación)	S	2001–2003	2003	Investigate human rights violations committed by both the state and insurgent guerrilla forces	Total number of deaths during the counterinsurgency war was between 61,007 and 77,552; the Shining Path organizations was responsible for 54% of the deaths and for most of the other human rights crimes
Uruguay 1973–1985	Commission for Peace (Comisión Para la Paz)	S	2000–2002	2003	Investigate fate of disappeared	State agents "disappeared" 26 Uruguayans; most died under torture and the rest were executed.

Legend: S = State-mandated, C = Catholic Church, T = treaty-mandated.

of guerrilla fighters. In Brazil and the Southern Cone, on the other hand, military rule followed sudden *golpes de estado* that removed civilian governments from power; there, the enemy was less likely to be an armed insurgent than an unarmed person or group suspected of disloyalty to the state.

Nowhere, however, could the estimates of the numbers of dead, disappeared and tortured provide more than a rough indicator of the toll of destruction and suffering. Besides body counts, the costs included the direct and indirect effects of such outrages as the liquidation of entire rural communities in Guatemala and El Salvador and the displacement (often abroad) of tens of thousands of their inhabitants; the illegal appropriation of victims' personal property by government officials in Paraguay and Argentina; the permanent disruption of family relationships, careers and educations; and the kinds of deep psychological wounds that heal only slowly if at all. Nor can the full responsibility for the damage be laid solely at the feet of the armed forces or their accomplices. In their efforts to achieve power, the self-styled revolutionaries and their collaborators undertook a terroristic program of assassination, bombing, kidnapping, extortion, robbery and assaults on public and private institutions. Nevertheless, the ultimate responsibility for the carnage rested with the governments, for in failing to adhere to their own constitutional norms of due process, they succumbed instead to vengeful strategies of reprisal far more brutal than the offenses of the insurgents. It was a reaction that pointed to the weakness, indeed the irrelevance, of the judicial institutions and the law codes of so many Latin American states, and of their governments' abiding lack of confidence in them to effectively repress criminal activity. This traditional indifference to the rule of law would likewise expose truth-commission members and their staffs to great personal risks. In 1998, two days after the Guatemalan Catholic Church issued its massive study of the human costs of the country's three-decade civil war, the director of the project, Juan José Gerardi, 75, an auxiliary bishop of the Catholic archdiocese of Guatemala City, was beaten to death. Gerardi had made the fateful decision to identify by name the principal military and police figures implicated in human rights crimes.

The habitual flouting of the law that made massive human rights crimes possible was not confined to military regimes. In 2006, the Mexican government announced the result of an investigation of crimes planned at the highest levels of government from the 1960s until the early 1980s, when it was governed by civilian presidents who exercised unquestionable authority over the armed forces. At least 645 persons considered to be political enemies were "disappeared" by government agents; at least another 99 were summarily executed and more than 2,000 tortured.

In some countries, the initial decision to redress the harm done by merely gathering and analyzing information (the phase represented by the truth commissions) gave way over time to a desire to punish the wrongdoers. Upon taking office in March 1990, President Aylwin of Chile created a Commission on Truth and Reconciliation to weigh the human costs of the military dictatorship. But it took more than a decade for the justice system to begin moving against individuals. Pinochet's constitution allowed him to occupy the office of army commander-in-chief until 1998, a privilege that he insisted on retaining and when his term expired he dutifully exercised his constitutional option to take a lifetime seat in the senate, immunizing himself from prosecution while provoking violent protests and confrontations in the streets outside the congress. For decades Chile's untouchable inquisitor, the haughty general was about to become, at the age of 83, the quarry of an increasingly globalized system of human-rights justice. Arriving in London for medical treatment in October 1998, Pinochet was arrested by British police in response to an extradition request issued by a court in Spain, charging the ex-dictator with genocide and terrorism. Detained under house arrest in Britain during a fourteen-month period of unprecedented international political and legal maneuvering, the general was finally allowed by the British government to return to Chile in March 2000 on grounds of ill-health.

The incident emboldened Chileans seeking a judgment against Pinochet, for in August the country's supreme court removed the immunity from prosecution that Pinochet enjoyed as a senator, opening the way for a criminal investigation of charges of kidnapping, torture and murder. Kidnapping and crimes linked to kidnapping, the court ruled, were not covered by the amnesty decree issued by Pinochet in 1978 to protect himself and other officers from prosecution. As a result, the court also opened the door for the prosecution of other retired military and police officers for kidnapping-associated crimes, including torture and murder. In December 2000, a Chilean judged accused Pinochet of fifty-five deaths and eighteen disappearances. The general died on 10 December 2006 while under house arrest in Chile, awaiting a trial continuously postponed because of his ill-health. But the time of reckoning had arrived. By 2010, about 600 armed forces personnel were facing prosecution for human rights violations during the dictatorship. Two hundred others had already been convicted and sixty-five were serving prison sentences.

Meanwhile, the Chilean army had already begun to seek reconciliation with the victims of dictatorship. In 2002, the army commander in chief, Gen. Juan Emilio Cheyre, paid public tribute to Gens. Schneider and Prats for their loyalty to the constitution. Two years later, Gen. Cheyre announced the army's unequivocal assumption of full responsibility for the human rights crimes committed by its members during the dictatorship. "Human rights violations are never ethically justifiable, for anyone," he stated. Until then, the army had denied any institutional responsibility for "excesses," blaming them on errors committed by individual soldiers, a stance still maintained by the navy and the police.

In Guatemala, the congress passed amnesty laws in 1986 and 1996 to protect the military from criminal prosecution for murder, torture and kidnapping. But as in most other countries that suffered from especially severe military repression, the pressure for a public accounting mounted over time. Besides the two "truth commission" reports of the late 1990s, in 2009 President Alvaro Colom announced that secret military archival records would be systematically inspected and published except for those that might compromise national security. The plan generated considerable opposition from military officers who feared that the release of the files would implicate the armed forces in human rights crimes. In 2011, Guatemala's public prosecutor charged retired Gen. Héctor Mario López Fuentes with genocide, crimes against humanity and forced disappearances for directing the killing of 317 Maya Indians during a counterinsurgency operation in 1982 and 1983.

Nowhere was the search for justice more capricious, dramatic and agonizing than in Argentina. Seventeen days after the newly elected Argentine congress took office in 1983, it abrogated the amnesty that the generals had bestowed on themselves by decree. A federal court charged the nine members of the three, three-man military juntas that had governed Argentina between 1976 and 1982 with 709 criminal offenses, including disappearance, torture, rape, theft and murder. Eight hundred witnesses testified. On 9 December 1985, the panel of judges acquitted three of the defendants but found the other six guilty, sentencing Gen. Videla and Adm. Emilio Massera to life imprisonment and the other four to terms of four and one-half to seventeen years. By then, citizens had filed more than 2,000 criminal complaints against 650 military officers. The prospect of hundreds of trials over many years led President Raúl Alfonsín to propose the Ley de Punto Final (Final Stop law). Adopted by congress on 23 December 1986, the law imposed a sixty-day limit on further criminal complaints. Nevertheless, ongoing prosecutions inspired military uprisings in 1987 and 1988 led by mid-level officers demanding an end to the trials. In response, Alfonsín proposed, and the congress adopted, the Ley de Obediencia Debida (Due Obedience law). It made most officers immune to prosecution on the grounds that they were carrying out orders from their superiors. The only exceptions were for theft, rape and the kidnapping of children.

Alfonsín's successor, Carlos Saúl Menem, showed considerably more sympathy for the military after taking office in 1989. That year he pardoned three junta members, and another thirty-nine military officers for crimes committed in the 1970s. The 174 officers and non-commissioned officers who had participated in the 1987 and 1988 rebellions were also pardoned. The following year, Menem pardoned five junta members, including Videla and Massera, and several other generals.

In 1995, a new phase in the reconciliation process opened with the stunning public admission of a guilt-stricken retired naval captain, Adolfo Francisco

Scilingo, that he had personally thrown living prisoners out of military aircraft into the Atlantic Ocean. Less than two months later, on 25 April 1995, a retired army sergeant, Victor Ibáñez, admitted in a live radio broadcast to having participated in the "death flights." Moved by the sergeant's statement, the army chief-of-staff, Gen. Martín Balza, went on national television later the same day. He astonished the country by admitting that the army had committed crimes. "The ends never justify the means . . . No one is obliged to obey an immoral order or one that violates military laws or rules." Within two days of his speech, a retired policeman and an army private provided more details of torture and murder during the Dirty War. The commanders of the navy, the air force and the national police added admissions of guilt on behalf of their own institutions. The sale of babies born of pregnant captives in a secret army detention center was officially confirmed.

The next turning point came with the election of President Néstor Kirchner in 2003. In his first speech to congress, he praised the Mothers and Grandmothers of the Plaza de Mayo, women who had initiated public protests against the military regime in 1977 by quietly demanding to know the fate of their "disappeared" children and grandchildren. In a calculated affront to the armed forces, Kirchner called the women the "ultimate moral reserve" of Argentine society, the very phrase that the military had long applied to themselves. On Kirchner's initiative, congress repealed the Punto Final and the Obediencia Debida laws and in 2005 the supreme court nullified them, finally opening the way for new trials. As a result, convictions for crimes against humanity committed by former members of the security forces rose steadily. To the forty-one who had been convicted by the end of 2007, another 171 were added by May 2011. Among the high-profile convictions were those of Gens. Videla and Reynaldo Bignone. At the age of 85, Videla was sentenced to twenty-five years in prison in 2010 for the murder and torture of thirty-one prisoners. Gen. Bignone, as the head of two of the junta's largest prisons, had overseen the torture and murder of thousands, for which he was sentenced to twenty-five years in prison at the age of 82. In 2011, Videla, Bignone and six other defendants went on trial for stealing babies from prisoners. Prosecutors estimated that at least 400 babies had been taken away from their imprisoned mothers during the dictatorship.

In concluding this chapter, we note that, of all the post-Cold War reckonings in Latin America, none achieved greater favor than the establishment of national truth commissions. As initial expressions of a search for justice, the commissions represented a deepening demand for the first and most important value in the democratic tradition: accountability. Initially, accountability took the limited form of an objective appraisal of the causes and outcomes of the violence. Only later would the concept be extended to embrace the pursuit of justice for wrongdoers. We saw the anti-democratic ideology of communism defeated, but at a terrible, and probably unnecessary, cost in innocent life. But we also saw how the response to that tragedy, in the form of the demand for accountability by the truth commissions, constituted one of the first, essential steps in the great transition toward the rule of law and democratic government, the theme we are now ready to consider in the next chapter.

Notes

1 Thomas E. Skidmore, *The Politics of Military Rule in Brazil, 1964–85* (New York: Oxford University Press, 1988), 18.
2 Salvador Allende, "First Message to the Congress by President Allende." In *The Chilean Revolution : Conversations with Allende*, ed. Régis Debray (New York: Pantheon Books, 1971), 170, 179.
3 Thomas C. Wright, *State Terrorism in Latin America: Chile, Argentina, and International Human Rights* (Lanham, MD: Rowman & Littlefield, 2007), 100.
4 Luis Alberto Romero, *A History of Argentina in the Twentieth Century* (University Park, PA: Pennsylvania State University Press, 2002), 243–4.
5 Kathryn Sikkink, *Mixed Signals: U.S. Human Rights Policy and Latin America* (Ithaca, NY: Cornell University Press, 2004), chapter 7.
6 Werner E. Michel, "Report of Investigation: Improper Material in Spanish Language Intelligence Training Manuals," Memorandum to the Secretary of Defense, 10 March 1992, U.S. Department of Defense. Published online by The National Security Archive (Washington, DC), www.gwu.edu/~nsarchiv.
7 U.S. Department of Defense, "Fact Sheet Concerning Training Manuals Containing Materials Inconsistent With U.S. Policy," 1996. Published online by The National Security Archive (Washington, DC), www.gwu.edu/~nsarchiv.
8 "Remarks in a Roundtable Discussion on Peace Efforts in Guatemala City March 10, 1999," in U.S., President, *Weekly Compilation of Presidential Documents* 35 (15 March 1999) 10:395.
9 Amnesty International USA., *"Disappearances," a Workbook* (New York, NY: Amnesty International USA, 1981), 2.

References

Allende, Salvador. "First Message to the Congress by President Allende." In *The Chilean Revolution : Conversations with Allende*, ed. Régis Debray, 168–201. New York: Pantheon Books, 1971.
Amnesty International USA. *"Disappearances," a Workbook*. New York, NY: Amnesty International USA, 1981.
Clinton, Bill. "Remarks in a Roundtable Discussion on Peace Efforts in Guatemala City March 10, 1999." *Weekly Compilation of Presidential Documents*, 15 March 1999, 395.
Michel, Werner E. *Report of Investigation: Improper Material in Spanish Language Intelligence Training Manuals*. Washington, DC: U.S. Department of Defense, 1992.

Romero, Luis Alberto. *A History of Argentina in the Twentieth Century*. University Park, PA: Pennsylvania State University Press, 2002.

Sikkink, Kathryn. *Mixed Signals: U.S. Human Rights Policy and Latin America*. Ithaca, NY: Cornell University Press, 2004.

Skidmore, Thomas E. *The Politics of Military Rule in Brazil, 1964–85*. New York: Oxford University Press, 1988.

United States, Department of Defense. *Fact Sheet Concerning Training Manuals Containing Materials Inconsistent with U.S. Policy*. Washington DC: Public Affairs Office, 1996.

Wright, Thomas C. *State Terrorism in Latin America: Chile, Argentina, and International Human Rights*. Lanham, MD: Rowman & Littlefield, 2007.

Chapter 5

The Turning toward Democracy

All four of the pre-1980s regime types – *caudillismo*, oligarchism, populism and direct or indirect military rule – discussed in the introduction to Part II were "authoritarian" because they were guided by principles of exclusion rather than inclusion. Almost inevitably, therefore, "democracy" became the name for the regime-type that contrasted most sharply with these varieties of authoritarianism. To those who had just been experiencing the dictatorial, and often brutal, hand of the armed forces, democracy was advanced as the system that at least held out the promise, if not the certainty, of rule by civilian governments accountable to the people through regular elections. Indeed, in countries like El Salvador, Honduras, Nicaragua and Paraguay, where the military, or military-backed autocrats, had held power for generations, the election of civilian governments, though minimally democratic, would represent epochal transformations in their political histories beginning in the 1980s and 1990s. Figure 5.1 compares the transition from authoritarianism in three subregions – South America, the Caribbean and Central America – starting in the 1960s.

But even in countries with substantial experience in constitutional, electoral government, such as Argentina, Chile and Uruguay, the military dictatorships of the 1960s and 1970s had lasted so long, and had destroyed so many lives and institutions, that the chance to once again elect civilian leaders would be counted as a major turning point in their histories.

As a result, as one military government after another fell in the 1980s, few Latin Americans were prepared for what turned out to be a slow process of democratic transition rather than the instantaneous democratization that many had hoped for. The transition coincided with what social scientist Samuel P. Huntington called the "third wave" of worldwide democratization, originating in southern Europe in the early 1970s, then spreading to Asia and Latin

Contemporary Latin America: 1970 to the Present, First Edition. Robert H. Holden and Rina Villars.
© 2013 Robert H. Holden and Rina Villars. Published 2013 by Blackwell Publishing Ltd.

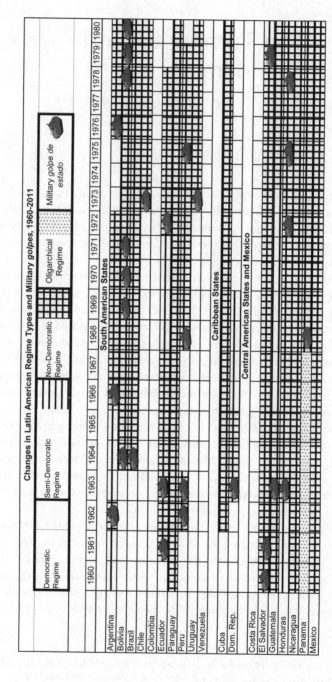

Figure 5.1 Changes in Latin American regime types and military golpes, 1960–2011. Data to 2001 (except Cuba) from Peter H. Smith, *Democracy in Latin America: Political Change in Comparative Perspective*. New York: Oxford University Press, 2005, App. 1 and 2.

	1981	1982	1983	1984	1985	1986	1987	1988	1989	1990	1991	1992	1993	1994	1995	1996	1997	1998	1999	2000	2001-2011
South American States																					
Argentina																					
Bolivia																					
Brazil																					
Chile																					
Colombia																					
Ecuador																					
Paraguay																					
Peru																					
Uruguay																					
Venezuela																					
Caribbean States																					
Cuba																					
Dom. Rep.																					
Central American States and Mexico																					
Costa Rica																					
El Salvador																					
Guatemala																					
Honduras																					
Nicaragua																					
Panama																					
Mexico																					

Figure 5.1 (Continued)

America. In most places, including Latin America, the transition would be measured in decades rather than in spans of a few years. Thus, by the late 1990s, with elected civilian governments still firmly in place almost everywhere in Latin America except for Cuba, it was clear that even the countries with the longest electoral experience were seriously confronting, for the first time, the need to build political institutions capable of *consolidating* democracy. Certain historical legacies, some of which we have already reviewed in Part I, continued to inhibit the formation of strong, stable, democratic polities. They included:

- the nearly autocratic powers of the president, and the relative weakness of the legislative and judicial branches, both of which remained vulnerable to presidential interference;
- the persistence of deeply personalistic loyalties that could easily override loyalty to the constitution, to a political ideology or to the nation;
- the entrenchment of corrupt political practices, long permitted under the patrimonial premise that to occupy a public office was to "own" it;
- the lack of consistent law enforcement and a corresponding tolerance for law breaking, and indifference to the rule of law.

Perhaps the greatest risk entailed by the persistence of these tendencies, and the frustration with the democratization process that they provoked, was the emergence of a cynical attitude toward democracy itself. In fact, evidence of disillusion and disenchantment with the process was not hard to find by 2005. Such views were further exacerbated by the failure of many governments to make significant progress in overcoming poverty, chronic unemployment and inequality, or in stabilizing the national economies.

Bailing out of the process of democratic consolidation became one option and as a result, democratically elected governments, deliberately drawing on the very legacies of authoritarianism identified above, advocated alternatives to democratization that essentially looked back to the populisms of earlier decades, and to the even less credible alternative of a Cuban-style, one-party "socialist" state. "While democracy has spread widely across Latin America," a team of experts concluded in 2004, "its roots remain shallow." Survey data showed that more than half of all Latin Americans were ready to sacrifice democratic gains if in return they could get "real social and economic progress." Among less well-educated groups – typically the poorest – support for democracy was lowest.[1]

In trying to understand the obstacles to democratization, more and more students of Latin American politics proposed that it wasn't enough for a regime to hold competitive elections. In 2010, Fernando Henrique Cardoso, the president of Brazil from 1995 to 2003, told an interviewer that Latin America had recovered the machinery of democracy, but not its soul. "There is still much to be done to achieve equality before the law and equality of opportunity."[2] Democracy "with soul" would thus be a *liberal* democracy. Free and fair elections needed to be accompanied by the core elements of constitutional liberalism – the rule of law, separation of powers, and guarantees of basic rights. Democratic procedures alone might yield an elected tyrant, corroding and ultimately nullifying the effectiveness of democratic procedures.

A merger of liberalism and democracy, of the kind that has characterized most of western Europe, the United States and Canada, would give Latin Americans a chance to achieve levels of democratic rule comparable to those prevailing in those countries. Of course, democratic government in North America and western Europe has never been free of corruption, abuses of power, lawless violence and crimes against human rights. Their democracies also need "consolidation," but for the most part they safeguard basic human and civil rights far more effectively and systematically than those of Latin America. Stronger guarantees of basic freedoms would also help Latin America reduce its world-record levels of economic inequality, while exerting more control over its exceptionally volatile economies – a theme we return to in Part III.

We can think of these basic principles of liberal political rule as partial indicators of "governance," or the *quality* of political power. Only since the late 1980s has governance been recognized as a problem at least equal in importance to that of economic development, and very likely a *precondition* of both democratic rule and economic development itself. The rising value placed on the concept of governance can be seen in the efforts of the World Bank to find ways to do for governance what social scientists began doing a long time ago for economic development: namely, identify a bundle of indicators that would allow one to measure and thus compare different countries' progress in achieving good governance. The Bank's researchers defined "governance" broadly as the "traditions and institutions" of rule, of which three were considered fundamental:

- the *process* of choosing, monitoring and replacing a government;
- the *capacity* of any given government to design and carry out policies;
- the *respect* that citizens have for the institutions of rule.

Two specific measures of each of these dimensions of governance were devised. For *process*, they were (1) Voice and Accountability and (2) Political Stability and Absence of Violence. For *capacity* they were (1) Government Effectiveness and (2) Regulatory Quality. For *respect* they were (1) Rule of Law and (2) Control of Corruption. Since 1996, the Bank has collected data from survey respondents, non-governmental organizations, public sector groups and business enterprises that capture their perceptions of the six indicators. In 2009,

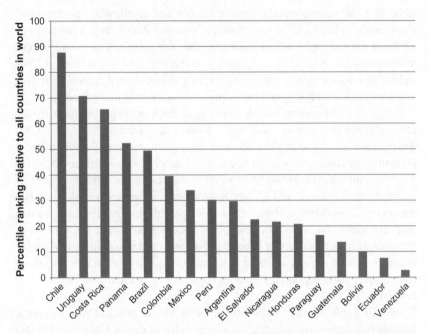

Figure 5.2   Perception of the rule of law in Latin America, 2009. Based on World Bank, World Governance Indicators, 2009. http://info.worldbank.org/governance/wgi. Confidence level: 90%.

on the average, the Latin American countries as a whole were seen as only half, or less than half, as well governed as the thirty developed countries of the Organization for Economic Cooperation and Development (OECD). But, as we have stressed repeatedly in this book, almost any Latin American average veils the region's remarkable diversity. For example, Figure 5.2 compares perceptions of a single indicator of governance, the rule of law, across all the Latin American countries. Chile stands out as the only country viewed as nearly equivalent to the OECD average in rule of law. While the other countries reveal an impressive range in worldwide rankings, from the seventieth percentile to the third, it is worth noting that after Chile, the standings descend very rapidly, with thirteen of the seventeen countries (76%) drawing a percentile ranking of less than 50%, meaning that more than half the world's countries outranked them.

In the face of widespread popular frustration with the lack of progress in economic and political development after 1990, some elected leaders resorted to two longstanding political tactics. "Chasing utopias and blaming others for our misfortunes" was how Costa Rican President Oscar Arias referred to them in his 2006 inaugural address. More than a decade and a half into Latin

America's democratic transition, Arias said, he could detect a feeling of uncertainty and confusion sweeping the region. He speculated that the democratization phase might turn out to have been little more than a long "parenthesis of rationality in a history marked by intolerance, violence and frustration." As the president of the Latin American country with the longest uninterrupted record of regular, competitive elections with moderately liberal institutions, Arias spoke with some authority. His credentials had already been enhanced by his success in piloting Central America out of the region-wide war that engulfed it in the 1980s, during his first period as president (1986–1990). Awarded the Nobel Peace Prize in 1987 for his efforts, he was elected again in 2006, after having worked in the intervening years as the head of an influential foundation he established with his Nobel Prize award money to promote peace and justice in Central America. A sign of the maturity of Costa Rica's liberal democratic institutions, relative to many elsewhere in Latin America, could be seen in the outcome of the 2006 election. Arias was declared the winner by the slenderest margin in Costa Rican history – 18,169 votes, or 1.1% of the total cast, after a tedious manual ballot recount that went on for a month after the election. Both sides were careful to avoid claiming victory prematurely, and both accepted the results peacefully.

In 2006, Mexico also held a presidential election. And like Costa Rica's, the victor won by a scanty margin. The political consequences of these two close votes were very different, however. On the one hand, Costa Rica and Mexico were alike in pursuing democratization; in fact, they shared the distinction of being the only two Latin American countries to have escaped military rule for most of the twentieth century. On the other hand, Mexico remained considerably behind Costa Rica in its progress toward establishing reliable democratic norms of government. In this sense, Mexico was more like the rest of Latin America, despite its freedom from military rule, and its experience showed that democracy meant more than just competitive elections.

The official count of the 2 July 2006 Mexican election gave the presidency to Felipe Calderón of the conservative Partido de Acción Nacional (PAN) over the nearest contender, Andrés Manuel López Obrador, the former mayor of Mexico City and the candidate of the leftist Partido Revolucionario Democrático. The winning margin of 0.56% was the slimmest ever recorded in a Mexican presidential election – only about 234,000 votes out of some 42 million cast. López Obrador reacted by accusing the government of having stolen the election from him, and he went on to declare himself the real winner. Organizing a series of protest rallies in the capital, he called on his followers to carry out acts of civil disobedience, and announced that he would live in the Zócalo (the main public square of the capital) until the country's special electoral court ruled in favor of a complete recount. He and thousands of his supporters camped out in the heart of Mexico City for seven weeks, disrupting daily life and refusing to abandon their posts. Even after the election tribunal confirmed Calderón's victory, López Obrador insisted he was the legitimate president of Mexico, even staging his own "inaugural" ceremony and appointing a "shadow government." A year later, he wrote *La mafia nos robó la Presidencia* (*The Mafia Stole the Presidency from Us*) and organized another protest rally.

While López Obrador found little support for his accusations except among his closest followers, Mexico's longstanding reputation for tainted elections and authoritarian government enhanced the credibility of his accusations, at least initially. A single party, the Partido Revolucionario Institucional (PRI) or the Institutional Revolutionary Party had controlled the presidency of Mexico from the 1920s until 2000, when the candidate of the PAN, Vicente Fox, defeated the PRI's Francisco Labastida. For decades, the PRI had acted almost as an arm of the state, successfully presenting itself as the only legitimate guardian of the ideas and aspirations of the Revolution of 1910–1920, a civil war that began as a national uprising against the three-decade dictatorship of Gen. Porfirio Díaz, and ended in a much bloodier factional struggle among the rebel forces.

Two revolutionary aspirations in particular were constantly held aloft by the PRI and by those who governed in its name: a fiercely nationalistic yet pragmatic posture in Mexico's relations with the United States, and a commitment to raising the living standards of the rural poor and the working class through various collectivist initiatives, such as the redistribution of rural land to the landless, and the encouragement of labor union organization. But Mexico's land-distribution goals had become much less ambitious by the 1950s as agribusiness interests began to dominate government policymaking. And the government's devotion to the working class was frequently vitiated by quiet support among the authorities for industrialists, and for labor-union leaders who could be depended on to control the rank and file.

Yet the ever-revolutionary oratory of government and party leaders, along with occasional spurts of action in favor of the downtrodden, were enough to preserve the loyalty of the majority of Mexicans. They accepted the authoritarian features of a constitutional system that endowed the presidency with extraordinary power. The PRI was the personal tool of the president, who always picked his own successor. While opposition parties and candidates were usually allowed to campaign, none could match the financial and political resources of the PRI, which sought to control every office from the lowest municipal post to the presidency and the national legislature.

Mexico's was thus a "soft" authoritarianism, famous for its flexibility and capacity to coopt and assimilate challengers – but also for doctoring election results, and for intimidating and killing its enemies whenever cooptation failed.

The system produced the most stable government in twentieth-century Latin America and, in a phrase made famous by the Peruvian novelist Mario Vargas Llosa, "the perfect dictatorship." Mexicans could proudly point to the fact that theirs was one of the very few Latin American states in which the military remained truly subordinate to civilian officials. While some of their presidents were known to have illegally amassed fortunes for themselves and their cronies during their terms of office, all of them scrupulously complied with the constitutional limit of a single six-year term. Until the 1980s, the PRI probably held the loyalty of most Mexican voters, who associated the party not only with the ideals of the Revolution but with the long period of peace and relative prosperity that began in the 1930s.

One of the heaviest blows to the legitimacy of the Mexican political system was delivered by the government itself on 2 October 1968, when Mexican security forces terminated months of increasingly disruptive pro-democracy demonstrations by firing into a crowd of about 5,000 protesters in the capital's Plaza de las Tres Culturas, in the district known as Tlatelolco. Estimates of the dead ranged from the government's forty-three to those of more credible witnesses who claimed up to 350. Many hundreds more were injured and some 2,000 survivors were jailed. With the opening of the 1968 Olympics in Mexico City only ten days away, the government had placed its desire to ensure a superficial tranquility above the lives of the demonstrators, most of whom were student-age. It was a decision that would unleash a period of reflection, debate, constitutional adjustments, and political realignments within the PRI that would gradually lead, over the following three decades, to a more pluralistic and competitive political regime.

An important sign of progress toward democracy was the creation in 1996 of a seven-judge special electoral court, empowered to make the final decision on disputed election results. Until then, a majority vote by the lower house of the national legislature, which was always controlled by the PRI, had been enough to confirm the election results that the PRI sought, regardless of the actual distribution of votes. The process culminated, at least in a symbolic sense, in Fox's electoral triumph in 2000.

By the first decade of the new century, the outcome of Mexico's ongoing transition to democracy was typical of the rest of Latin America. Reasonably fair, regular elections were putting civilian governments in power. But almost everywhere, the biggest political challenge – the interrelated problems of corruption, crime and indifference to the rule of law – threatened further progress in democratic consolidation. In some cases, as we will see when we turn to the problem of organized crime in Chapter 7, they became so severe by 2011 as to undermine the capacity of the state to even guarantee public order, overshadowing the question of progress toward a liberal-democratic regime.

Has Latin America Vanquished Military Rule?

The decade of the 1980s saw only four *golpes de estado* in three Latin American countries: Bolivia (1980), Guatemala (1982 and 1983), and Paraguay (1989). It was the fewest in any decade since independence in the 1820s. After the 1980s, traditional forms of military intervention in politics continued to decline almost to the vanishing point. But the military's role in political change did not disappear.

Paraguay

Paraguay, burdened with a legacy of almost unbroken dictatorial rule ever since 1811, ended the thirty-five-year dictatorship of Gen. Alfredo Stroessner in 1989 with a military coup led by Stroessner's number-two man, Gen. Andrés Rodríguez. He was the father of the woman who married Stroessner's youngest son Alfredo, and a billionaire investor in a wide range of Paraguayan enterprises. Pushed out of the inner circle by Stroessner's oldest son Gustavo, who expected to succeed his father in power, Rodríguez ordered troops under his command to arrest President Stroessner at the home of the president's mistress on the evening of 2 February 1989. After a gun battle that killed several soldiers, Stroessner escaped. The next day, Rodriguez's troops attacked the president's own Escort Regiment in a gun battle that killed at least 150 troops. Stroessner surrendered but Rodríguez allowed him to move to Brazil, where he died in 2006 at the age of 93.

Gen. Rodríguez went on to win election as president on 1 May. Under a new constitution adopted in 1992, Paraguay elected its first civilian president in thirty-nine years, the businessman (and preferred candidate of the military leadership) Juan Carlos Wasmosy, in 1993. But when Wasmosy decided to sack the army commander, Gen. Lino César Oviedo, in 1996, the general refused to quit. With the support of 5,000 troops, Gen. Oviedo revolted, threatening to kill Wasmosy, who took refuge in the U.S. embassy. Negotiations led to Wasmosy's return to office and the arrest of Gen. Oviedo, convicted of rebellion in 1998 by a military court and sentenced to ten years in prison. Oviedo was released in 1998 when a political ally, Raúl Cubas, won the presidential election and commuted his sentence to time served. A second coup attempt, thought to be organized on Oviedo's behalf, was defeated in 2000.

Venezuela

The most unexpected revival of militarism occurred in Venezuela in 1992, when Lt. Col. Hugo Chávez led an unsuccessful attempt to overthrow the elected civilian government of Carlos Andrés Pérez. It was unexpected because of Venezuela's conspicuous adherence to competitive electoral procedures even as almost every other Latin American country succumbed to military rule in the 1960s and 1970s. Venezuelans, it was widely believed, had somehow managed to banish the ghost of authoritarianism after the collapse of the dictatorship of Gen. Marcos Pérez Jiménez (1952–1958). His regime, much like that of Gen. Juan Vicente Gómez (who ruled from 1908 to 1935), incarnated the popular image of the ruthless, vainglorious and extravagantly corrupt Latin American military dictator.

After Pérez Jiménez's removal from power, the political and economic leadership of Venezuela met and, in classic patrimonial fashion, "pacted" among themselves. They devised a system by which the country's three main political parties would control successive governments by sharing power through regular elections. Known as Punto Fijo (after the house where the pact was negotiated in 1958), the system was designed to avoid both another disastrous descent into military rule and the opposite extreme of a social revolution like the one whose leaders were even then preparing to seize power in Cuba. A system like Punto Fijo could only have been conceived and arranged by leaders committed to traditional corporatist and patrimonial assumptions about the distribution of political power. It allotted no space for genuine popular participation or the expression of popular interests except for the electoral channels controlled by the major parties. The system's success depended on an essential, and exceptional, lubricant – Venezuela's rising tide of petroleum revenues, which mounted to spectacular levels over the next two decades. They allowed the leadership to keep taxes low while rewarding collaborators and clients with petroleum-derived gratuities in the form of jobs, government contracts and social welfare programs. The corruption and economic mismanagement that led to the collapse of Punto Fijo will be analyzed in Chapter 9.

The deep-seated disgust for Punto Fijo within the middle ranks of the army and among non-commissioned officers led to the organization of a secret society within the army, the Movimiento Bolivariano Revolucionario, in the early 1980s. Because the major political parties controlled promotion above the rank of lieutenant colonel, many officers considered their generals to be corrupt and incompetent. The Movement's conspirators blamed Venezuela's poverty on the politicians and businessmen who utilized the Punto Fijo system as a source of personal enrichment. Their outlook seemed to be confirmed in the bloody nationwide uprising of February 1989, in which close to 400 persons died at the hands of the security forces during protests against the economic austerity program of President Pérez. Mobilized during the uprising to defend a system they detested, the military conspirators sympathized with the protestors. As news of more government corruption scandals followed, Pérez's popularity declined even more.

The Movement acted on 4 February 1992. Under the leadership of Chávez and another officer, Lt. Col. Francisco Arias, more than 1,000 rebel soldiers attacked the presidential office building in Caracas. Other units moved against government installations elsewhere in the country but loyalist forces defeated the insurrectionists within hours, arresting Chávez and his co-conspirators. While they were in prison, senior officers attempted another coup in November. By then, Chávez, who had been allowed to make a statement on national television after he was captured, had achieved heroic status among many Venezuelans for having challenged the Punto Fijo system. Released from prison in March 1994, Chávez called himself a "revolutionary" and organized a campaign for the presidency, which he won with 56% of the vote on 6 December 1998. Chávez's plans for "twenty-first century socialism" provoked a faction of the military to rise up on 11 April 2002 and remove him from power, but its government only survived forty-eight hours before yielding to popular pressure and restoring Chávez to office. The president purged the armed forces of officers suspected of sympathizing with the coup, and in 2008 he decreed a law giving himself more direct control over all four services of the armed forces, which he renamed the Fuerza Armada Nacional Boliviariana, now more thoroughly politicized than at any time since the 1950s.

Ecuador

Ecuador's military, which last governed the country from 1972 to 1979, played a decisive role in President Jamil Mahaud's ouster in January 2000, not by initiating action but rather by stepping aside and allowing others to force Mahaud from office. Massive demonstrations protesting government austerity measures, a catastrophic banking crisis and political corruption had practically paralyzed Ecuador. On 21 January, troops deployed to protect the congress and the supreme court from the protesters received orders to withdraw. Rushing both buildings, the protest leaders joined with an anti-Mahaud faction in the congress to declare the formation of a temporary government, one of whose leaders was Col. Lucio Gutiérrez.

The support of several hundred junior officers for the new government was interpreted by the high command as an act of disobedience, and after a tense confrontation with his superiors, Col. Gutiérrez agreed to withdraw from the government. At the same time, in response to President Mahaud's rejection of the army high command's recommendation that he resign, the army simply ordered the presidential guard to return to its barracks. Defenseless before thousands of furious citizens, Mahaud fled his office and took refuge in the Chilean embassy. The army commander's endorsement of Vice President Gustavo Noboa as the congressionally-backed successor to Mahaud, as well as the firm opposition of the United States to any military participation in government, extinguished any lingering hope for a joint military-civilian junta, a plan that had been strongly endorsed by prominent civilian politicians and activists.

Honduras

In 2009, the armed forces of Honduras executed a Supreme Court order to arrest President José Manuel Zelaya for defying various court orders enjoining him to desist from his attempts to amend the constitution so that he could run for a second term as president. However, instead of bringing the president before a magistrate to face the charges, the military officers illegally put him on a plane to Costa Rica, forcing him into exile. The next day, 29 June, Congress voted 122 to 6 to remove Zelaya from office, and appointed his constitutional successor, Roberto Micheletti, the president of the Congress, as president of Honduras. Widely reported as a "military coup," the arrest and expulsion from Honduras of President Zelaya incited the greatest wave of international condemnation against any Latin American government in memory, owing in good part to the inferior status Honduras occupied in the international system. The UN General Assembly refused to recognize the Micheletti government and demanded Zelaya's "immediate and unconditional" restitution. The Organization of American States' General Assembly suspended Honduras' right to participate in the organization, a move it last took in 1962 when it suspended Cuba. Governments in Latin America and Europe withdrew their ambassadors from Honduras in protest, discontinuing loan agreements, economic assistance programs and trade relations. In Honduras, Zelaya's removal inspired a furious wave of popular protest. Not until 2011, after negotiations mediated by the presidents of Colombia and Venezuela, was the crisis resolved. The Honduran judicial system annulled the charges against Zelaya, opening the way for Zelaya and President Porfirio Lobo to sign a nine-point accord establishing Zelaya's right to return to Honduras and participate fully in politics.

Peru

In two other cases, civilian presidents themselves sought to extend their power and their terms in office by organizing what became known as *autogolpes* or self-coups. Their success depended on the disposition of the armed forces to cooperate. The term was first applied to the surprise announcement by President Alberto Fujimori of Peru on 5 April 1992, two years after his election, that he was suspending the constitution, dissolving congress, and ruling by decree with the full support of the armed forces. Owing largely to his success in subsequently defeating the Sendero Luminoso insurgency and restoring economic stability, Fujimori went on to win the 1995 election with 64% of the vote and a large majority in the congress, illustrating once again that political legitimacy in Latin America does not necessarily depend on any given government's commitment to basic civil liberties or constitutional guarantees. But Fujimori's increasingly authoritarian style evidently exceeded the electorate's tolerance during his second term. He announced he would run for a third term in 2000 despite the constitutional limit of two terms, and after he manipulated the law (and electoral procedures) to ensure his victory with 52% of the vote, Fujimori's inauguration on 28 July was greeted with violent protests, provoked largely by evidence of massive vote fraud. In September, hundreds of videotapes were released showing his security adviser, Vladimiro Montesinos, bribing numerous public officials. As the crisis deepened, Lt. Col. Ollanta Humala led sixty men in an abortive revolt, taking his own commanding general as a hostage and demanding Fujimori's immediate resignation.

Disgraced and desperate to avoid arrest, Fujimori fled to Japan in November, where he announced his resignation as president. Despite the Peruvian government's persistent efforts to seek his extradition in order to try him on numerous charges of corruption, murder and kidnapping, Fujimori declared his candidacy for president in the elections scheduled for 2006. After arriving unannounced in Chile in 2005 to direct his campaign, he was arrested and extradited to Peru. In 2009, a Peruvian court sentenced Fujimori, then 70 years old, to twenty-five years' imprisonment for creating a military death squad called the Colina Group that killed twenty-five people, including an 8-year-old boy. Fujimori remained a popular figure among many Peruvians. His daughter Keiko nearly won the presidency with 49% of the vote in 2011, having declared during the campaign that her father was not only innocent but had been "the best president of Peru."

Guatemala

Fujimori's successful *autogolpe* in 1992 appeared to inspire President Jorge Elias Serrano of Guatemala to suspend the constitution, close congress and the supreme court, and impose censorship on the news media on 25 May 1993. Like Fujimori, Serrano intended to rule by decree. Unlike Fujimori, however, he had acted without first consulting the leadership of the armed forces, which consequently divided between those who supported Serrano and others who argued that to support the *autogolpe* would jeopardize the military's legitimacy. Fujimori could also count on considerably more popular backing than Serrano. Unable to convince Guatemala that it was facing a security threat sufficient to justify the self-coup, Serrano faced a wave of protest that temporarily united almost every sector of society. Ironically, the army itself restored constitutional order by arresting Serrano on 1 June and putting him on a plane for El Salvador.

While the military had intervened in both facilitating Serrano's *autogolpe* and then in removing him, in neither case had it acted independently and since the crisis the military has clearly accepted its constitutional subordination to elected civilian governments. On the other hand, the military's control over its own internal operations, and thus its freedom from full civilian control, persisted. In response to the accelerating rates of violent crime that have been sweeping Guatemala since the 1990s, the military's responsibility for domestic security has been expanded along with its budget, while military officers have repeatedly been implicated in the criminal activities that they were assigned to investigate, as we will see in Chapter 7.

Conclusions

By the start of the new century, the classic military *golpe de estado* appeared to have faded as a key feature of Latin American authoritarianism. In the period that followed the 1980s, the armed forces demonstrated a clear aversion to interrupting constitutional procedures. On the other hand, the post-1980s period revealed that Latin America has not succeeded in eliminating political instability. Now, however, instability could no longer be blamed on a historical legacy of military intervention. As we have just seen, most of the post-1980s interruptions of constitutional order in which the military participated were directed by civilian politicians, and often propelled by mass demonstrations of popular discontent. The military men who did move independently against a government represented factions of officers, usually in the middle or upper-middle ranks. Their revolts – Chávez in Venezuela in 1992, Oviedo in Paraguay in 1996, and Ollanta Humala in Peru in 2000 – were both rare and unsuccessful, owing to a lack of support for their moves within the armed forces.

Yet officers who took leading roles in abortive traditional revolts or in the broader interruptions of civilian-led constitutional order after the 1980s were often exalted by the public as heroic defenders of the nation, rather than as criminals or misfits. In flouting the constitution, disobeying orders and resorting to violence, these modern incarnations of the nineteenth-century man on horseback regularly launched new and often successful careers as candidates for legislative office or the presidency. Among them were Lt. Col. Hugo Chávez (president of Venezuela, 1999–), Col. Lucio Gutiérrez (president of Ecuador, 2003–2005), Lt. Col. Ollanta Humala (president of Peru, 2011–) and Gen. Lino Oviedo of Paraguay, who won 22% of the vote in the 2008 presidential election and built his political party into the country's third largest. Since the 1970s, the appeal of the military *caudillo* as the ultimate defender of order and dispenser of justice had abated, but it clearly had not disappeared.

Notes

1 United Nations Development Programme, *Democracy in Latin America: Towards a Citizens' Democracy* (New York: United Nations Development Programme, 2005), 13, 29.
2 Fernando Gualdoni, "Entrevista: Fernando Henrique Cardoso Ex presidente de Brasil," *El País* (Madrid), 15 June 2010.

References

Gualdoni, Fernando. "Entrevista: Fernando Henrique Cardoso Ex presidente de Brasil." *El País* (Madrid), 15 June 2010.
United Nations Development Programme. *Democracy in Latin America: Towards a Citizens' Democracy*. New York: United Nations Development Programme, 2005.

Chapter 6

Religion, Politics and the State

The Catholic Church and Politics

Like other institutions, the Catholic Church passed through some important changes in Latin America in the latter half of the twentieth century. None was greater than the spirit of political and social activism that penetrated the priesthood, religious orders, lay leadership, and the highest pastoral authorities, including the bishops. As they spoke out and took action, both individually and collectively, they made the Catholic Church a highly influential participant in the politics of reform, revolution, militarization and demilitarization almost everywhere in the region. At the same time, both civic and Church leaders reappraised and in some cases reordered the historically intimate, but often antagonistic, relations between state and Church, a topic that will be addressed in a separate section of this chapter.

Two consequences of the spirit of activism that suffused the Church from the 1960s onward have affected the Church's standing to the present day. The first was the emergence of a division within the ranks of the clergy, separating those campaigning for rapid political and economic change from those who resisted what they considered an undue politicization of the faith. To speak of a "liberal–conservative" split, or a "church of the rich and a church of the poor," as some have done, is simplistic. Conflicting political ideologies – Marxism, liberalism, social democracy – have indeed divided the clergy, in part; but the deeper and longer-lasting division centered on the proper role of the clergy in the political sphere, and on the relative importance of their more strictly spiritual duties. While some clergy argued that their pastoral duties required them to endorse and even lead movements for progressive social change, others

Contemporary Latin America: 1970 to the Present, First Edition. Robert H. Holden and Rina Villars.
© 2013 Robert H. Holden and Rina Villars. Published 2013 by Blackwell Publishing Ltd.

insisted that such activities could only derail or undermine their obligations to provide spiritual leadership.

As the option for thoroughgoing social and political change appeared to captivate many of the clergy, the second effect followed: the Church was increasingly identified in the public mind with social change, often of a radical kind, and less with the salvation of souls. The image of a highly politicized clergy preoccupied with social change discouraged individuals who were looking primarily for spiritual guidance, and at the same time increased the appeal of the rising Protestant communities, which for the most part were militantly apolitical. Three developments, all rooted in the 1960s, drew the Catholic Church into movements for social and political change in Latin America.

The first was the rise of the politics of radical reform and socialist revolution. While some churchmen sided with the authorities, many sympathized with the reformers and the revolutionaries, at least intellectually. They cited the longstanding teaching of the Church that social justice was the essential condition for social peace. A fairer distribution of wealth, guarantees of basic freedoms for all men and women, and the cessation of dictatorial rule were increasingly seen as matters of urgent spiritual as well as practical significance.

Clergymen who took that stand found encouragement in the second development, a pair of institutional changes within the Church. The first was the establishment in 1955 of the Consejo Episcopal Latinoamericano (CELAM – Latin American Episcopal Council), a permanent organization of all the region's bishops. The second was the Catholic Church's Twenty-First Ecumenical Council of bishops, better known as Vatican Council II. It met in Rome from 1962 to 1965 to consider how to present Church teaching in ways that responded more effectively to the vast social changes that had occurred since the previous council (1869–1870). *Aggiornamento* or renewal was Vatican II's byword, and the world's poor were to be a special beneficiary of that process. "While an immense number of people still lack the absolute necessities of life, some, even in less advanced areas, live in luxury or squander wealth," the Council declared. "Extravagance and wretchedness exist side by side. While a few enjoy very great power of choice, the majority are deprived of almost all possibility of acting on their own initiative and responsibility, and often subsist in living and working conditions unworthy of the human person."[1] This message would be amplified considerably, and redirected mainly to Latin America and Africa, when in 1967 Pope Paul VI denounced the "flagrant inequalities" of wealth, culture and political power in his encyclical letter "Populorum progressio," which was addressed to "the bishops, priests, religious, and faithful of the whole Catholic world, and to all men of good will." One widely commented section even seemed to justify revolutionary violence wherever one finds "manifest, longstanding tyranny which would do great damage to fundamental personal rights and dangerous harm to the common good of the country."[2]

Both the pope's letter and Vatican II inspired broad experimentation in doctrine and practice, and the boldest of all experiments in Catholic-led social change emerged first in Latin America. CELAM's second general meeting in 1968 in Medellín, Colombia – perhaps the single most important event in the twentieth-century history of the Catholic Church in Latin America – was convened to reflect on the implications of Vatican II for Latin America. There, in the midst of a continent torn between popular demands for change, on the one hand, and the repressive response of a rising number of military dictatorships preoccupied with national security, on the other, the bishops arrived at a somber conclusion: In spite of all the efforts to overcome the tragedies of underdevelopment, Latin Americans continued to live with "hunger and poverty, widespread sickness and infant mortality, illiteracy and marginality, profound inequalities of income, tensions among social classes, outbreaks of violence and minimal participation by the people in the management of the common good." The bishops called for a "new order of justice" as well as a "new evangelization" embracing the rich as well as the poor.[3]

The language of these documents and many similar expressions of concern issued by the Church's hierarchy were subjected to contradictory interpretations. Those who favored more intensive engagement in social change confronted those who argued for a response that would preserve the primacy of a more traditional spirit of evangelization and interior conversion. The result was a Latin American church whose priests, bishops and laity found themselves increasingly divided by the scope and depth of their commitments to social change.

The confidence of those most impatient for change was vastly strengthened by the third development, the forging of a "theology of liberation" among Latin American theologians in the mid-1960s. By the late 1970s, "liberation theology" had become one of Latin America's most famous cultural exports, having matured into a tool of religiously inspired social analysis that was cited, studied and adopted by intellectuals and activists around the world. Its classic expression came in a book first published in 1969, *Hacia una teología de la liberación* (*Toward a Theology of Liberation*), by a Peruvian priest, Gustavo Gutiérrez. The core teaching was that God, having revealed himself above all *in* the poor and oppressed, desired their emancipation from poverty and political oppression. In its broadest application, such as at Medellín and among a good many Latin American churchmen, liberation theology provided a method for identifying and denouncing "structural sin," understood as social arrangements that permitted the systematic exploitation and oppression of the weak and poor. More importantly, it became a means of encouraging the poor to act to change their living conditions through the study of specifically "liberationist" interpretations of Christian scripture

Taken together, these three developments – the surge in popular demands for social change, organizational and doctrinal modifications within the Church, and a distinctively Latin American theology – magnified and energized the Catholic Church's traditional teachings on justice as the criterion of morality in the social sphere. As early as 1962, the bishops of Guatemala and Chile issued pastoral letters denouncing what they called the unjust distribution of land, and demanding its redistribution in favor of the rural poor. Four years later, the bishops of Brazil's impoverished Northeast declared themselves in favor of the redistribution of land and workers' rights. In 1971, Mexican bishops criticized that country's dependence on the United States and accused the government of "institutionalized lying," and of a "kind of subfascism" responsible for the rise of "a new oligarchic and monopolistic minority in collusion with foreign forces to the detriment of the oppressed and exploited." In the late 1970s, the bishops of Mexico's eight southernmost dioceses agreed to make the defense of their region's Indian population (the most highly concentrated in the country) the highest priority in their dioceses. Acting under the leadership of Samuel Ruiz, the bishop of San Cristóbal de las Casas from 1959 to 2000, the region's churchmen encouraged both Indian and non-Indian peasants to mobilize in favor of land redistribution and their human and political rights.

The politicization of Catholic teaching that liberation theology encouraged was at times expressed in ways that explicitly challenged the legitimacy of the state. The exemplar of the politically-committed priest was Camilo Torres, who was killed in action against the Colombian army four months after he joined the revolutionary guerrilla army, Ejército de Liberación Nacional (ELN) in 1965. The most broadly political application of liberation theology helped to stoke the revolutionary violence that erupted in Central America during the 1970s and 1980s. In Honduras, the U.S.-born Jesuit priest, James F. Carney, quit his work as a missionary to join a guerrilla column bent on overthrowing the Honduran government in 1983. Within weeks, the Honduran army captured him and other insurgents as they marched north from their sanctuary in Nicaragua. Carney's body has never been found, and the cause of death has not been firmly established. In Nicaragua, numerous priests joined the insurgency led by the Frente Sandinista de Liberación Nacional (FSLN), which overthrew the Somoza dictatorship in 1979. Some subsequently received posts in the government of the FSLN (1979–1990). But the Sandinistas' highly liberationist interpretation of Christianity in defense of its program of revolutionary change sharply divided the clergy while drawing the stern opposition of the archbishop of Managua, Miguel Obando y Bravo.

Priests and bishops who rejected violence and remained detached from partisan politics in Central America were nevertheless threatened or killed for defending human rights or advocating for the poor. In Guatemala, seven priests who were assassinated in the performance of their duties between 1978 and 1983 have been proposed for sainthood by the Church authorities of Guatemala. In 1977, death threats drove the Honduran bishop of Juticalpa to desert his post, while in El Salvador, a secret society calling itself the Unión Guerrera Blanca threatened to execute all of the country's Jesuit priests, whom the country's military government also accused of disloyalty. During the 1980s, as a coalition of armed rebel groups tried to overthrow the U.S.-supported and military-dominated government of El Salvador, Catholic leaders and missionaries were constantly singled out as targets by the government and its paramilitary allies. El Salvador's highest-ranking church leader, Archbishop Oscar Romero, was shot to death in 1980, in retaliation for his frequent denunciations of political violence and government repression. Later that year, four Catholic women missionaries from the United States, three of whom were nuns, were apprehended and shot to death by members of the Salvadoran armed forces. In the midst of a fiercely fought offensive by El Salvador's revolutionary guerrilla army in 1989, a squad of Salvadoran soldiers broke into the residence of six Jesuit priests, lined them up and shot them to death, along with their housekeeper and her daughter.

In countries ruled by military dictatorships in the 1960s, 1970s and early 1980s, the Catholic Church and some Protestant communities were among the few institutions that managed to evade direct control by the state. Individual churchmen as well as national bishops' conferences often defended the victims of state political repression, and in doing so emerged as those countries' only consistent voices in favor of human rights and economic justice. The Catholic Church of Brazil gradually took on this role during the 1970s, the period of the most intense political repression by the country's military government, which ruled from 1964 to 1985. The Brazilian church even investigated and publicized individual cases of flagrant violations of human rights, directly challenging the authority of the government. In the regime's last year in office, the Church collaborated in the publication of *Brasil: Nunca Mais* (subsequently published in English as *Torture in Brazil: A Report*), which sought to provide a case-by-case accounting of the victims of the dictatorship. Similarly, the Catholic Church of Chile emerged as the principal adversary of the military regime that ruled the country from 1973 to 1990. The leadership of the Chilean Church denounced the government's policies, and provided material support and protection for the poor and victims of political repression. It also played a key role in organizing civilian political opposition to the regime, hastening the transition to democracy. Like their Brazilian counterparts, Chilean priests, bishops and lay activists who criticized the government risked intimidation, arrest, assassination and torture.

Another example of resistance to dictatorial rule emerged in Paraguay under the one-man rule of Gen. Alfredo Stroessner from 1954 to 1989. The tense and often hostile character of the relations between Stroessner and the Church since the inception of the dictatorship did not discourage Church leaders in the 1980s from trying to mediate the conflict between the dictatorship and the rising number of its opponents. When Paraguay's bishops organized and directed a "national dialogue" in the 1980s, opposition groups participated in the process but the government strongly resisted, claiming exclusive authority to control public debate. As government interference with the dialogue intensified, more and more political opponents utilized the protective cover of the Church while deploying traditional Christian religious symbols to express their resistance. Two silent religious processions (on 30 October 1987 and 6 August 1988) that drew 35,000 to 40,000 marchers marked decisive moments in the military government's decline. Between the two marches, Pope John Paul II visited Paraguay in May 1988 and deftly communicated his support for political change.

In Argentina, where military rule (1976–1983) was the harshest of any South American country, the leadership of the Catholic Church spurned the oppositional role assumed elsewhere. As already noted in Chapter 4, more than 10,000 Argentines perished at the hands of the military during the dictatorship, the highest death toll of civilians recorded by any South American military government. Churchmen denounced flagrant human rights violations and frequently expressed their opposition (if only in private) to the dictatorship's signature terror tactic – the kidnapping, torture and "disappearance" of suspected political opponents. Nevertheless, many bishops remained openly sympathetic to the regime, and as a result, clerical defiance of military rule tended to take the form of individual acts that were in turn swiftly punished. After Bishop Enrique Angelelli of La Rioja began to investigate the 1976 kidnapping and murder of two priests, he was murdered and the documents he had collected on the deaths of the priests were taken by his killers. Most of the country's bishops said nothing about his murder and one who did denounce it, Bishop Carlos Ponce de León of San Nicolás, was himself killed in a suspicious car accident a year later.

In 1996, Argentina's bishops publicly asked forgiveness for the moral failures of those Catholics who, during the 1960s, 1970s and 1980s, supported the violent path of the Marxist guerrillas, as well as those Argentines who took part in "immoral and atrocious" acts connected with the repression of the insurgents. They acknowledged that many Argentines believed the bishops should have cut off all communication with the military regime, instead of merely denouncing the human rights crimes of the military government. "Only God knows what would have happened had we taken that path. But without a doubt, all that was done wasn't enough to stop the horror," the bishops conceded. Four years later – seventeen years after the end of the dictatorship – the head of the bishops' conference, at an extraordinary public liturgy attended by more than 100,000 Argentines, begged pardon, in the name of all the country's Catholics, for the silence and the participation of so many "in crimes against freedom, in torture and in action as informers, in political persecution and ideological intransigence, in the struggles and wars, and in the absurd killing that bloodied our country."[4]

The Church's engagement in social change unfolded in yet another way in Peru. Church-inspired social change after the 1950s typically led to hostile relations between the Church and military governments that usually opposed those changes. Then, on 2 October 1968, just as the country's bishops were moving toward stronger action on behalf of the poor and oppressed, the armed forces carried out an unusual coup d'état. The generals declared themselves to be "revolutionaries" who were taking the side of the masses. Promising a thoroughgoing reconstruction of Peruvian society, the armed forces redistributed land and water rights to the poor, took a nationalistic stance against foreign economic interests, and reformed the educational system and the economy.

As a result, the leadership of the Catholic Church and that of the military government found common ground. The military government even justified its reforms by citing Catholic social doctrine. While the Church welcomed the changes associated with the regime's slogan of "a social democracy of full participation," leading Churchmen nevertheless criticized the government's violations of human rights and encouraged moves toward democratic, civilian rule. Church–state tensions over the government's authoritarian policies persisted to the last days of the presidency (1975–1980) of Gen. Francisco Morales Bermúdez, who paved the way to an elected civilian government. About the same time, the guerrilla warriors of Sendero Luminoso were beginning to kill members of the clergy and religious orders while targeting Church-affiliated rural development projects and anyone associated with them. As a result, the Peruvian Church was in no position to take on the kind of mediating role between the government and the insurgency that churchmen elsewhere in Latin America accepted during this period.

Peru and Argentina therefore turned out to be exceptional in the period of military rule. Peru owed its singularity to the rare commitment of a military government to Church-supported social change, and to the principal guerrilla group's hatred of the Church. What made Argentina so different was the timidity and even complicity of the national Church's response to South America's bloodiest dictatorship. Except in Argentina, as military governments seized power and cancelled civil liberties across Latin America from the 1960s onward, the Catholic Church stood out, in the words of church historian Jeffrey Klaiber, as "the only national institution which the great majority, whether of the left, the center, or the right, could accept as a common meeting ground."[5]

Change within the religious sphere was not limited to clergy-directed social activism or political mediation. An institutional innovation with strongly political overtones, widely adopted throughout Latin America, and then imported by Catholic and Protestant leaders elsewhere, were the *comunidades eclesiales de base* (CEBs) or "Christian base communities." Springing up in the 1960s, they were small groups of lay Catholics who met regularly to read the Bible and reflect on its implications for social change. Priests and members of religious orders, as well as specially trained lay leaders, encouraged base-community members to identify and analyze the conditions responsible for their problems, to judge them according to particular passages of the Bible, and to consider corrective action. Here, the theology of liberation interacted with the pedagogical innovations then championed by Paulo Freire (1921–1997), the Brazilian professor of education who taught that literacy instruction and basic education could be tools of social emancipation. His work will be discussed in Chapter 11.

Encouraged by the new emphasis on social justice in Church teaching and the support of individual clergymen influenced by liberation theology, base-community members called on carefully selected elements of Christian doctrine leavened with Freire's pedagogy and the Marxist theory of class conflict. An early example of mobilization inspired by base communities appeared in eastern Paraguay, where nearly 10,000 land-seeking peasants organized themselves into cooperatives in the 1960s. Launched with the encouragement of some priests and religious orders, the "ligas campesinas" or peasant leagues began seizing vacant land in the early 1970s. The rising militancy of the movement's leadership provoked the hostility of both the government and Church leaders. By the late 1970s the movement had been completely suppressed through mass arrests and detentions, and the Jesuit priests connected with it were expelled from Paraguay. In 1976, a pastoral letter issued by the country's bishops condemned the government's harsh repression as well as political extremists among their clergy, while encouraging a more thorough spiritual formation of the populace by means of the CEBs.

The contemporary history of the Catholic Church as a political force in Latin America can be divided into two phases. The first began in the 1960s, a time of accelerating activism on behalf of the poor and oppressed, accompanied and justified by shifts of emphasis in official doctrine and in speculative theology, as well as by institutional innovations. Doubts about the propriety of such activism could be found among some priests and theologians who warned that the Church could lose sight of the primacy of its sacramental and spiritual obligations to poor and rich alike. They also feared that intervention in the political arena risked associating the Church with political ideologies and programs that might end up discrediting it.

As these criticisms began to mount, they came to dominate the second phase, which opened in the early 1980s. Enthusiasm for promoting rapid social change diminished, activism was increasingly redirected toward evangelization and spiritual formation, and doctrinal corrections were issued. The seeds of phase two were sown in 1979 at the third meeting of the Latin American bishops, inaugurated by the just-elected Pope John Paul II, in the Mexican city of Puebla. "Your principal duty," he told them, "is to be teachers of the truth," safeguarding the purity of Catholic doctrine and putting faith in Jesus Christ at the center of their work. Political, social or economic liberation should not be confused with spiritual salvation, the pope warned. The bishops seemed to be listening, for in their concluding report they warned against the politicization of the faith, yet narrowly voted to keep alive the spirit of Medellín with a sharply debated paragraph proclaiming a "preferential option for the poor."

The tide turned against the theology of liberation with the release by the Vatican in the mid-1980s of two letters to the Brazilian theologian Leonardo Boff and two sets of instructions to the Latin American bishops. While reaffirming the validity of the Puebla conference's "preferential option for the poor," the Vatican interpreted that phrase to include all persons rather than just a single economic class. And while insisting on the Church's commitment to social justice, it also declared that "The Church's essential mission, following that of Christ, is a mission of evangelization and salvation." At their fourth conference in Santo Domingo in 1992, the Latin American bishops upheld the renewed emphasis on both personal salvation and the struggle for social justice, while explicitly widening the definition of the marginal population to include not just those who were economically poor, but women, Indians and Afro-Americans. The most controversial of their conclusions, in the year that marked the 500th anniversary of Christopher Columbus's first voyage to the Americas, was the bishops' "request for pardon" for abuses committed by Catholics in the name of their faith over the course of Latin American history. After a special, Vatican-convened meeting of the region's bishops in 1999, a papal document again reminded the bishops of their fundamental duty to undertake a Christ-centered "new evangelization – new in its spirit, methods, and expression" that would include the leaders of society as well as its most marginalized members.

Church–State Relations

During the period of Spanish and Portuguese rule, the Iberian monarchies exercised immense control over the Church in the Americas. After independence, most of the new national governments insisted on their right to inherit the same sort of authority over the Church that the monarchies had wielded. Eager to assert its autonomy after so many centuries of domination by the monarchies, the Church resisted. The ensuing struggles between those largely liberal forces that sought to limit the Church's traditional influence while seizing most of its wealth, and conservatives who fought to defend the Church's colonial-era status and privileges, accounted for a good deal of the political conflict and violence that consumed Latin America after independence. By about the mid-1960s, two broad categories of Church–state relationships could be detected. Nine countries had adopted the principle of a "soft" separation between Church and state, having conceded some kind of constitutional privilege to the Catholic Church over other religions (Argentina, Bolivia, Colombia, Costa Rica, Dominican Republic, El Salvador, Paraguay, Peru and Venezuela). A more decisive and less flexible or "hard" separation characterized the situations in the other ten countries: Brazil, Chile, Cuba, Ecuador, Guatemala, Honduras, Mexico, Nicaragua, Panama and Uruguay. But even in this group, a continuum of practices could be discerned: At one end was Mexico, where the government strictly regulated the Church and even held formal title to all ecclesiastical property. At the opposite end were the countries closest to true separation, where the state remained neutral and religious freedom prevailed: Brazil, Chile and Uruguay. Everywhere, of course, constitutions guaranteed religious freedom, though in practice limitations on freedom were common. They were strongest in Cuba and Mexico.

A general trend toward stricter separation and state neutrality has continued since the mid-1960s but has by no means prevailed. By 2005, all of the region's governments generally respected religious freedom except for Cuba's, where the one-party Communist state, in power since the early 1960s, continued to impose legal and practical restrictions on religious freedom. Cuba's 1976 constitution declared that the "socialist state bases its activities on, and educates the people in, the scientific materialist conception of the universe," and went on to criminalize religious opposition to state directives. That language was removed in 1992 and replaced by numerous references to religious freedom, along with others asserting the state's right to regulate religion. In a speech welcoming Pope John Paul II to Cuba in 1998, Castro compared Cubans to the Christian martyrs of ancient Rome, and the United States to the Roman imperial government that persecuted them: "Like those Christians horribly slandered to justify the crime, we who are as slandered as they were, we choose a thousand times death rather than abdicate our convictions." John Paul's successor, Pope Benedict XVI, planned a visit to the island in March 2012.

Nine countries continued to favor the Catholic Church over other religious denominations in a diversity of ways, ranging from constitutional recognition and direct financial subsidies, at one extreme, to little more than the recognition of certain Catholic feast days as national holidays, at the other. They were Argentina, Bolivia, Chile, Colombia, Costa Rica, Dominican Republic, El Salvador, Panama and Peru. The Argentine, Bolivian (until 2009) and Costa Rican constitutions asserted their states' commitment to supporting the Catholic religion, and all of them directly subsidized Church activities in various ways. The Church was receiving some public subsidies in the Dominican Republic, and the Panamanian constitution required that Catholicism be taught in the public schools but made attendance at such classes voluntary. In Peru, the state extended financial, educational and other privileges to the Church. In 2009, Bolivia adopted a new constitution ending the state's moderate support for Catholicism by declaring that "the state is independent of religion." As a result, in 2010 the country's legislative assembly terminated the teaching of the Catholic religion in public schools, and required a new course, "Religions, Spirituality, Ethics and Values."

Nowhere in twentieth-century Latin America were Church-state relations more turbulent than in Mexico, which claims the second-highest number of Catholics in the world after Brazil. The constitution of 1917, adopted in the heat of a revolutionary civil war, prohibited the establishment of monastic orders and the celebration of religious rituals outside of a church building. Religious instruction of any kind was prohibited, even in private schools. No church was allowed to own real estate or any buildings, and those already owned by any church became state property. No priest or minister was allowed to vote, comment publicly on matters of government or even to wear clerical garb in public. State governments were authorized to regulate the number of priests or ministers in their states, and numerous other restrictions were imposed on religious expression. The legislative implementation of these provisions in the 1920s led to the bloodiest war of religion in Latin American history, the Cristero Rebellion of 1926–1929, which took as many as 70,000 lives. As a result of the war, the government relaxed enforcement of some of the laws that provoked it. But a highly uneasy *modus vivendi* between Church and state persisted.

With the exception of Cuba after 1960, Mexico remained the least tolerant of religion in Latin America until at least 1992. That year, as a result of negotiations between leaders of the Catholic Church and President Carlos Salinas, some of the anti-religious language of the constitution was softened, and some of the implementing legislation was repealed or amended. Certain religious ceremonies could now be conducted outside of church buildings, limited property rights for Church institutions were restored, and while clergy were now allowed to vote, their freedom to speak on political matters was still restricted. The prohibition on religious education even in private schools also remained in effect. When President Vicente Fox (2000–2006) waved a banner impressed with the image of the patron saint of the Americas, the Virgin of Guadalupe, at a pre-election campaign rally in 2000, he was fined $1,800 for violating a law against mixing religion and politics. After his election, his attendance at a Mass inspired front-page headlines. But with the exception of some cases of religious discrimination attributed mainly to local or state government offi-cials, and the shadow still cast by the restrictive language of the constitution, religious freedom by the first decade of the new century was not markedly inferior in Mexico to that of most other Latin American countries.

What continued to distinguish state–Church relations in Latin America as compared to, say, those of the United States, was revealed in the way in which the Mexican reforms of 1992 were undertaken and settled. The problem was understood to be less about religion and more about calibrating the rela-tionship between two institutions. In this we see reflected the Latin American tradition of corporatism and the preference for settling contentious matters by means of pacts among leaders assumed to speak for all the "members" of their respective corporate bodies. To have conceived of the problem in terms of individual religious freedom and therefore the protection of a human right superseding institutional interests would have entailed, in the case of Mexico, a different framework for reform, and probably a different kind of outcome. Instead, the baseline remained the presumed superiority of the rights and interests of the state over those of individuals or religious institutions. The legal existence and standing of religious institutions has continued to depend, in most of Latin America, on explicit recognition by the state.

Conclusions

From the 1970s onward, Latin America moved decisively away from military rule and other forms of authoritarian government, even as the continuing popular appeal of individual military figures persisted in many places. Demo-cratic institutions gradually embedded themselves in the political culture of the region. Social revolution largely disappeared as an alternative path of politi-cal and economic development, for with the waning of arbitrary and repressive government, the main political motive for rebellion faded. Yet if the democra-tization of Latin America owed something to the wave of guerrilla insurgency, it owed even more to steady, nonviolent popular pressures for such basic politi-cal reforms as fair and competitive elections, governmental accountability, respect for individual rights, and the surrender of the armed forces to civilian rule. Owing to its long near-monopoly on religious practices and beliefs in Latin America, no single institution contributed more to the process of politi-cal change than the Catholic Church. Energized by a series of internal reforms beginning in the 1960s, the Church almost everywhere devised new ways to apply ancient teachings about the essential dignity of the person. At the same time, and despite an unprecedented wave of conversions to Protestant forms of Christian belief, the Catholic Church in many (but not all) countries continued to benefit from its traditional though diminished status as a kind of semi-official church.

Notes

1 Pope Paul VI, in Vatican Council II, "Pastoral Constitution on the Church in the Modern World: Gaudium et spes," promulgated by His Holiness, Pope Paul VI on 7 December 1965, §63, www.vatican.va/archive/hist_councils/ii_vatican_council/documents/vat-ii_cons_19651207_gaudium-et-spes_en.html.
2 Pope Paul VI, Encyclical Letter, "Populorum progressio," 26 March 1967, §§30–1, www.vatican.va/holy_father/paul_vi/encyclicals/documents/hf_p-vi_enc_26031967_populorum_en.html.
3 Consejo Episcopal Latinoamericano, "Mensaje a los Pueblos de América Latina," in *La iglesia en la actual transformación de América Latina a la luz del Concilio. Medellín: Conclusiones. Segunda Conferencia general del espiscopado latinoamericano Bogotá, 24 de Agosto. Medellín, Agosto 26-Septiembre 6. Colombia 1968* (Bogotá: Secretariado General del CELAM, 1981), 18, 20.
4 Conferencia Episcopal Argentina, "Caminando hacia el tercer milenio: carta pastoral para preparar la celebración de los 2000 años del nacimiento de Jesucristo," 27 April 1996, reprinted in *Boletín de Lecturas Sociales y Económicas* 3, no. 11 (1996): 88–94. Conferencia Episcopal Argentina, "Reconciliación de los bautizados," 8 September 2000, reprinted in *Boletín Semanal* (Agencia Informativa Católica Argentina), no. 2283 (20 September 2000); Jorge Rouillon, "Histórico pedido de perdón de la Iglesia argentina," *La Nación*, 9 September 2000.
5 Jeffrey L. Klaiber, *The Church, Dictatorships, and Democracy in Latin America* (Maryknoll, NY: Orbis Books, 1998), 7.

References

Conferencia Episcopal Argentina. "Caminando hacia el tercer milenio: carta pastoral para preparar la celebración de los 2000 años del nacimiento de Jesucristo." *Boletin de Lecturas Sociales y Económicas* 3, no. 11 (1996): 88–94.
Conferencia Episcopal Argentina. "Reconciliación de los bautizados," *Boletín Semanal* (Agencia Informativa Católica Argentina), no. 2283 (20 September 2000), http://aica.org/aica/documentos_files/CEA/Otros_documentos/Reconciliacion.htm.
Consejo Episcopal Latinoamericano. *La iglesia en la actual transformación de América Latina a la luz del Concilio. Medellín: Conclusiones. Segunda Conferencia general del espiscopado latinoamericano Bogotá, 24 de Agosto. Medellín, Agosto 26-Septiembre 6. Colombia 1968.* Bogotá: Secretariado General del CELAM, 1981.
Klaiber, Jeffrey L. *The Church, Dictatorships, and Democracy in Latin America.* Maryknoll, NY: Orbis Books, 1998.

Pope Paul VI, Encyclical Letter. "Populorum progression." 26 March 1967. www.vatican.
    va/holy_father/paul_vi/encyclicals/documents/hf_p-vi_enc_26031967_
    populorum_en.html.
Rouillon, Jorge. "Histórico pedido de perdón de la Iglesia argentina." La Nación (9
    September 2000).
Vatican Council II. "Pastoral Constitution on the Church in the Modern World:
    Gaudium et spes." Promulgated by His Holiness, Pope Paul VI on 7 December 1965.
    www.vatican.va/archive/hist_councils/ii_vatican_council/documents/vat-ii_cons_
    19651207_gaudium-et-spes_en.html.

Chapter 7

Lawless Violence, Impunity and the Democratic Transition

Guatemala is a good place to commit a murder, because you will almost certainly get away with it.

Philip Alston, Special Rapporteur, Human Rights Council,
UN General Assembly, 2007

As Latin America became more democratic, prosperous and politically stable after the 1980s, it became more dangerous. Crime and lawless violence rose spectacularly. More ominous still, governmental authorities in many places reacted with indifference, and even engaged in criminal violence on their own or in collaboration with the outlaws. Philip Alston's comment on Guatemala, cited above, could have applied to a number of other Latin Americans countries.

From the 1960s to the 1980s, the term "impunity" – freedom from punishment – was applied almost exclusively to the way authoritarian military regimes escaped accountability for illegally depriving their enemies of their rights or even their lives, while enriching themselves and their friends. But since the 1980s, impunity has come to refer more often to the freedom of criminals to get away with almost anything, and the corresponding failure of police officers, prosecutors, judges, military officers and other public officials to even investigate crimes, let alone to capture and punish wrongdoers.

If the primary function of the state was to protect civil society, this sort of corruption stood to undermine the legitimacy of even freely elected governments. It inspired serious doubts about the efficacy of liberal democracy as a political regime. In many places, people felt both victimized by criminals (who might also be government agents) and abandoned by the government agencies responsible for protecting them. By the first decade of the new century, the

Contemporary Latin America: 1970 to the Present, First Edition. Robert H. Holden and Rina Villars.
© 2013 Robert H. Holden and Rina Villars. Published 2013 by Blackwell Publishing Ltd.

greatest problem faced by several Latin American countries was not the poverty or the economic inequality that continued to afflict the region but the personal security of its people. In those countries, sustained levels of extreme violence rolled back earlier gains in economic development and threatened to turn democratic procedures into a meaningless sideshow. The violence afflicting them was invariably transnational in scope, because the crimes associated with it, like drug trafficking, were committed in more than one country. At the same time, criminal violence blended with political violence, as elected officials and government agents, including police and military forces, entered the fray.

Quantitative comparisons of criminal violence from one world region to another, and from one time period to another, continue to be hampered by extreme variations in both the availability and quality of data, as well as the precise definitions of crime and violence. Nevertheless, ranges of magnitude can be estimated that offer reasonably accurate comparisons of change from place to place and from time to time. As a kind of proxy for criminal violence, analysts typically count annual murders – broadly defined as intentional homicide – which are then standardized by population. While one might think that acts of murder happen rarely enough to be easily identified and counted by authorities at the national level, it turns out that even these statistics are often completely unavailable (sometimes for many consecutive years), contradictory or otherwise unreliable. A country's criminal justice system might report numbers substantially higher or lower than those of the same country's public health system. Even criminal justice figures can vary according to the particular reporting agency, as in El Salvador, where the police, the national forensic science institute, and the prosecutor's office all report different annual murder counts. Independent counts by non-governmental human rights organizations often contradict the official data. Moreover, governments classify killings according to different criteria, frustrating exact comparisons. While murder is normally a crime of intent, determining intent is a matter of judgment, not fact. For example, killing in self-defense or in defense of others – which would include most killings by police officers – would be an act of intentional homicide but not necessarily murder.

In comparing rates of criminal violence, most analysts draw on the intentional homicide counts submitted by national governments to the UN's Office of Drugs and Crime (UNODC). Taken together, they show that in the period 2003 to 2008, the world regions with the highest intentional homicide rates were probably southern Africa, the isthmian countries of Central America, and the island nations of the Caribbean. The lowest rates were found in Europe, Oceania and eastern Asia. While in most countries of the world the homicide rate was steady or declining, it was rising in both Central America and the Caribbean during the first decade of the twenty-first century. The world homicide rate of about 7.6 per 100,000 persons in 2004 corresponded to about

490,000 intentional killings. The homicide rate in the United States that year was 5.4. In some countries of Latin America, the intentional homicide rate was 9 to 11 times that of the United States. In 2008, El Salvador reported 52 per 100,000 persons, Venezuela 47, Honduras 61 and Brazil 22. In 2007, Colombia reported 40 and in 2006, Guatemala 45.

Few countries in the world could match these rates during the first decade of the new century. But how did they compare to those of, say, the 1970s or 1990s? Did they represent a significant increase? The answer is probably yes. On a global scale, intentional homicide rates rose slowly from at least the early 1970s then accelerated in the 1980s and 1990s. Much of that increase occurred in low-income countries. From the 1970s onward, Latin America's intentional homicide rate was consistently the highest of any world region, at around 8 per 100,000 until the mid-1980s. It jumped to more than 12 by the late 1990s, outpacing all other world regions. Only Argentina and Chile reported declines from the 1970s through the 1990s, while Colombia's homicide rate increased more than any other, from about 16 per 100,000 in the early 1970s to more than 80 by the mid-1990s.

Figure 7.1 compares the average intentional homicide rates for the period 1970–1994 to the latest year available, which ranges from 2003 to 2008. Three groups of Latin American countries can be distinguished:

- Six never reported a homicide rate in excess of 10 per 100,000: Argentina, Chile, Costa Rica, Cuba, Peru and Uruguay.
- In seven countries, high homicide rates (i.e., above 10) have been a feature of their societies since at least the 1970s: Brazil, Colombia, El Salvador, Guatemala, Mexico, Nicaragua and Panama.
- A third group that reported low rates through the 1990s were suddenly coping with high rates after 2000: Ecuador, Honduras and Venezuela.

The most extraordinary rates of increase in the period 2003–2008 can be found in three Central American countries (El Salvador, Guatemala and Honduras), and in Ecuador and Venezuela. Only Colombia reported a significant decline, from 64 in 2001 to 38.8 in 2007. In any case, inferences drawn from comparisons between the pre-1995 period and the first decade of the new century must be treated with caution, owing to the extremely inconsistent character of the data, especially for the period 1970–1994. For five countries (Cuba, Ecuador, El Salvador, Nicaragua and Panama) the average homicide rates for 1970–1994 were computed on fewer than ten years each; El Salvador's was based on only four years (1970–1973) and Nicaragua's on five (1990–1994). Bolivia and Guatemala reported no homicide data at all during the pre-1995 period.

The Central American countries present a perplexing example of accelerating rates of criminal violence and impunity because the increases immediately

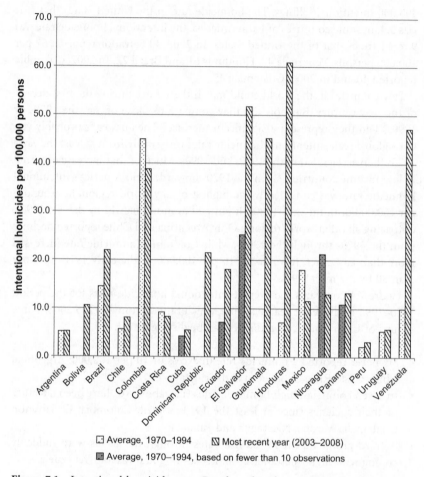

Figure 7.1 Intentional homicide rates. Based on data from Pablo Fajnzylber, Daniel Lederman and Norman Loayza, "Determinants of Crime Rates in Latin America and the World: An Empirical Assessment" (Washington, DC: World Bank, 1998), p. 37. Also, United Nations Office on Drugs and Crime, "UNODC Crime and Criminal Justice Statistics," www.unodc.org/unodc/en/data-and-analysis/homicide.html.

followed the negotiation of peace agreements that had ended decades of murderous political violence. As we noted in Chapter 3, civil wars in El Salvador, Guatemala and Nicaragua spilled over into Honduras and Costa Rica in the 1980s. Peace was finally declared in Nicaragua in 1990, El Salvador in 1992 and Guatemala in 1996. While no one will ever know just how many died in those wars, the standard estimates were 200,000 in Guatemala over 34 years (an annual average of 5,880), some 75,000 in El Salvador over 12 years (an annual average of 6,250), and perhaps 50,000 in Nicaragua over 18 years (an average of 2,780).

Yet to many Central Americans, life seemed no less dangerous a decade after the last peace treaty was signed In 1996. The 14,257 murders in the seven countries of Central America in 2006 were 42 times the 336 reported that year in Spain, whose population was slightly larger than Central America's. Worse, state organs charged with preventing and investigating criminal conduct, and punishing outlaws, were seen in most countries as irrecoverably incompetent, corrupt, influenced by criminal organizations, and largely indifferent to the rule of law. For example, the murder of 6,292 people in Guatemala in 2008 yielded a homicide rate of 49 per 100,000, the highest ever recorded in the country. Yet no more than 2% of all murder cases were ever brought to trial because the justice system had practically ceased to function.

Much of the violence in Central America stemmed from the explosive growth of youth gangs from the 1990s onward. Two separate developments encouraged their formation. The first was the demobilization of combatants following the peace settlements of the early 1990s. After returning home, some veterans organized vigilante groups for neighborhood self-defense that evolved into criminal gangs or *pandillas*. The second development was the passage by the U.S. Congress of the Illegal Immigration Reform and Immigrant Responsibility Act of 1996, which required the repatriation of non-U.S. citizens imprisoned for a year or more. Close to 46,000 convicts were returned to Central America between 1998 and 2005, along with 160,000 unauthorized immigrants. More than 90% of them returned to El Salvador, Guatemala and Honduras. Many returnees had been members of criminal gangs in Los Angeles and reestablished their gang affiliations upon arrival in Central America. These transnational groups became known as *maras*, in contrast to the more traditional *pandillas*. In addition to petty crime and murder, often as a result of turf wars between rival gangs, both types of groups quickly established themselves as criminal organizations that were notably more violent, better organized and armed, and more defiant than the typical youth gangs of earlier decades. At the same time, after about 2000, *maras* and *pandillas* turned increasingly to drug trafficking as Central America emerged as a transit route from the drug-producing areas of South America to the consumer markets in the United States (see Chapter 10).

The surge in violent crime attributed to the gangs was widely seen as the most serious national security threat in the isthmus since the civil wars of the 1980s, inspiring the governments of El Salvador and Honduras to adopt "iron fist" (*mano dura*) policies beginning in 2003. All seven countries undertook cooperative enforcement strategies but mass arrests and imprisonment only seemed to intensify the violence, as the gangs counterattacked and applied more extreme measures – including decapitations and mass killings designed to inspire terror – in explicit reprisal for the government crackdowns. A clear evolution from youth gangs to professional criminal organizations was taking place. In El Salvador in 2010, the gangs demonstrated their ability to respond effectively to government enforcement efforts by forcing public transport drivers to stay home for three days or risk death. El Salvador's two main rival gangs collaborated in enforcing the stoppage, which paralyzed the country's transportation system. They even issued a joint statement explaining that they were protesting a new law that made gang membership a crime punishable by up to six years in prison.

Horacio Castellanos Moya, the Honduran-Salvadoran novelist, wrote from exile in the United States in 2010 that the violence in his homelands had surpassed the levels of the worst years of civil war, and exceeded in volume and brutality anything he could imagine as a novelist. As an example, he pointed to the case of the three Salvadoran politicians – Eduardo D'Aubuisson, William Pichinte and José Ramón González – and their driver, Gerardo Ramírez. While attending a meeting in Guatemala of the Central American parliament, the regional legislative body, all four were shot to death and their bodies burned on 19 February 2007. Four days later, four Guatemalan policemen – including the head of the National Police's organized crime unit – were imprisoned and charged with the murders. Three days after that, the four policemen were themselves shot to death in their prison cells by men who entered the prison carrying assault rifles and then left. Within days, twenty-two prison guards were arrested for allowing the killers to enter and leave the prison.

Castellanos Moya recalled that in discussing these events with another Salvadoran novelist, both agreed that "our imaginations were not able to fly high enough to conceive such a plot for a novel. Reality went beyond our fiction."[1] His comment recalled the observation of Colombian novelist Gabriel García Márquez in his 1982 Nobel Prize for Literature lecture: Latin Americans, he said, "have had to ask but little of imagination, for our crucial problem has been a lack of conventional means to render our lives believable." (For a discussion of the emergence of drug-driven violence as an important Latin American literary theme in the 1990s, see Chapter 13.)

In Guatemala, much of the criminal violence was driven by the rise in drug trafficking, often in partnership with Mexican gangsters. But it also depended on other forms of contraband trade, including human trafficking, illegal child adoptions and money-laundering. A tradition of impunity allowed organized crime to thoroughly penetrate the law enforcement offices of the Guatemalan state. As criminal gangs operated more and more freely, protected by military officers and politicians at every level, by 2002 a serious crisis of legitimacy was putting into question the state's very ability to govern. Corruption charges against cabinet officers and high-ranking security officials were now routine, but convictions practically unheard of.

An example of the way the Guatemalan government had yielded to the superior strength of criminal bands could be seen in 2006, when 3,000 soldiers and police armed with tear gas, tanks and assault rifles invaded the Pavón prison outside of the capital of Guatemala City. Ten years earlier, the government had formally turned over the administration of the prison to the most powerful gangsters among its 1,500 inmates. In return for keeping order and preventing escapes, they were given the freedom to govern themselves as they wished. Over the course of a decade, the prisoners built laboratories to make crack and cocaine, as well as stores, bars, brothels, restaurants and plush living quarters for the leaders. Prisoners regularly left the prison (and returned) to carry out assassinations and kidnappings for extortion as well as to sell drugs. At the time of the 2006 government raid, some suspected that the assault had actually been inspired by rival gangsters. In fact, in 2010, the same government officials who had ordered the raid on Pavón (Alejandro Giammattei, the director of the country's prisons, and Carlos Vielmann, the interior minister) were charged with being members "of a criminal organization ... dedicated to murder, drug-trafficking, money-laundering, kidnapping, extortion and the theft of drugs" as well as "extrajudicial executions of prisoners," including those killed at Pavón, according to the prosecutor.

Organized crime had become so powerful in Guatemala that it threatened the ability of even the most traditionally influential elements of society to shape government action. It was a situation that provided common ground for action among rival interest groups that could agree on one thing: that impunity was having a deeply corrosive effect on public life. Knowing that crimes would not be investigated, and fearing the criminals in part because the police themselves were often known to be collaborating with them, people quit reporting crimes. Knowing that justice would not be done, people inflicted their own punishment on suspected wrongdoers. Others hired the services of private security firms to defend themselves and their property, further eroding respect for the authority of state institutions. Both tendencies reinforced impunity, encouraged other forms of corruption, and inspired cynicism about the prospects of democratic rule. At the same time, the political system itself became a target of criminal gangs, who saw access to political office as an opportunity to plunder public revenues and resources. The 2007 election campaign led directly to the murder of fifty-eight people, including persons linked to all the major political parties.

Impunity had embedded itself so deeply in Guatemala's political culture that outside help was needed to extirpate it. Provoked to act in part by the serial killings of the four Salvadoran politicians and of the police who had been charged with their killings, the Guatemalan government in August 2007 allowed the United Nations to establish the International Commission Against Impunity in Guatemala, with the support of voluntary donations by UN member states and other groups. In turning over to an international body the task of helping the government to investigate and prosecute the corruption of its own law-enforcement agencies, as well as the criminal networks that had penetrated them, Guatemala in effect gave up some of its own sovereignty. It was a remarkable acknowledgement of state failure.

As the Commission gathered evidence and brought charges against Guatemalan military officers, police officials and former cabinet ministers, as well as former president Alfonso Portillo (2000–2004), it was clear that prosecutorial integrity alone would not suffice to end impunity. In 2011, Guatemalan judges dismissed the charges against Portillo, and later against Alejandro Giammattei, for "lack of evidence." Days later, the worst organized crime massacre in Guatemalan history was discovered on a ranch in the Petén region, where a Mexican drug-trafficking gang murdered twenty-seven laborers (beheading twenty-five of them) because they failed to give their killers any information on the whereabouts of the ranch's owner. That massacre was followed by the murder of the beloved Argentine singer Facundo Cabral on 9 July 2011, who was performing in a series of concerts in Guatemala. Cabral, 74, was caught in a hail of bullets evidently intended for a businessman who offered him a ride to the airport. The next day, President Alvaro Colom told an interviewer that the drug gangs had acquired an ability to "kill and to buy anyone who gets in their way." The countries of Central America "can do no more," he said, denying that Guatemala's had become a "failed state."

Yet Colom himself had only months before astonished the country by announcing that he and his wife of eight years, Sandra Torres, would seek an amicable divorce in order to circumvent the constitutional ban on presidential candidacies of close relatives of the incumbent. The divorce was granted in April and Sandra Torres prepared for the presidential election in September, perpetuating the Latin American tradition of presidential *continuismo* in spite of legal and constitutional obstacles. "Divorce is the only solution for defending the advances that have been achieved during the government of Colom," Torres declared, insisting on her "great and solid" love for her husband. The divorce was clearly no more than a legalistic fraud, and in this sense, it revealed as little respect for the rule of law as did Cabral's killers.

The threat of state breakdown also loomed in Mexico. In his inaugural address on 1 December 2006, President Felipe Calderón announced a battle against organized crime, impunity, and any government officials who collaborated with criminals. Because so much of the recent rise in violence was owing to competition among rival drug-trafficking organizations, the country's police and military mounted direct assaults on their leadership. The result was a massive increase in drug-related killings. From 2007 to 2010, what became known as "the Mexican drug wars" claimed 34,611 lives – four times the number of such killings (8,901) that had taken place during the entire six-year administration of the previous president, Vicente Fox (2000–2006). As the number of murders rose every year, the range of victims and the brutality with which they were killed shocked the world. Torture, dismemberment and decapitation were now commonplace; elected officials, journalists and innocent bystanders (including young children) were increasingly targeted for death. To supplement their income, criminals kidnapped for extortion. Ongoing war between two criminal gangs in Juárez, a city of 1.2 million on the northern border with the U.S. state of Texas, earned Juárez the title of "the most dangerous city in the world." The city's 2,738 murders in 2010 – a rate of 228 per 100,000 – were mostly drug-related, and often included the massacre of entire groups, such as children attending birthday parties. Juárez' reputation for danger had been growing since the early 1990s, as a result of more than 500 unsolved murders of young women between 1993 and 2010.

As Mexican government forces were deployed against the drug organizations, some officials, tempted by huge bribes, continued to collaborate with them. One of the Calderón administration's first moves was to arrest the head of the Fox administration's organized crime unit, now charged with having received $450,000 a month from a gang of drug dealers in exchange for advance warnings about police investigations and raids. After Calderón assigned the Mexican armed forces to fight drug-smuggling because of police corruption, the Mexican police and the Mexican army confronted each other violently, with guns drawn and sometimes exchanging gunfire, more than sixty-five times in 2009 alone. Days after Brig. Gen. Juan Arturo Esparaza was appointed police chief of García, a Monterrey suburb, he was assassinated and five García policemen were among the first suspects apprehended.

Though accustomed to spectacular displays of official corruption, even Mexicans were astonished by news of the arrest in 2010 of the director of a prison in the state of Durango and her top five aides. They were charged with having allowed groups of inmates to leave the prison, kill their enemies with automatic weapons supplied by the prison guards, and then return to their cells. Corruption penetrated the justice system, which killers had little reason to fear because of their ability to buy non-enforcement and to make credible threats. Documented cases in which army personnel tortured suspects to extract confessions or obtain information, often from innocent persons who were then presented to the news media as confessed killers, accumulated during President Calderón's war against drugs.

As drug-related violence continued to soar in 2010 and 2011, some Mexicans blamed Calderón's government for confronting the drug gangs. While there is little doubt that Calderón's offensive encouraged counterattacks by criminal organizations, thus intensifying the violence, students of Mexican politics suggested that much of it was an ironic consequence of Mexican democratization. The transition from a stable, one-party, authoritarian state in the 1980s to a more politically diverse and competitive electoral democracy beginning in the 1990s, contributed to the rise in violence among the drug gangs. New political movements and fresh office holders who successfully challenged the authoritarian Partido de la Revolución Institucional (PRI) disrupted the arrangements that had been worked out between criminals and top officials of the highly centralized one-party state in the 1980s and early 1990s. Now the drug organizations found themselves in a new and considerably less predictable environment. At the same time, the U.S. drug market was shrinking and authorities there were better able to detect and halt drug shipments into the country. The result was a sharp increase in violence as the Mexican gangs competed over trafficking routes, markets, and access to government officials.

In both Guatemala and Mexico, the ability of criminal organizations to survive and even flourish depended heavily on the clandestine assistance of a wide range of public officials, from judges and prosecutors to generals and police officers. Their collaboration could be secured by immense bribes or death threats. The ease with which criminals could penetrate and influence the very institutions of a government pledged to destroy them constituted an important source of their continuing strength. The problem, therefore, was not weak or inept states facing an implacable foe, but rather the capacity of criminal groups to suborn some government agents in order to promote the criminal violence that the government claimed to be resisting.

Similar patterns of interaction could be seen elsewhere in Latin America after the onset of the democratic wave of the 1980s. For example, Brazil's military dictatorship formally ceded power to elected civilian leaders in 1985. But the impunity associated with military rule persisted, and criminal violence rose. Drug-traffickers in the *favelas* or slums of Rio de Janeiro skillfully exploited longstanding traditions of political patronage. They established ties with politicians in exchange for votes and bribes, enhancing their popular support in hundreds of neighborhoods by providing public services and incidentally protecting their freedom to deal drugs. From the mid-1980s to 2000, cocaine use among 10- to 20-year-olds in Brazil's cities quadrupled. Impunity for drug dealers and other criminals was matched by impunity for the politicians who protected them.

The police became a notorious source of arbitrary violence, especially in the major cities. In the states of Rio de Janeiro and São Paulo alone, police killed more than 11,000 people between 2003 and 2009. In São Paulo, police killed an average of 691 civilians a year from 1990 to 1998 but they would be outdone in 2007 by the Rio police, who killed 1,330 persons that year. By comparison, justifiable homicides by police in the entire United States averaged 350 a year from 2000 to 2005. While many such killings were no doubt legitimate, both Brazilian government authorities and human rights groups gathered evidence that most were extrajudicial executions. Police murders in Brazil first came to public attention in the late 1960s, when "death squads" of police-men in São Paulo enforced their control over drug, prostitution and protection rackets by assassinating their enemies. Police there and in Rio and other cities continued to kill, torture and illegally detain suspects with almost complete impunity because their victims were typically seen as "undesirables" or crimi-nals, and the rule of law an obstacle to public security – a view also shared by many Brazilians.

As Brazil was preparing to host the 2014 World Cup soccer tournament in Rio, São Paulo and thirteen other cities, and the Olympic Games in 2016 in Rio, some questioned the government's capacity to ensure the security of ath-letes, spectators, game officials and journalists in cities where lawlessness had become a way of life. The scale of the challenge became apparent in December 2010, when it took combined army, marine, military police and special police forces a week to recover control of one of Rio de Janeiro's slum districts (Com-plexo do Alemão) from the drug gangs that had been governing it for years. The operation took thirty-seven lives and resulted in the military occupation of the district for an indefinite period, though its success was undermined by the ability of some gang leaders to escape by calling on their allies in the police department. In other *favelas*, the ruling gangs – in some cases composed of retired and off-duty police officers called "militias" – prepared to defend their territory against further military-police mobilizations to dislodge them.

Beyond the cities of Brazil, the country's vast frontier zone, as well as its long-settled rural areas, remained scenes of intense and often violent conflict over access to the land and its resources. Sharpened by the extreme poverty and inequality that have plagued rural as well as urban Brazil for many decades, the strife pitted the interests of ranchers and developers against those of agri-cultural workers, who demanded access to land of their own or improved working conditions and higher wages. In the northern state of Pará alone from 1964 to 1992, conflicts over land resulted in the killing of 563 persons, of whom two-thirds were landless farmers. Across Brazil, an average of forty killings a year were attributed to land conflicts from 1994 to 2006, including two mass killings by police: In 1995, thirteen workers occupying land in the western state of Rondônia were shot in a predawn raid; the following year in Pará, police armed with machine guns fired on a crowd of 2,000 land-seeking demon-strators, killing nineteen. In both cases, some of the victims were shot at point-blank range after they were captured.

Perhaps the best-known case of rural violence was the killing in 1988 of Francisco ("Chico") Mendes Filho (1944–1988), a rubber-tapper known as the "Amazonian Gandhi" for his advocacy of non-violent methods of civil disobe-dience to protect the Amazon rainforest from destruction by ranchers and loggers, while preserving rubber-tappers' traditional access to the region's rubber trees. Mendes earned international recognition, including the UN's

Global 500 Prize. He traveled widely to promote the causes of the rural poor and the rainforest while condemning the indifference of both government and business interests, despite numerous death threats, arrests and imprisonment. Probably because of Mendes' international stature, his death in an ambush led to an official investigation and a rare conviction. A wealthy landowner and his son were sentenced to nineteen years in prison in 1990.

Despite the murder of Mendes, however, many like him continued the campaign to stop illegal logging. In 2010, Jose Claudio Ribeiro da Silva, 54, a rubber-tapper and nut-harvester in Pará, told a group of supporters he had received numerous death threats for denouncing illegal logging: "I will protect the forest at all costs. That is why I could get a bullet in my head at any moment." In May 2011 he was found slain, execution-style, along with his wife Maria do Espirito Santo, 53, in the forest not far from their home. Government officials held an emergency meeting to discuss new measures to protect rural activists and resolve land disputes.

The extreme violence and lawlessness that Brazil, El Salvador, Guatemala and Mexico were known for by 2010 had begun building in the 1990s. By that decade, however, the level of criminal violence in Colombia had already achieved legendary status. To a reporter in 1995, President Ernest Samper remarked that for Colombians, violence was so routine that it was now a *forma de convivencia* – a way of living together – that had become the only way to resolve problems. Colombia's rise to prominence as a major supplier of marijuana in the 1970s, then of cocaine and opiates from the 1980s onward (see Chapter 10), contributed significantly to the country's status as one of the most violent countries in the world. The criminal organizations that produced, transported and sold illegal drugs murdered their enemies, or suspected enemies, in vast numbers. In addition, leftwing guerrilla groups, originally organized in the 1960s with the aim of overthrowing the government and carrying out a social revolution, joined the illegal drugs industry. By the 1990s the guerrillas controlled and "taxed" drug-traffickers and the land where coca and poppy were cultivated, as well as the labs where cocaine and heroin were made. To defend themselves against the guerrillas, the major drug gangs began to organize and finance separate paramilitary organizations, many of which had direct ties with military and police officers. Thus, in addition to the war between rival drug organizations or "cartels" and their enemies, a second internal war erupted between the guerrillas and the paramilitaries. Avoiding direct confrontation with one another, they tended to kill the civilians they suspected of aiding their enemy. Finally, the drug trade spawned a number of ancillary criminal enterprises, such as kidnapping for ransom and murder for hire, that added to the toll in homicides. *Sicarios* or freelance killers, employed initially by the drug lords, gradually diversified into political assassination for hire and other, more mundane categories of homicide. All told, the drug-related violence of the 1980s and 1990s spawned about 350,000 deaths and 2 million internal refugees in Colombia.

But it would be a mistake to assume that the drug trade alone was responsible for Colombia's exceptional record of violence. Before the era of drug violence, the watershed event of Colombia's modern history was a period known simply as "La Violencia." It began in 1946. By the time it ended in 1966, more than 200,000 Colombians had died in a war among the armed bands associated loosely with the two principal political parties (Liberals and Conservatives) and the armed forces. In some obvious ways, therefore, the drug wars could be seen as a continuation of La Violencia, drawing on attitudes toward authority and techniques of coercion and terror, already perfected in the 1950s and early 1960s, such as massacres, abductions and the ubiquity of the contract killer and the informer. The sweeping disorder and violence that characterized Colombia from the 1940s onward were undoubtedly nourished by some longstanding conditions that, if not unique in Latin America, seemed particularly influential in Colombia:

- an exceptionally diverse geographical configuration that fettered the reach of the state, enhancing the power of the regional *caudillos* entrenched in hundreds of isolated communities;
- a land tenure system dominated by great estates, giving rise to violent struggles between landless rural workers and the estate owners;
- a state too feeble to establish its independent authority.

No central government had ever been able to prevent smuggling, guarantee property rights, or enforce the law across the national territory; as a result, impunity reigned. Indeed, some parts of Colombia have *never* been under the control of the central government, making it possible for armed groups to enrich themselves by simply controlling access to various parts of the national territory, especially those abundant in exploitable resources such as emeralds, oil or drug crops. Rivalry among different armed groups for control of the same resources or territory led in turn to bloody encounters between them and their local adherents. Because of these conditions, any given government's survival typically depended on the ability of its leaders to negotiate informal (and therefore unstable) pacts among diverse groups, many of which were well armed and could survive indefinitely by plundering and killing. Further justifying a longstanding disposition to resolve problems violently was a code of honor that encouraged revenge and retaliation.

Thus, the historical and structural conditions in Colombia for the overlapping operations of the drug cartels, the rural guerrilla armies and the paramilitary groups in the late twentieth century could scarcely have been more favorable. Outside the cities, these groups became the effective rulers of much of Colombia from the 1980s and into the twenty-first century. The death toll, as measured in police reports of intentional homicides, climbed steadily, reaching 26,539 in 2000; at a rate of 62.7 per 100,000 persons, Colombian violence was practically matchless on a world scale. As a result of the violence, the country also had one of the world's highest levels of internal displacement of persons (at least 3 million in 2008). Many others were displaced beyond the national borders; in 2009, more than 200,000 Colombians were taking refuge in Venezuela.

The tide began to turn after the election of President Alvaro Uribe in 2002. Pledging to restore control of Colombian territory to the Colombian state, Uribe increased the size of the armed forces by one-third. With major financial support from the U.S. government, Uribe's administration achieved the biggest security gains of any Colombian president in decades while eradicating much of the country's coca crop and putting the guerrilla armies as well as the paramilitary groups on the defensive. Murder and kidnapping rates fell drastically. Arrests of paramilitary leaders led to the unveiling of a massive corruption scandal linking members of the Colombian congress and other public officials. The Uribe administration showed that the spiral of violence that had afflicted the country for so many decades could be stemmed and even reversed. Nevertheless, Colombia's status as the world's biggest source of cocaine remained untouched and it still seemed unlikely that any combination of public policies, even when coordinated across national borders, could ever overcome the undiminished power of attraction of the illegal drugs market.

From Mexico to Central America, and from Brazil to Colombia, the production and sale of illegal drugs probably accounted for most of the rise in lawless violence since the 1980s. But to blame the violence solely on drugs, or on their consumers (whether in the United States and Europe, or in Latin America) would be a mistake. Violent disorder, corruption and impunity were nothing new in Latin America history, and the two-decade trend in favor of electoral democracy had in most places done little or nothing to abate them. The basic source of the violence remained the chronic indifference to the rule of law that continued to pervade so much of the region. Criminal gangs, insurgent armies, private militias and ordinary criminals, as well as their collaborators in the government, flourished because society, and the state it spawned, habitually *allowed* them to flourish. The law still counted for little in most of Latin America. That fundamental permissiveness has been exploited, over time and across countries and regions, in ways that varied with local circumstance and opportunity: levels of unemployment and income inequality, the demand for criminal services, the quality of political leadership, and any given government's commitment to law enforcement.

No one understood these conditions better than Latin Americans themselves. A 2008 opinion poll by Latinobarómetro revealed that *more than half* the citizens of El Salvador, Guatemala, Honduras, Mexico, Nicaragua and Peru would support a military coup "when there is a lot of crime." Between 36% and 47% of the people in six other countries responded affirmatively to the same question. The findings underscored the circular nature of the problem of impunity, and its phenomenal resistance to abatement: In order to put an end to one sort of impunity (for criminals and their accomplices in government) many Latin Americans would accept another and perhaps more traditional sort of impunity: That accorded to the armed forces for unconstitutional interventions in the political process, and for breaching basic human and civil rights that typically accompanied military rule. If democratic consolidation depended on the rule of law, it seemed that the electoral revolution of the last three decades would have to be followed by a cultural revolution.

Note

1 Horacio Castellanos Moya, "Notes on the Culture of Violence and Fiction in Latin America," in *Sampsonia Way*, www.sampsoniaway.org/literary-voices/2009/10/31/notes-on-the-culture-of-violence-and-fiction-in-latin-america-by-horacio-castellanos-moya.

Reference

Castellanos Moya, Horacio. "Notes on the Culture of Violence and Fiction in Latin America." In *Sampsonia Way*, www.sampsoniaway.org/literary-voices/2009/10/31/notes-on-the-culture-of-violence-and-fiction-in-latin-america-by-horacio-castellanos-moya.

Part III
Wealth

Introduction

The quality of our lives depends in part on access to material goods and the satisfactions they provide. As goods or access to goods ("wealth") and payments received ("income") for producing wealth accumulate in a given society, the results can be analyzed to identify the main *sources* of wealth and income, and also to see how they were *distributed* among different groups and individuals. In comparing wealth and income among a number of different societies, we will want to understand why some prosper and others struggle to survive. As we look at these problems of analysis and comparison in Part III, we will move back and forth among the global, regional, national and family levels, trying to capture both the diversity and the uniformities of the Latin American economies since the 1970s.

The most spectacular economic transformations in world history have taken place precisely during the two centuries of the Latin American countries' existence as independent republics. Between 1820 and 2001, world income *per person* rose 800%, after having increased by only about 50% in the eight centuries before 1820. The period of fastest growth (almost 3% a year) was recorded from 1950 to 1973. The second-fastest was the period covered in this book, when East Asia turned in the best performance of any world region. Everywhere else, the economic slowdown that began in 1973 stimulated a major reorientation of economic-growth strategies. The slowdown was most damaging in Latin America, and as a result, it was the region whose political systems undertook the most radical changes in economic policy.

The second biggest change in the last two centuries was the ever-accelerating increase in the *disparity* between the highest-performing economies (western Europe, the United States, Canada, Australia, New Zealand and Japan) and the rest of the world. While the income of all world regions was roughly the same in 1000, by 2000 the gap between the just-mentioned leading performers and

Contemporary Latin America: 1970 to the Present, First Edition. Robert H. Holden and Rina Villars.
© 2013 Robert H. Holden and Rina Villars. Published 2013 by Blackwell Publishing Ltd.

the rest had widened by a ratio of almost 7:1, as the first group's average per-capita income had climbed to $22,500 compared to an average of $3,400 in the rest of the world.

The ratio of per-capita income in Latin America to that of the leading group of countries was only 1:1.6 in 1820. But by 1950, the gap had widened to 1:2.2, and in 2002, it stood at 1:3.8. The Latin American economies had grown dramatically, but those of the top performing regions had expanded even more. That disparity was faithfully duplicated inside Latin America to an even greater extent, as seen in the stark differences even today between standards of living in, say, Bolivia, Guatemala or Honduras, on the one hand, and those in Uruguay, Chile or Venezuela on the other. The same pattern can be found within countries, as between, say, Brazil's chronically poor Northeast and its wealthy South.

In a way, these two global transformations – per-capita growth but accelerating disparity – define the core problems that invariably frame any discussion of Latin America's economic history. The first is the region's aspiration for raw *growth* – for the production of ever-more goods and services. The second is its longing for *development* – for a more equitable distribution of the benefits of growth, both on a world scale (between the better-off nations and Latin America), and within Latin America itself (between the poor and the better-off classes).

Let us define development, therefore, as the achievement of higher standards of living for everybody, or almost everybody, but above all for Latin America's numerous poor, a step that would narrow the gap separating the Latin American nations from the world's preeminent performers. If economic growth is about how to make more of everything, development is about how to distribute the gains more fairly.

By the early twentieth century, with the dramatic expansion of the electorate and the rising influence of public opinion on government policy, national leaders across Latin America understood that their tenure in office depended in large part on their ability to use the power of the state to raise or at least maintain living standards for all, or nearly all, of their constituents. As a result, political leaders typically sought to encourage overall growth in the hopes that doing so would redistribute income in favor of the middle and lower classes. The hoped-for outcome was more votes for the incumbent politicians, and a dampening of economically induced discontent, which could lead to disorder or rebellion. But growth-abetting policies alone did not seem to be enough to substantially narrow the gap between the rich and the poor. As a result, from the 1930s onward, governments increasingly sought to improve living standards by seizing private assets and redistributing them. The range, depth and thus the impact of these measures varied considerably from place to place, but commonly included action to:

- confiscate large landholdings and divide them among the landless inhabitants of the countryside;
- reduce food prices by either limiting the prices that producers could charge or by purchasing food supplies directly and then reselling them to consumers at lower prices;
- start up or buy ("nationalize") key industrial enterprises or services in order to control prices, ease access to their products, or diminish dependence on imports;
- establish mandatory social-insurance funds for the payment of old-age pensions, unemployment benefits or medical expenses.

At the same time, a range of political movements and ideologies emerged proposing to implement these ideas, deepen them, resist them, or to completely remake the political and economic systems by force of arms. Often, the result was more growth-inhibiting disorder and instability. As the Latin American economies collapsed in the 1980s, another development strategy that relied more on market decisions and less on state intervention rapidly gained adherents.

In the following chapters, we first define economic growth and discuss its causes. We then analyze growth trends in Latin America while comparing them to other world regions. Next, we review Latin America's experience over the last half-century as it struggled to apply the two different doctrines (one state-centered, the other market-centered) of growth and development. We then focus on what it may take to turn growth into development, and introduce short discussions of three aspects of hemispheric economic relations that achieved great prominence after the 1970s: the illegal trade in drugs, the migration of peoples and the mitigation of poverty and economic inequality. Finally, we evaluate the performance of the economy of Cuba, so far the only country to have chosen a fully socialist path to economic development.

Chapter 8

The Challenge of Sustained Growth

Increases in the total output of goods and services of a country (or, what is the same thing, increases in its income) is "economic growth," and the normal way to measure it is to divide the value of the country's output by its population. Doing so standardizes income by holding population constant. The result is "gross domestic product" per person, or GDP per capita – the single most important bit of data you can have about any country's year-to-year economic performance.

Even small differences in annual per-capita GDP rates can add up over time to big differences in standard of living. Unless a country with a rising population creates *more* wealth every year, its inhabitants will be materially worse off every year, on the average. Precisely what sorts of conditions either encourage or inhibit growth across time, territory and cultures are themselves so numerous and so variable that they are still not fully understood in all their complexity. Nevertheless, at the most basic level, economic growth is thought to depend in part on the *accumulation* of "factors" like labor, capital (both physical and human) and natural resources, as well as on the acquisition of new knowledge and more efficient ways of doing business. We might call all of these the immediate or proximate causes of growth.

But it would not be hard to expand this short list to include a good many long-term or "ultimate" sources of growth. An idea of their variety and complexity can be inferred from the following list suggested by the Chilean economist Andrés Solimano: "Incentives, institutions, macroeconomic and political stability, terms of trade and other external shocks, the quality of the political regime, the respect given to property rights, the degree of distributive conflict, geography and others."[1] Clearly, the effective range and weight of these "ultimate" factors have varied considerably from place to place, as well as over time.

Contemporary Latin America: 1970 to the Present, First Edition. Robert H. Holden and Rina Villars.
© 2013 Robert H. Holden and Rina Villars. Published 2013 by Blackwell Publishing Ltd.

A recent study of late twentieth century growth rates around the world found strong *positive* correlations between growth and the following variables: the value of the stock of "human capital," as expressed mainly in average levels of schooling, literacy and the quality of health and nutrition; the extent to which the rule of law is respected; and the levels of investment (both private and governmental). Having densely populated coastal areas also helped. *Negative* correlations, or variables that inhibited growth, included high levels of government expenditures (excluding those for defense and education), and higher fertility rates. Having lots of land in tropical zones also hurt growth.[2]

Other economists took a more holistic approach, arguing that to reduce the sources of growth to a few measurable variables would be too simplistic. They stressed the *systemic* nature of a given country's growth record, and the complex ways that multiple variables interacted over time. On this view, growth or lack of growth was the result of a panoply of institutional incentives and con- straints, historical legacies and social settings, cultural conditions (such as the level of respect for the rule of law), ethical beliefs, levels of trust, ideas about the identity of the nation and its history, and attitudes toward minorities and women. Together, these factors made up a particular "growth system." Rather than the search for statistical correlations among discrete "factors," the research question of this approach focused on the emergence and operation of the system and the relationships that it entailed.

Of course, any attempt to settle the theoretical question of the determinants of growth would be well beyond the scope of this book, not to mention the competence of the authors. We raise the matter at the outset mainly to empha- size that while common sense may point to a number of fairly obvious condi- tioning factors, just how they interact, change over time, respond to and affect external influences, and in turn vary in their impact on growth across space and time, are far from being well understood. As we will see, economists and policy-makers have frequently changed their minds about what it might take to get sustained, stable growth and development.

If we observe Latin America at two moments in time, 1960 and 2000, we will see that in comparison to the rest of the world, most of the Latin American countries started out in the middle range of world GDP per capita in 1960 and were still there in 2000. In that period, Nicaragua and Venezuela ranked among the world's twenty slowest-growth countries; all the rest were in sub-Saharan Africa. No Latin American country was among the twenty fastest-growth coun- tries, nine of which were in East Asia. Until 1980, Latin America as a whole grew well above the world average before dipping sharply and finishing slightly below the world average. Sub-Saharan Africa grew even more slowly, and so in 2002 it was still the poorest region. In 1960, Asia started poorer than Latin America (but only slightly richer than Africa), but grew considerably faster than either region after 1980, and so in 2000 found itself mostly in the middle along with Latin America. The richest countries in 1960, mostly those of western Europe and North America, were still the richest in 2000, having reported growth rates in the middle range of the world average.

Perhaps the most outstanding feature of the recent Latin American experience with economic growth has been its instability. An analysis of twelve Latin American countries over a forty-three-year period (1960 to 2003) showed that the average number of years of *negative growth* was twelve – in effect, an economic crisis every three to four years. Moreover, the frequency of such crises more than doubled after 1980. Thus, instead of the smooth growth trends typically seen in the world's wealthiest economies, in Latin America we see volatility, and a good deal of diversity at the country level, with alternating episodes of growth, stagnation and contraction. Externally induced disruptions such as the collapse of currency-exchange rate parities in the early 1970s, the oil price rises of the same decade, and the Russian and Asian financial crises of the late 1990s, typically hurt Latin America, but rarely in a uniform way – some countries absorbed the shocks and recovered quickly, while others languished. Within Latin America, growth trends have also been affected by shifts in government economic policy concerning trade and borrowing, and by reorientations of grand economic strategy.

The last two decades of the twentieth century showed much less growth compared to the previous two decades. From 1961 to 1980, the average annual growth rate across all nineteen countries was a moderate but healthy 2.4%. Over the next two decades, average annual growth slowed to a mere 0.5%, a period that also saw a good deal more volatility in growth rates compared to the previous two decades. Most Latin American countries found it difficult to recover from the damage caused by the huge foreign debts they contracted in the 1970s. That problem was accompanied by unwelcome changes in capital flows and commodity prices, as well as a series of global financial crises that undermined growth. The recovery of 2003–2007 brought with it an average annual growth rate of 4%, which collapsed to 1% a year in the world financial crisis of 2008–2009.

Theory and Practice

In their pursuit of economic growth and development over the last 100 years, Latin American leaders took stances that tended to cluster around two starkly different economic development doctrines.

The first favored a regime of private enterprise, free markets and international trade, with economies oriented principally toward the production of raw or semiprocessed commodity exports, such as minerals like copper or foods like sugar or coffee. This doctrine of export-led, market-oriented development ("liberalism") dominated in Latin America from the late nineteenth century to the 1930s, and then again from the 1980s until today ("neo-liberalism").

The second option envisioned a much more active role for the state in directing the economy. This one reigned almost everywhere in Latin America during the middle years of the twentieth century, from the 1930s to the 1970s. Called "statism" or "dirigisme" (from the French for *diriger* or "direct"), it took numerous forms, but in the largest countries it was aimed primarily at accelerating industrialization, a policy known as "import-substitution industrialization" or ISI. The overall objective was to reduce both the negative effects of external shocks such as wars and economic depressions emanating from the developed economies, and Latin America's dependence on them as the main markets for its exports and as the source of the bulk of its investment capital and manufactured goods. Ideally, ISI would thus serve the cause of nationalism, reducing reliance on foreign consumers and investors and making the economies of the region more responsive to national interests and popular welfare.

Under ISI, governments sought to protect national industries from foreign competition through a variety of measures. They included the imposition of extremely high tariffs on imports, limits on the quantity of certain imports, and a system of government-controlled currency exchange rates that could be used to manipulate the ultimate prices of imports and exports. In addition, governments established industrial development banks that not only provided low-interest loans to industrial enterprises, but also purchased equity in them. That policy often led to government bailouts of firms that performed poorly but were "too big to fail," and resulted in government ownership of a wide range of uncompetitive enterprises whose product prices were subsidized by taxpayers.

Operating in the historical context of the patrimonial state, the ISI development strategy also meant that partisan and personal considerations constantly intervened in government decisions, deforming markets, corrupting politics, and vastly complicating private-sector investment decisions. At the same time, with their national industries protected from competition, consumers found themselves stuck with inferior and overpriced goods that could not compete on the world market. Then, in 1973, the first of two giant increases in the world price of oil drained the foreign currency reserves of many oil-importing countries, aggravating their balance of payments deficit.

In the face of mounting evidence of the counterproductive effects of the statist development approach, only Chile succeeded in extinguishing the system of government subsidies and establishing a largely market-driven economy. Everywhere else, governments sought to borrow their way out of trouble by turning to international bankers, who at that very moment were seeking customers for big loans on exceptionally attractive terms. Instead of rescuing the statist model, however, the decision to borrow delivered the *coup de grâce*. Interest rates rose sharply after 1980 just as a worldwide recession further limited the market for Latin American exports. The Latin American debt jumped from $184 billion in 1979 to $314 billion in 1982; the ratio of debt service to exports climbed to the completely unsustainable level of 59%. Imports continued to rise as private investors moved their money out of Latin America in anticipation of currency devaluations aimed at discouraging imports and expanding exports. Even the oil-exporting countries of Ecuador, Mexico and Venezuela faced huge budget and trade deficits. In fact, it was Mexico, considered immune to financial crisis because of its huge reserves of crude oil, that became the first to announce, in August 1982, that it could no longer meet its debt obligations. Banks suddenly stopped lending to Latin America, and the debt crisis had arrived. Fewer than twenty international banks had lent so much money to Latin America that the specter of a wave of defaults now threatened to unleash a worldwide financial crisis.

In order to service their debts, Latin American countries at first concentrated on restricting imports in order to free the necessary hard currency for loan payments to the overseas bankers. That strategy failed because the value of exports was also falling. The result was the "lost decade" of the 1980s, and it turned out to be the turning point in Latin America's late-twentieth century economic history. Per-capita GDP shrank in every country but Chile, Colombia and the Dominican Republic between 1981 and 1990. Not until after Brazil announced a moratorium on debt payments in 1987 did the major international creditors negotiate an arrangement that finally provided debtors with the relief they were seeking. The Brady Plan, named after U.S. Treasury Secretary Nicholas Brady, ended the crisis in July 1989 by allowing indebted governments to write off some of their debts if they carried out market-oriented reforms of their economies and ended dirigisme.

Across the region in the late 1980s and 1990s, a reprise of the mainly market-oriented doctrines that had dominated in Latin America before the 1930s began to shoulder aside policies associated with ISI. As foreign loan sources evaporated and their economies floundered, governments were forced to reduce spending, collect more taxes more efficiently, sell off government-owned enterprises, ease state regulation of the business and financial sectors, and drastically cut subsidies and transfers of all kinds. Once again, export promotion took a preeminent role. Growth was now understood to depend on the ability of Latin America to fully engage global economic forces that it had tried to shield itself from for decades. Above all, that meant lowering the barriers to trade, forcing national producers to compete with imported goods while encouraging a more diversified mix of exports.

Slowly, policy-makers realized that by holding fast to the inward-looking strategy of development, they had failed to seize opportunities for trade-induced growth created by the post-World War II boom in international trade. Even as the value of world trade expanded at an annual rate of close to 10% from 1948 to 1973, Latin America's share of world exports declined from 14% in 1946 to 7% by 1960. Furthermore, the region's exports were still heavily concentrated in agricultural commodities, precisely the kind of products still subject to protectionist policies in the developed countries, as well as to increasingly stiff competition from other regions that succeeded in eroding Latin America's share of the market. Resistance to more open trade arrangements was already being worn down by the external shocks of the early 1970s – above all, the collapse of fixed exchange rates tied to the U.S. dollar and the quadrupling of world oil prices. Further enhancing the lure of freer trade were rising demand among multinational manufacturers for cheap labor, the spectacular success of export-led growth policies in the industrializing Southeast Asian countries, and a sudden boom in commodity prices.

The first to move away from statism and ISI in the 1970s, while building on a foundational commitment to trade liberalization, were Argentina, Chile and Uruguay. Others – notably Brazil, the Dominican Republic and Mexico – tried to encourage the export of manufactured goods while preserving ISI and its protectionist environment. While they succeeded in increasing manufactured exports, by clinging to protectionism and fixed exchange rates they held back growth. Some countries – Bolivia, Ecuador, Paraguay, Venezuela and the five republics of Central America – concentrated on promoting primary exports but only oil-rich Ecuador and Venezuela were able to significantly increase export earnings, at least in the short term.

By the early 1990s, all the region's republics had finally recognized the need to diversify their exports away from commodities and to loosen or eliminate the ISI era's restrictions on foreign trade. In short, they gradually accepted what by then had become (and remains today) the orthodox view of professional economists: that reducing trade barriers encourages exports, for two reasons: free trade lowers the costs of the imports needed to make the exported products, and tends to prevent the overvaluation of the national currency (an overvalued currency inflates the price of exports, diminishing their competitiveness). Most countries, led by Mexico in 1985, proved their "conversion" to economic liberalism by joining the General Agreement on Tariffs and Trade (GATT). The GATT was a loose association of countries that promoted free trade while forbidding members to discriminate either *among* foreign producers, or *against* them in favor of domestic producers. Members had to open their markets equally to all comers, with some exceptions for less developed countries. Until the 1980s, most Latin American countries had stayed away from the GATT but by 2000 all of them had joined it or its successor organization, the World Trade Organization, which replaced the GATT in 1995.

In liberalizing trade, the Latin American countries joined a worldwide trend that saw exports as a share of world GDP nearly double from 13% in 1970 to 24% in 2003; among developing countries, exports almost tripled. That shift in the overall volume of trade constitutes the single most important (and controversial) aspect of globalization, a trend that encompasses the rise of a good many other "flows" – welcomed and unwelcome, legal and illegal – that are nevertheless closely linked to trade, such as capital, labor and information. From 1990 to 2005, the years of greatest expansion in the region, exports and imports rose by a little more than half in the Latin American countries, which also succeeded in raising the volume of their manufactured exports by 50% while substantially reducing primary exports.

In 1994, the GATT expanded the freedom of member countries to establish "regional trade agreements" (RTAs) aimed at liberalizing trade among the signers only, a kind of second-best option for governments wary of the political costs of full global integration. A highly controversial move, it contradicted GATT's founding principle of treating all GATT members equally, for RTAs in effect establish free trade by discriminating against non-members of the group. Whether regional agreements can achieve the same improvements in overall growth and welfare claimed for wider agreements remains an open question, but RTAs proved to be extraordinarily popular. Before the 1990s, fewer than a dozen existed worldwide, including no more than two or three Latin American agreements that had either languished or collapsed completely. Their numbers have exploded since the early 1990s, and by 2010, about 280 RTAs were in force worldwide.

The countries of the western hemisphere contributed substantially to this wave of economic regionalism, and the effect has been to make the Americas one of the most integrated trade areas in the world. On the other hand, a number of the hemisphere's RTAs carry restrictions and limitations that inhibit their ability to evolve toward an "open regionalism" that would extend liberalization beyond the members of the individual free-trade associations. Some economists also expressed concern at the "spaghetti-bowl" proliferation of RTAs (forty-one between 1991 and 2006) across the hemisphere, a trend that threatened to undermine the achievement of a single, grand hemispheric RTA which they assumed would enhance the benefits of trade for all.

The largest single RTA was the North American Free Trade Agreement (NAFTA) of 1994, which connected the United States, Canada and Mexico. At about the same time, a number of other RTAs were either created or reestablished: the Andean Community (Bolivia, Colombia, Ecuador and Peru), the Central American Common Market (CACM) and the Southern Common Market or Mercosur (Argentina, Brazil, Paraguay, Uruguay). The plan for a thirty-four-nation Free Trade Area of the Americas, launched in 1994, proved overly ambitious. As negotiations stagnated, more subregional RTAs emerged, including the Mercosur-Andean Community in 2004, the U.S.–Central America–Dominican Republic Free Trade Agreement (DR-CAFTA, 2006) and various bilateral arrangements.

While the first RTAs of the 1990s linked countries within the hemisphere, the larger trend since the turn of the century was to form RTAs linking countries in different continents. Between 2003 and 2006, Chile joined RTAs connecting it with New Zealand and five Asian countries; Mexico, Peru, Panama and Guatemala made similar agreements with various East Asian countries in 2005 and 2006. The European Union (EU) entered into bilateral trade partnerships with Mexico and Chile. In 2010 the EU adopted its first ever region-to-region agreement when it signed a free trade deal with the six members of Central America's Sistema de Integración Centroamericano (SICA), which committed all the signers to the unimpeded importation of each other's industrial products. It also suspended Central American duties on European-made vehicles for ten years, reduced European tariffs on Central American bananas, and eliminated EU tariffs on isthmian beef and rice.

The increase in hemispheric RTAs did little for trade with Europe but stimulated trade within the hemisphere. The East Asian trade rose modestly except in Argentina, Brazil, Chile and Peru, which saw significant increases in commerce with China. Canada and the United States together continued to receive the vast majority of Latin American exports – rising from 41% in 1990 to peak at 59% in 2000 before falling back to 43% in 2006. The 13% share of Latin American exports destined for Latin America itself in 1990 climbed to 19% in 1995 before declining to 15% in 2006. As usual, deviations from the regional average can be quite large; only about 5% of Mexico's exports were going to Latin America around 2000, while the Latin American share of Bolivian and El Salvadoran exports exceeded 60%. Many economists agreed that international trade and the integration of production processes within Latin America had scarcely reached their potential.

With one exception, neoliberal economic doctrine and a commitment to democratic principles of government drove the post-1980s process of regional trade integration. The exception was the creation in 2004, by presidents Hugo Chávez of Venezuela and Fidel Castro of Cuba, of the Alianza Bolivariana para los Pueblos de América (Bolivarian Alliance for the Peoples of the Americas) or ALBA. Bolivia, Ecuador, Nicaragua, and the three ex-British colonies of Antigua & Barbuda, St. Vincent & the Grenadines, and Dominica joined between 2006 and 2009; Honduras was a member until 2009. Explicitly opposed to market-driven development and free trade, ALBA declared that its treaties sought only the "exchange of goods and services to satisfy the needs of the peoples" and were founded on the principles of "solidarity, reciprocity, technology transfer." The members of ALBA claimed that all other Latin American free-trade arrangements were imposed by the United States with the aim of wiping out national economies and promoting "the penetration of big imperialist capital."[3]

While the leaders of few other Latin American countries shared ALBA's interpretation of U.S. motives in promoting free trade, or the socialistic aims of ALBA's Bolivian, Cuban and Venezuelan administrations, there is no doubt that by the first decade of the new century, enthusiasm for rigidly free-market policies had cooled everywhere. The skeptics argued that the state would have to assert, and perhaps deepen, its legitimate regulatory function of protecting consumers and investors, and guaranteeing competition in sectors where cronyism or monopolies threatened to distort the market. The opponents of the neo-liberal turn also insisted on the state's responsibility for ensuring access to basic goods and services for the poorest, or to oversee and finance projects aimed at improving the country's infrastructure, or to cultivate the conditions necessary for reducing inequality and poverty.

But it was also obvious that dirigiste doctrines that had turned the state into the primary economic force had failed, and ALBA risked reintroducing ideas that were already known to be defective. The most compelling evidence of statism's failure was the massive debt burden, acquired in the 1970s and 1980s precisely to rescue the economies from the distortions created in large part by the statism of ISI. The shift to neo-liberalism had also been encouraged by external factors, for the debt crisis had endowed powerful international financial institutions like the International Monetary Fund, the U.S. government and big multinational corporations with tremendous leverage over national economies. Faced with desperate appeals for help from the debtor countries, those institutions used their power over them to encourage market-oriented reforms.

Even after the "lost decade" had ended, indebtedness remained a long-term problem. In fact, the debt burden continued to rise, though now (as permitted by the terms of the Brady Plan) in the form of bonds sold to foreign investors rather than as syndicated bank loans. In 1994, Mexico narrowly avoided default thanks to a bailout by the U.S. government and the International Monetary Fund. The Asian financial crisis of 1997 and the Russian default in 1998 tended to discourage further speculative lending to Latin America. Some countries managed their debts successfully by boosting exports or by attracting more direct foreign investment. Others, mainly the smaller countries with less attractive investment climates, turned to subsidized loans and grants supplied by public entities such as foreign governments and multilateral agencies like the World Bank.

Two other external developments coincided with Latin America's "lost decade," and seemed to point toward the wisdom of returning more control over the Latin American economies to national and international market forces. The first was the late-1980s collapse of the communist system in the

Soviet Union and its longtime allies in Eastern and Central Europe. The second was the success of the East Asian developing countries in achieving industrialization through what was widely interpreted as a strongly market-oriented strategy of economic growth. The core idea shared by both trends, consistent with liberal ideology, was a philosophical commitment to human freedom in both the economic and the political realms. Both events also coincided with economic globalization and the fading of national barriers to exchanges of all kinds, not just economic ones. Finally, the shift from ISI to neo-liberalism occurred just as the "third wave" of democratization swept Latin America and other countries starting in the 1970s, again emphasizing the values of personal freedom and individual rights. In summary, the neo-liberal turn in Latin America reflected a worldwide shift that no Latin American government could resist, at least initially.

Since the late 1990s, however, sustained growth has continued to elude Latin America as a whole. The modest expansion phase that began gathering force in 2003 was cut short by the global financial crisis of 2008, which originated in the U.S. subprime home-mortgage market. The scale and impact of the economic disruption generated by that crisis have been compared to those of the Great Depression of the 1930s, which also originated in the United States and Europe. And like the crisis of the 1930s, that of 2008 was also caused by the explosion of an asset-price bubble that took the financial system down with it. The effects, in both cases, spread around the world almost immediately. In the crisis that began in 2008, GDP per capita fell by 3.2% to 4.2% in the developed countries. Growth rates in Latin America were hit harder, dropping from an average of 4.1% in 2008 to *negative* rates of around −2% throughout the region in 2009. As a result, unemployment rose, the volume of international trade fell, and capital flows declined sharply; not since the early 1980s had foreign direct investment in Latin America fallen so steeply. Nevertheless, in the judgment of the UN's Economic Commission for Latin America and the Caribbean, the overall shock of the 2008 crisis was less damaging than previous ones, in part because of a superior capacity to manage economic policy on the part of most Latin American governments, which tended to respond by borrowing less, renegotiating debt payments and building currency reserves while controlling inflation and reducing the public debt.

High-Growth Performers: Chile and the Dominican Republic

Since the debt crisis of the 1980s and the adoption of more market-oriented policies, only one country, Chile, established a clear record of outperforming its ISI-era growth record. As the pioneer in neo-liberal doctrine, Chile not only survived the lost decade with an average per-capita annual growth rate of 2.6% (the best in the region), but grew at an average annual rate of 4.1% from 1992 to 2002, nearly triple the average for all the Latin American countries. Moreover, unlike the Latin American pattern of volatility, its growth record was remarkably steady, interrupted only by a moderate recession in 1999. The elected governments that took power after the end of military rule in 1990 accelerated efforts to reduce social inequalities even while maintaining the strongly market-friendly policies initiated during the Pinochet dictatorship.

Why Chile has done so well in recent decades in comparison both to its own experience and to that of the rest of the region before the 1970s has been the subject of much debate among scholars. Two factors clearly played a major role. The first was dramatic improvements since the 1970s in the quality of institutions, including political stability, accountability, government effectiveness, the rule of law, and the control of corruption. The second was the timely adoption of complementary and mutually supportive growth-enhancing economic policies – in other words, smart management. Those policies succeeded in two areas: First, in stabilizing the economy by controlling inflation, public debt and exchange rates; and second, in remaking the old statist economic structure by liberalizing the financial and capital markets, opening the country to international trade and finance, privatizing state-owned enterprises, deregulating the private sector, and taking steps to reduce poverty and inequality. But to sustain its remarkable growth record, Chile will nevertheless have to tackle some widely acknowledged weaknesses, beginning with the quality of its public education system. More investment in research and development, as well as improvements in the efficiency and accountability of government services, were needed. The share of Chileans who lived in poverty, estimated at about one-fifth the population by 2010, had to be reduced.

From 1992 to 2002, the Dominican Republic exceeded even Chile's record, with an average annual growth rate of 4.3%. Like Chile's, the Dominican growth spurt also took shape in the 1970s. Foremost among the sources of growth was the enhanced political stability that followed the turmoil ignited by the assassination of dictator Rafael Trujillo in 1961. Major improvements in the curriculum of the country's secondary school system, as well as enrollment increases, were carried out in the 1970s. A reform of government banking regulations resulted in a significant rise in private bank lending. Economic growth flattened out in the 1980s but recovered spectacularly in the 1990s owing largely to structural measures that improved trade (by eliminating export taxes and cutting tariffs) and strengthened the country's electrical, transportation and communication infrastructure. A comprehensive program of stabilization policies reduced inflation, solidified the exchange rate and reduced the external debt. Foreign direct investment rose substantially after legislation passed in 1996 removed restrictions on capital flows.

In comparison with Chile, however, the Dominican Republic continued to lag in the reform most needed for sustainable growth: designing and maintaining institutions and accountability mechanisms capable of keeping the confidence of investors. In government effectiveness, rule of law and the control of corruption, the Dominican Republic declined during the first decade of the twenty-first century, according to the World Bank.

The fact that the Dominican Republic shares the island of Hispaniola with Haiti, the hemisphere's perennially poorest country, provides an opportunity for a comparison that can help explain why some economies grow and others stagnate. Besides similar geographies, the historical institutions of the two countries were quite similar well into the twentieth century, though the Dominican Republic's political history may have been even less stable than Haiti's until the early twentieth century. Both countries experienced long-term, near-simultaneous occupations by U.S. military forces aimed at stabilizing the political systems: the Dominican Republic, from 1916 to 1924, and Haiti, from 1915 to 1934.

Their paths began to diverge almost immediately after the occupation. Successive Haitian governments concentrated on the personal enrichment of their leaders and did little to maintain the social services and public infrastructure that the U.S. military occupation authorities had built up. On the other hand, Trujillo's dictatorial regime (1930–1961) did more than the Haitians next door to advance public works, industry, agriculture and education. The Dominican economy, and with it the middle class, expanded. From the 1960s onward, while the Dominicans enjoyed largely favorable growth trends generated by improvements in productivity and capital accumulation, Haiti regressed. Since 1960, sustained positive GDP per capita growth in Haiti only occurred once, in the 1970s, averaging 2.5%, largely as a result of liberalized trade regulations, more accessible bank credit, and educational improvements. For Haiti, the "lost decade" was a much bigger calamity (–2.4% growth) than for Latin America as a whole (–0.9% growth). Politically, the 1980s was also "lost" to Haiti, as popular resistance to the Duvalier family dictatorship (François Duvalier from 1957 to 1971, then his son Jean-Claude from 1971) led to its collapse in 1986, followed by almost continuous disorder and lawless violence, failed elections and military coups d'état. Unrestrained government spending led to debt arrearages, followed by exchange rate instability and inflation.

The 1990s, far from being a decade of recovery for Haiti as it was elsewhere, saw average growth plunge at the same rate as the 1980s. After the Haitian military overthrew an elected government in 1991, the United States, the United Nations and the Organization of American States all imposed trade embargos to pressure the military regime to restore electoral democracy. That led to a catastrophic decline in trade. A U.S.-led military intervention in 1994 ended military rule, but another military rebellion in 2004 crowned a decade of intense political instability.

Haiti fell behind the Dominican Republic in the implementation of stabilization policies and structural reforms. But there is little doubt that the Haitian economy's failure to thrive has been owing primarily to the deficient capacity of the Haitians to govern themselves.

Notes

1   Andrés Solimano, "Introduction and Synthesis," in *Vanishing Growth in Latin America: The Late Twentieth Century Experience*, ed. Andrés Solimano (Cheltenham: Edward Elgar, 2006), 3–4.
2   Robert J. Barro and Xavier Sala-i-Martin, *Economic Growth*, 2nd edn. (Cambridge, MA: MIT Press, 2004), 14–15; 521ff; 554.
3   Portal ALBA-TCP, www.alianzabolivariana.org.

References

Barro, Robert J., and Xavier Sala-i-Martin. *Economic Growth*. 2nd edn. Cambridge, MA: MIT Press, 2004.

Solimano, Andrés. "Introduction and Synthesis." In *Vanishing Growth in Latin America: The Late Twentieth Century Experience*, ed. Andrés Solimano, 1–10. Cheltenham, UK: Edward Elgar, 2006.

Chapter 9

Poor Countries, Rich Countries

The Stragglers

The poorest Latin American countries also reveal a persistent incapacity to acquire the habits of governance required for democratic consolidation. In Chapters 1 and 3, we reviewed some of the underlying causes of this political failure. Here we wish only to call attention to the interactive character of governmental incompetence and economic backwardness. If bad government holds back economic development, extreme poverty and inequality also hinder political stabilization, to say nothing of democratic consolidation. The performance of Latin America's consistently poorest countries – Bolivia, Honduras, Nicaragua and Paraguay – is charted in Figure 9.1.

Paraguay

In 1960, the poorest Latin American country was Paraguay, then still in the springtime of Gen. Alfredo Stroessner's one-man military dictatorship, which ended in 1989 when he was removed by his own armed forces. As low as it was, Paraguay's per-capita GDP in 1960 was nevertheless 60% higher than Haiti's average per-capita GDP from 1991 to 2009. By 1980, Paraguay had climbed up to the fifth-lowest position, having registered the fastest growth rates of any Latin American country in the 1970s. Driving Paraguay's ascent was a boom in soybean and cotton prices, and the completion of a major highway that linked the capital of Asunción to Brazilian seaports and to underdeveloped agricultural lands in the east. Perhaps the greatest contributor to Paraguay's economic growth was the construction, with Brazil, of the colossal Itaipú

Contemporary Latin America: 1970 to the Present, First Edition. Robert H. Holden and Rina Villars.
© 2013 Robert H. Holden and Rina Villars. Published 2013 by Blackwell Publishing Ltd.

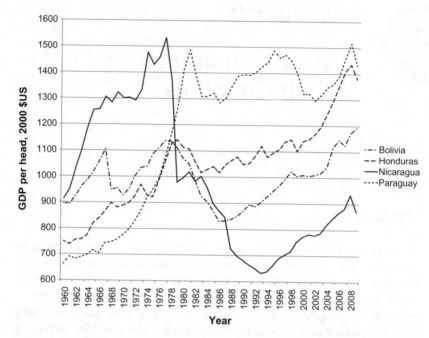

Figure 9.1   The stragglers: lowest-income Latin American countries, 1960–2009. Based on data from the World Bank, "World Development Indicators and Global Development Finance," http://databank.worldbank.org/ddp/home.do.

hydroelectric dam between 1975 and 1982. None of these events depended on political democracy, but they did require political stability, the one benefit that Stroessner's thirty-five-year reign delivered.

Nicaragua

As Paraguay surged ahead, Bolivia and Nicaragua fell behind. In 1960, Bolivia was the fourth poorest Latin American country and Nicaragua the sixth poorest. By 1980, however, both had anchored themselves firmly at the bottom, Nicaragua as the poorest and Bolivia as the second poorest, positions they continued to hold for the next three decades. From 1991 to 2009, Nicaragua's per-capita income averaged $758 per year, followed by Bolivia at $1,020. What accounted for their descent?

By 1970, Nicaragua's steady growth had lifted it to the seventh-poorest country in Latin America. But in the decade to come, the Nicaraguan dictator Anastasio Somoza had to confront a challenge that Gen. Stroessner never did: a powerful and ever-growing opposition movement eventually spearheaded by a guerrilla army led by Marxists who promised "national liberation" and a socialist revolution. Steady gains in popular support for the removal of the Somoza dictatorship led to the victory of the insurgents in 1979 and the subsequent rule of the Frente Sandinista de Liberación Nacional (FSLN) until 1990.

As the rest of Latin America began its historic shift away from economic statism during the 1980s, the FSLN embraced it. Determined to redistribute the country's wealth in order to reduce economic inequality, the revolutionary government seized large and medium-sized rural properties as part of its land reform program; nationalized much of the banking, mining, insurance and transportation sectors; imposed price and wage controls; and devoted up to 20% of the national budget to transfers and subsidies. The government merely tolerated the continued existence of the private sector, whose total output by the mid-1980s had been whittled down to about half of the country's GDP. The FSLN's long-term goal was the complete socialization of the economy.

From the moment that it seized state power, however, the Nicaraguan government labored under two obstacles that together proved to be insuperable. The first was the physical destruction and capital flight caused by the civil war that had brought it to power. The second was the relentless opposition of the U.S. government, which launched an aggressive program of military, political and economic destabilization aimed at the removal of the FSLN from power. The politico-military dimension of the destabilization program depended on a U.S. trained and supplied force of anti-FSLN Nicaraguan guerrilla raiders based in neighboring Honduras. In response, the FSLN devoted an increasing share of its budget to national defense, which included compulsory military service for most Nicaraguans. U.S.-imposed economic sanctions, including the blockage of both commercial credit and multilateral development assistance, as well as a trade embargo, helped drive the Nicaraguan economy into a severe recession, intensifying the crippling effects of the U.S.-sponsored guerrilla war.

After the FSLN lost the presidential election of 1990 to the U.S.-backed party of Violeta Chamorro, Nicaragua took steps to establish a competitive, market economy. Yet despite a 1992–2002 average annual growth rate of 1.5%, in 2010 it was still reporting the lowest GDP per capita among all the Latin American countries, and was tied with Guatemala for the lowest standard of living, as measured by the Human Development Index, a measure of economic welfare that will be discussed in Chapter 10. Nicaragua remained highly dependent on primary product exports such as coffee, cotton, sugar and beef and thus continued to suffer from the periodic price declines that characterize the commodities markets. As a result, the country's trade balance was chronically negative; the value of imports typically totaled nearly twice that of exports. This failure to compete in an increasingly globalized economy continued to undermine Nicaragua's chances for sustainable economic growth. Its weak infrastructure, high rates of crime and official corruption, coupled with wide-spread disregard for the rule of law, and low rates of educational attainment, diminished its attractiveness to investors.

Nicaragua's political system mirrored its chronic economic weaknesses. Instead of progressing toward a consolidated democracy after the 1990 election, Nicaragua moved in the opposite direction. In a political ambience framed by disorder and violence, leading politicians continued to rely on the old patrimonial techniques of rule to circumvent the constitution and the law, undermine public accountability, and reduce voter choice. As in Haiti, chronic deficiencies in governability loomed as first-order obstacles to economic development.

Bolivia

Few national economies have been as decisively and durably crippled by war as Bolivia's. Nothing could make up for the loss of 523 km of Pacific Ocean coastline or the immense deposits of copper and nitrates in the territory that Bolivia lost to Chile in 1880. Much the same could be said of the 234,000 sq. km that the Paraguayan army seized from Bolivia in 1935. To those losses must be added the economic disadvantages of an extremely mountainous and variable geography that has impeded the development of a transportation and communication infrastructure, and a society sharply divided by class and ethnicity.

A three-day civil war in 1952, launched by tin miners bent on social revolution, forced the surrender of the Bolivian army and led to the installation of a government that nationalized the country's tin mines, redistributed its largest agricultural enterprises to landless peasants, and granted universal suffrage. The revolution succeeded in greatly extending the political influence of the country's poor and middle class. But as the revolutionary party split into moderate and radical factions, the economy faltered, and the army seized power in 1964. In 1982, after a general strike that nearly led to another civil war, the military stepped down and returned the country to constitutional rule. The last years of military rule, marked by economic mismanagement, extreme corruption, and a massive foreign debt, had practically destroyed the economy. The collapse of tin prices in 1985 pushed it to the brink.

As a result, three weeks after taking office in August 1985, President Victor Paz Estenssoro launched one of the two most radical neoliberal restructuring programs of a Latin American economy since the 1970s. Only Chile's was comparable in scope and impact. Bolivia's subsequent success in reducing both inflation and its fiscal deficit, and encouraging foreign investment and economic growth by opening the economy and closing state enterprises, was widely recognized. Neoliberal restructuring was deepened in the early 1990s, and led to a period of robust economic growth averaging nearly 5% a year through 1997. Poverty rates fell. But after 1998, the all-important growth rate began falling too. Unemployment rose and poverty increased, despite a price-rise bonanza in natural gas and soy exports. Political pressures derailed plans for continuing structural reforms and in response, public spending jumped. Consolidating its reputation for instability, the country had four presidents between 2000 and 2005.

By the first decade of the twenty-first century, Bolivia's economy was about as large as that of Akron, Ohio, a city of 200,000 people. Bolivia was as big as Austria, Belgium, France, Germany and Switzerland combined, but its population of 9 million was smaller than that of metropolitan Paris. Looking back over the previous half-century, a team of World Bank economists observed in 2005 that Bolivia's economy had not grown, and that average incomes were actually lower in 2000 than they were in 1950. While the main causes of low growth in the 1990s had been poor management and a weak financial sector, after 2000, the main cause was a rise in political and social conflict, which in turn increased uncertainty about the future of Bolivia and thus discouraged investment. Serious doubts were raised about Bolivia's commitment to the rule of law and the protection of property rights, a situation aggravated by violent protests, rising fiscal deficits, and abrupt changes in government policy. Until Bolivia achieved more social and political stability, the economists argued, growth could not be sustained and neither, therefore, could economic development. "Clear and stable rules are essential for investors . . . [T]he rules of the game have to be the right rules that encourage efficient, labor intensive investment in line with Bolivia's comparative advantages. Today, the rules of the game, and the institutions which implement and enforce them, are not the right ones."

Underlying the recent surge in social and political conflict, the authors of the report went on to note, were four deeply rooted features of Bolivian life:

- a weak, corrupt and incompetent state incapable of maintaining law and order;
- a highly unequal society in which wealth was concentrated in the hands of an elite who had managed to keep the poor indigenous majority excluded from any meaningful participation in the country's institutions;
- deep divisions of opinion over the management of Bolivia's natural resources; and
- the failure to complete the transition from a state-centered to a market-centered economy.[1]

Yet it was hard to miss a glaring paradox in their analysis. A concerted effort to correct any of the four weaknesses would almost inevitably lead to even more conflict, which was likely in turn to hold back growth even more. In fact, at the very moment that the World Bank released its report, on 31 October 2005, Bolivia found itself embroiled in a highly polarized election campaign in which the principal candidates and their followers debated solutions to precisely the four problems identified in the report. The election of 18 December swept into office the candidates of Movimiento al Socialism (MAS, Movement Toward Socialism) including Evo Morales, who drew 54% of the vote to become the first fully indigenous president of Bolivia upon his inauguration on 22 January 2006.

True to his party's name, over the next four years Morales led Bolivia in just the direction that the World Bank economists had warned against, restoring a heavily statist economic strategy, nationalizing key sectors of the economy, imposing new government controls on the market, redistributing agricultural land to landless Bolivians, and vastly increasing the country's social welfare budget. A new constitution greatly augmented the political power of the country's indigenous population. Yet, buoyed by rising prices for the country's principal exports, natural gas and electrical energy, the economy grew between 2006 and 2008. Even though it declined in 2009, Morales, more popular than ever, easily won reelection in December 2009 by appealing (as he had in 2005) to the poor majority (particularly indigenous voters) and condemning capitalism and the neoliberal development model. He promised to continue his program of state-sponsored wealth redistribution and economic regulation.

The Leaders

Since 1960, the ranking of the highest-income Latin American countries has varied significantly only in one respect: the steady decline of Venezuela, from the country with the highest GDP per head to the sixth-highest in 2009. Except during Venezuela's ascendancy from 1962 to 1968, Argentina reported the highest GDP per head every year. Venezuela occupied second place throughout the 1970s before descending further. Uruguay has been in second place since 1986, and Mexico in third since 1996. While Venezuela's per-capita income has scarcely changed over the last half-century (from $5,425 in 1960 to $5,638 in 2009), Argentina's rose from $5,237 to $9,880, Uruguay's from $4,340 to $8,942 and Mexico's from $2,554 to $6,099. (All income figures have been standardized by converting them to U.S. dollars at 2000 prices.) Figure 9.2 charts the performance of the leaders in per-capita income – Argentina, Mexico, Uruguay and Venezuela; Figure 9.3 illustrates the tremendous rise in absolute terms of the three countries with the highest output: Argentina, Brazil and Mexico.

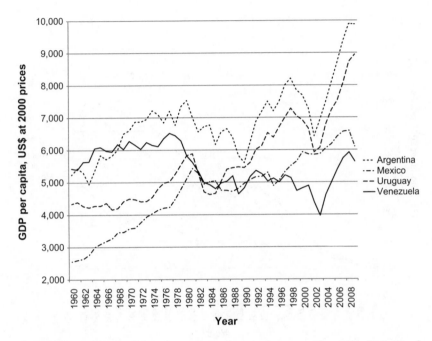

Figure 9.2   The leaders: highest-income Latin American countries, 1960–2009. Based on data from the World Bank, *World Development Indicators and Global Development Finance*, http://databank.worldbank.org/ddp/home.do.

Venezuela

Venezuela's descent was tied to the structural difficulties created by two closely related circumstances. Not only did its economic growth depend almost exclusively on the country's huge reserves of crude oil, but an exceptionally corrupt political system had become no less addicted to oil revenue. After the collapse of the military dictatorship of Gen. Marcos Pérez Jiménez in 1958, the leaders of Venezuela's three main political parties pacted to establish a controlled democracy in which elections would be limited to their own candidates, power would be shared among them on a rotating basis and income from the sale of petroleum would be spent to raise the living standard of the average Venezuelan, thus ensuring electoral support for the official parties.

The country's status as the world's largest exporter of petroleum (from 1929 to 1970), and the site of the hemisphere's largest proven oil reserves, encouraged the government to keep taxes low and spending high. Both before and after the nationalization of the petroleum industry in 1976, the state's fiscal arm basically funneled oil revenues into an ever-increasing number of public

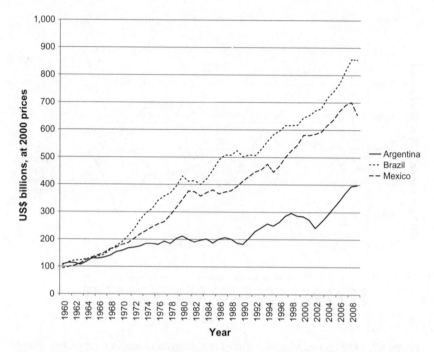

Figure 9.3 Gross domestic product, 1960–2009, of top three producers. Based on data from the World Bank, *World Development Indicators and Global Development Finance*, http://databank.worldbank.org/ddp/home.do.

jobs and contracts that enriched the politically powerful and their friends. They in turn sought to protect their wealth by transferring much of it to foreign banks, thus decapitalizing their own economy.

Thus in Venezuela, a strategic natural endowment of stupendous value had met its master: a patrimonial and clientelistic political culture indifferent to the rule of law yet flexible enough to exploit for public and private gain the new opportunities provided by globalization and the techniques of modern capitalist enterprise. Little effort was made to separate public power and private interests. As world petroleum prices rose fourfold in the early 1970s, the Venezuelan treasury became El Dorado, the source of funding for everything from huge development projects to massive imports of basic foodstuffs.

But like other Latin American governments in the late 1970s, even Venezuela had to turn to foreign banks to cover its fiscal deficits. Oil prices slumped, borrowing and interest rates rose, and the economy stagnated, crippled less by external factors than by Olympian-scale mismanagement and corruption. The decline of Venezuela, from its long-assumed exceptional status as a prosperous, stable, electoral democracy in a continent famous for its military dictatorships, had begun. As economic conditions worsened, the voters returned Carlos Andrés Pérez to the presidency in 1988 with 55% of the vote. He was the candidate of Acción Democrática, one of the political parties that had founded the post-1958 political system and long considered a model party of Latin America's "democratic left." Pérez had served as president in the mid-1970s, during the El Dorado years of oil-driven bounty.

Hopes that he could return Venezuela to its golden age were dashed on 16 February 1989, two weeks after his inauguration, when he announced "El Paquete" ("the package"), a neoliberal bombshell that, among other severe austerity measures, doubled the price of gasoline and raised the price of public transportation by 30%. When the price increases took effect on 27 February, violent student-led protests broke out across Caracas and other cities. The violence, looting and destruction quickly overwhelmed the capacity of the police forces to respond, while in some cases the police supported the protesters. Pérez imposed martial law and called out the army. The army and elements of the police force concentrated their fire on the poorest neighborhoods, where resistance was strongest, and order was restored on 3 March. The nationwide death toll of what became known as the *Caracazo* ("Caracas uprising") or the *Sacudón* ("violent shaking") was placed at 396 persons by independent investigators; thousands were wounded and thousands of retail businesses were destroyed. The disaster revealed the authoritarian and oligarchic core of Venezuela's vaunted social-democratic institutions, as well as the distance that had opened up between the political leaders and the people they governed. For the rest of his life, Pérez insisted that his austerity program had not caused the riot, which he attributed instead to police insubordination.

The *Caracazo* led directly to the collapse of the post-1958 power sharing arrangement, which turned out to be little more than a gigantic investment swindle in which oil revenue was used primarily to coopt the popular classes rather than to achieve sustainable economic development. Its success depended on the flow of fresh investment income in the form of oil revenue, which in turn depended on the world price of oil, a factor that Venezuela's leaders could not control. In this sense, Venezuela's "lost decade" was fundamentally a political and cultural crisis rather than an economic one. By 1991, Pérez's public-opinion approval rating had fallen below 10%, and the three-decade old power-sharing system had already lost much of its legitimacy. On 4 February 1992, a secret society of nationalistic junior military officers led by Lt. Col. Hugo Chávez attempted unsuccessfully to overthrow the Pérez government and the power-sharing regime, denouncing its exclusiveness and proposing a new system that would be more responsive to the needs of the poor, whose numbers had multiplied since the early 1970s despite Venezuela's status as an oil superpower.

Despite, or because of, his imprisonment for rebellion, Chávez's popularity soared as Pérez was charged with stealing public funds and removed from office in 1993. A plurality of Venezuelans elected Rafael Caldera, who had served from 1969 to 1974, as president. One of Caldera's first official acts upon taking office in 1994 was to release Chávez and his military co-conspirators from prison. In doing so, Caldera unintentionally launched the political career of the man whose election as president with 56% of the vote on 6 December 1998 would establish a completely different political regime and a new economic agenda aimed at the radical redistribution of wealth and income. Chávez came from behind to defeat the two frontrunners, who had endorsed programs of neoliberal structural reform. The public was in no mood for economic ortho-doxy, and had become deeply hostile to candidates associated with the country's traditional political elite.

Calling on the memory of Simón Bolívar, the statesman and military leader of South American independence, Chávez pledged to undertake a "Bolivarian revolution" of Venezuela's political and economic institutions. This he accom-plished by campaigning successfully, after his inauguration as president, for a new constitution that greatly enhanced the state's responsibility for the eco-nomic welfare of Venezuelans. Following his reelection as president in 2000 with 60% of the votes, Chávez began to veer leftward, away from his initial preference for a kind of humanistic capitalism or "third way" between capital-ism and socialism.

Increasingly, Chávez identified communist-ruled Cuba as his preferred eco-nomic model. After he won a recall referendum in 2004 by polling 59% of the vote, he speeded up land redistribution programs, boosted social welfare spending substantially, opened a chain of government-run and subsidized food markets, and subsidized industrial enterprises that had been seized by their workers after the owners closed them. About 20,000 Cuban doctors arrived to staff newly built medical clinics to serve the poor. After winning a third term in 2006 with 63% of the vote, Chávez announced plans to speed up his program of "Twenty-First Century Socialism," further expanding state control over the economy, particularly in the petroleum, communications and energy sectors.

Oil exports, however, remained the economic mainstay of Venezuela; the country's proven reserves of 99 billion barrels in 2009 were the sixth largest reserves in the world, just after Kuwait. Higher world prices from 2003 onward financed much of Chávez's socialist reform agenda, and in 2005, 2006 and 2007, the economy grew at annual rates of 6% to 8%. But Chávez's efforts to diversify away from oil exports were no more successful than earlier attempts. In 2007, Venezuela still depended on petroleum for 85% of its export revenue and close to one-fifth of the country's GDP. As a result, the Chávez government found itself in the paradoxical position of condemning global capitalism and big business, while relying on the world market's thirst for oil to finance a socialistic and nationalistic transformation of the Venezuelan economy.

Mexico

Like Venezuela, Mexico has been among the most important oil-producing countries in the world since the early twentieth century. But Mexico's relatively more successful record of managing its oil wealth was owing largely to a much more stable and ultimately more flexible (if authoritarian) political system that also enjoyed a considerably higher level of popular acceptance than Venezuela's.

Like most other Latin American countries, Mexico followed the statist doctrine of ISI after World War II, seen as the quickest way to supply the jobs and the higher living standards that its growing population – still largely dependent on agriculture – would require. Mexico had already nationalized the foreign-owned oil industry in 1938, redirecting that sector's substantial revenues into domestic development. To expand the industrial base, the government raised tariffs and established import quotas aimed at insulating Mexican industry from the burden of competition with foreign producers. The government spent heavily on the development of infrastructure, and put up barriers to foreign investment in order to "mexicanize" the economy, a measure that forced the government itself to provide increasing amounts of investment capital as well as subsidies and tax exemptions.

By the 1960s, these policies of economic nationalism had multiplied the country's gross output and achieved the goal of producing Mexican-made substitutes for most imported goods in the light industrial sectors, such as textiles, paper, shoes, rubber and glass, and of creating entirely new industries, such as petrochemicals and synthetic fiber. Economic nationalism provided Mexico with average annual growth rates of 7% during the "miracle years" of 1963 to 1971. But it also produced a manufacturing sector deliberately trained on a domestic market (rather than foreign markets) whose expansion was unsustainable, just as a balance of payments crisis called for export-led growth to pay for a rise in imports.

At the same time that the countries of South Asia and East Asia were turning their new, state-nurtured industries into export-oriented engines of national growth and development, Mexico, ever-faithful to the policy of import substitution, was discouraging manufactured exports. Had it acted otherwise, it is not clear that export-promotion would have succeeded, considering the high costs and poor quality of most of the goods that carried the proud label, "Hecho en México." The capital and technology required to make most industries competitive on the world market would have forced the country to look abroad, which was just what the policy of economic nationalism had been designed to prevent. Only a strong export sector could have generated enough revenue to remake key industries and to deepen industrialization, going beyond light consumer goods and developing the capital-goods sector.

The problem of capital scarcity was aggravated by the government's refusal to enlarge a Lilliputian tax base that should have generated considerably more revenue. At the same time, ISI had drawn capital away from the agricultural sector and further weakened it by imposing government caps on food prices, thus discouraging private investment in agriculture. The land reform policies inherited from the Revolution of 1910 led to the creation of ever-smaller and less efficient farming units. Production of the basic grains of the Mexican diet – corn, wheat and beans – stagnated, forcing the country to rely increasingly on imports from the United States. Among the most serious social consequences of agricultural decline was a rise in income inequality and a rapid increase in rural–urban migration as poor rural families sought jobs and basic services in the cities. ISI had also produced an economy whose key beneficiaries depended more and more on the patronage of Mexico's one-party political system, aggravating official corruption.

By the early 1970s, it was already clear that Mexico's economy required a radical course correction if it was going to generate the investment capital and tax revenue required to sustain the growth rates of the "miracle years" of the 1940s-1960s, and provide jobs for an expanding population. But as the economy began to break down in the mid-1970s, in a crisis of capital flight, falling output and rising inflation, a *deus ex machina* appeared in the eastern and southern peripheries of Mexico: the discovery of new, massive reserves of crude oil in the Gulf of Mexico and the states of Tabasco and Chiapas. (The oil sector had diminished to just 2.5% of GDP and 3.5% of federal government tax revenues by the early 1970s.) The government, as the owner of the oil fields, allowed production to rise from about 800,000 barrels a day in 1976 to 2.3 million a day in 1980, turning Mexico into the world's fourth largest oil producer in a short-lived era of rapidly rising world prices. Oil as a share of total exports rose from 68% in 1980 to nearly 80% in 1982, its all-time high. The widely shared assumption that Mexico's economic future now burned more brightly than ever encouraged the government to avoid facing the structural problems that lay behind the growth bonanza of the 1960s, and had nearly capsized the economy in the mid-1970s.

As it turned out, however, the oil boom would undermine both economic growth and the longstanding ideal, inherited from the Revolution of 1910, of national self-reliance. Rising oil prices drove a tremendous increase in public investments, which in turn produced spectacular average annual growth rates of 8.4% between 1978 and 1981. But this would be the last boom until the late 1990s, for excessive optimism about future oil revenues led to excessive government spending and a growing budget deficit. The higher oil prices rose, the more the government spent. During the 1970s, the number of state-owned enterprises quadrupled.

One result of excessive spending was a drastic rise in the value of imports over exports, an imbalance aggravated by the government's refusal to devalue the currency, a move that would have discouraged imports and encouraged more exports. To cover the deficit, the government increased its borrowing from foreign lenders; private enterprises followed suit. Interest rates on these foreign loans rose and so did domestic inflation, which jumped from 30% in 1976 to 60% by early 1982. Disaster struck in the middle of 1981. Contrary to expectations, oil prices slid and the government borrowed even more in an attempt to protect the over-valued currency. Oil prices continued to fall through 1982, and investors withdrew more and more capital to foreign safe havens. When the government finally stopped trying to protect the peso, the currency collapsed to its true value: from 12.5 to the dollar in 1976 to 144 by the year's end.

Mexico ended its six-year oil boom in an economic crisis that vastly surpassed that of 1976 in scope and impact. In mid-1982, foreign lenders reacted by turning off the flow of credit, and Mexico announced that it could no longer make payments on a foreign debt that stood at $84 billion in 1982 and would balloon to an incredible $105 billion by 1988, while the peso's worth would plummet to 2,945 to the dollar in 1990. Instead of a panacea, the stupendous oil discoveries of the 1970s had sucked Mexico into the worst economic crisis in its history, worsening poverty and inequality instead of alleviating them. At the same time, Mexico's political institutions and the regime's ideological commitments had evolved in ways that limited the government's policy options, reducing its flexibility and its openness to rival economic management strategies. After the 1940s, the presidency became increasingly autocratic and clientelistic, paving the way for the mismanagement of the economy by a small circle of self-selected leaders who justified their moves with populistic appeals to national pride and the Revolution of 1910.

With an economy shrinking every year from 1982 to 1988 (except for a slight rebound in 1984–1985), it fell to the presidency of Miguel de la Madrid (1982–1988) to begin the demolition of the Mexican variant of dirigisme, although few at the time anticipated the extraordinary scope of the restructuring to come. Limited reforms and some macroeconomic tinkering would suffice, it was widely assumed. In fact, what awaited Mexico on the economic front was a Herculean undertaking, vastly complicated politically by the way that economic institutions had become intertwined over the decades with those of the ruling party, its state-approved affiliates, and a dense web of clientelistic networks.

Introducing effective market-oriented reforms without disrupting the party's grip on power would prove to be impossible. At first, De la Madrid, a Harvard-educated technocrat, rose to the occasion by prosecuting two of the most corrupt officials of the previous administration, devaluing the currency, reducing government subsidies, selling some of the most unprofitable state-owned enterprises, and cutting the federal payroll. His administration negotiated a debt-restructuring arrangement with Mexico's largest lenders, entered the GATT, and began to liberalize foreign trade. But, unable to arrest inflation sufficiently, and faced by persistent balance of payments deficits and shrinking output, the government was forced to consider sterner measures. Among other things, Mexico's continued dependence on oil exports had to be curbed, for the world price of oil had fallen from $25.50 a barrel in 1985 to $12 a barrel in 1986, leading to huge losses in foreign exchange. On top of the country's economic woes, an 8+ earthquake in Mexico City on 19 September 1985 killed more than 8,000 people and caused some $4 billion in damage.

During the last three years of the De la Madrid administration, the pace of economic reform picked up, and accelerated drastically with the election in 1988 of Carlos Salinas, whose victory in the most bitterly contested election since 1929 was widely believed to be the result of government fraud. The holder of a Harvard doctorate in economics, Salinas had supervised De la Madrid's economic reforms as his budget director. By the time Salinas's term in office was ending in 1994, Mexico's economic crisis seemed to be in retreat. The government had conquered inflation, reorganized and reduced its still-massive foreign debt, opened itself to world trade, vastly reduced oil's share of export revenue, and dismantled most of the remaining government-owned enterprises. Salinas even decreed a constitutional reform allowing for the privatization of the *ejidos*, the vast network of politically sacrosanct, community-owned farming enterprises brought to life by the Revolution of 1910. Salinas sealed the country's commitment to free trade by joining the North American Free Trade Agreement in 1992. Encouraged by the deregulation of the economy, foreign direct investment increased to $8 billion by 1994.

But election years in Mexico were now becoming moments of grave political and economic crisis, and 1994 was no exception. Much of Salinas's success was founded on unsustainable exchange-rate controls, and an overvalued peso was leading to a growing balance of payments deficit. Then suddenly, the specter of political instability – a hitherto unthinkable scenario – touched off a massive withdrawal of foreign capital, and by the end of 1994 foreign exchange reserves were only a quarter of what they had been a year earlier. 1 January 1994 was not only the day that Mexico's membership in NAFTA took effect, but also the day that a guerrilla army named after Emiliano Zapata, the legendary leader of Mexico's 1910 Revolution, declared war on the Mexican state and called on the people to "overthrow the dictator" Salinas. A ceasefire and subsequent peace talks ended hostilities after twelve days, but worse was to come. In March, Salinas's handpicked successor, PRI candidate Luis Donaldo Colosio, was assassinated on the campaign trail. In September, Francisco Ruiz Massieu, the secretary-general of the PRI and Salinas's ex-brother in law, was murdered.

Colosio's replacement as the PRI's presidential candidate was Colosio's campaign manager, Ernesto Zedillo. The holder of a Ph.D. in economics from Yale University, Zedillo would have to face the country's worst economic crisis since 1982 within three weeks of his inauguration on 1 December 1994. Forced to allow the overvalued peso to float, Zedillo could not control the rate of devaluation. Because the government's new debt obligations of some $30 billion were denominated in dollars, the cost of servicing it was essentially doubled by the devaluation. The threat of a debt default and a banking collapse, on a scale that dwarfed even that of 1982, loomed. The U.S. government came to the rescue in January 1995 with a stopgap loan of $20 billion that was conditioned on further market-oriented reforms, higher taxes and more careful fiscal management. The economy, now more integrated than ever into the U.S. market via NAFTA, and firmly committed to economic liberalization, began to recover in 1996.

With rising economic freedom came democratic reforms. Zedillo renounced the customary presidential privilege of choosing his successor, and took steps to detach the PRI from the state. The public's disgust with the regime of "institutionalized revolution" soared after Salinas's brother Raul was arrested in 1995 and charged with murdering Ruiz Massieu, who had been married to the Salinas brothers' sister Adriana. In 1999, Raul Salinas (who had ties to drug dealers and accumulated hundreds of millions of dollars during his brother's presidency) was convicted of murdering Massieu. Few Mexicans thought that his brother the president, now living in exile, was innocent. In 1997, Mexicans voted the PRI out of office in state and local elections. Three years later, the candidate of the conservative Partido de Acción Nacional (PAN), Vicente Fox, won the presidency, defeating the PRI candidate and terminating the regime that had ruled the country since 1920.

As Mexico liberalized its economy, its reliance on oil exports declined in comparison to Venezuela. Mexico's 31 billion barrels of proven reserves in 1980 (fifth largest in the world) dipped to 11 billion in 2009 (fifteenth largest), and oil's share of total exports fell progressively, from 1982's nearly 80%, to the 10–15% range after 1998 as the government succeeded in encouraging the diversification of exports. Major contributors to that diversification were the free-trade agreement with the United States, and the boom in the establishment of a novel form of manufacturing enterprise, the *maquiladora* or bonded assembly plant. Exploiting Mexico's low wage rates and its proximity to the huge U.S. consumer market, the government in the mid-1960s began to allow foreign-owned companies to temporarily import manufacturing parts duty-free, which were assembled by Mexican workers and then exported duty-free. By the first decade of the twenty-first century, close to 4,000 *maquiladoras* were employing more than 1 million Mexicans. Their exports alone accounted for more than half of the nation's overall manufacturing revenues.

   The Mexican state, however, still depended on oil income to meet its budgetary obligations. Every year since the early 1990s, the federal government drew about one-third of its revenues from the government-owned oil company, PEMEX (Petroleos Méxicanos). Despite the sharp decline in Mexico's proven reserves, output remained higher than Venezuela's, and the government's fiscal reliance on oil production was having two deleterious effects. First, it deprived PEMEX of sufficient funds for exploration, expansion, and overall maintenance. Instead of an engine of economic growth, PEMEX was being exploited as a convenient source of revenue, an unsustainable situation. Second, overreliance on oil revenue allowed the government to continue to postpone a frontal assault on a problem common to all the Latin American states: the massive evasion of taxes (particularly on income) and the related one of inefficient tax collection methods. Like many other countries exceptionally rich in natural resources, Mexico was unable to resist the temptation to use oil revenues to expand the government budget rather than to seek revenues in other, politically risky ways, such as enforcing the tax code. In the meantime, Mexico's proven oil reserves continued to shrink.

Argentina

On a per-capita basis, Argentina's economy has produced the highest income of any Latin American country every year since 1969. In 2009, with a GDP per head of $9,880, Argentina ranked thirty-first in the world, between Trinidad & Tobago ($10,541) and Saudi Arabia ($9,827). Yet despite its capacity to outproduce all other Latin American economies year after year, Argentina's economy is perhaps best known for its exceptional volatility, even by Latin American standards. In 1988 and 1989, as the administration of President Raúl Alfonsín relied more and more on loans to pay the government's bills, interest rates skyrocketed and so did inflation, further increasing the government's budget deficit. Hyperinflation seized Argentina in early 1989. After prices had risen 9.6% in February, then 18% in March and 30% in the first week of April, they rose 70% in the last week of April before peaking at the end of May at a monthly rate of 150%, the worst in Argentine history. In late May, crowds of shoppers began walking out of supermarkets without paying, a tactic that quickly escalated to outright looting as mainly low-income consumers banded together to plunder stores, private homes and factories for food and other merchandise. Declaring a state of siege, the Alfonsín government suspended civil liberties for thirty days. The riots left sixteen people dead and thousands under arrest.

Again in 2001, with inflation spiraling upward and the public debt rising in the midst of a recession, panic-stricken Argentines withdrew more than $15 billion from the country's banks between March and July, provoking a credit crisis and the flight of another $5 billion. By December, Argentina was out of money and out of credit, and provincial governments were issuing their own quasi-currencies to pay their bills and their employees. The International Monetary Fund (IMF) withheld action on a major loan and on 7 December, Argentina announced it could no longer service its foreign debt. With unemployment approaching 20%, workers everywhere went on strike. Once again, hungry Argentines looted supermarkets. Riots in major cities killed 28 people and the government declared a state of siege. President Fernando de la Rúa resigned on 20 December 2001. His congressionally-appointed successor, Adolfo Rodríguez Saá, resigned ten days later amid continuing rioting, but not before declaring the end of the neoliberal economic development model, and defaulting on the public debt, to the cheers of the entire Congress. The survival of the state itself seemed to be in play when on 31 December the Congress selected Sen. Eduardo Duhalde to complete De la Rúa's presidential term. A Peronist in the populist tradition, Duhalde blamed the crisis on the free-market policies of the De la Rúa administration.

The economic crisis of 2001–2002 was the deepest and most intractable in Argentina's history; after three straight years (1999, 2000 and 2001) of negative growth, total output plunged another 12% in 2002. And yet, the crisis came on the heels of one of the country's greatest periods of growth and prosperity. Under a classic regime of neoliberal restructuring, the years 1991 to 1995 saw growth rates explode – to 11% and 10% in 1991 and 1992, followed by two more years of 4%+ growth. But by the time the gradual disintegration of the economy reached its most extreme levels in 2002 and 2003, some 52% of the Argentine population were living below the poverty line.

Was neoliberalism to blame for the collapse of 2001–2002? Many Argentines thought so. After all, Argentina had practically blazed the way toward statist economic management in Latin America, and had done so under the highly nationalistic, populist regime of President Juan Perón in the 1940s and early 1950s. Perón was so popular that his own name became the name of Argentina's particular brand of corporatist-populist ideology, "peronism," the labor-based movement that dominates Argentine politics to this day, despite attempts by four separate military governments (between 1955 and 1983) to purge it from the country's political system. The last *golpe de estado* occurred in 1976, when a peronist government had presided over yet another economic catastrophe compounded of the usual elements: escalating inflation and a balance of payments crisis.

The military junta of 1976–1983 liberalized the economy, lowered export taxes, removed price controls and reduced wages, then welcomed a flood of new foreign investment capital. Inflation subsided and exports soared. Yet the junta refused to cut state spending or the government's own immense holdings in the national economy, even as it demanded a larger share of the national budget for warmaking. The junta's mismanagement of its own halfhearted liberalization plan led to soaring deficits and inflation, and economic collapse coincided with the Argentine military's defeat in the Falklands War of 1982. After the armed forces withdrew from power in 1983, Argentines elected the mildly populist (but not peronist) government of Raúl Alfonsín, but its commitment to root-and-branch economic reform was no more profound than the junta's had been. As it implemented one short-term stabilization plan after another, the Alfonsín administration found itself presiding over an economy that was actually becoming even more dependent on state spending and direction. By 1983, the state had accumulated 707 enterprises that together accounted for about 85% of the government's budget deficit. The state-owned petroleum monopoly, YPF, became the only major oil company in the world to *lose* money. The state-owned airline and the state-owned telecommunications company were also run at a loss. In the mid-1980s, Argentina ranked 117th out of 126 countries in trade openness, according to the World Bank. The country's external debt of $46 billion equaled 80% of its GDP. Unable to resist the immense popular opposition to the privatization of state-owned enterprises and to inflation-reduction measures, Alfonsín made little headway in dismantling the peronist state.

The election of a peronist, Carlos Menem, to the presidency in the midst of the economic crisis in 1989 was widely expected to push the economy out of the crisis zone and into a catastrophic free-fall. Like a traditional peronist, Menem had campaigned as a populist, and his electoral support derived overwhelmingly from urban workers. Personable and even charismatic, Menem sharply criticized the reformism of the Alfonsín administration. He presented himself as Perón's legitimate successor during the campaign and like his mentor, Menem blamed Argentina's economic troubles on foreign interests.

But upon taking office in July 1989, Menem assembled an economic policy team of conservative business leaders, and relaunched the neoliberal revolution that the military had initiated in the 1970s and then extinguished. It would take a populist to liquidate the populist economic model and to invent a new ideology to justify the unthinkable: "populist liberalism." In its emphasis on the personal leadership of the great man or *caudillo* rather than institutions, and in calling for sudden, revolutionary change, the new ideology was consistent with traditional populism. As construed by the political scientist David E. Leaman, the "liberalism" of the new populism was represented by Menem's accent on efficiency over popular participation, and on liberty over equality. His administration applied a strict policy of spending reductions, trade liberalization, more effective collection of income taxes, deregulation, massive privatizations, and financial and currency reforms. International creditors agreed to write off one-third of the face value of the current debt and to restructure payment of the remainder over thirty years. The early to mid 1990s were years of prosperity, but as we have seen, the one thing that Menem's reforms could not transform was the economy's endemic instability. As inflation fell, so did the government's incentive to restrain spending in order to keep interest rates down. Government deficits widened, which led to more public debt at higher and higher interest rates. Unemployment remained unacceptably high.

The fundamental problem was less economic than institutional and cultural, which put it beyond the reach of Menem's technocrats. Corruption tended to mount in time of rapid growth and easy money, and the temptation to profit from the liquidation of government-owned enterprises was irresistible. Far from trying to curb institutionalized corruption, both Menem and his successor, Fernando de la Rua, appeared to be promoting it, and they did little to control the government spending that fed it. A second obstacle to economic stability correlated with corruption but had much wider implications, especially for Argentina's crucial need to attract foreign capital: the traditional indifference to the rule of law seemed to deepen during the Menem years as the president himself bent the constitution to move his policies forward. Finally, Argentina's electoral system tended to produce members of the national Congress who were politically obligated to provincial governors. In a country that divided key responsibilities among twenty-four provincial governments and the federal government, the system could easily inhibit cooperation between the federal executive and the Congress, as it did on sensitive fiscal questions. When external financial shocks disrupted the liberalization program in 1994 (the effects of the Mexican crisis) and 1999 (the effects of the Brazilian crisis), political support for it declined rapidly in the provinces and in Congress, where traditional populist ideas remained strong.

Just because of its hybrid character, "populist liberalism" preserved and protected a number of patrimonial enclaves across Argentina's institutional landscape. Despite the sweeping character of Menem's reforms, they were proposed and implemented by a peronist, in a way that not only failed to repudiate peronist populism, but sought justification in peronism itself – a clearly contradictory situation. As a result, at the first signs of difficulty from

1994 onward, it was not hard for anti-reformers to rally the traditional peronist base against liberalization. At the same time, the full effects of the reforms remained stunted by extensive corruption, widespread tax evasion, impunity and factionalism.

In 2003, aided by a brutal devaluation of the peso and the fiscal relief provided by the debt default, the Argentine economy began to recover. In that year's presidential election campaign, most of the candidates represented different factions of the peronist movement. The victory of Néstor Kirchner, who was backed by Duhalde, stood for continuity in peronist-style economic policy. Kirchner established himself as a more belligerent populist than Duhalde, as well as one devoted to peronism's highly personal and clientelistic style of leadership. After his government won a remarkable 75% write-down from creditors on the defaulted debt in 2005, fiscal surpluses gave Kirchner the leverage he needed to secure the cooperation of provincial governors and other groups. As inflation declined, exchange rates stabilized and commodity exports rose, the government began to spend more on social services while taking a traditionally nationalistic stance in dealings with foreign creditors and with economic rivals Chile and Brazil.

Kirchner shored up his peronist credentials by sealing ideological alliances with Latin America's premier left-wing populist, President Hugo Chávez of Venezuela, and with Bolivia's President Evo Morales. Like Perón, Kirchner promoted his wife Cristina Fernández as his political successor and as a result, she swept to victory with 45% of the vote in 2007, the first woman to be elected president of Argentina. Her husband continued to play a central governing role, above all in economic policy, from behind the scenes until his sudden death by a heart attack on 27 October 2010.

For many years, what might be called "the riddle of Argentina" has been posed in terms very much like those chosen in 2004 by the Argentine journalist Jorge Carlos Brinsek: "How can a country, ultraprivileged in natural resources, without racial or religious problems, with a scarce population in relation to its extensive territory, without famines or disasters like hurricanes or earthquakes, and with a sea abundant in riches of all kinds, remain stagnant for decades and instead of growing, go into reverse . . . ?" Referring to the research of that year's recipients of the Nobel Prize in economics (Finn E. Kydland and Edward C. Prescott), Brinsek proposed the following solution to the Argentine riddle: "Countries are like families. They have to work long and hard, live austerely, and not spend more than they earn, besides training and preparing themselves for the future. For many years our Argentina has functioned like a whimsical family gone astray." In a reference to the startling success of Chile, for so long considered inferior by Argentines, Brinsek concluded: "The mirror we have before us, piercing the Andean cordillera, is a faithful reflection of our capacity to ruin everything."

Brazil

If Argentines saw much to envy in Chile's stable growth record, to their north they watched as their traditional rival Brazil loomed ever larger on the regional and the global economic horizons. In 1960, the output of the Argentine and Brazilian economies was practically identical, and Mexico's was only slightly lower. Little by little, Brazil pulled away, vastly surpassing Argentina and Mexico in total production. Since 1969, Brazil has outproduced every other Latin American country in absolute terms, rising from an annual GDP (measured in 2000 U.S. dollars) of $105 billion to $856 billion in 2009, when it accounted for one-third of the entire region's output. Mexico, Brazil's closest rival every year, turned out $655 billion in goods and services in 2009. From 1960 to 2009, as Argentina's total output rose by a factor of 3.7 and Mexico's seven-fold, Brazil's expanded eight-fold. By 2009, Brazil boasted the world's ninth-largest economy (after India but before Canada) and Mexico the thirteenth (after Spain but before Australia).

Of course, when Brazil's annual income is controlled for its immense population – it accounts for one-third of all Latin America's people, as well as one-third the region's total income – its achievement shrinks. In per-capita terms in 2009, Brazil stood eighth among the Latin American countries, below Costa Rica and above the Dominican Republic. And Brazil continued to lead the region (and much of the world) in income inequality, a problem that will be taken up in Chapter 10.

Even though the benefits of Brazil's spectacular overall growth record have done little to improve the lot of the average Brazilian, its ascent was so impressive that in 2003 an international financial services company predicted that in forty years, Brazil, along with Russia, India and China, might together surpass the output of the six biggest economies at the time (the United States, Japan, the United Kingdom, Germany, France and Italy). The startling possibility that "the BRICs" could be in the take off phase of world domination, circulated so widely and rapidly in financial circles that it quickly lofted Brazil out of the relative obscurity of Latin America into a select global club of developing or "emerging" superstars.

A publicity windfall for Brazil, the circulation of the BRIC idea coincided with a rush of investment capital into Brazil and its three associates. Suddenly, there were BRIC forums, BRIC seminars, and BRIC research centers; thousands of articles and scores of books on the BRICs were published. The heads of state of the BRIC nations, now seeing themselves as the up-and-coming alternative to the G-8 (the "Group of 8" largest industrial economies, which Russia joined in 1997), began to meet annually in 2009 at a series of "BRIC summits" to advance their common interest in a multi-polar world free of protectionist trade policies and the domination of the U.S. dollar as a global currency. They also sought a stronger voice in world economic matters for themselves and other developing countries. But beyond those broad interests, a shared record of rapid growth, and some serious but quite diverse problems of governance, the four countries had little in common. Brazil had the most to gain from its celebrity economic status, and tried to leverage it in favor of its larger goal of becoming a world political heavyweight. In failed, however, in its bid for a permanent seat on the UN Security Council in 2011, as well as in its attempt in 2010 to mediate the conflict between Iran and the NATO countries over Iran's nuclear weapons program.

Brazil's rise to global economic stardom accelerated after 1990, the year of two major turning points. The first was the inauguration of President Fernando Collor de Mello, Brazil's first directly elected president since 1961. The second was President Collor's immediate announcement of a thoroughgoing economic reform that would gradually dismantle the system of state-directed capitalism under which Brazil had labored for more than three decades. When he took office, the public sector was producing half the country's output, and nineteen of Brazil's twenty largest corporations were state owned. Two-thirds of the country's credit came from state-owned banks. The external debt stood at $120 billion and rising; and the corrosive effects of an 80% monthly inflation had led to insistent demands for corrective action. Meanwhile, during the 1980s all four of the Asian "tiger" economies (Hong Kong, Taiwan, Singapore and South Korea) had surpassed Brazil's per-capita income. The timing of Collor's reform program coincided closely with that of President Menem in Argentina, and like Menem, Collor presented himself as a crusader whose powerful personality would save Brazil. Like the Argentines, Brazilians craved a miracle-worker.

Within two years of taking office, the Brazilian congress impeached Collor for acts of corruption extravagant even by Brazilian standards. He resigned on 29 December 1992 and was succeeded by his vice president, Itamar Franco. But Collor's reform package had already established the main policy lines that would be followed over the next two decades: trade liberalization, privatization, market deregulation and fiscal reform. Another "Brazilian miracle," like that of 1968–1973, was in the making, now framed by a political system of electoral democracy rather than military dictatorship, and a more conservative, market-oriented economic structure that depended far less on external debt than did the first "miracle." Franco toned up Collor's reform program at a critical moment with the appointment of Fernando Henrique Cardoso, an academic economist widely known for his advocacy of dependency theory, as head of the Finance Ministry in 1994. Cardoso's main assignment was to control inflation, a problem whose political dimensions typically overwhelmed the fairly straightforward economic solutions. The "stabilization" demanded by the International Monetary Fund shrank wages and credit, making it politically inexpedient. The centerpiece of Cardoso's anti-inflation strategy was an ingenious plan to introduce a new currency, the real, replacing the cruziero. It worked spectacularly well. In April 1994, inflation was rising 50% a month; by October, it was down to 2%. By then, Cardoso was campaigning for the presidency. He won the election on 3 October with a first-round absolute majority of 54% of the vote, an electoral record last surpassed in 1945. Brazilians had found their *real* savior, an exceptionally agile politician and strategist who had exchanged his academically inspired notions of state-directed development for belief in the superiority of market-oriented economic policies. As Cardoso went to work, further trimming government spending and pushing Brazil into the global marketplace, exports skyrocketed and the country's superstar status seemed assured. Cardoso assured his own status as a political superstar by becoming the first president to win two consecutive terms, with 53% of the vote in 1998.

When Cardoso's successor, Luiz Inácio Lula da Silva, was elected in 2002, he seemed unlikely to maintain Cardoso's policies. A former union organizer and Worker Party leader whose formal education ended in the fourth grade, da Silva nevertheless declared his respect for the market while increasing state spending on measures aimed at raising the living standards of the poorest Brazilians. Preserving the liberal framework he inherited from Cardoso, da Silva had the good luck to preside over the discovery of huge reserves of deep-sea oil and gas in 2007. The technological challenges of bringing the oil to the surface were immense, but so were the risks to the country's economic and political stability, as the experience of both Mexico and Venezuela attested. When he left office on 1 January 2011 after serving the constitutional limit of two terms, the popularity of "Lula" exceeded even that of Cardoso. He endorsed his own chief of staff, Dilma Rousseff, as the Worker Party candidate and Rousseff became Brazil's first woman president, pledging to continue the economic policies of her two predecessors.

Great strides had been made in restructuring and priming an economy geared for globalization. Owing to the efforts of the Cardoso and da Silva governments, Brazil had never been more thoroughly integrated into the world economy. The share of national income stemming from trade rose from 15–20% during the 1970s through the 1990s, to 25–30% in the first decade of the new century. Brazil benefitted substantially from the rise of the middle classes in China and India, whose demand for Brazilian food products and other commodities surged as personal income rose in those countries and elsewhere. Brazil responded by increasing production, and in 2005 it was the world's leading producer of chicken, coffee, beef, orange juice, sugar and tobacco, and the world's second-largest producer (after the United States) of soy and ethanol, a biofuel. Land and water are not scarce in Brazil, the fifth-largest country in the world and one of the few left with land – at least 15 million hectares – still available for agricultural exploitation. As the fourth-largest agricultural exporter in the world, Brazil had the potential to rise even higher as long as demand for food and fuel continued to expand.

From the 1990s onward, Brazil had profited from exceptionally high commodity prices – which invariably fall, sometimes precipitously and unexpectedly, destabilizing an entire economy. Diseases and weather conditions regularly dislocate agriculturally dependent economies. Brazil's badly underdeveloped transportation system depended heavily on trucking rather than more economical railways and waterways. Environmental sustainability was another concern. Finally, neither Cardoso nor da Silva – each of whose administrations were disrupted by major corruption scandals – had managed to surmount the massive political and cultural obstacles to the badly-needed reform of state institutions, whose legendary corruption and inefficiency were widely seen as impediments to sustained economic growth.

Conclusions

Reversing an economic development strategy that had pushed them into a decade of stagnant or negative growth and an intolerable debt burden in the 1980s, the Latin American countries recovered with moderate-to-high rates of economic growth. At the same time, they demilitarized and democratized their political systems. Altogether, it was an achievement impressive enough to establish the 1970s as the decade that marked the start of a new era in Latin American history. Nevertheless, not one country proved unable to shed its longtime status as "developing," in both a political and an economic sense. In the next chapter, we take a close look at three interrelated problems that rose to international prominence over the period, and that exemplified the "developing" dimension of the Latin American economies: the tremendous growth of the illegal drugs trade, the surge in migration across and out of Latin America, and the persistence of extreme poverty with high rates of economic inequality.

Note

1   World Bank, *Bolivia: Country Economic Memorandum; Policies to Improve Growth and Employment* (Washington, DC: 2005).

Reference

World Bank. *Bolivia: Country Economic Memorandum: Policies to Improve Growth and Employment.* Washington, DC: World Bank, 2005.

Chapter 10

Agonies of Underdevelopment

The Informal Sector: Drugs and Other Illicit Flows

Nowhere can people do business in complete freedom. Governments impose taxes, control prices and wages, and regulate the quality of products and the working conditions of employees. They also license or prohibit entirely the manufacture and sale of certain goods. It follows that smugglers, bootleggers, and other "unlicensed" manufacturers, processors and traders – as well as the people who work for them – do not pay taxes on their income. Their earnings can only be estimated by the statisticians who compute GDP. In the urban zones of Latin America in 2008, at least one-third and as much as one-half or even more of the workforce was employed in the so-called "informal economy," also known as the black market, or the shadow, parallel or underground economy. Most were engaged in the petty commerce of street-corner trade and services, from washing windshields at busy intersections to selling cold drinks, moving furniture, repairing appliances or working as freelance electricians, carpenters or plumbers.

But the informal sector also included multinational criminal organizations specializing in such illegal transactions as trafficking in human labor or in human organs for transplant, kidnapping for ransom, selling adoptable children, or making and selling illegal drugs. The transnational reach of such outlaw enterprises expanded enormously after the 1960s, their markets globalized by massive increases in international passenger travel, and in the volume of shipping, trade, electronic communications and migration. As access to new markets and financial resources increased, so did the growth potential of lawful and unlawful transactions alike. Government spending to detect and halt transnational crime, and to prosecute and punish the

Contemporary Latin America: 1970 to the Present, First Edition. Robert H. Holden and Rina Villars.
© 2013 Robert H. Holden and Rina Villars. Published 2013 by Blackwell Publishing Ltd.

perpetrators, multiplied. New bilateral and multilateral arrangements linked investigators and enforcers across borders and even gave rise to a new field of study, international crime and justice.

In the sheer scale of both their economic impact and their maleficence, the manufacture and sale of illegal drugs dwarfed all other "informal" and other openly criminal enterprises that have operated in Latin America since the 1970s. The flow of foreign currency into the major drug producing and re-export countries contributed substantially to economic growth. Estimates of the impact on Colombia's GDP in the 1980s and 1990s, for example, range from 1.5% to 3.8%. In Mexico, as much as 2.7% of GDP may have been attributable to the drug trade in 2005.[1] But drug-trafficking, and the criminal violence associated with it, have also destroyed thousands of lives; corrupted police, military, judicial and political institutions; diverted substantial government revenues to investigative and enforcement efforts; and occasionally threatened political stability. The negative effects clearly overwhelmed any conceivable gains in economic growth. They were most obvious in Bolivia, Colombia, Guatemala, Peru and Mexico but had become a major problem in other countries as well. Like any other commodity, the production of illegal drugs grew in response to rising demand, above all in the United States and Europe, the regions with the highest levels of disposable income. Three illegal drugs have dominated the world market over the last four decades.

The first is marijuana (*Cannabis sativa*). Between 121 and 191 million people smoked it at least once in 2008, making it the most widely consumed illicit substance. Although marijuana was increasingly being cultivated in the country of consumption, most of Mexico's crop – which is thought to have doubled over the five years ending in 2008 to about 22,000 metric tons – was exported to the United States. Because marijuana was produced and consumed practically everywhere, precise data on world supply and demand were harder to ascertain than for the other drugs.

The second are opiates, a class of drugs that includes opium, morphine and heroin, all made from latex extracted from the seedpods of the opium poppy (*Papaver somniferum*). Between 13 and 22 million people worldwide were consuming opiates illegally in 2010, mostly in the form of heroin, the most dangerous illegal drug and addiction to which is the most costly to treat. In 2008, the value of the worldwide heroin market alone was estimated at $55 billion a year, or 85% of the total market for opiates. Asia accounted for more than half the world's opiate users, followed by east and southeast Europe. Of the estimated 2 to 2.5 million heroin users in the Americas, slightly more than half were in the United States but close to 900,000 lived in South America. During the decade ending in 2010, Afghanistan accounted for around 90% of the world supply of opiates while Latin America – mainly Mexico and Colombia – contributed about 4%.

The third drug, cocaine, is an entirely Latin American product derived from the leaves of the coca plant (*Erythroxylum coca*), a bush that grows wild in Bolivia, Ecuador and Peru. No other illegal drug market came close to cocaine in value. In 2008, the world's 15–19 million users – distributed more or less as indicated in Map 10.1 – paid $88 billion for the product. Although North America remained the largest single market with some 6 million users, consumption in the United States and Canada began to decline after 2005 and rose in Africa, Asia and Europe.

A worldwide boom in legal cocaine production died out in the 1920s. Then, in the 1970s, Colombian traffickers reintroduced cocaine into the United States, building on their success in growing and exporting marijuana to the United States in the 1960s. As U.S. cocaine demand soared, so did the cultivation of coca leaf, peaking in 2000 at about 221,000 hectares, of which about three-quarters were in Colombia, one-fifth in Peru, and the rest (about 7%) in Bolivia.

Colombian entrepreneurs, taking advantage of the country's historical and structural conditions discussed in Chapter 7, and eager to supply the nascent U.S. market, began importing semi-processed cocaine paste from Peru and Bolivia in the early 1970s. They constructed clandestine laboratories to convert the paste into the fine white powder known as cocaine before exporting it by air to the United States. The next step in the gradual "colombianization" of the cocaine trade was the establishment of coca plantations in remote areas of eastern Colombia. As the criminal groups that controlled the production and distribution of cocaine diversified into opium in the 1990s, Colombia cemented its reputation as the world's preeminent source of illegal drugs. Wrecked by crime, violence and social disorder, Colombia did not begin to demonstrate a capacity to recover until 2002, with the election of President Alvaro Uribe – a development analyzed in Chapter 3.

As Colombia slowly reconquered its territory and society from the forces of drug-driven lawlessness, Mexico succumbed to them. The production of coca leaf and cocaine in Colombia peaked in the mid to late 1990s before declining dramatically toward the end of the first decade of the new century, the result of intensified leaf-eradication and enforcement efforts by the Colombia government, with heavy financial, technical and military aid from the U.S. government. But the "balloon effect" – the tendency of producers and traffickers to respond to enforcement pressures by shifting to another territory – can be seen in the corresponding surge in cocaine and opium production in Mexico. Exploiting that country's 2,000-mile long border with the United States; its vast, mountainous and sparsely settled northern region; and its traditional detachment from the rule of law, criminal organizations turned Mexico into the hemisphere's main cultivator of poppies and its principal heroin producer, as well as the conduit for 90% of the cocaine destined for the United States

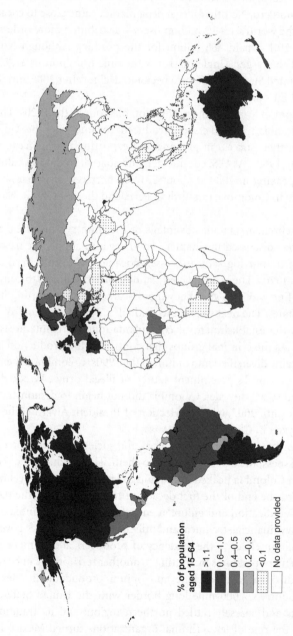

Map 10.1 Use of cocaine c. 2008, showing the percentage of the population who used cocaine at least once in the survey year. Based on United Nations, Office on Drugs and Crime, *World Drug Report 2010* (New York: United Nations, 2010), p.180 (see pp. 282–6 for exact years illustrated). Data from UNODC ARQ/DELTA; Government reports; US Departments of State and Health and Human Services; EMCDDA; DAINAP; CICAD; UNODC Rapid Assessment Surveys; Council of Europe; ESPAD.

% of population aged 15–64
>1.1
0.6–1.0
0.4–0.5
0.2–0.3
<0.1
No data provided

from its sources in the labs of Bolivia, Colombia and Peru. Chapter 7 analyzed the disastrous impact on Mexican society.

As enforcement efforts intensified in Mexico, more northbound cocaine passed through the "northern triangle" of Central America – Belize, El Salvador, Guatemala and Honduras. Their porous seacoasts and proximity to the Mexican border made these countries the natural complements of the Andean–Mexican connection, as well as feasible alternatives to the Mexico–U.S. route. So did traditions of political violence, corruption and impunity that equaled Mexico's. The drug-induced miseries heaped on the people of the isthmian nations soon surpassed those of Mexico, as the analysis of the violence in Chapter 7 indicated.

After four decades of explosive growth, two aspects of the drug trade stood out. The first was its extraordinary resilience and apparently inexhaustible capacity for innovation – from cultivation and processing to financing, warehousing, packaging, transportation, marketing and in the use of violence against enemy rivals and the agents of law enforcement. The second was the corresponding inability of state institutions in both the countries of supply (primarily Latin American) and those of demand (primarily the United States and Europe) to liquidate a business that they not only outlawed but repeatedly declared to be the target of all-out "war." Time and again, governments tasted defeat at the hands of loosely organized and barely visible legions of laborers, clerks, technicians, executives and the killers who protected them. In 2009, frustration over the failures of so many "wars on drugs" led a commission of seventeen prominent Latin Americans headed by three ex-presidents (César Gaviria of Colombia, Ernesto Zedillo of Mexico and Fernando Henrique Cardoso of Brazil) to call for the decriminalization of drug use both in Latin America and in their main markets, the United States and Europe. At the same time, however, "Public security forces should focus their efforts and resources on the fight against organized crime and arms trafficking associated with it, seeking to dismantle the great web of drug and arms trade and money laundering."[2]

Of all the solutions to ending the illegal drug trade, legalization seemed both the surest remedy, and the least likely to be adopted. Besides the still-strong cultural resistance to legalization everywhere, the commission's remedy also overlooked the underlying reason for the flourishing of the drug business and other criminal enterprises (from the routine subornation of public officials to kidnapping and murder for hire) in Colombia and many other Latin American countries: namely, a chronic indifference to the rule of law. The commission's proposal for the Latin American countries to adopt new "laws, institutions and regulations" to make legalization work failed to explain why such legislation would be respected in societies that have historically paid little heed to laws and regulations.

Migration

The lure of stupendous wealth for those at the top, and a decent living for those at the bottom, motivated and sustained the illegal drug trade. The appeal of a better life likewise drove another globalized commodity with both legal and illegal dimensions – the flow of human labor. Like the drug trade, the volume of Latin American migration has also expanded exponentially over the last four decades. And like the drug trade, the demand for Latin American workers was kept in motion largely by demand in the United States, and to a lesser extent in Europe. As the flow of migrants broadened and deepened, the effects in both the sending and receiving countries became both more obvious and controversial.

Viewed in historical perspective, however, the surge in migration from Latin America fades in comparison to the massive movement of peoples from Europe and Asia to the Americas during an earlier phase of globalization, that of the late nineteenth to the early twentieth centuries. Then, many countries in the New World encouraged the migration of workers and settlers from Europe and Asia to toil on plantations and in factories and mines, to build railroads, and to settle the vast interiors of Argentina, Brazil, Mexico and the United States. But after two hideously destructive world wars, Europe (the main source of immigrants to Latin America) embarked on an era of unprecedented political peace and economic growth in the 1950s. Now, Europeans tended to stay home. Immigrants from outside Latin America declined from 3.9 million in 1970 to 1.9 million in 2000. At the same time, prosperity in Europe encouraged many European migrants to return to the Old World.

From a region that for nearly five centuries had primarily received immigrants, Latin America changed to one that produced emigrants, thus joining in a global movement of peoples from the less developed regions to the more developed ones, or from south to north, as Figure 10.1 shows. Migration to the "developed regions" of Australia/New Zealand, Europe, Japan and North America rose by a factor of 4.6, from an average of 646,000 persons a year in the 1960s to an average of 3 million a year during the first decade of the twenty-first century. By 2005, two-thirds of all the world's migrants (i.e., 120 million persons out of a total of 190 million) were concentrated in the developed regions, in contrast to 42% in 1960. Over the same period, the three major developing regions (Africa, Asia and Latin America) sent more people abroad than they received, especially from the 1980s onward. Latin America's net annual average of 67,000 emigrants a year in the 1960s rose to 1,099,000 a year in the first decade of the new century, only slightly less than Asia's 1,286,000 but considerably more than Africa's 521,000. Given the extremely low fertility rates of the developed regions, and the resulting decline in their working-age

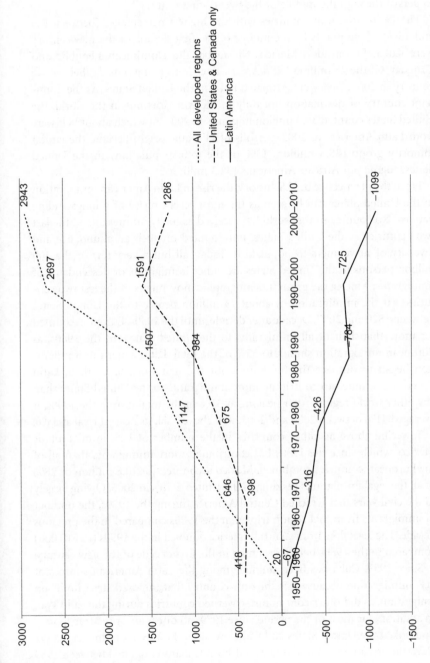

Figure 10.1 Average annual net number of migrants (in thousands) by decade. Based on data from United Nations, Department of Economic and Social Affairs, Population Division. *World Population Prospects: The 2008 Revision.* Vol. 1. 2 vols. (New York: United Nations, 2009).

Note: The net number of migrants is the number of immigrants minus the number of emigrants.

populations, the south-to-north pattern of international migration was likely to persist through the middle of the twenty-first century.

The Latin American countries with the highest percentages (between 8% and 15%) of emigrants by the middle of the first decade of the new century were Cuba, El Salvador, Mexico, Nicaragua, the Dominican Republic and Uruguay. Of the 25 million Latin American citizens living outside their native country in 2005, 74% were estimated to be in the United States. As the dominant country of destination not only in the Americas but in the world, the United States counted 38.3 million migrants in 2005, of which about half were from Latin America. In 2002, persons of Hispanic origin became the largest minority group (38.8 million, 13% of the total population) in the United States, edging out African-Americans (38.3 million).

From the perspective of U.S. history, the rise in Latin American immigration to the United States can be seen as the most recent phase of a longstanding pattern. No country in the world has received as many immigrants in the last two centuries as the United States, nor counted on such an abundance and diversity of newcomers to populate it. Today, all but a very few of the 300 million persons in the United States are either immigrants or descendants of immigrants. Among the greatest demographic movements of the last two centuries was the immigration of about 73 million people to the United States between 1820 and 2007. Decade after decade, until the 1950s, Europe accounted for more than half of all immigrants to the United States. In the 1960s, as European immigration shrank to 35% of the total, Latin American immigration began to outpace that of Europe for the first time. Since then, Latin America continued to contribute more immigrants to the United States than any other world region. After peaking at 51% of the total during the 1990s, it averaged 41% between 2000 and 2007, well above Asia, its nearest rival at 33%.

Towering above all other countries in the number of U.S. immigrants is Mexico, which since the 1980s has contributed more immigrants than all of the European countries combined. Mexico accounted for 10.8 million or 28% of all the legal immigrants residing in the United States in 2005. Owing largely to the civil wars that wracked Central America during the 1980s, the number of immigrants from that region tripled in the 1980s compared to the previous decade. The legal flow from Central America doubled in the 1990s (to 610,000) compared to the 1980s before declining in the first decade of the new century.

Since 1959, Cuba has been unique among the Latin American sources of U.S. immigration because it is the only country that imposed strict limits on emigration, as did other communist-governed countries during the Cold War. In addition, for most of the period since 1959, no direct air or sea transportation linked the United States and Cuba owing to the U.S. economic embargo. Nevertheless, about 1.4 million natural-born Cubans emigrated between 1959 and 2004, representing 12 to 15% of the island's population and all but a very few headed for the United States. They sought political, economic and personal freedoms; they rejected the ruling communist ideology; and, especially after the 1980s, they wanted to escape the increasing material deprivation of life on the island. So intense was the desire to leave that many abandoned all their property and risked death by sailing in open boats on the high seas.

When in April 1980 the Cuban government announced that U.S. residents would be allowed to pick up any Cubans who wanted to leave from the port of Mariel, over the next six months nearly 125,000 Cubans flocked to Mariel to board vessels sent by exiles living in Florida. In the late 1980s, increasingly desperate Cubans began building their own rafts and tried to leave the island secretly, navigating the 90 miles of open sea that separated Cuba and Florida. Between 1985 and 1992, 5,791 Cubans reached U.S. shores, some after they were rescued at sea. As economic conditions worsened in Cuba, the numbers rose until in August 1994, the Cuban government again announced it would let anyone leave who wished to do so. More than 34,000 Cubans set sail over that summer alone, usually on precarious home-made rafts, some in nothing more than tire inner-tubes lashed together. Many died at sea. By 2006, there were 1.5 million Cubans in the United States and more than two-thirds of them lived in Florida.

In addition to the aliens admitted as lawful permanent residents, the United States also attracted a rising number of undocumented or unauthorized aliens who lived there illegally. In 2007, they were estimated at about 11.8 million (compared to the 2.5 million estimated in 1990) – about twelve times the number of persons granted permanent-resident status in 2007. Most entered the United States from Mexico, undetected by U.S. authorities; another one-fourth to one-third of the undocumented population entered legally, but remained beyond the term of their visa. Most of the unauthorized population entered with a low level of formal education, crossing the border primarily to find work and typically taking jobs that native-born Americans spurned.

About 60% of the unauthorized immigrants in 2007 were Mexicans. The next largest group came from El Salvador, Guatemala and Honduras, which together accounted for about 11% of the unauthorized population. They too crossed the U.S.–Mexican border. As a result, the political debate in the United States over illegal immigration has largely been about Mexican workers and the security of the U.S. –Mexican border. While some U.S. citizens considered the rise in undocumented immigration an intolerable defiance of U.S. sovereignty, and a drain on government-funded health, education and welfare programs that served the immigrants, others defended the rights of illegal immigrants to public services and supported legislation aimed at regularizing their status.

At the same time, more Latin American emigrants were choosing countries other than the United States. By 2005, about 3 million Latin Americans were living outside the region, in countries other than the United States. Spain was the preferred non-U.S. destination. From 1991 to 2001 the number of Latin Americans residing in Spain quadrupled, from 210,000 to 840,000. By 2004, Spain counted 1.2 million residents born in Latin America. The most numerous were Ecuadorans (218,351) followed by Colombians (174,405) and Argentines (103,831). In part, the surge in emigration to Spain was the result of legislation encouraging the return of descendants of Spaniards who had immigrated to Latin America between the late nineteenth century and the mid-twentieth century. Nearly a third of the Latin American emigrants became naturalized Spanish citizens. At the same time, a rising number of Latin Americans – estimated in 2004 at half of all those living in Spain – entered illegally. Women accounted for most Latin American immigrants, a reflection of rising demand for labor in traditionally feminine jobs like domestic service and elder care.

During the last third of the twentieth century, international migration *within* Latin America also expanded. The 1.2 million Latin American immigrants found within the region in 1970 rose to 2 million within a decade, and by 2000 stood at 3 million. Typically, the "pull" factor was socio-economic, in the form of greater opportunities, often complemented by the "push" of political violence and repression, civil war and economic disruption in the countries of origin. Throughout the period, the favored destinations for migrants within Latin America were Argentina, Costa Rica and Venezuela – the only countries in the region in which the number of immigrants still exceeded that of emigrants. The Argentine agricultural, manufacturing, construction and service sectors drew Bolivians, Chileans, Paraguayans and Uruguayans. Venezuela's oil boom mainly attracted Colombians and political refugees from Argentina, Brazil, Chile and Uruguay during the years of military rule in those countries. Costa Rica's agricultural and service sectors traditionally attracted Nicaraguans. With the restoration of democracy in the 1990s, and a record of stable economic growth, Chile began to attract more immigrants than at any time in its recent history. Since the 1990s, violence-torn Colombia has exceeded all other countries in Latin America in the share of migrants within the region. Of the 700,000 Colombians living elsewhere in Latin America, 90% had settled in Venezuela by the early 2000s.

While emigration offered migrants and their families back home opportunities to improve their standard of living, they faced enormous risks, particularly those trying to cross international borders without permission of the authorities in the destination country. As the flow of migrants rose, so did two kinds of crime: the smuggling of migrants, officially defined as obtaining illegal entry for migrants in return for a fee; and trafficking in migrants, meaning recruiting or transporting migrants by force or fraud in order to enslave them or submit them to some other form of forced labor. Despite the scarcity of estimates of the number and type of victims, since the 1990s governments and international organizations adopted legislation to outlaw human trafficking and devoted more resources to investigating and denouncing it. In its 2009 *Global Report on Trafficking in Persons,* the UN noted: "One of the key unanswered questions remains: Just how big is the human trafficking problem globally? Without a sense of the magnitude of the problem, it is impossible to prioritize human trafficking as an issue relative to other local or transnational threats, and it is difficult to assess whether any particular intervention is having effect." In its tenth annual *Trafficking in Persons Report,* issued in 2010, the U.S. State Department estimated the number of adults and children held in forced labor, bonded labor and forced prostitution around the world at 12.3 million, and the total of successful prosecutions at just 4,166. Mexico, according to the report, was "a large source, transit, and destination country for men, women, and children subjected to trafficking in persons, specifically forced prostitution and forced labor." The majority of the victims were from El Salvador, Guatemala and Honduras. The report identified Brazil as another major source of human trafficking, estimating that more than 25,000 Brazilian men were enslaved on cattle ranches, in logging and mining camps, sugar plantations and other large agricultural enterprises. Women and girls were forced into prostitution within the country and abroad, and child sex tourism was a "serious problem," particularly in northeast Brazil. Forced prostitution and child sex tourism were also serious problems in Costa Rica, where forced labor was also prevalent in the agricultural, fishing, construction and domestic services sectors of the economy.

As the worldwide scale of south-to-north migration increased, so did the flow of remittances, the share of earnings that migrant workers send home to their families. In 2006 alone, 150 million migrants sent more than $300 billion to their families in developing countries, typically in small amounts of $100 to $300 at a time. The impact on household consumption, savings and investment was such that remittances had become "the world's largest poverty alleviation program," in the words of the Rome-based International Fund for Agricultural Development. The $1.1 billion received in Latin America in 1980 had risen to $68 billion in 2006, equaling 3% of the region's GDP and 13% of exports. About $45 billion originated in the United States. Mexico took in more than any other country except for India – $24 billion, the same amount received in all of South America. After Mexico, the major recipients were (in order) Brazil, Colombia, Guatemala and El Salvador.

In some small-economy countries, remittances accounted for a significant share of GDP – as high as 24% in Haiti, 14% in El Salvador, and 10% in the Dominican Republic, Nicaragua and Honduras in 2004. Remittances in almost all such economies typically amounted to more than three times the amount of foreign direct investment. However, much remains unknown about the amount, source, destination and impact of remittances. And while some economists believed that their impact on poverty-alleviation was substantial, others found little evidence for that conclusion. It seemed likely that the impact was greatest at the level of the household, for the effect on the population as a whole was less obvious. Equally uncertain were the migrant's motivations in remitting part of her or his income to the family back home – whether to invest in a small business or to provide for basic consumer needs.

Poverty and Inequality

From 1970 to 2000, the proportion of poor people in the world fell spectacularly. While 20% of the world's population was classified as poor in 1970, three decades later only 7% were poor. At the same time, the world average GDP per capita rose just as spectacularly – by 71%, from about $4,200 to about $7,200.

What accounts for the dramatic decline in world poverty rates? Regional breakdowns showed that poverty reduction rates corresponded to rises in GDP per capita. The regions whose economies grew the most also reported the biggest reductions in the number of poor people. In Africa, where per-capita growth rates were flat or negative for thirty years, poverty increased dramatically. The Latin American poverty rate declined sharply from about 10% of the population in 1970 to around 3% in 1980, reflecting the big growth gains of the 1970s, but made little progress after that, when growth rates began to plummet. Numerous studies have shown that as long as national income rises faster than the population, average incomes even among the poorest sectors of the population usually increase.[3]

Of course, growth alone can never guarantee a more equitable distribution of the benefits of growth, for income inequality can increase even as per-capita GPD rises. Looking back over the period 1990 to 2010, the administrator of the United Nations Development Program pointed out that some countries with only modest growth records nevertheless managed to make big improvements in health and education, while some big-growth countries failed to translate that growth into proportionately better living standards for their people. "Improvements are never automatic," said the administrator, Helen Clark. "They require political will, courageous leadership and the continuing commitment of the international community."[4]

In other words, improvements in human welfare depended on factors other than income alone. While increases in GDP per capita seemed to be a necessary *condition* for the reduction of poverty and improvement in the quality of life, they may not be enough to improve the quality of life of the poor. But how can quality of life be measured? One way is to compare, from year to year and from country to country, certain kinds of socio-economic data that can indicate trends in the ways that changes in GDP per capita likely affect the poor.

The large-scale collection and analysis of such "indicators" by the United Nations Development Program (UNDP) led to the formulation, in 1990, of the UNDP's Human Development Index (HDI), now the standard measure of overall quality of life.

The HDI gauges development by isolating three basic dimensions of quality of life – health, education and income. While the exact indicators it uses to assess change in these areas, and the weights assigned to them, varied slightly over the years, by 2010, the UNDP settled on four: life expectancy at birth, mean years of schooling, expected years of schooling and gross national income (GNI) per capita. The latter, a slightly broader measure of income than GDP, takes into account not just the income of a country's residents but also the amount of income that flows into a country from abroad, including, for example, remittances sent to family members by emigrants working abroad.

How does Latin America compare to the developing countries of other world regions? Over the last few decades, when comparing the national averages of the standard HDI indicators, the Latin American countries consistently outperformed, by wide margins, all other developing regions except for those of Europe (mainly eastern) and Central Asia. Narrowing our focus to the country level, however, we see a diverse range of development outcomes. At the top of the list, Chile, Argentina and Uruguay ranked 45th, 46th and 52nd in worldwide terms in 2010, making them comparable in economic development terms to the eastern European countries of Lithuania (44), Latvia (48) and Romania (50). Latin America's least developed countries – Guatemala (116), Nicaragua (115) and Honduras (106) – ranked with some of the better-off African countries, such as Cape Verde (118), Morocco (114) and South Africa (110). It is worth emphasizing that the HDI is only an *aggregate* measure of achievement for the population as a whole. As such, it indicates the probable direction of distribution, in the sense that a higher HDI suggests a higher standard of living for the country as a whole – not just for the poor but also for the middle class and the rich. If more people are going to school and if more are receiving better healthcare, then it is likely that the poor are among them.

But the HDI discloses very little about inequalities in the way the dimensions of development are distributed across the whole population. Within the same country, one region may be much better off then another; and some groups do better than others in one or more of the selected development dimensions. In two countries with identical HDIs, one may have managed to distribute the benefits of growth to almost everyone in a fairly even way, while in another, the benefits remain skewed in favor one or another group or area.

One way to capture the level of inequality of income is to estimate the proportion of households receiving different amounts of income. Conventionally, economists place all households into five groups – the poorest 20%, the next-poorest 20%, and so on, to the richest 20%. The share of total national income received by each of the five groups is then estimated and compared. In a society of perfect equality, each of the five levels would receive one-fifth of national income. In the United States, the richest 20% receive about half of all income; the second richest group receives about one-fourth, and the lowest quintile receives about 3.5%. Often, these distributions can be reduced to a single number called a Gini index (after the statistician Corrado Gini), such that an index of 0 would be perfect equality and 100 would be perfect inequality. The Gini index is the most-cited formulation for comparing degrees of inequality within countries and among countries.

Despite its relatively high world HDI standings, Latin America has for decades reported the highest levels of income inequality in the world. Uruguay, the Latin American country with the least income inequality, is still substantially more unequal than any of the developed countries. From 1970 to 2000, Latin America's average Gini index was 50.5, compared to Asia's 40.6 and the developed countries' 33. From the 1970s to 2000, Latin American inequality rose from an average of 48.4 to an average 50.5, even as its HDI score improved significantly during the same period. In the United States in the late 1990s, the richest 10% of households received only 31% of total income. That was a more equal distribution than that of the most equal Latin American countries – Uruguay and Costa Rica, in both of which the top 10% took 35% of national income. In Brazil and Guatemala, the richest 10% received 47% of all income. Although Brazil was one of the few countries to record a slight decline in inequality from the early 1990s to the early 2000s, it continued to maintain its status as the country with the highest inequality in Latin America.

Income inequalities on this scale imply massive disparities in access to such basic services as potable water, health, education, electricity and telephone service. That, in turn, implies still wider inequities in the distribution of power and influence, and in the responsiveness of the police and justice systems. Here is just where economic development and the democratization trend discussed in Chapter 5 can be seen as interactive rather than independent variables. Gross economic disparities can retard democratic consolidation because they inhibit participation in the political process by those who lack basic human resources that others may possess in abundance. At the same time, political change in the shape of more responsive institutions and fairer access to more government services can in turn abate economic inequalities. Among the most highly visible dimensions of inequality are those associated with race and ethnicity. In Latin America, disproportionate numbers of indigenous peoples and those of African descent, both long subject to discriminatory treatment, occupy the poorest sectors of the population.

Of course, inequalities of wealth and income can never be made to disappear. Some may even be necessary to stimulate people to work, save and invest. But extreme levels of inequality not only translate into higher poverty rates. They also constrain the beneficial effects of economic growth, slowing down the rate of national development. Think, for example, of the missed opportunities for individual and communal advancement when access to credit is so constricted as to deter profitable investments, or of children with great natural talents who cannot even learn to read and write because their poverty forces them to beg or engage in petty commerce to survive. Deep inequalities of opportunity waste resources and hold back per-capita growth, and thus restrain economic development. The crime and social violence that commonly accompany high levels of inequality further diminish the life chances of the poorest and waste human assets.

At certain extremes of poverty and inequality, it seems clear to most of us that an intrinsic injustice in the way opportunities have been distributed needs to be corrected. "Brazil is not an underdeveloped country anymore," remarked Fernando Henrique Cardoso in his successful campaign for the presidency of Brazil in 1994. "It is an unjust country."[5] Of course, Brazil is both, and there can be little doubt that its exceptionally unjust social structure has limited its overall development. Perhaps no one intended such an outcome, but the social structures that made such injustice possible did not just happen. They were built by individuals over the course of centuries. Recall the dependence of the Europeans who settled the Americas on the forced labor of indigenous peoples and Africans for more than three centuries. In the case of the Iberian monarchies, the ownership of land and other kinds of property, including access to natural resources, was not considered an individual prerogative but rather a privilege extended by the monarchs to the few, as a reward for their service. From the beginning, political institutions were designed to protect the power of the most privileged families and individuals over the majority of the population. The strength of these barriers to equality varied from place to place. They were weakest in places that lacked high-value mineral or agricultural resources and an easily subjugated population of nonwhites to extract and process them. But what still stands out is the extraordinary persistence of the institutions and the habits of mind first formed centuries ago. Figure 10.2 illustrates that persistence across Latin America. But it also reveals important national differences, owing to the distinct histories of the relatively better-off countries on the left side of the Latin American chart and the poorer ones – associated historically with large populations of nonwhites, forced labor and concentrated resources – on the right.

The search for a quick solution to the injustices associated with extreme poverty and inequality led to the rise of the Marxist-oriented insurgencies discussed in Chapter 3. Seeking a revolution that would both remake the state and turn society itself upside down, by expropriating the wealth of the rich and redistributing it to the poor, many Latin Americans placed their hopes in

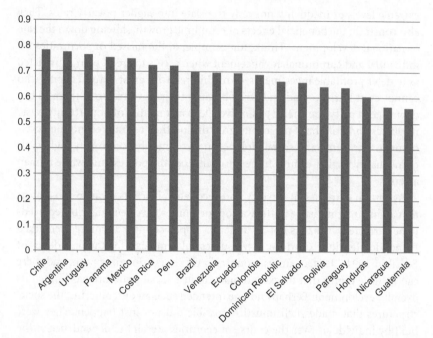

Figure 10.2 HDI of Latin American countries, 2010. Based on data from United Nations Development Program, *Human Development Reports*, http://hdr.undp.org/en/statistics/data.

socialism during the 1960s, 1970s and 1980s. Nothing provided them with more encouragement and inspiration than the example of Cuba, the only Latin American country to fully adopt the socialist model of economic development. We discussed the politics of the Cuban revolution in Chapter 3. We now evaluate the revolution as a model of economic development.

The Cuban Model

Cuba alone, beginning in 1961, took a third path, rejecting both statist capitalism and liberal capitalism. In adopting a fully planned, government-owned and -controlled economy ("socialism"), Cuba made all enterprises state property and nearly all Cubans employees of the state, which also claimed the exclusive right to educate them, under conditions dictated by the Communist Party, the only legal political party.

Between 1959, the year that Fidel Castro's 26th of July Movement took power, and 1968, the regime seized 100% of all private property in the industrial, construction, retail trade, wholesale trade, foreign trade, banking and education sectors of the economy. By 1988, the agricultural sector was 97% state-owned or managed, and 99% of the transportation sector had fallen under state ownership. The Cubans who publicly questioned socialism or proposed an alternative economic development strategy were jailed or fled into exile. "The duty of every revolutionary," Castro declared in 1962, "is to make the revolution."[6] In effect, loyalty to the revolution and to the fatherland were treated as equivalents, and already in 1961 the official slogan "Socialismo o muerte" (socialism or death) had laid out the two basic options available to Cubans under the revolutionary regime.

Until the 1980s, most Cuban probably benefited materially under socialism. Cuba consistently reported impressive gains in education and health, as well as notable successes in reducing unemployment and redistributing income. These achievements depended in large part on aid supplied by the Soviet Union, which totaled about $65 billion between 1960 and 1990, as well as additional assistance from other countries in the socialist bloc. With a population of just 10 million, $65 billion can go a long way, even over three decades. On a per-capita basis, Cuba became the world's most subsidized economy, and its real economic growth relative to the rest of Latin America deteriorated markedly. In 1950, it ranked seventh in per-capita GDP but by 2001, it was ahead of only Nicaragua and Haiti. In the same period, while Latin America's average per-capita GDP increased 132%, Cuba's rose 21%. In fact, annual average GDP per capita growth from 1950 to 1958 (the year before Castro seized power) was four times that of the period after the revolution took power. Considering the level of external subsidies and the mutual isolation of the U.S. and Cuban economies, it seems doubtful that the U.S. economic embargo accounted significantly for Cuba's failure to thrive. Only during the period of Cuba's highest dependence on Soviet bloc subsidies, from 1971 to 1989, did it outpace Latin America's GDP per-capita growth rate, averaging 2.2% per year, compared to Latin America's 1.3%, a time that embraced the region's "lost decade" of stagnation and negative growth.[7]

Besides Cuba's growing dependence on external subsidies, it also became increasingly tied to the economies of the Soviet bloc countries as a member of the Council for Mutual Economic Assistance (CMEA). From the mid 1970s to 1989, the share of the island's commerce accounted for by the CMEA countries rose from 52% to more than 85%. Not surprisingly, therefore, the collapse of socialism in the bloc countries in the late 1980s, the dissolution of the Soviet Union itself in 1991 and the resulting liquidation of the CMEA shattered the Cuban economy. The markets for Cuban exports practically disappeared. In 1993, the value of trade fell to one-fourth that of 1989, and Cuba remained deeply in debt to Russia and other countries. Almost all the revolution's social gains suffered serious setbacks, while poverty and inequality rose. In response, the government took the unprecedented steps of encouraging tourism and foreign investment, bitter medicine for a proudly nationalistic and collectivistic regime that had gone out of its way to condemn these "imperialistic" mainstays of the pre-revolutionary era. Still worse for socialism was a series of modest, market-oriented reforms that the regime was practically forced to implement starting in 1993 if it was to survive at all. The changes, including the right to very limited self-employment, seeded a moderate recovery but the overall trend diverged unmistakably from the old dream of collectivistic prosperity.

From 1991 to 2000, Cuba's annual average GDP growth declined to –1.4%, the lowest in Latin America. Even after 2000, rates of investment, production and export continued to languish well below those of the late 1980s. First China, then Venezuela – oil rich and governed by Hugo Chávez – stepped into the breach as trade partners and suppliers of credits and development projects. Nevertheless, by 2005, the main sources of Cuba's foreign exchange resembled those of many another developing economy: tourism and money remitted by Cubans abroad. Meanwhile, food rationing – a fixture of the revolution since its inception – not only persisted but the amount of rationed food had to be cut owing to a decline in food production, which in turn forced Cuban families to buy more food at rising prices in government-controlled markets.

In response to the steady deterioration of the economy, President Raúl Castro announced on 1 August 2010 a series of adjustments to what he called the "Cuban economic model." The most dramatic was the decision to reduce the number of state employees from 5.5 million (85% of all the country's workers) to about 5 million by April 2011. Cutting the "considerably bloated" state payroll, Castro added, was an important step toward "the necessity of erasing forever the notion that Cuba is the only country in the world where one can live without working." Redundant workers were to be retrained and encouraged to start their own businesses, in effect accelerating the capitalistic reforms of the early 1990s and emulating communist-governed China's move toward free enterprise. In September, Cuba authorized a major expansion of the private sector by identifying 178 occupations in which Cubans would now be allowed to work independently of the state; in the case of 83 of them, they could even hire non-family employees. Before the announcement, the private sector of the economy had consisted of about 600,000 workers, most of whom were family farmers, plus another 140,000 self-employed individuals working in approved occupations.

The reforms of 2010 conformed to a policy cycle that, according to U.S. economist Carmelo Mesa-Lago, had characterized the regime ever since it introduced socialism in 1961. Idealistic, anti-market phases alternated with pragmatic, pro-market policies adopted to correct the disruptions caused when the more idealistic modes of socialist economic policy failed to achieve their goals. To head off popular discontent, save the system and retain their hold on power, the leaders of the regime adopted the market-oriented policies in order to raise living standards and fortify the economy sufficiently to prepare it for yet another cycle of collectivist, idealistic policies designed to correct the new inequalities introduced during the pragmatic cycle.[8]

A few weeks after Raúl's speech, his brother Fidel (who had ceded power to Raúl when he fell ill in 2006) seemed to endorse Raúl's reforms by suggesting that the revolution, or at least the way it had been administered, was a colossal failure. Asked by a sympathetic journalist whether he thought the Cuban model of revolutionary change still merited emulation elsewhere in the developing world, the 84-year-old Fidel replied to his astonished guest: "The Cuban model doesn't even work for us anymore."[9] The comment might well have earned an ordinary Cuban a jail sentence. Nothing daunted, a few months later Fidel told a select group of a university students: "A conclusion that I have drawn after many years is that among the many errors that we have all committed, the most important was to have believed that anyone understood socialism, or that anyone knew how to build it."[10]

Much like Fidel's evolving views of socialism, the reforms of 2010 represented the most radical reversal of economic collectivization since 1961. The key question was whether they portended the onset, in a few years' time, of yet another cyclical correction of the "errors" of pragmatism, or the beginning of the end of socialism. In the short term, economic growth would depend on the ability of the nascent private sector to absorb hundreds of thousands of sacked government workers. Yet by heaping taxes and regulations on them and their employers, the government risked stunting the growth of the entrepreneurial sector and its capacity to employ enough Cubans to lead the economic takeoff that even the communist leadership of the island now acknowledged eluded them for decades.

Conclusions

In recent decades, Latin America's leaders struggled to find a functional and politically durable balance between two obvious goods: On the one hand, ensuring sufficient freedom for groups and individuals to invest, produce and consume according to their own needs and interests; on the other, discharging the state's responsibility to oversee and regulate the national economy in the interests of the common good, while attending to the welfare of the neediest. We have seen that the high road to economic ruin nearly always passed through the territory of the state. Too much intervention inhibited individual initiative and often wound up protecting the extravagant privileges of a parasitical elite that prospered by buying and selling government-sponsored favors. External pressures and inherited structures impeded growth and development, but the equally rich legacies of patrimonialism and populist-oriented dirigisme were no less unfriendly to both democratic consolidation and economic prosperity.

Notes

1 Sir Keith Morris, "Economy," in "Colombia," *South America, Central America and the Caribbean 2009* (London: Routledge, 2009), 291–7, here 294; United States, Government Accountability Office, *Drug Control: U.S. Assistance Has Helped Mexican Counternarcotics Efforts, but Tons of Illicit Drugs Continue to Flow into the United States* (Washington, DC, 2007), GAO–07–1018, n. 18, p. 13.
2 Latin American Commission on Drugs and Democracy, *Drugs and Democracy: Toward a Paradigm Shift*, www.drogasedemocracia.org/Arquivos/livro_espanhol_04.pdf, p. 40.
3 Dwight H. Perkins, Steven C. Radelet and David L. Lindauer, *Economics of Development*, 6th edn. (New York: W.W. Norton, 2006), 221.
4 United Nations Development Programme, *Human Development Report 2010. The Real Wealth of Nations: Pathways to Human Development* (New York: United Nations Development Programme, 2010), iv.
5 Anthony Pereira, "Brazil's Agrarian Reform: Democratic Innovation or Oligarchic Exclusion Redux?" *Latin American Politics and Society* 45, no. 2 (2003): 41–65, here 48.
6 Fidel Castro, "The Second Declaration of Havana," in Robert H. Holden and Eric Zolov, *Latin America and the United States: A Documentary History* (New York: Oxford University Press, 2011), 233–6, here 236.
7 Because it is not a market-based economy, estimates of Cuba's real output can vary considerably; the source for these data is Frank W. Thompson, "Cuban Economic Performance in Retrospect," *Review of Radical Political Economics*, no. 37 2005).
8 Carmelo Mesa-Lago, "Economic and Ideological Cycles in Cuba: Policy and Performance, 1959–2002," in *The Cuban Economy*, ed. Archibald R. M. Ritter (Pittsburgh: University of Pittsburgh Press, 2004), 25–42.
9 Jeffrey Goldberg, "Fidel: 'Cuban Model Doesn't Even Work for Us Anymore,'" *The Atlantic* (2010), www.theatlantic.com/international/archive/2010/09/fidel-cuban-model-doesnt-even-work-for-us-anymore/62602.
10 Fidel Castro, "Mensaje de Fidel a los Estudiantes," 17 November 2010, *Círculo de Periodistas Cubanos contra el Terrorismo*, www.cubadebate.cu/fidel-castro-ruz/2010/11/17/mensaje-de-fidel-a-los-estudiantes.

References

Castro, Fidel. "Mensaje de Fidel a los Estudiantes." *Círculo de Periodistas Cubanos contra el Terrorismo*. www.cubadebate.cu/fidel-castro-ruz/2010/11/17/mensaje-de-fidel-a-los-estudiantes.

Castro, Fidel. "The Second Declaration of Havana." In Robert H. Holden and Eric Zolov. *Latin America and the United States: A Documentary History.* 233–6. New York: Oxford University Press, 2011.

Goldberg, Jeffrey. "Fidel: 'Cuban Model Doesn't Even Work for Us Anymore,'" *The Atlantic* (2010). www.theatlantic.com/international/archive/2010/09/fidel-cuban-model-doesnt-even-work-for-us-anymore/62602.

Latin American Commission on Drugs and Democracy, *Drugs and Democracy: Toward a Paradigm Shift,* 2009, www.drogasedemocracia.org/Arquivos/livro_espanhol_04.pdf.

Mesa-Lago, Carmelo. "Economic and Ideological Cycles in Cuba: Policy and Performance, 1959–2002." In *The Cuban Economy,* ed. Archibald R. M. Ritter. 25–42. Pittsburgh: University of Pittsburgh Press, 2004.

Morris, Sir Keith. "Colombia." *South America, Central America and the Caribbean* 2009. 291–7.

Pereira, Anthony. "Brazil's Agrarian Reform: Democratic Innovation or Oligarchic Exclusion Redux?" *Latin American Politics and Society* 45, no. 2 (2003): 41–65.

Perkins, Dwight H., Steven C. Radelet and David L. Lindauer. *Economics of Development.* 6th edn. New York: W.W. Norton, 2006.

United Nations, Department of Economic and Social Affairs, Population Division. *World Population Prospects: The 2008 Revision.* Vol. 1. 2 vols. New York: United Nations, 2009.

United Nations Development Programme. *Human Development Report 2010. The Real Wealth of Nations: Pathways to Human Development.* New York, NY: United Nations Development Programme, 2010.

United Nations, Office on Drugs and Crime. *World Drug Report 2010.* New York: United Nations, 2010.

United States, Government Accountability Office. *Drug Control: U.S. Assistance Has Helped Mexican Counternarcotics Efforts, but Tons of Illicit Drugs Continue to Flow into the United States.* Washington, DC, 2007, GAO-07–1018.

Part IV
Culture

Introduction

Rooted etymologically in the Latin term for agricultural cultivation, *colere*, culture in its primary sense refers to the work of "cultivating" the person, forming and perfecting her or him toward becoming more fully human, according to the ruling ideals of any given place or epoch. Culture understood as "the cultivation of the individual" coexists with a related definition of culture that emerged in the nineteenth century. In this secondary meaning, culture refers to the common features of any given society. In this wider sense, culture is what we humans make, and what in turns remakes us – ranging from the deepest presuppositions about the meaning of life to language, forms of government, modes of entertainment, scientific discoveries, technologies and economies. The utility of this secondary way of understanding culture is obvious whenever we reflect on the astonishing diversity of human conduct over time, from region to region and group to group.

But even in this secondary meaning of culture, which takes in everything that is specifically human, we find a route back to the primary meaning of culture as individual cultivation, formation or improvement. For to speak of distinct groups according to ideas and behaviors that coalesce and persist over time is to recognize the universal practice of *conveying* some particular bundle of beliefs and behaviors – a "way of life" – that we call a culture. We might refer to that act of conveyance or transmission as "socialization" or even (in a broad sense) "education," a process that takes forms both seen and unseen, formal and informal, intentional and unintentional, innovative and customary.

In accord with the primary meaning of culture as cultivation, the *education* of children and adolescents can therefore be understood as forming the individual and thus the society as a whole according to prevailing standards and norms. In fact, in the Spanish language, the verb *educar* ("to educate") often

Contemporary Latin America: 1970 to the Present, First Edition. Robert H. Holden and Rina Villars.
© 2013 Robert H. Holden and Rina Villars. Published 2013 by Blackwell Publishing Ltd.

refers to this wider process of formation, and so encompasses the shaping of a person's character and behavior as well as his or her formal schooling.

The essential traits of any given culture do not transfer easily from place to place, despite the tremendous increase in the flow of culture-specific ideas and images around the world in recent decades. And while they are flexible enough to absorb limited modifications, they resist transformation. In Chapter 2 we reviewed the core beliefs and values, or the ethos, associated with the culture of Latin America. Here, we examine developments in the *means* by which that ethos has been propagated, instilled, and occasionally modified since about 1970. Of the many practices that could qualify as channels or vehicles of cultural propagation, we have selected only a few of the most prominent. Beginning with scholarship and learning, we focus on changes in basic literacy, primary and secondary education, and university education. Scientific research and technology, particularly in respect to the distribution of information, will be discussed, along with changes in the media of mass communication, followed by developments in literature, the visual arts, cinema and sports.

Chapter 11

Education

The leaders of the independence movements and the liberal reformers of the nineteenth century saw education as the principal means of leading Latin America to "modernity" – meaning toward the standards, qualities and styles of life as it was being lived in the most advanced countries of western Europe and the United States. Basic or primary education was seen as the main tool for the construction of modern nations of responsible citizens. As a result, national educational policies aimed above all at promoting universal access to basic education while increasing literacy.

Literacy

As recently as the 1950s, one could find dramatic contrasts in Latin American adult (i.e., 15 years of age or older) literacy rates. In Guatemala, 70% were illiterate while Argentina reported just 14% and Mexico 44%. Regional leaders considered the widespread inability to read to constitute a serious crisis, and throughout the 1950s and 1960s, numerous intergovernmental meetings, as well as conferences and seminars sponsored by non-governmental organizations and international agencies, proclaimed commitments to eradicating illiteracy.

The effort reflected the common belief that the inability to read and the lack of a basic education held back democratic rule as well as economic development. By the 1970s, more and more specialists in education and development were pointing to Article 26 of the United Nations' Universal Declaration of Human Rights of 1948, with its bold assertion that "Everyone has the right to education." As a result, a more sharply political critique of the neglect of

Contemporary Latin America: 1970 to the Present, First Edition. Robert H. Holden and Rina Villars.
© 2013 Robert H. Holden and Rina Villars. Published 2013 by Blackwell Publishing Ltd.

illiteracy and basic education emerged. The single most prominent voice in the politicization of illiteracy and basic education was that of the Brazilian professor of education, Paulo Freire (1921–1997), a specialist in the teaching of adult literacy. His widely republished and translated *Pedagogy of the Oppressed*, written in the late 1960s, urged teachers to encourage their students to understand literacy and basic education as tools for social change and personal liberation. "Freierian pedagogy," one of the better-known instances of a "globalized" product of Latin American thought, was adopted throughout the world.

Between 1950 and 1980, the overall rate of adult illiteracy in Latin America fell by half, owing in part to the expansion of basic educational opportunities by governments throughout the region, as well as improvements in the quality and efficiency of public education. Nevertheless, the slow pace of change and the gathering economic crisis of the late 1970s prompted Latin America's governments to issue the "Mexico Declaration" of 1979. In it, they acknowledged the persistence of such "serious shortcomings" as extreme poverty, low school enrollments, an unacceptably high proportion of adult illiterates, and a high primary-school drop-out rate. They also criticized educational systems that were overcentralized, poorly administered and "very often ill-suited to the population for which they were intended." The signatories called on the region's governments to ensure "the general introduction of complete primary or basic education for all children of school age" and to eliminate illiteracy. These and other goals were eventually embodied in the "Major Project in the Field of Education in Latin America and the Caribbean," a twenty-year program adopted by the Latin American governments at Quito in 1981 with the support of UNESCO.

Delegates to that meeting were by then aware of the spectacular claim of the government of Nicaragua, controlled from 1979 by the Sandinist Front for National Liberation (Frente Sandinista de Liberación Nacional or FSLN), that it had chopped the illiteracy rate among Nicaraguans aged 10 and above from 50% to 13% in just six months – from March to August of 1980. Even considering the government's incentive to exaggerate its achievement, the Nicaraguans nevertheless demonstrated the potential for speedy improvements in basic adult literacy, when spearheaded by tens of thousands of highly motivated volunteers and government employees. Nicaragua's National Literacy Crusade was succeeded by a structured program of "adult popular basic education" that sought to deepen and extend the Crusade's impact. Although some UNESCO experts questioned the measures used by the Nicaragua government, the organization awarded four prizes for literacy gains in Nicaragua during the period of FSLN rule, 1979–1990. The FSLN's model was Cuba's National Literacy Campaign, undertaken in 1960 by the revolutionary Marxist government led by Fidel Castro. The Nicaraguans followed the Cuban strategy of a concentrated attack on illiteracy that doubled as a means of instilling loyalty to the government by using specially written reading exalting the revolution.

Primary Education

During the 1980s and 1990s, the "Major Project" goals identified above became a key point of reference in educational policy across Latin America. Twenty years after its adoption, UNESCO experts assessed the results. By 1991, all countries had established basic education programs of seven to ten years per pupil. At the same time, more children were attending school than ever before, at both the primary and secondary levels. Nevertheless, the experts concluded, "Achievements in coverage during the two decades have not been sufficient to meet the goal of universal enrollment in basic education. Significant inequalities persist in the distribution of opportunities for education." The UNESCO panel also noted that merely making education compulsory could not guarantee that all children would receive a basic education. Extremely poor children, the children of indigenous parents, those with special education needs, and children living in rural areas faced the greatest obstacles to receiving a basic education. Moreover, while every country reported reductions in "absolute illiteracy," the goal of eliminating illiteracy had not been reached; some 14% of the population (39 million people 15 or over) were considered illiterate in 1999 (though the rate would fall to about 10% in 2006), and huge disparities could be found within and between countries. The report estimated that 110 million Latin Americans had not finished primary school. "If we consider together the number of illiterates with those with low levels of literacy, or who have not completed primary school, we are speaking of a very large number of people, especially young people, who do not possess the basic skills needed to develop and to participate in society, in the full exercise of their citizenship."

Perhaps the most discouraging news was UNESCO's conclusion that the increases in enrollment had often come at the expense of quality and efficiency in school systems that were already below par. Latin American governments required fewer school hours than developed countries, a minimum that was reduced further by extraordinary rates of absenteeism among both students and teachers. Curricular improvements and reforms in classroom teaching methods remained high priorities. But when educational reform programs, including better teacher-training norms, were adopted, their implementation was often slowed or checked entirely by the continuing need to overcome the deficits in basic education and literacy. A UNESCO ranking of Latin American countries in 2007, according to overall educational quality, highlighted the disparities within the region, and the sizeable gap between Latin America as a whole and the developed countries. The top performers were Chile, Costa Rica and Cuba. But in the Dominican Republic and Nicaragua, no more than 60% of the children who entered primary school made it to the last primary grade. In Guatemala, no more than half of the secondary-school age group was enrolled in secondary school. No more than 70% of the over-15 population in Guatemala and Nicaragua was considered literate. In most countries, no more than 80% of primary teachers and no more than 70% of secondary teachers had any pedagogical training. Compared to North America and western Europe, in Latin America a child received on average three years less schooling – thirteen rather than sixteen. Furthermore, the quality of the schooling was considerably inferior; students in Argentina, Brazil, Chile, Mexico and Peru consistently ranked at the lowest levels of proficiency in a forty-three-country study of literacy, math and science skills among 15-year-olds carried out in 2003.

University Education

Within a span of just seven decades after Columbus's first voyage to the New World in 1492, the Spanish monarchy had founded five universities in its American territories, and another twelve would follow before the independence revolts swept away Spain's hold on its American territories in the early nineteenth century. Portugal never established a university in Brazil. In Hispanic America, the universities preserved their status as havens for the sons (and, very rarely, the daughters) of the most privileged families. Largely geared to training in the professions (law, medicine and engineering), the universities by the early twentieth century had lost much of their colonial-era intellectual independence. Faculty appointments and financing were largely controlled by the state, while a few powerful faculty members dominated the administration of the university. The central mission of the university was understood to be that of consolidating a strong national identity, a task that inevitably turned it into an agent of political mobilization.

Social changes brought on by sizeable increases in European migration (especially in Brazil and the Southern Cone countries), rapid urbanization, incipient industrialization, and the rise of a large entrepreneurial class led, after 1900, to increasing demands for university self-government (including a participatory role for students) and the liberalization of rules governing student and faculty conduct. The pace of change accelerated abruptly after 1918, when students in Argentina's Universidad de Córdoba launched one of the most successful Latin American social movements of the century. Besides the university's autonomy from the state, and more freedom and flexibility for students, the students and their faculty allies demanded term appointments of faculty members with tenure subject to periodic review. That goal was joined by a desire to extend the benefits of university training beyond the families of the well-to-do, in part by eliminating or reducing tuition. By the end of the 1950s, most of these goals had been enacted into law in eighteen Latin American countries.

Nevertheless, the new model of the Latin American public university as an autonomous, nearly tuition-free institution governed in part by its own students, with a strong commitment to extending the benefits of education to all, had the effect of further politicizing the campuses. Students became a political constituency that few governments could ignore, and that dictatorial governments in particular came to fear. Across Latin America, students earned a level of influence in national political affairs beyond that of any other world region. Campuses became ideological and organizational centers of radical social change. As a law student at the University of Havana in the early 1950s, Fidel Castro drew largely on fellow students to organize the guerrilla army that would lead the successful revolutionary war against the Cuban government. But Castro was following a well-established tradition in Cuba, for at the same university in the early 1930s, the student-led movement to oust the Gerardo Machado dictatorship had led to the closing of the university for three years. Well aware of the potential for disruption posed by organized student movements, when Castro seized power in 1959 he almost immediately purged the university, relieving his government of the burden of student opposition for the rest of the period of revolutionary rule, now exceeding six decades.

No other Latin American government, not even those of Argentina, Brazil and Chile during their respective military dictatorships, disposed so effectively of student agitators as did Cuba's. In Venezuela in 1958 and Bolivia in 1964, governments fell to social movements in which students played important roles, while the guerrilla armies that sprang up across Latin America in the 1960s and 1970s found a ready source of volunteers on university campuses. In 1968, the Mexican army fired on students who were demonstrating peacefully for democracy, killing up to 300, wounding hundreds more, and eventually hardening popular opposition to the country's authoritarian government.

By then, violent confrontations between students and government security forces were a regular feature of the region's politics. Within three years of Peru's transition from military to elected civilian rule, students protesting new laws that limited their role in the government of universities, as well as cuts in state funding for higher education and bus fare increases, helped ignite a nationwide wave of strikes and demonstrations in 1983 and 1984. Coinciding with gains by two guerrilla armies in their war against the government, student protests were increasingly identified as threats to Peru's national security. The result, by the end of 1984, included legislation limiting civil liberties and increasing the military's power to deal with the insurgents and their allies. A particularly important target of the military was the University of San Cristobal de Huamanga in Ayacucho, which had emerged as the headquarters of one of the guerrilla armies, Sendero Luminoso or Shining Path, in 1981.

In neighboring Chile, students joined labor and human rights groups in demanding the end of military rule. Army and police forces used helicopters and assault trucks in 1986 to arrest 600 students who had taken over university classrooms in Santiago. The students demanded a civilian replacement for the army general whom the dictatorship had appointed to head the University of Chile. Student–government tension continued in Chile long after elected civilian government had been firmly reestablished. In March 2011, high-school and university students, school teachers and professors began a months-long campaign of street demonstrations, hunger strikes, occupations and other protest measures to support their demand for free university education for all, and the banning of private for-profit universities, which had been authorized by the military government before it fell in 1989 "Nothing is free in life," declared President Sebastián Piñera, whose offer to increase state aid for individual students was dismissed by the leaders of the protest movement.

In Venezuela, famed at the time for its relatively stable system of elected civilian governments, a series of violent, nationwide confrontations in 1987 between university students demonstrating for educational reforms and state security forces killed at least two students and wounded dozens of others. In justifying its action to stop the protests, the government asserted that the student groups were subversives intent on destabilizing Venezuela. A wave of selective tortures and killings of professors and student leaders by death squads in Colombia in 1987 led to strikes and marches joined by thousands of university students. In Mexico in 2000, a strike by 200,000 students and teachers paralyzed Latin America's largest university, the National Autonomous University of Mexico, for nine months. The strike, aimed at protesting the government's decision to raise the annual tuition from a few cents to the equivalent of $140, ended after 2,260 police officers raided the campus and arrested 430 students, who had added other demands after the university agreed to drop the tuition increase.

Evaluations of the impact of the university reform movement on higher education have been mixed. On the one hand, it has not been difficult to find evidence that university autonomy and student co-government inhibited academic freedom and sometimes replaced education with ideological indoctrination. As traditional standards for admitting students and promoting faculty members collapsed, the overall quality of education fell, depriving many countries of the intellectual leadership they most needed for stable, democratic development. Advocates of the reform countered that the true role of the university was precisely to empower students to become confrontational agents of social change in class-stratified societies where economic disparities remained among the sharpest in the world.

In any case, university autonomy was always subject to any given government's threshold of tolerance for student activism and rebellion, as well as its willingness to support its universities financially. Traditionally authoritarian regimes such as Mexico's, as well as the outright military dictatorships that took power in many countries during the 1960s and 1970s, intervened directly in the universities, violating academic freedom and self-government in harshly repressive and sometimes violent ways. In Brazil, where the movement to reform the university had never achieved the level of success recorded elsewhere in Latin America, the military government that took power in 1964 issued decrees that in effect instituted a counter-reform. Governmental agencies so controlled the universities that little freedom remained for students or faculty, who were often the targets of state-directed ideological purges. In Argentina and Chile, military governments from the late 1960s onward imposed similar measures.

President Hugo Chávez of Venezuela, an admirer of Cuba's socialist system, sought to emulate Cuba's success in controlling its students. On 22 December 2010, his administration together with the National Assembly adopted legislation to abolish the autonomy of the country's public and private universities and place them under the direct control of the presidency. The purpose, according to the legislation, was to ensure that university education fomented "attitudes, values, and capacities oriented to participation in the endogenous, integral and sustainable development of Venezuela in the attainment of socio-productive sovereignty for the construction of the socialist Fatherland."[1] Perhaps more importantly, the Venezuelan universities had long been the scene of persistent protests against the Chávez government, and the new law would enable the president to eliminate another source of political opposition. Eleven days after its passage, in response to intense protests by students and university administrators, President Chávez announced he would veto the law. Despite having insisted earlier on its passage, he now called for a wider debate on university education. The law was immediately abrogated by the National Assembly.

Already by the early 1960s, as politicization and state intervention intensified, the quality of higher education was suffering. As a result, students began to enroll in ever-greater numbers in private (including Catholic) universities. Both public and private enrollments exploded across Latin America between 1960 and 1975, with annual increases averaging 13%. Extraordinary demands were placed on publicly funded universities, and critics highlighted the weak admissions standards, the lack of library and laboratory facilities, poor research performance, the paucity of post-graduate programs, and widespread dissatisfaction with dogmatic teaching methods and poorly qualified professors. Too many students were dropping out or attending part time. Student strikes and political organizing consumed too much time and attention. What had become, by the 1970s, a widely acknowledged crisis in higher education was further aggravated by the gathering international debt crisis of that decade.

The economic recession that began to sweep Latin America in the early 1980s forced policy-makers to undertake major changes in higher education policy – raising tuition, cutting budgets, decentralizing control and encouraging the growth of private institutions of higher education. Higher education became more diverse in both kind and quality as demand continued to grow. Accessibility increased as enrollments of women and rural inhabitants expanded. When it took power in 1973 by overthrowing the elected socialist government of President Salvador Allende, the military government of Chile took measures that would be followed by other governments within a decade. To meet rising demand for higher education, while promoting private investment in universities, Chile adopted a market-driven scheme that demoted the state from its traditional status as the central source and authority in higher education, to that of market regulator. A tripartite system of universities, professional institutes and private technical training centers was created, each with discrete functions, governing methods and funding mechanisms. The military dictatorship's legal framework for higher education continued to govern the system into the twenty-first century, well after military rule had ended.

If, until the 1970s, the Latin American university had in theory been trusted to regulate and govern itself, subject to occasional intervention by the state, by the 1990s a new role for the state consistent with demands for democratic accountability had emerged. Now, the state would both assure the quality of education and guarantee the widest possible access to education. Several countries created systems of evaluation and accreditation to protect the consumers of higher education. At the same time, new communications technologies opened the way for distance education, innovative teaching methods, and even the internationalization of formal education. European and U.S.-based institutions opened campuses in Latin America, while some Latin American universities took reciprocal action by offering distance-learning programs over the Internet. All these trends favored the expansion of enrollments. In the decade ending in 2003, higher-education enrollments of all kinds had nearly doubled across Latin America, from 8 million to 14 million, with 65% of that total concentrated in Argentina, Brazil, Colombia and Mexico, and more than 40% in private institutions. The increase far outstripped the rise in the population of 20- to 24-year-olds, meaning that the overall proportion of the college-age population rose dramatically. By 2003, higher education enrollments had climbed to the equivalent of 32% of the 20–4 age group (compared to 17% in 1994), a rate still well below the 57% recorded in North America and western Europe. While the thirty most developed countries belonging to the Organization for Economic Co-operation and Development were turning out one new Ph.D. for every 5,000 people, the Brazilian rate was one for every 70,000 and in Chile, one per 140,000.[2]

Despite the rise in enrollments, the Latin American university was still mired in crisis at the start of the twenty-first century. A scarcity of teaching materials, rigid and underdeveloped curricula, poorly prepared faculty, a lack of responsiveness to changing opportunities in the job market, and a deficiency in researchers with strong international reputations were among the shortcomings regularly singled out by education specialists. Most university libraries lacked specially trained librarians; their collections were very small by North American standards, and were updated only sporadically. Students rarely bought books required for courses and instead borrowed copies provided by the library, a practice that diverted library funds from collection development. Notable exceptions were Brazil's University of São Paulo and the National Autonomous University of Mexico, where bibliographical resources matched those of the developed countries. Despite gains in accessibility, higher education was still mainly for the better-off sectors of society.

Thus, two of the biggest questions that confronted the students of Córdoba in 1918 – the proper role of the state and the quality of education – still awaited a definitive resolution in most countries of Latin America. Two rival approaches to education policy dominated the region, the Inter-American Development Bank concluded in 2005: that of seeking expansion and growing enrollments, or preferring improvements in quality and efficiency. Whereas proponents of "quality-first" typically confronted resistance to change, "expansionists" could usually count on a friendly reception because almost all interested parties – parents, children, teachers and government authorities – stood to gain from increasing the number of schools and teachers.[3] Unlike changes in quality, expansion was not only easier done but more easily measured.

Educational Access and Achievement

Gauged according to the proportion of the relevant age group enrolled in school, accessibility rose but significant disparities remained from one country to another, and among certain groups within countries. In the mid-1970s, only two countries, Argentina and Costa Rica, could report that 92% or more of their primary-school-age children were enrolled in primary schools. Among the lowest was Guatemala with 53%. Bolivia, Brazil, Ecuador, Panama, Paraguay and Venezuela reported that between 71% and 87% were being schooled. Over the following decade, significant changes in those rates were difficult to find, probably because of the sharp drops in government spending that characterized the economically depressed decade of the 1980s. While the share of

Table 11.1   Net enrollment ratios, primary school. Data for 1975 and 1985 from *Statistical Abstract of Latin America* 1990 V. 28, Table 904, pp. 201ff; for 2000: Economic Commission for Latin America and the Caribbean, *Statistical Yearbook for Latin America and the Caribbean* 2005, p. 59.

	1975	1985	2000
Argentina	96	n/a	100
Bolivia	73	79	95
Brazil	71	82	97
Chile	96	92	87
Colombia	n/a	76	87
Costa Rica	92	87	90
Cuba	n/a	94	94
Dominican Republic	n/a	68	96
Ecuador	78	n/a	100
El Salvador	n/a	62	90
Guatemala	53	n/a	87
Haiti	n/a	44	n/a
Honduras	n/a	87	87
Mexico	n/a	98	99
Nicaragua	65	76	86
Panama	87	89	100
Paraguay	85	86	89
Peru	n/a	97	100
Uruguay	n/a	91	90
Venezuela	81	86	91
Average			**93**

Note: Gross enrollment is total enrollment of all ages divided by the total population of the appropriate age group; net is only that share of total enrollment that corresponds to the relevant age groups of each level, divided by the total population of the appropriate age group.

Bolivia and Venezuela's children who were in primary school had risen only modestly, the rate declined slightly in Chile and Costa Rica. Only Brazil and Nicaragua reported notable increases.

The greatest period of expansion in primary education since the 1960s was registered in the 1990s (Table 11.1). By 2000, the school enrollment average in Latin America was 93%, and the lowest enrollment was 86% (Nicaragua). Argentina, Ecuador, Panama, Peru and Mexico reported full or nearly full enrollment of its primary-school-age population. Secondary-school enrollment rates disclosed a similar pattern of stagnation in the 1980s, followed by explosive growth in the 1990s, reaching an average rate of 64% by 2001; Bolivia's more than doubled in the 1990s from 29% to 68%, while Brazil's nearly quintupled, from 16% to 72%. The highest rate in 1990 was reported by Cuba at 70%; its 83% in 2001 was exceeded by no other Latin American country.[4]

Disparities between male and female rates of educational achievement across Latin America as a whole have been considerably less than those recorded in other world areas, and comparable to those of the United States and western Europe. The percentage of females enrolled in all three levels of education was 47% in 1950 and rose to 48% by 1966, a period when total enrollments at all three levels rose from 17 million to 45 million. On the whole, male–female enrollment rates across all three levels of education were so close by 2007 that the gap had practically disappeared everywhere; only Bolivia and Guatemala reported enrollment ratios and literacy rates that strongly favored males. The biggest shift was recorded in higher education; in 1950, only one in four post-secondary students were women (exactly the same as western Europe's share) but in 2003, more than half (54%) of all post-secondary students were women, with the lowest rate (45%) recorded by Peru and Bolivia. By 2004, Latin America had the highest adult female literacy rate of all the "developing" world regions; at 90%, it was nearly identical to the male rate.

Perhaps the most glaring disproportion in education access and achievement continues to be that which separates the indigenous from the non-indigenous populations. A World Bank study of educational disparities in Bolivia, Ecuador, Guatemala, Mexico and Peru (the countries with the highest concentrations of indigenous peoples) in 2006 concluded that in all five countries, the gap in average years of schooling between indigenous and non-indigenous people 15 and older ranged from 2.3 years in Peru to 3.7 years in Bolivia. Among all five countries, Guatemala reported the lowest level of average indigenous educational achievement (2.5 years of schooling), and Peru the highest (6.4 years).[5]

As governments and researchers focused on ways to overcome this gap in educational achievement, they increasingly turned in the last three decades to programs of bilingual education as a means of keeping indigenous children in school and improving their learning. About 500 indigenous languages, distributed among some 100 linguistic groups, were spoken in Latin America, with Aymara and Quechua (the Andes), Quiché (Guatemala and Mexico), Mapuche (Chile), and Nahuatl (Mexico) accounting for the highest number of speakers. Yet it was not until the 1960s that many educators and policy-makers began to see indigenous languages, not as threats to Hispanization or national unity, but as valuable expressions of Latin America's pluricultural heritage. In Peru, for example, a pilot project in bilingual education was launched in the 1960s by the country's oldest and most prestigious university, that of San Marcos. The project, which drew on the direct participation of Quecha-speaking people, became the basis for Peru's bilingual education development program in the early 1970s, and in 1975, Peru became the first Latin American country to endow an Indian language (Quechua) with official status.

Since then, native languages have been granted official standing in the constitutions of Bolivia, Colombia, Ecuador, Nicaragua and Paraguay. The majority of Latin American countries now recognize the right of the indigenous people to be taught in their own languages, and have adopted programs aimed at preserving and developing both the languages and their cultures. By 2004, all but four countries (Belize, El Salvador, Guyana and Uruguay) lacked bilingual programs for indigenous populations, and studies carried out in several countries in the last fifteen years report significant achievement gains as a result of bilingual education.[6] Nevertheless, the gap between indigenous and non-indigenous schooling persisted. In Guatemala, for example, bilingual education expanded rapidly from the mid-1980s, and the number of languages increased from four to fourteen. Yet in 2003 less than a third of indigenous primary-school children were receiving a bilingual education.

In Bolivia, government policy required indigenous children to learn to read and write in both Spanish and their mother tongue, and to hear math, science and other subjects taught in both languages in rural areas. As a result, by 2001, twice as many schools were teaching bilingually as compared to 1997. Still, both enrollment and drop-out rates remained considerably higher among the indigenous population compared to the non-indigenous. A team of researchers reported that, while some of the gap was owing to income inequality, "a large part of the gap remains unexplained," and could be attributable to a variety of other factors, such as reduced access to basic services by indigenous families, the tendency for indigenous children to be concentrated in schools with fewer resources and fewer teachers, and the persistence of language barriers. Another possibility was that teachers treated indigenous pupils differently than they treated non-indigenous pupils.[7]

While the achievement gap between indigenous and non-indigenous peoples has clearly diminished, the failure of these educational gains to translate into higher earnings for the indigenous continued to puzzle researchers. Part of the answer may lie in the quality of the education they received. Or, it may be explained by the tendency of indigenous children to participate, to a far greater extent than non-indigenous children, in the labor force, and therefore keeping them out of the classroom. These and other dimensions of life in Latin America's indigenous societies will be treated in Chapter 16.

Notes

1   "La Asamblea Nacional de la República Bolivariana de Venezuela Decreta la Siguiente, Ley de Educación Universitaria," Bolivarian Republic of Venezuela, Ministry of University Education, www.unesur.edu.ve.

2   The post-secondary statistic is the Gross Enrollment Ratio, which divides total
    enrollment, regardless of age, by the total population of the corresponding age
    group, in this case 20–4 years of age. Instituto Internacional de la UNESCO para la
    Educación Superior en América Latina y el Caribe, *Informe sobre la educación supe-
    rior en América Latina y el Caribe 2000–2005: la metamorfosis de la educación
    superior* (Caracas, Venezuela: Instituto Internacional de la UNESCO para la Edu-
    cación Superior en América Latina y el Caribe (IESALC), 2006).
3   Inter-American Development Bank, *The Politics of Policies: Economic and Social
    Progress in Latin America; 2006 Report* (Washington: Inter-American Development
    Bank, 2005), Ch. 10.
4   The percentages reported here are Net Enrollment Ratios, computed by dividing
    the total enrollment of children in the age bracket that corresponds to primary
    school, by the total population of that age group. The sources consulted were James
    Wilkie, ed., *Statistical Abstract of Latin America* (Los Angeles: UCLA Latin American
    Center Publications, 2001); James Wilkie, ed., *Statistical Abstract of Latin America*
    (Los Angeles: UCLA Latin American Center Publications, 1990)Economic Com-
    mission for Latin America and Comisión Económica para América Latina, *Statisti-
    cal Yearbook for Latin America and the Caribbean 2005 / Anuario estadístico de
    América Latina y el Caribe 2005* (Santiago, Chile: ECLAC/CEPAL, 2006). Not all
    countries reported ratios in the selected years.
5   Gillette Hall and Harry Anthony Patrinos, "Key Messages and an Agenda for Action,"
    in *Indigenous Peoples, Poverty and Human Development in Latin America*, ed. Gillette
    Hall and Harry Anthony Patrinos (Basingstoke: Palgrave Macmillan, 2006), 221–40,
    here 224–5.
6   Gillette Hall, Heather Marie Layton and Joseph Shapiro, "Introduction: The Indig-
    enous Peoples' Decade in Latin America," in *Indigenous Peoples, Poverty and Human
    Development in Latin America*, ed. Gillette Hall and Harry Anthony Patrinos (Bas-
    ingstoke: Palgrave Macmillan, 2006), 12–17.
7   Wilson Jiménez Pozo, Fernando Landa Casazola and Ernesto Yañez Aguilar,
    "Bolivia," in *Indigenous Peoples, Poverty and Human Development in Latin
    America*, ed. Gillette Hall and Harry Anthony Patrinos (Basingstoke: Pal-
    grave Macmillan, 2006), 40–66, here 57–62.

References

Economic Commission for Latin America and Comisión Económica para América
    Latina. *Statistical Yearbook for Latin America and the Caribbean 2005/Anuario
    estadístico de América Latina y el Caribe 2005*. Santiago, Chile: ECLAC/CEPAL, 2006.
Hall, Gillette, Heather Marie Layton and Joseph Shapiro. "Introduction: The Indigenous
    Peoples' Decade in Latin America." In *Indigenous Peoples, Poverty and Human Devel-
    opment in Latin America*, ed. Gillette Hall and Harry Anthony Patrinos, 1–24. Bas-
    ingstoke: Palgrave Macmillan, 2006.
Hall, Gillette, and Harry Anthony Patrinos. "Key Messages and an Agenda for Action."
    In *Indigenous Peoples, Poverty and Human Development in Latin America*, ed. Gillette
    Hall and Harry Anthony Patrinos, 221–40. Basingstoke: Palgrave Macmillan, 2006.

Instituto Internacional de la UNESCO para la Educación Superior en América Latina y el Caribe. *Informe sobre la educación superior en América Latina y el Caribe 2000–2005: la metamorfosis de la educación superior.* Caracas, Venezuela: Instituto Internacional de la UNESCO para la Educación Superior en América Latina y el Caribe (IESALC), 2006.

Jiménez Pozo, Wilson, Fernando Landa Casazola and Ernesto Yañez Aguilar. "Bolivia." In *Indigenous Peoples, Poverty and Human Development in Latin America*, ed. Gillette Hall and Harry Anthony Patrinos, 40–66. Basingstoke: Palgrave Macmillan, 2006.

Statistical Abstract of Latin America. Vol. 28, ed. James Wilkie. Los Angeles: UCLA Latin American Center Publications, 1990.

Wilkie, James, ed. *Statistical Abstract of Latin America.* Los Angeles: UCLA Latin American Center Publications, 2001; 1990.

Chapter 12

Research and Communications

Scientific Research and Technology

Exact knowledge of the material world, the discovery and validation of that knowledge, and its practical applications are what we will refer to here as "science." One of the central features of modernity itself has been the rise since the nineteenth century of the global authority of science, scientists and scientific methods. As a result of this trend, to call an idea "unscientific" is practically to banish it from serious consideration. While globalization has in many ways been a force for diversification, in its scientific guise it has acted in favor of *conforming* the world's cultures to the general assumptions, methods and institutions of modern science. Hardly any topic is now exempt from the authority of evidence and testimony said to be "scientific," ranging from family and health issues to educational policy, economic organization and even political arrangements. Few people speak with more authority than scientists, in part just because what they say is assumed to have universal value and applicability. If there is a global authority structure, it is composed not of powerful politicians, nation-states or multinational corporations but of individuals and groups who ground their status in science. Almost invariably, they speak from within the university, an institution that has propagated itself in a remarkably uniform way across the globe, with standard disciplinary specialties divided among the humanities, the natural sciences, the social sciences and various professional schools. As a result, what came to count as suitably scientific – whether the subject was human society, the planetary system, a biological organism, or a geological formation – everywhere became the standard according to which knowledge was evaluated and decisions were made. That made science itself a global force – perhaps the core "culture" or ethos of

Contemporary Latin America: 1970 to the Present, First Edition. Robert H. Holden and Rina Villars.
© 2013 Robert H. Holden and Rina Villars. Published 2013 by Blackwell Publishing Ltd.

globalization – and thus an inescapable theme in the study of any world region since 1970.

Scientific knowledge and the institutions associated with it have become part of every local culture. National, regional and global networks of innovation and knowledge transmission interact, creating local traditions of scientific and technical learning and application. Institutions – universities, research institutes, museums, laboratories – profoundly affect the scope and creativity of those interactions. The institutions themselves largely depend on the initiative and interests of national governments and non-national organizations of all kinds, which is to say that "politics" matters a great deal. The highly inequitable distributions of wealth and trained personnel across the world also condition the way science unfolds in any given place. Varying levels of commitment to universal, public education can also make a big difference. These background conditions need to be kept in mind as we consider the development of scientific knowledge across Latin America since the 1970s. We will begin with general patterns in the unfolding of the "culture of science" across the region, and then analyze some of the diverse ways in which that culture has been expressed.

While scientific activity has never been absent from Latin America, its contemporary formation was critically influenced by the large-scale immigration of European scientists in the late 1930s who were driven out of their homelands by the civil war in Spain (1936–1939) and by the expansion of Germany's totalitarian Nazi regime (1933–1945). In Latin America, these scientists became the catalysts for the transformation of the region's science-oriented institutions. At the same time, the massive wartime destruction inflicted on Europe by World War II (1939–1945) made the United States the world's supreme source of scientific knowledge and education, and the effect on Latin America was two-fold. On the one hand, the tremendous growth of the U.S. economy, increasingly oriented to scientific and technological production, attracted Latin American scientists, creating a "brain drain" that weakened the possibilities for science in Latin America. On the other hand, as increasing numbers of younger Latin American scientists, freshly trained in the United States and elsewhere, returned home, a "scientific ethos" or worldview began to emerge in the 1950s, along with a sense of solidarity among Latin American scientists in various fields.

Scientists organized specialized associations that set out to institutionalize the exchange of scientific information through new journals and conferences, and to encourage support for science education and research. Between the late 1950s and the late 1970s, nearly every Latin American government created a science research council to help shape policy and funding priorities. But governments, particularly non-democratic ones, could also inhibit scientific research. Military-led *golpes de estado* overthrew popularly elected governments across Latin America in the 1960s and 1970s, interrupting the institutional stability (and funding) required for a tradition of research to grow and mature. The 1966 Argentine *golpe* put the country's universities into the hands of military officers whose policies pushed hundreds of scientists into exile. The pattern was repeated, with even more severe consequences, after the coup of 1976. After the Chilean coup of 1973, the Universidad de Chile's sciences faculty scattered into exile, and in the 1980s the Universidad de El Salvador was occupied for months by the armed forces. Demilitarization restored both the institutional stability and the atmosphere of free inquiry that are the foundations of serious scholarship everywhere. Yet military regimes also had the capacity, as we will see in the case of Brazil, to concentrate resources in a way that could encourage scientific research in selected fields.

If one field of scientific research in Latin America stood out in the twentieth century, it was the life sciences. Researchers in Argentina and Brazil established strong traditions in the field of genetics before the middle of the twentieth century. In biomedicine, Argentina's Bernardo Houssay had set up a world-class research institute by the 1940s, and went on to share the 1947 Nobel Prize in medicine for discovering, to quote the award, "the part played by the hormone of the anterior pituitary lobe in the metabolism of sugar." Houssay's Instituto de Biología y Medicina Experimental (Institute of Biology and Experimental Medicine) trained a generation of researchers, one of whom, Luis Leloir, won Latin America's second Nobel Prize, for chemistry, in 1970, for his work on sugar nucleotides and their role in the biosynthesis of carbohydrates. The Argentine institute was among a number of similar labs in Mexico, Brazil, Chile and Venezuela whose researchers were closely associated with the lab established at Harvard University by the experimental physiologist Walter B. Cannon (d. 1945).

Separately, world-class research in high-altitude medicine emerged as a specialty in the Andean nation of Peru in the 1930s and 1940s, a tradition that continued there and in neighboring Bolivia. The reception by Mexico in the 1930s of numerous exiled Spanish researchers in biology and biomedicine led to the establishment of strong programs of research in pharmacology and related specialties. Elsewhere in Latin America, important discoveries in the field of bacteriology in the early twentieth century were recorded in Paraguay and Cuba.

The emphasis on life sciences research persisted into the twenty-first century. About six out of ten research units in Latin America were linked to the biological sciences by about 2000, and a study of scientific articles published by Latin American researchers in 2001 concluded that nearly half were in the life sciences – clinical medicine, biomedical research and biology. This was unusual, for among almost all other "emerging and developing" countries (i.e., those of low to middle income) the favored fields were engineering and technology, mathematics and the physical sciences. The contrary emphasis on the life sciences in Latin America originated in the preference, especially among the government agencies that funded research, for supporting research that promised to solve practical problems in the fields of health and natural resources, including agricultural production. On the other hand, the region's comparative weakness in chemistry, physics and mathematics has been said to be responsible in part for Latin America's lag in the development of modern technologies. The once-strong preference for encouraging "applied" rather than "basic" science for its supposedly practical advantages was seen, by the early twenty-first century, to have been based on a mistaken assumption, because – it was now said – technological prowess depended in good part on the continuous development of "pure" or basic science.

The foundation for Brazil's leadership in scientific research was laid during the period of military rule (1964–1985), when a nationalistic ethos dominated among the leadership of the armed forces and found expression in a desire to make the country self sufficient in science and technology. To that end, the government centralized all planning and funding in research and development. The new National Fund for Scientific and Technological Development (Fundo Nacional de Desenvolvimiento Cientifico e Tecnológico) received an annual budget in the mid-1970s of about $200 million, a sum that did not begin to diminish until the 1990s. Degree programs in advanced engineering – biomedical, chemical, electrical, mechanical, metallurgical, naval and nuclear – were set up, and work in solid-state physics and lasers received immediate support. At the same time, separate initiatives in nuclear technology (including both nuclear power generation and a secret weapons program), space exploration, jet aircraft construction and computers were launched. Research in the fields of petroleum, telecommunications and electrical generation was funded through the state-owned corporations that monopolized these fields.

But Brazil's self-sufficiency program had contradictory effects. For one thing, it was inconsistent with the government's policy of economic openness to international capital and to the importation of new technologies, with the result that Brazilian research findings often went underutilized. And yet when the government decided to protect the Brazilian microcomputer industry from foreign competition in the 1980s, in an effort to force national development in that field, opponents of the policy argued that by restricting access to cheaper and better foreign computer technology, the government was hurting the country's economic competitiveness, which was the very goal of the self-sufficiency program. The protectionist policy in information technology was finally abandoned in the early 1990s. By then, the civilian leadership of the country was taking steps to strengthen links between the research sector and private industry.

A military-initiated space program, which was firing test rockets by the mid-1980s with the aim of launching communication satellites, quickly moved

Brazil into first place among Latin American countries with space programs. The $470 million Centro de Lançamento de Alcântara (Alcântra Launching Center) in the state of Maranhão gave Brazil the launching center closest to the equator of any in the world, providing sizeable fuel savings compared to North American sites. The first completely Brazilian-made satellite, used primarily for collecting weather and other environmental data from the Amazon region, was launched in 1993. As the space program expanded to include the development of missile systems, concern mounted elsewhere about Brazil's potential to launch a nuclear-armed missile. The United States sought to restrict missile development in Brazil during the late 1980s and early 1990s, and in response to that pressure Brazil sought ties with other countries, including China and Russia, to enhance its satellite launch vehicle and ballistic missile programs. Later, Brazil requested admission to the Missile Technology Control Regime, a voluntary association of countries committed to non-proliferation of unmanned delivery systems that could carry weapons of mass destruction. Brazil was accepted as a full member in 1995. In 2006, Brazil and South Africa began the joint development of air-to-air missiles, with production scheduled to begin in 2013.

When in 1981 the armed forces built its underground Laboratorio de Estudios Avançados, equipped it with one of the largest computers in the world, and declared that it would develop a fast-breeder, gas-cooled nuclear reactor, the move was widely viewed as a step toward the manufacture of nuclear weapons. Nine years later, the elected civilian administration of President Fernando Collor de Mello (1990–1992) announced that the military government had in fact planned to test a nuclear device once it obtained enriched uranium. Collor's and successor administrations forged ahead with the construction of a uranium enrichment plant whose purpose was to make the country a net exporter of uranium by 2014, amid continuing speculation that the plant's output, intended exclusively for use as fuel in nuclear power plants, would increase the risks of nuclear weapons proliferation. On the other hand, Brazil and Argentina repeatedly pledged during the 1980s and 1990s to limit their nuclear development programs to peaceful uses, and in 1994 both countries finally ratified the 1967 Treaty of Tlatelolco, which prohibited nuclear weapons in Latin America. While Argentina became the first country in Latin America to build and operate a nuclear power plant in 1974, the performance of Brazil's nuclear program has been disappointing. One power plant that cost $2 billion to build had been in operation, off and on, since 1983. A second began operations in 2001 after a twenty-five-year construction period. The building of a third, halted in the 1980s, resumed in 2008 and was scheduled to begin operations in 2016 at a cost of nearly $5 billion.

Throughout Latin America, better conditions for the rapid expansion of scientific and technological research, long inhibited by political instability and economic underdevelopment, were emerging by the 1990s. Democratization and civilian rule tended to protect scientists from the blunt political interference that had been common under the military governments of the 1960s, 1970s and early 1980s. The globalization of technical and scientific knowledge reduced the costs of access to information and encouraged new research. Government and non-government organizations alike took steps to regionalize the promotion of scientific research and technical innovation by creating a number of cross-national cooperative networks. They included the Regional Network for the Popularization of Science and Technology in Latin America and the Caribbean ("Red-Pop"), the Pan-American Foundation for Science and a Common Market for Knowledge (MERCOCYT), the Latin American Academy of Sciences (ACAL); and the Ibero-American Science and Technology Program (CYTED). In 1992, the Bolivar Program linked research and development programs in universities with business enterprises.

One sign of improving conditions was the nearly threefold increase (a growth rate exceeding that of any other developing world region) in the number of scientific articles by Latin American researchers published in the world's most influential journals between 1988 and 2001. No Latin American country produced more scientific publications than Brazil (whose output quadrupled between 1988 and 2001), followed by Mexico, Argentina and Chile. Together these four countries accounted for nearly 90% of all Latin America's scientific articles. Moreover, the number of citations to those articles nearly tripled in the same period, and in three countries (Argentina, Brazil and Chile) most of those citations were by non-Latin American authors. In comparison with all developing countries in the world in 2001, Brazil ranked first and Mexico third in the relative rate at which its authors' articles were cited in the field of earth and space sciences. By the same measure, Chile ranked first and Mexico third in the field of biomedical research. Chile's record in mathematics made it the most widely cited developing country in that field. The always-strong relationship between international collaboration and scientific productivity could be seen in the sharp increase in articles by Latin Americans authors with international coauthors between 1988 and 2001, from 29% to 43%, reflecting the appearance on the scene of new countries (mainly of the former Soviet Union) as well as the Internet.

About four out of every five science and technology research units in Latin America in 2005 could be found in Argentina, Brazil, Chile and Mexico, plus Venezuela and Colombia. All six countries historically boasted per-capita incomes above the Latin American average, suggesting that scientific and technological prowess depended heavily on overall levels of development. On the other hand, a strong scientific and technological sector was increasingly seen as a prerequisite for economic growth and success in the highly competitive global marketplace. Developing countries could always depend on experts elsewhere to help them reduce inequalities, a special UN task force concluded in 2005. Nevertheless, it warned, "if long-term goals are to be achieved and growth and problem-solving are to become indigenous and sustainable, developing countries need to develop their own capabilities for science, technology, and innovation." The underlying premise of this view was that technological innovation must eventually replace natural-resource exploitation as the basis of development.[1]

Some of the political and economic obstacles to that goal can be illustrated in the career of Salvador Moncada, who was born in Tegucigalpa, the capital of Honduras, in 1944. Because the country had no medical school, Moncada moved to neighboring El Salvador to earn his medical degree, and stayed on to do research in cardiovascular science. But after he joined popular protests against the country's military dictatorship in the late 1960s, Moncada was deported back to Honduras. He won a fellowship at England's Royal College of Surgeons in 1971, and after three years returned to Honduras hoping to continue his research. But with "no infrastructure, no money and no connections with the outside world to do scientific research," as he put it, Moncada returned to the United Kingdom, going on to set up and then direct the Wolfson Institute for Biomedical Research at University College, London. The author of numerous highly-cited papers on the treatment of cardiovascular disease, and the recipient of honorary degrees and prizes for his research, Moncada was ranked in 2003 as the scientist with the second-highest record of citations in the world; he was one of only nine among the top fifty not working in the United States.

The migration of highly talented individuals like Moncada from Latin America to Europe or the United States has until recently been considered a net loss for the region, and a severe setback to economic development. However, concern about the "brain drain" has been balanced by an awareness that natives educated and trained outside the country produce knowledge that can flow back to the sending country in different ways, including through the collaboration of the natives themselves. Many eventually return to their home country, bringing their skills back with them. Another local positive effect is the increased incentive provided for others to seek to improve their skills, while the prospect of emigrating with those skills lowers the risks of investing in personal education.

Here, also, we see the transforming impact of globalization at work. "In a more global world the best and the brightest might, in fact, be potentially hyper-mobile entrepreneurs who are now able to stay at home with the new emergence of technical industries in developing countries or, when they do move, use transnational networks and contribute to the economic development of their countries and regions of origin," a team of researchers concluded in 2002. In addition, thanks to globalizing technologies themselves, "migrants, ideas, knowledge, information and skills sets" now routinely move back and forth around the world, at greater rates than were imaginable even two decades ago. Skilled and unskilled migrants alike have created a pattern of "trans-local interconnectivity" to their home localities.[2] All these changes may be transforming the "brain drain" from an outright liability into a trend with some positive aspects.

Thus, the experience of Salvador Moncada should be considered alongside that of Marco Tulio Medina of Honduras, who received his medical degree at Honduras' Universidad Nacional Autónoma in 1985. Subsequently trained in neurology in Mexico, France and the United States, Medina concentrated on research in epilepsy. He returned to Honduras to become director of his alma mater's training program in neurology. The author or coauthor of more than 100 papers and book chapters, he received credit in 2004 as the co-discoverer, with an international team of researchers, of a gene considered to be the principal cause of a common type of epilepsy. Medina went on to co-found and lead Honduras' Fundación Salvador Moncada para el Avance de la Ciencia – The Salvador Moncada Foundation for the Advancement of Science.

Communications in the Age of Information

Among the near-universal advances most responsible for reducing the isolation of Latin American researchers is the Internet and allied technologies of communication and information. The gains in economic productivity resulting from ever-increasing use of the Internet have been matched by tremendous leaps in the dissemination of all kinds of knowledge by means of distance learning, digital libraries, medical consulting, and e-mail communication. Many now see these new tools of information technology as indispensable weapons in the war against poverty and other aspects of underdevelopment, as well as the means of encouraging more participatory democracy and government accountability.

Since 1970, entirely new communications media have appeared, and existing ones transformed. The leading advance was no doubt the breathtaking gains in digitization – the reduction of text, speech and images to numerical digits. The result: An immense expansion of the quantity of information in circulation, and a tremendous increase in the speed of its transmission and the range of its reception. Information of all kinds – from music and other forms of entertainment to news and technical data – became more accessible than ever to greater numbers of people, by means of an ever-greater variety of media. What linked all those who generated, distributed and used this information was what one communications scholar called "the biggest single machine that has ever been created," namely, the "global information infrastructure," a network of networks able to accommodate multiple users and an amazing diversity of content.[3]

If one had to pick a date for the birth of the "big machine" of global information it would probably be 1980. That was the year the International Telecommunications Union, an association of 191 nations established in 1865 to standardize and coordinate telecommunications networks and services, decided to adopt global standards for the creation of a worldwide network for the transmission of all types of information. The result was the Integrated Services Digital Network (ISDN). The fruit of the convergence of two technologies (computing and communications), ISDN could not have happened without digitization. In the very same year, Wilbur Schramm, the century's foremost theoretician of mass communication, observed that what the world was witnessing was less a change in the *kind* of information available than in the rate of increase in both the size and speed of its *flow*. We were at the threshold, he declared, of "an Age of Information."[4]

The first serious international debates about the way information of all kinds was being produced and distributed across the globe had also just begun to take place in the 1970s. Who was generating the news and entertainment programs that dominated the world's media? Who controlled the world's telecommunications systems? For what purposes, and with what effects? Answers supplied by radical critics of capitalism hinged on the assumption that the political and cultural content of any given medium must be dictated by the presumably monolithic economic interests of the owners. In fact, the highly industrialized countries of the North Atlantic world practically monopolized control over the content of the global information networks, as well as the conditions of access. Many in Latin America, but especially intellectuals, interpreted that domination as a deliberate assault by the most developed capitalist countries, whom they accused of "cultural imperialism," or of trying to alter the values and beliefs of the inhabitants of the poorer countries in order to ensure they would continue to cooperate in their own victimization as the targets of capitalist exploiters. As a discourse in the ideological rivalry that stoked the Cold War, cultural imperialism found its most influential expression in a book coauthored by Ariel Dorfman, a Chilean, and Armand Mattelart, a Belgian intellectual working in Chile. *How to Read Donald Duck: Imperialist Ideology in the Disney Comic* was first published in Chile in 1971 as *Para Leer el Pato Donald,* then translated into fifteen languages:

> According to Disney, underdeveloped peoples are like children, to be treated as such, and if they don't accept this definition of themselves, they should have their pants taken down and be given a good spanking. That'll teach them! When something is said about the child/noble savage, it is really the Third World one is thinking about. The hegemony which

we have detected between the child-adults who arrive with their civilization and technology, and the child-noble savages who accept this alien
authority and surrender their riches, stands revealed as an exact replica
of the relations between metropolis and satellite, between empire and
colony, between master and slave.

Critiques like these led to proposals, centered in the United Nations, for a
"new world information and communication order" whose aim would be the
establishment of a separate global communication system for the developing
countries, under which every poor country would achieve "information sovereignty." The UN chose Latin America as the most propitious site for its First
Intergovernmental Conference on National Communication Policies, which
drew representatives from twenty Latin American countries to San José, Costa
Rica in 1976. Two conditions made Latin America an attractive site to launch
a global movement for communications reform. First, almost all print and
electronic media in the region were privately owned, a fact interpreted by the
reformers as evidence of social inequality and as a major obstacle to information sovereignty. Second, the intense social upheavals and the rise of guerrilla
insurgencies that marked the mid-1970s seemed to be a favorable moment to
propose the establishment of publicly-owned media enterprises, which would,
it was assumed, automatically represent the interests of the poor majority.
Reformers also favored government regulation of privately owned media in
order to force them to become more responsive to popular interests and
needs.

Needless to say, the San José meeting was not welcomed by the owners of
the mass media. They feared that its goal of encouraging governments to adopt
national "communications policies" would lead to government limitations on
freedom of expression. In the end, the meeting's recommendations for more
balance in news coverage, government guarantees of wider access and popular
participation in the media, and media support for certain development goals,
were largely ignored. Nevertheless, the San José meeting of 1976, and the global
debate that formed it, raised fundamental questions that persist today about
the role of communications in economic development generally, and especially
the way new communication and information technologies interact with political, cultural and economic institutions.

What did change, beginning in the 1980s, were the basic conditions
governing the discussion. First, the national and international markets in communications turned from being dominated by a handful of huge public and
private corporations to ones that were becoming increasingly open and competitive. That transformation was facilitated by technological innovations
(such as microwave telephone networks) that made monopolistic practices less
justifiable, and by the global policy move toward economic liberalization.

Second, after 1989, the year that most of eastern Europe's communist dictator-ships fell, global communications issues could be discussed in an entirely new ideological environment. The Cold War rivalry that pitted liberal capitalist principles against a state-centered socialist model of economic development with limited personal freedoms was rapidly displaced by the broad acceptance of democratic procedures and guarantees of fundamental rights and freedoms.

As a result, by the early 1990s, Dorfman and Mattelart's once-canonical interpretation seemed obsolete. Information was still flowing faster and in greater quantities than ever, but it was ever-more diverse in viewpoint and subject matter, as well as increasingly accessible to more people. The ownership and nationality of the biggest global communications companies had diversi-fied considerably since the 1970s. Moreover, the notion of a passive audience available for manipulation and exploitation by powerful monopolies suc-cumbed to the realization that individuals and groups actively engage with what they hear and see, and utilize it for purposes that they themselves devise. Pluralism and openness, under conditions of increasing freedom in both the reception and the transmission of information, were quickly emerging as the criteria of justice in a "new world information and communication order" whose contours were very distant from what the critics of the 1970s had advo-cated on the eve of the Age of Information.

Internet

The most telling expression of this new order was the spectacular growth of the Internet, a medium at once personal, public and universal. Even if one could show that information-media ownership was too concentrated in "foreign" hands, the impact on values and beliefs in any given region of the world could not plausibly be reduced to the preferences of any single ideology or economic interest. By the first decade of the new century, the general tendency was not toward a homogenization of cultures but rather a kind of selective hybridization. People assimilated or rejected distinctive facets of once-distant cultures, even as they gave voice to their own versions of the local culture, in surprising ways and in unexpected venues. In suburban Washington, DC, immigrants from Mexico and Central America open the morning newspapers – published in places like Guanajuato and Tegucigalpa – before breakfast, without leaving their homes, and without having to actually buy the papers, by directing the Internet browser on their home computer. They call their families in San Salvador or Zacatecas for a few cents a minute using tele-phone cards purchased in a local convenience store or on the Internet, or place Internet calls without spending a cent. They tune in a cable TV channel – or their home computer – to watch television programs originating in their home countries. Of course, similar scenes unfolded in countries across Latin America, among immigrants and travelers as well as among individuals still rooted in the localities they were born into. One result was that the cultural assimilation of immigrants, once taken for granted in, say, the United States or Brazil, could seemingly be resisted or postponed indefinitely.

Like any technologies, however, access to those of the Age of Information was often subject to the limits imposed by wealth and income. The tension between the potential scope of information technologies and their effective application was reflected in the "digital divide," the gap between "information-rich" societies and individuals and those that are "information poor." In a global sense, the gap separated developed and developing countries, while from a national perspective, the division applied to sizeable groups of individuals, some of whom enjoyed high rates of access to the new technologies, while others could count on little or none.

Two important measures of access were the rate of Internet penetration and the quality of the connections and related services, including the basic tele-communications infrastructure. Of course, a certain level of education and technical skill was also needed to obtain and make good use of information. In other words, disparities in the new information technologies tended to reinforce disparities in traditional technologies; a UN report in 2004 found that 81 out of 100 of the world's Internet users lived in just 20 countries. Finland with a population of 5 million had as many Internet users as all of sub-Saharan Africa with a population of 643 million. In 2007, only about 17% of the world's population used the Internet but the average access rate of 54% in North America, Europe and Oceania was five times more than that of the rest of the world (10%). The OECD countries owned 93% of Internet hosting services. Finland had more Internet hosting services than all of Latin America, and New York City more than all of Africa. All of Latin America's bandwidth (the rate at which data can be transferred) was roughly equal to that of Seoul, the worldwide leader in broadband Internet access.

In Latin America, some of the prerequisites for overcoming the digital divide began taking shape during the 1990s. The most notable was the rise in literacy and general education rates, and the deregulation of the telecommunications industry. In addition, initiatives directed to Latin America by various interna-tional agencies were applying nonregional resources to overcoming the digital divide. The Institute for Connectivity in the Americas (ICA)'s Network of E-Government Leaders in Latin America and the Caribbean (Red GEALC), encouraged the use of the new information technologies in the public sectors of eighteen Latin American countries and supplied training and technical assistance. The ICA was a project of the Canadian government. In 2002, the European Union began promoting periodic Ministerial Information Society Forums aimed at planning cooperative projects in information technologies between Latin American countries and those of the European Union. Some countries set up "digital community centers" offering free Internet access in public libraries, museums, schools, health clinics. By 2007, about 16% of the population in Latin America was using the Internet, compared to about 70% of the U.S. population.

Some specialists argued that the Internet tended to intensify inequality and exclusion because those with higher skills and education were also best able to exploit it. The introduction of any new technology in a setting of scarce, unevenly distributed resources typically meant that access to them would be used to gain still more resources, including those associated with communications and information. Those few with the capacity to work with and benefit from computers were likely to benefit disproportionately from the information revolution, while disadvantaged groups without access to even basic education were likely to be excluded from the start. In a region like Latin America, where class and ethnic-group relations draw on deep economic and social inequities, a domestic digital divide was to be expected. By 2000, close to 20% of the richest 15% of the population had Internet connections, compared to a 3% overall rate, and that discrepancy was likely to "increase significantly," a UN study predicted in 2003.[5] In the higher-income countries of Argentina, Chile, Costa Rica, Mexico and Uruguay, 20–25% of households were estimated to have Internet access in their homes in 2008–2009; the rate in Bolivia, El Salvador and Guatemala ranged from 2 to 5%.

Newspapers and Broadcast Media

In what follows, we focus on changing trends in the mass media of Latin America since the early 1970s in two areas, newspapers and broadcast media. Their importance derives from their peculiar standing as commercial enterprises that also provide an indispensable service as the principal public forums for the exchange of news, information, values and opinion. As a result, they shoulder certain ethical responsibilities and social obligations that some commentators have identified as "civic journalism," such as commitments to accuracy, fairness, balance and comprehensiveness in their news coverage. The ability of the Latin American countries to consolidate democracy will therefore depend partly on the quality of the news media and their freedom from government interference, and thus on the depth of their allegiance to the principles of civic journalism, as opposed to the journalistic practices associated with Latin America's authoritarian tradition.

In the Latin American countries, daily newspapers continued to play a vigorous role in national life during the four decades ending about 2010. Between the late 1960s and the late 1990s, as the population of Latin America grew by about 80%, the number of daily newspapers grew 30%, to a total of 1,258. Despite that strong growth, however, the number of copies printed per 1,000 inhabitants, when averaged across all 19 countries, rose only modestly, from about 82 to about 86, a trend that mirrored the general global tendency across countries identified as "developing," in which the average circulation rose from 23 per 1,000 inhabitants in 1970 to 28 in 1995. (By comparison, U.S. daily newspapers printed about 212 copies per 1,000 inhabitants in 1996).

Regional and national trends within Latin America varied enormously in response to such diverse influences as levels of literacy, urbanization, economic prosperity and government regulation. The competition of other media, such as radio, television and the Internet, also affected the newspaper industry, as well as trends in the lifestyles of readers and in national and regional demographic structures. And of course, since advertisers provided most of the revenue of any newspaper, shifts in the cost-effectiveness of different media influenced the quality and durability of newspapers. From about 1970 to about 2000, the number of newspapers in Brazil rose from 250 to 465, the highest in Latin America, but circulation rose slightly, from 42 copies per 1,000 inhabitants to 45. In Mexico, the second-largest producer of newspapers, the number also increased dramatically, from 196 to 311, but circulation stagnated at about 92 per 1,000. The country with the highest circulation over the period was Uruguay; at 293 copies per 1,000 inhabitants in the late 1990s, it was far ahead of second-place Venezuela (with 206) and third-place Argentina (123). Everywhere by 2000, newspapers were turning to the World Wide Web to publish daily electronic editions; close to 300 Latin American newspapers were publishing online editions by the end of 2000.

The trends toward economic and political liberalization that we have identified as the keynotes of our era clearly favored both the growth of daily newspapers in Latin America, and their freedom to report the news and publish a diversity of opinions. Latin American governments have never been shy about exercising political control of the media by means of outright censorship or by asserting a right to license (and unlicense) media enterprises. Governments also used their considerable economic power to purchase advertising from friendly media and to withdraw it from unfriendly media. Nationalistic and populistic policies aimed at influencing access to media and to their content were common in the 1950s and the 1970s, and, as we shall see below, reemerged after 2000. In Brazil and Mexico, the two countries in which states had the most success in developing a collaborative relationship with commercial broadcasters, the broadcast markets have been monopolized by one or two powerful corporations that flourished under government protection. And it is no coincidence that they grew and achieved dominance precisely during periods of authoritarian rule in Mexico (beginning in the 1930s and lasting until 2000) and Brazil (1964–1984). Elsewhere in Latin America, state efforts to control the media have been more intermittent, and the result has been more competitive broadcasting sectors.

Thus, both television broadcasting and newspaper publishing appear to be permanently subject to the longstanding tension in Latin America between two different ideas about development: On the one hand, the belief that populist-oriented governments should expand their reach and control in the name of a collective and nationalistic development model; on the other, a free-enterprise model of economic development and political freedom based on a belief in the superiority of individual initiative and private interests. While this is a rivalry familiar to Europeans and North Americans, it is one that has long been even more prominent in Latin America. The region's history of authoritarian and dictatorial rule has in some ways worked to undermine public trust in government, while increasing the legitimacy of the media as independent sources of leadership in the political and cultural arenas.

The most dramatic changes in Mexico's newspaper and broadcast industry since the 1970s paralleled the country's transition, beginning in the late 1980s, from rule by an authoritarian, one-party state toward electoral democracy. That was also when Mexico's press and broadcast media undertook their own fitful transition from informal state oversight to independence. Since the 1930s, the Mexican state and the ruling Partido de la Revolución Institucional (PRI) had disciplined the country's newspapers to ensure favorable coverage for the regime through an ingenious variety of measures that turned the media into an instrument of the state. One government agency practically monopolized the supply of newsprint, an essential commodity that could be withheld from uncooperative publishers. Regular cash transfers and other gifts by government agents to individual journalists, editors and publishers became a routine part of Mexican newsgathering. The government informally exempted media companies from property and income taxes and provided lavish subsidies in the form of government-paid advertising. The few journalists who failed to cooperate were threatened or killed. More journalists were killed in Mexico between 1970 and 1998 than in any other Latin American country, although the main source of that violence was not the government but drug-dealers and corrupt policemen who were often the targets of journalistic investigations.

As a result of the Mexican government's policies of informal coercion and censorship, "The press quickly grew accustomed to using information spoon-fed to it by government officials or commercial sources that, to this day, dominates the front pages of almost all newspapers," Murray Fromson, a specialist in Mexican journalism, wrote in 1996. Among the few to resist was Julio Scherer, the editor of *Excelsior* of Mexico City, the country's largest newspaper, long considered the voice of the PRI. In the early 1970s, Sherer was making the newspaper one of the most respected in Latin America for its aggressive coverage, criticisms of the administration of President Luis Echeverría and investigations of official corruption. In early 1976, the government began applying pressure to *Excelsior* by withdrawing advertising and refusing to speak with its reporters. Finally driven out of the paper by the administration of President Luis Echeverría in 1976, Scherer and other staff members founded the critical news magazine *Proceso* in late 1976, despite being forced to borrow newsprint from other publications and to buy it on the private market at much higher rates when the government paper agency refused to sell it the newsprint it needed. *Proceso* survived, becoming the leading Mexican newsweekly, still famed for its independence and investigative reporting.

Another publisher who made a career of resisting government control and intimidation was Alejandro Junco de la Vega, who inherited ownership of his family newspaper, *El Norte* of Monterrey, in 1971 at the age of 24, soon after he graduated from the University of Texas with a bachelor's degree in journalism. Overcoming attempts by the administration of President Echeverría to sabotage *El Norte* by cutting off newsprint, eliminating government-sponsored advertising, and subsidizing the establishment of a rival newspaper, Junco de la Vega went on to establish the successful daily, *Reforma*, in Mexico City in 1993. *Reforma* became a model of the civic journalism that was beginning to transform the Mexican news media, winning praise for its commitment to balance and diversity in news coverage, aggressive reporting and autonomy from governmental control. Another example emerged in Guadalajara, Mexico's second-largest city, when Alfonso Dau and Jorge Cepeda launched *Siglo Veintiuno* in 1992.

As the Mexican state sold off more and more public enterprises in the 1980s, its financial leverage over the mass media declined and private-sector demand for advertising rose. When the PRI lost more elections to opposition parties at the local and state levels, journalists had no choice but to turn to the opposition for information. At the same time, a wave of political violence and corruption scandals in the late 1980s and early 1990s further reduced the credibility of the PRI and the presidency that it still controlled. Readers began to prefer newspapers that demonstrated independence and integrity. As a result, by 1997 most Mexico City readers were buying one of the new "civic style" newspapers – *Reforma*, *La Jornada* or *El Financiero*. In 2000, the election of Vicente Fox indirectly exposed details of the corrupt relationship that had endured over the decades between the PRI-controlled governments and the news media. *Excelsior* lost its secret government subsidies and had to pay $70 million in back taxes. And in a country where circulation reports were rarely audited, it turned out that *Excelsior* had inflated its circulation by a factor of 2.7 – instead of 180,000 copies daily, it was printing 65,000.

Elsewhere in Latin America during the 1980s and 1990s, similar transitions to a civic-minded approach to news coverage encouraged the region's gradual democratization, a process that in turn abetted the turn toward more civic-oriented journalism. In Chile, writers and editors who challenged the military government of President Augusto Pinochet (1973–1990) were subject to arrest, exile or assassination. When the regime loosened its grip on public information in the mid-1980s, the daily newspaper *La Epoca* went out of its way to cover all political viewpoints, including that of the government, but made no secret of its preference for a democratic transition. As in Mexico, the example of *La Epoca* encouraged journalists at other Chilean publications to take a more critical stance toward the government, and public support for those moves in turn encouraged more daring coverage.

As Guatemala's armed forces slowly yielded its control of the country to elected civilians, a group of entrepreneurs established a new daily newspaper, *Siglo Veintiuno*, in 1990. For the first time in decades, Guatemalans were offered stories about public corruption and human rights problems. As the paper's circulation increased, its rivals responded by imitating *Siglo Veintiuno*'s critical style. Even the country's largest newspaper, *Prensa Libre*, turned away from its tradition of pro-government coverage. When the military attempted a *golpe de estado* in 1993, only *Siglo Veintiuno* and the smaller *La Hora* openly defied the armed forces' attempts at censorship, but *Prensa Libre* collaborated with the censors. With the failure of the military takeover seven days after it started, *Siglo Veintiuno*, *La Hora* and the magazine *Crónica* were widely seen as having contributed to broad public resistance to the resumption of military rule.

As commercial enterprises, newspapers must return a profit if they are to survive. They also require access to capital for investment in new technologies. With few exceptions, therefore, the future of the newspaper industry will turn more and more on financial considerations. Survival in many countries has meant the acquisition of independent newspapers by large newspaper chains or media corporations, which could inhibit editorial independence and diversity. At the same time, competition by the Internet – where anyone with a computer connection can, in theory, publish an unlimited number of words accessible to everyone in the world, around the clock – posed the greatest technological challenge to the survival of the newspaper in its history.

No country's newspapers or magazines, however, could match the reach of radio and television broadcasting, owing in part to widespread illiteracy, in part to the accessibility of electronic media. By the 1990s, radio claimed the largest audience of any communications medium, covering nearly 100% of Latin America; Brazil alone had almost 3,000 radio stations. Estimates of the proportion of households with radios in 2006 ranged from about 80% in Honduras to around 90% in Brazil, Mexico and Uruguay. Rates of television ownership were still more disparate. In 2006, about two out of three households in Bolivia and Honduras had a TV while for Argentina, Brazil, Chile,

Mexico and Uruguay the rates were in the mid to upper 90% range. In some countries, sizeable shares of the population were still living out of range of a radio signal (19% in Panama, 12% in Brazil, 10% in Honduras) in 2002. No terrestrial TV signal was available to 42% of Panamanians, 23% of Peruvians, 20% of Paraguayans, 11% of Brazilians, and 10% of Hondurans. While some households in such excluded areas undoubtedly subscribed to either cable or satellite services, people living in rural areas so remote as to be out of range of terrestrial signals were also more likely to be too poor to purchase such services. Although these figures reveal some significant disparities from country to country in access to radio and TV broadcasts, the overall share of households without radios or TVs is evidently quite small – probably no more than 10% – in relation to the total population of Latin America, and terrestrial TV signals reach at least 90% of the population in almost all countries.

At its birth in the mid-1940s, television (like radio in the 1930s) was introduced everywhere in Latin America according to the U.S. free-enterprise model, rather than the state-operated model that would predominate in Europe. In many cases, U.S. equipment manufacturers and television networks supplied financial and technical support to Latin American entrepreneurs, as well as U.S.-produced TV programs. U.S. programming and U.S. financial investment in the Latin American television industry soared in the 1960s, with the support and encouragement of the U.S. government. At the same time, U.S. corporations became major advertisers in Latin American TV markets. During its first two decades of its existence, then, Latin American TV was a transnational medium that depended on transnational investors, programmers and advertisers. But that dependence dwindled in the 1970s as U.S. networks divested themselves of their Latin American properties and Latin America producers replaced more and more U.S. programs with locally made shows.

In Mexico, the Televisa network monopolized the commercial television market from 1973 to 1993, when the government sold its own network of 140 TV stations to a private investor who christened his new property "TV Azteca." As a result, these two networks came to control 95% of the Mexican television market, the most highly concentrated in Latin America by the turn of the century. About 80% of Mexico's 465 television stations were doing little more than repeating the programs of one of the two networks. From its first days, Televisa made itself the mouthpiece of the PRI and the Mexican government, and responded to news events according to their estimated impact on corporate interests. Emilio Azcárraga, Televisa's principal shareholder, whose personal wealth was estimated at $5 billion, liked to identify himself as a "loyal soldier of the PRI" and a major financial contributor to the party. In the highly contentious presidential election of 1988, Televisa almost entirely ignored the political opposition to the PRI. "We are of the PRI, members of the PRI," Azcárraga said in 1988. "We do not believe in any other option. And as members of our party, we will do everything possible so that our candidate triumphs. This is very natural."[6]

The coverage of the 1994 presidential election by both Televisa and TV Azteca continued the pro-PRI tradition. In response to widespread criticism, both networks began to take a more objective stance in their reporting after the 1994 election. They gave nearly equal time to all the top candidates in future elections, particularly as opinion polls revealed higher and higher public support for opposition figures. With the death of Azcárraga in 1997 and the appointment of his 29-year-old, U.S.-educated son Emilio to succeed him, Televisa promptly shed its identity as a PRI organ. "What we are looking for today in Televisa's news programs is the truth," the younger Azcárrago announced at a staff meeting within days of his father's death.[7]

The dramatic expansion of the Latin American TV markets encouraged the exportation of locally made programs within the region. Contrary to the fears of those who accused the United States of "cultural imperialism," television ownership and programming became strongly Latin American from the 1970s on. Latin Americans clearly preferred, and got, programming that was linguistically and culturally Latin American. Mexico and Brazil emerged as the principal TV programming exporters within the region, followed by Venezuela and Argentina.

The most characteristically Latin American TV programs were the *telenovelas*. Like their U.S. counterpart, the soap opera (named for the dominance of detergent-manufacturers as program sponsors), telenovelas were serial melodramas broadcast at the same time every day. Unlike the U.S. version, which indefinitely postponed a plot resolution, the telenovela story usually had a definite beginning and ending. The plot was more likely to be based on a storyline already familiar to national viewers, who would therefore have a rough idea about how the story would end. Telenovelas also differed from the U.S. version in that they were usually shown at prime evening viewing hours rather than during the day, showcased well-known stars, and called for more elaborate productions than the assembly-line, indoor-studio style familiar to U.S. audiences.

No type of TV program in Latin America produced more revenue than the telenovela. As a thoroughly transnationalized product, the telenovela eventually found its principal distribution center in Miami, which also became the main residence of telenovela actors, directors, producers and technicians, and therefore a popular production location as well as a distribution center. Close to the geographic heart of the Latin American and U.S. Hispanic markets, Miami's diverse and plentiful Hispanic population, and its position as a major air transport hub, accounted for its status as the telenovela capital. By the 1990s, Latin American telenovelas – mostly produced by Televisa of Mexico, TV

Globo of Brazil, and Venezuela's Venevisión and RCTV – were being exported
throughout Europe and were especially popular in the post-communist societies of eastern Europe. The extraordinary popularity of the genre, both in Latin
America and elsewhere, probably owed little to any particularly "Hispanic"
qualities, but rather to its universal appeal. Delia Fiallo, a Cuban-born resident
of Miami and one of the most prolific and successful writers of telenovela
scripts, told a Venezuelan interviewer in 2001:

> I believe that the success, the force of penetration, of the telenovelas
> consists of nothing more than emotions. Emotion is the common
> denominator of the human species, throughout time and in all countries
> around the world. Love, hate, ambition, envy, and jealousy are common.
> It is the common denominator that explains how a telenovela written for
> Venezuela can be successful in Santo Domingo, can be successful in
> Greece, in Turkey, in Japan. Because we are not beings from the planet
> Mars, we are all human beings who respond to the same emotions. That
> is the whole secret.[8]

Despite the successes recorded by journalists and news organizations committed to more serious, independent and balanced reporting in the early years
of democratization, civic journalism had generally failed by 2005 to put down
roots in more than a few countries in Latin America. What one team of
researchers called "independent, pluralistic, and assertive" reporting continued
to encounter major obstacles. The first was violence against journalists, an
expression of the general lack of support for the rule of law in Latin America.
While state-sponsored censorship and informal authoritarian control had
ended almost everywhere except in Cuba, threats and pressures of a different
order persisted. In fact, standard surveys of press freedom reported less freedom
in Latin America in the first years of the new century than in the early 1990s.
Between 1988 and 2003, 273 journalists were murdered in Latin America; in
Guatemala alone, twenty-one were killed between 1988 and 2002. Typically, the
killers were drug-dealers and members of paramilitary and guerrilla organizations, and they usually went unpunished.

The second barrier to a more aggressive style of journalism were laws that
harshly punished libel and defamation, crimes often interpreted very broadly,
and laws that kept much government information off limits to the public.
Third, the ownership of broadcast media remained highly concentrated almost
everywhere. The markets in Mexico, Brazil and Venezuela were nearly controlled by duopolies, while those in Chile and Argentina qualified as oligopolies.
Usually, these networks were family-owned and operated, and thus hesitated
to undertake aggressive reporting that might embarrass political allies or big
advertisers. The ownership of the print media and radio stations appeared to

be much more diffuse. A fourth obstacle was journalists' lack of training in the requisite skills and attitudes required of a more aggressive and pluralistic approach to news gathering and reporting. Finally, most Latin Americans continued to rely mainly on television broadcasts for their news because of the higher costs of access to newspapers, magazines, cable television and the Internet.

If the consolidation of democracy depended in part on the development of a civic-oriented media, removing these barriers or reducing their negative effects could be considered an essential step in favor of democratization. But the overall trend in Latin America in the decade ending in 2010 was toward less freedom to report and interpret the news, effectively stalling and in some cases reversing the liberalization of the 1980s and 1990s. While this was part of a larger global pattern, the setbacks in Latin America were probably greater than anywhere else in the world, with the possible exception of the countries of the former Soviet Union.

Outside of Cuba, where the communist government has monopolized all communications media since the early 1960s, the most formidable obstacles toward liberalization were encountered in Venezuela during the presidency of Hugo Chávez (1999–). In 2003, the Inter-American Commission on Human Rights began calling on the government to halt attacks on journalists and to refrain from interfering with the free flow of ideas. But in the following years, the Chávez government expanded its censorship and control of the mass media. One of its most effective tools was the state's power to require all elec-tronic communications media in the country to simultaneously transmit Chávez's speeches and other public acts, without time limit, a practice known as *cadenas presidenciales* or blanket broadcasts. Between 1999 and 2009, Ven-ezuela's communication media were forced to transmit the equivalent of more than fifty-two days of uninterrupted presidential broadcasts, effectively turning them into arms of the state for hours every week.

At the same time, Chávez and other government officials took to publicly condemning communications media and individual journalists in ways that both intimidated them and incited violence against them. For example, in his blanket presidential broadcast of 14 May 2009, Chavéz asserted that Ven-ezuela was

> in the presence of a terrorist attack from within: we must tell them, the white-collar terrorists, bourgeois terrorists [who] have radio stations, television stations, and newspapers . . . This cannot be permitted . . . We all know who I am talking about . . . We will do what we have to do, and here we will wait for them . . . They are playing with fire, manipulating, inciting to hatred, every day . . . I only tell them, and the Venezuelan people, that this will not continue.[9]

As it closed down television and radio stations and harassed others, the Chávez administration also moved to increase its direct control over the airwaves, so that by 2007, it owned six television stations, three national radio stations, and more than 400 community-level radio and TV stations. In 2008, the government launched the $400 million "Simón Bolívar" telecommunications satellite, the country's first, to expand TV, radio and Internet services to the 20% of the population that it said were underserved by these media. As anti-government news and commentary migrated to the safety of Internet web sites, Chávez responded by announcing in 2010 that "the Internet cannot be something open where anything is said and done," and called for government oversight of websites.[10]

While Venezuela's move away from media freedom remained the most salient in Latin America, setbacks were regularly reported in Ecuador, Honduras, Mexico and Nicaragua during the first decade of the new century. Clearly, many governments in the region had come to resent the newly aggressive reporting of the 1990s, and to react defensively to the vastly increased flow of critical commentary enabled by the new technologies. They responded, not by protecting the media's watchdog role, but rather by seeking out new ways of slowing down or derailing the expressions of civic journalism.

Everywhere in Latin America, the traditional family-owned media companies were disappearing by the late 1990s, as economic liberalization and the acceleration of global capital flows transformed more and more such firms into corporate conglomerates. At the same time, programming content became less international and more local and national in character for the simple reason that audiences overwhelmingly preferred it to foreign content. Prime-time markets in the larger and wealthier Latin American countries were soon dominated by locally produced shows, while smaller and poorer countries (with less production capacity) tended to broadcast more programs imported from other Latin American countries. Thus, to see "globalization" as the annihilator of national cultures, at least in the Latin American media context, would be a grave oversimplification. As in the case of the telenovelas, we have seen how both global and regional-level forces interacted with political interests at the national level, and with national demographic and economic structures, in myriad ways that resist easy generalization.

Notes

1   United Nations Millennium Project 2005, *Innovation: Applying Knowledge in Development. Task Force on Science, Technology, and Innovation* (London: Earthscan, 2005), 21, 28.

2   Dominique Guellec and Mario Cervantes, "International Mobility of Highly Skilled Workers: From Statistical Analysis to Policy Formulation," in *International Mobility of the Highly Skilled: OECD Proceedings* (Paris: OECD, 2002), 85–6.

3   Sandra Braman, "Technology," in *The SAGE Handbook of Media Studies*, ed. John D. H. Downing (Thousand Oaks, Calif.: SAGE Publications, 2004), 123–44, here 133.

4   Wilbur Schramm, "The Effects of Mass Media in an Information Era," in *Propaganda and Communication in World History*, ed. Harold Lasswell, Daniel Lerner and Hans Speier, vol. 3: A Pluralizing World in Formation (Honolulu: University Press of Hawaii, 1980), 297.

5   United Nations Economic Commission for Latin America, *Road Maps toward an Information Society in Latin America and the Caribbean* (np: United Nations Economic Commission for Latin America, 2003), 12.

6   Sallie Hughes, *Newsrooms in Conflict: Journalism and the Democratization of Mexico* (Pittsburgh, PA: University of Pittsburgh Press, 2006), 165–9; Murray Fromson, "Mexico's Struggle for a Free Press," in *Communication in Latin America: Journalism, Mass Media, and Society*, ed. Richard R. Cole (Wilmington DE: Scholarly Resources, 1996), 115–38, here 124–7.

7   Hughes, *Newsrooms in Conflict*, 168–79.

8   Daniel Mato, "The Transnationalization of the Telenovela Industry, Territorial References, and the Production of Markets and Representations of Transnational Identities," *Television & New Media* 6 (November 2005) 4: 441.

9   Quoted in Inter-American Commission on Human Rights, "Democracy and Human Rights in Venezuela," 30 December 2009, www.cidh.org.

10   "Venezuela's Chavez calls for internet controls," 13 March 2010, Reuters, www.reuters.com.

References

Braman, Sandra. "Technology." In *The Sage Handbook of Media Studies*, ed. John D. H. Downing, 123–44. Thousand Oaks, CA: Sage Publications, 2004.

Fromson, Murray. "Mexico's Struggle for a Free Press." In *Communication in Latin America: Journalism, Mass Media, and Society*, ed. Richard R. Cole, 115–38. Wilmington, DE: Scholarly Resources, 1996.

Guellec, Dominique, and Mario Cervantes. "International Mobility of Highly Skilled Workers: From Statistical Analysis to Policy Formulation." In *International Mobility of the Highly Skilled: OECD Proceedings*, 71–98. Paris: OECD, 2002.

Hughes, Sallie. *Newsrooms in Conflict: Journalism and the Democratization of Mexico*. Pittsburgh, PA: University of Pittsburgh Press, 2006.

Mato, Daniel. "The Transnationalization of the Telenovela Industry, Territorial References, and the Production of Markets and Representations of Transnational Identities." *Television & New Media* 6, no. 4 (2005): 423–44.

Schramm, Wilbur. "The Effects of Mass Media in an Information Era." In *Propaganda and Communication in World History*, ed. Harold Lasswell, Daniel Lerner and Hans Speier, 3: A Pluralizing World in Formation, 295–345. Honolulu: University Press of Hawaii, 1980.

United Nations Economic Commission for Latin America. *Road Maps toward an Information Society in Latin America and the Caribbean*. Np: United Nations Economic Commission for Latin America, 2003.

United Nations Millennium Project 2005. *Innovation: Applying Knowledge in Development. Task Force on Science, Technology, and Innovation*. London: Earthscan, 2005.

Chapter 13

Literature and the Visual Arts

Literature

A preoccupation with history and identity has long been a constant in Latin American literature. The Nicaraguan writer Sergio Ramírez (b. 1942) even *defined* literature as a search for identity – "the most splendorous way to look for and find ourselves, in a common, diverse, contradictory, bitter and dark territory." Adding that his own readings of Latin American authors had always been a search for his own identity, he speculated that "our Latin American identity resides in the very fact of looking for it."[1] Ramírez's comments came in a speech accepting a prize for his 1998 novel *Margarita, está linda la mar* (*Margarita, How Beautiful the Sea*), which contrasted the life and death of two major, though dissimilar, figures of Nicaraguan history: the poet Rubén Darío (1867–1916) and the dictator Anastasio Somoza García (1896–1956). In joining reality and legend, the novel also illustrated Latin American literature's second great obsession: its attachment to history.

The blending of reality and legend, or of reality and fantasy, is known as *realism*, and in the history of twentieth-century Latin American literature it has taken three basic forms: natural realism, social realism and magical realism. Natural realism or the "novel of the land," typical of the 1920s, attempted to make the duality of nature *vs.* man the basis of Latin American identity. Social realism was a defining feature of the Spanish American *novela indigenista* (nativist novel) of the 1930s and 1940s, which presented the native American peoples as a basic source of national identity. Another expression of social realism could be found in the Brazilian regionalist novels of the 1930s, of which the most representative were those of Jorge Amado, who made African-Brazilian culture a central theme.

Contemporary Latin America: 1970 to the Present, First Edition. Robert H. Holden and Rina Villars.
© 2013 Robert H. Holden and Rina Villars. Published 2013 by Blackwell Publishing Ltd.

In the 1940s, social realism began to yield to magical realism, one of the styles associated with the emergence of what critics began to call "the new novel." Unlike natural and social realism, in which the imagined characters and their situations never departed from reality, magical realism audaciously juxtaposed fantasy and reality, while practically reinventing the narrative line of the novel. Magical realists interrupted and fragmented the old novel's lineal progression. Multiple narrators replaced the omniscient third person, while linguistic experimentation sometimes made language itself a theme of the novel rather than a mere vehicle. At the same time, the boundaries separating traditional genres of narrative, poetry, and the essay were reshaped, if not broken entirely.

The new novel movement culminated in the so-called "Boom" of the 1950s and 1960s, when Latin American literature began to draw international attention and found a place within the mainstream of Western literature. For some critics, the source of the Boom could be found in the work of the Argentinean novelist Jorge Luis Borges (1899–1986), particularly in his seminal *Ficciones* (*Fictions*), a collection of stories written between 1941 and 1944. Not only did *Ficciones* apply many of the narrative methods associated with the fiction of the Boom, but its author achieved a level of recognition among European critics that few if any Latin Americans had ever matched.

The subject of the novel of the Boom was the complex nature of the individual person, rather than the "needs of the people" with which the writers in the natural and social realist traditions were concerned. As the Peruvian writer Mario Vargas Llosa, one of the best-known Boom writers and the winner of the Nobel Prize for Literature in 2010, said in 1968, the new novelists "make no effort to express 'a' reality but rather personal visions and obsessions: 'their' reality."[2] Thus did the "new novel" emphasize the individual's solitude, pessimism and incommunicability by appealing to irony, humor, fantasy and the reader's sense of the absurd. The most representative product of the Boom were thus the magical realist novels, whose greatest practitioner was Gabriel García Márquez (1928–) of Colombia. In his 1982 Nobel Prize acceptance speech, García Márquez observed that the real eventually overcomes the fantastic. Latin Americans, he said, "have had to ask but little of imagination, for our crucial problem has been a lack of conventional means to render our lives believable. This, my friends, is the crux of our solitude."[3]

By 1975, a different form of narrative characterized by less formal experimentation, a more optimistic and reader-friendly tone, and a more overt concern with social problems appeared. Referred to as "post-Boom" fiction, it represented a radical break with the novel of the Boom for some critics, while for others, the post-Boom was simply a shift toward a less oblique engagement with social reality, and, hence, a partial return to the tradition of social realism. In just the way that some Boom writers had been inspired by the artistic experimentation of the 1959 Cuban Revolution, the Boom also owed its decline in part to the deterioration of revolutionary Cuba's artistic culture. By the mid-1970s, the Cuban revolutionary government had narrowed the limits of freedom for writers and other artists with its slogan, "Within the Revolution everything; outside the Revolution nothing." No longer did Cuba represent utopia for Latin American artists, as it had to many in the 1960s.

In addition, the late 1970s saw the beginning of a shattering economic crisis across Latin America. Military regimes governed most countries, and the Central American countries were sinking deeper into the maelstrom of war and revolution. The Boom novel was now interpreted as "elitist" because of its preoccupation with language and narrative techniques. Some called for a literature more accessible to the ordinary reader, more directly connected to daily life. The Argentine writer Julio Cortázar (1914–1984) responded by defending the Boom, and insisting that his and others' writing had always been anchored in the "the historical present of man" and sought to encourage "his long march toward the best of himself as collectivity and humanity."[4] Likewise, the Mexican Carlos Fuentes (1928–) argued that "the use of power" could always be found in the background of the Boom novel.[5]

In fact, since the late 1960s, when the Boom hit its peak, fiction that tended to focus more on everyday life was already being published. In Brazil, a literature of resistance to the military dictatorship that took over in 1964 emerged, linking historical events with fictional texts. Persisting until the 1980s, it distanced itself from the experimental, individual-centered fiction of the 1950s. Antônio Callado's novel *Quarup* (1967), the story of a Catholic priest who became progressively politicized while living among the Xingu people, and who ultimately embraced the armed struggle against the military regime, was perhaps the most representative novel of the literature of resistance during the 1960s. In 1969, Ignácio de Loyola Brandão finished his novel *Zero*, a critique of the abuses of the military regime that had to be first published in an Italian translation in 1974 because of military censorship. The German edition appeared in 1979; the same year the novel was finally allowed to be published in Brazil.

In 1968 a Mexican literary group, *La Onda* ("wave"), emerged as a transitional movement between the Boom and the post-Boom. The novels of the two leading figures of *La Onda*, José Agustín (1944–) and Gustavo Zaíns (1944–), depicted the youth counterculture of Mexico with its rock music and contemporary slang. The same interest in popular culture was also found in the work of the Argentine Manuel Puig (1932–1990), a novelist whose experimentation with narrative styles and linguistic registers placed him in the Boom, but whose more direct, representational style also made him a transitional figure from the Boom to the post-Boom. In his first two novels, *La traición de Rita Hayworth* (*Betrayed by Rita Hayworth*) (1968) and *Boquitas Pintadas* (*Heartbreak Tango*) (1969), Puig recreated the lives of townspeople in a narrow and oppressive society where the passive consumption of mass culture (Hollywood movies, tangos, soap operas, women's magazines and the like) became a means of both alienation and conciliation. Puig's 1976 novel, *El beso de la mujer araña* (*Kiss of the Spider Woman*), an international success, linked the themes of Marxist revolution, homosexuality, political repression and insurrection in a South American dictatorship.

The theme of political protest was in fact central in post-Boom fiction, especially in the work of writers of the Southern Cone and Central America, where dictatorships and insurgency during the 1970s directly affected literary production. An example could be seen in the work of the Chilean Antonio Skármeta (1940–), a prominent post-Boom writer. In the 1960s, his short fiction displayed the pessimism and use of imaginative fantasy characteristic of the Boom. But his novels of the 1970s and 1980s referred directly to socio-political reality while celebrating human warmth and solidarity. Behind that change was the electoral victory in Chile of the Marxist government headed by Salvador Allende in 1970 and then its overthrow by the military in 1973. Before Allende's election, Skármeta criticized his own writing as "individualistic and egocentric," a tendency that he reversed as socialism became a reality under Allende. The political engagement of Skármeta's fiction found its most radical expression in *La insurrección* (1982), a literary interpretation of Nicaragua's Sandinista revolution of 1979.

The Nicaraguan revolution was a central theme of *La mujer habitada* (*The Inhabited Woman*) (1988), the first novel of the Nicaraguan poet Gioconda Belli (1948–). The main character, Lavinia, a politically insensitive upper-class architect, joined the struggle to overthrow the dictatorship of Anastasio Somoza after she encountered social injustice and the horrors of political repression. Sergio Ramírez, who also portrayed the political struggle against the Somoza dynasty, argued that the function of the novelist was to fulfill a "political act" by novelizing the material supplied by "political reality."[6]

Ramírez's view of the novelist as a political actor drew on the Latin American tradition of engagement between intellectuals and politics that had begun in the independence era. In the particular case of Central America, writers nearly always saw themselves, and were seen by others, as mentors of the popular classes. This perception was crystallized in the frequently quoted phrase of the Guatemalan writer Miguel Angel Asturias (1899–1974): "To be a writer is to be the moral consciousness of his people." The tradition of the writer as political thinker gave rise to another Latin American phenomenon: the writer as politician. Ramírez was vice-president of Nicaragua during the period of Sandinista rule (1984–1990). The Salvadoran poet Roque Dalton (1935–1975) died a guerrilla fighter, and Vargas Llosa, whose right-wing politics set him apart from the vast majority of Latin American writers, ran unsuccessfully for president of Peru in 1990.

The political motive in Latin American writing culminated in the emergence of the so-called testimonial novel and non-fictional testimonial narratives. The Salvadoran Manlio Argueta (1935–) gained an international reputation for novels documenting the history of the civil war in El Salvador in the 1970s and 1980s. Non-fictional testimonial narratives gained large readerships during the same decades. *Testimonio* as the voice of witnesses sought to reveal aspects of reality as lived by oppressed individuals. *Si me permiten hablar* (*Let me Speak! Testimony of Domitila, a Woman of the Bolivian Mines*) (1978) by Domitila Barrios de Chungara and *Me llamo Rigoberta Menchú, y así me nació la conciencia* (*I, Rigoberta Menchú: An Indian Woman in Guatemala*) (1982), were among the most celebrated non-fictional testimonial works of the time, though the author of the latter was later accused by a U.S. anthropologist, David Stoll, of inventing some of the material in her book.

Among the most important features of the post-Boom period was the salience of women writers, whose presence was scarcely detectable during the Boom, with the exception perhaps of the Brazilian Clarice Lispector (1920–1977), who along with João Guimarães Rosa (1908–1967) were the only two Brazilians that critics associated with the Boom. However, some female authors who earned international reputations in the post-Boom had begun publishing in the 1960s: the Mexican writers Elena Garro (1920–1998) and Elena Poniatowska (1933–), and the Argentine Luisa Valenzuela (1938–). Garro's first and most celebrated novel, *Los recuerdos del porvenir* (*Recollection of Things to Come*) (1963), was judged by Octavio Paz as "one of the most perfect creations of contemporary Spanish-American literature." The novel was considered a seminal example of magical realism, and some critics suggested that it influenced García Márquez. With her testimonial novel *Hasta no verte Jesús mío* (*Here's to You, Jesusa!*) (1969), Elena Poniatowska became a leading figure in the introduction of non-stereotypical female images in Latin American literature. The novel was based on the life of Jesusa Palancares, a working-class woman who joined the Mexican revolution of 1910 and survived poverty. Poniatowska presented Palancares as a sort of androgynous figure with both masculine and feminine traits. This convergence seems to be essential, according to some feminist criticism, in the breaking of stereotyped female characters in literature. Valenzuela's work shared defining features of both the Boom and the post-Boom. Her emphasis on language in some of her novels, and on the psychological dimension of her characters, along with the interplay of fantasy and reality, placed her in the Boom mainstream. But her political questioning of reality associated her with the post-Boom.

Among the most clearly representative women writers of the post-Boom were the Chileans Isabel Allende (1942–) and Diamela Eltit (1949–), the Puerto Rican Rosario Ferré (1942–), the Uruguayan Cristina Peri Rossi (1942–) and the Mexicans Laura Esquivel (1950–) and Ángeles Mastretes (1949–). All these and many other female figures of the post-Boom challenged the Boom not only because they brought "feminine writing" to the center of contemporary Latin American literature, but also because of the way they presented women as anti-patriarchal figures. According to Isabel Allende, the post-Boom broke a "conspiracy of silence" around the writing of Latin American women that she claimed had existed since the seventeenth century.

In the 1990s, a trend against the literature of the post-Boom emerged. In Mexico, this new movement was founded by a group of young authors who in a manifesto identified themselves as the *Grupo Crack*. Adopting the term "crack" for its onomatopoeic association in both Spanish and English with the noise made when something splits open, the *Crack* authors – Miguel Angel Palou, Eloy Urroz, Ignasio Padilla, Ricardo Chávez Castañeda and Jorge Volpi, all born in the late 1960s – challenged the literature produced immediately before them. They depicted it as "cynically superficial and dishonest," nurtured by a "doubtful magical realism" and by the use of slang and the "rock discourse." Against what they called a *lite*, "trick" literature, the Crack authors offered their own "profound," "total" novels, written in a renewed language, and committed to "formal and aesthetic risk" which they associated with continuity rather than rupture.[7] They preferred themes that were not tied to Latin American reality, thus distancing themselves from the traditional quest for national and continental identity that had characterized literary production in Latin America for so long. When replying to critics about the strangeness of his novel *En busca de Klingsor* (*In Search of Klingsor*) (1999), which dealt with Nazism, Jorge Volpi said:

> I feel very Latin American, which made it absolutely natural for me to write a novel in which Latin America doesn't appear at all. There were some critics who denounced its foreignness, but for me it was always normal to admire novels such as *Doctor Faustus* by Thomas Mann or *The Man Without Qualities* by Robert Musil . . . Literature has never recognized the restrictive borders of the actual world. We belong to multiple traditions, and that does not make us any less Latin American or Mexican.[8]

A cognate trend aimed against the Boom and the post-Boom was the *McOndo* movement, named for a book published in 1996. *McOndo* was an anthology of short stories by seventeen Spanish and Latin American writers, published in Spain in 1996 and edited by the Chilean writers Alberto Fuguet and Sergio Gómez. The contributors intentionally sought to distance themselves from the influence of magical realism and the exoticism popularly associated with Latin America, particularly in Europe and the United States. The *McOndo* authors avoided both social commentary and any explicit preoccupation with the search for a Latin American identity. Instead, they revealed a much more intense concern with their own lives and their identity as individuals.

Depicted sometimes as individualistic, pseudo-intellectual and socially insensitive, the McOndo style reflects both the interests of a younger generation of writers and the larger social, political and economic changes that Latin America passed through in the 1990s, such as globalization and neo-liberalism. The McCondo writers were born in the 1960s and thus largely missed the political effervescence and repression experienced by the post-Boom writers. Their writing, by comparison, was almost entirely non-political. "McOndo" was a satirical reference to the fictional town of *Macondo* in García Márquez's great Boom novel, *Cien Años de Soledad* (*One Hundred Years of Solitude*), the paragon of magical realism, mocked by associating its numerous literary imitators with the worldwide chain of McDonald's restaurants.

According to McOndo's practitioners, the exploration in their writing of the audiovisual culture of movies and television shows, and the impact of new technologies on individuals and societies, were not signs of "alienation." Rather, their work expressed a "visceral reaction against magical realism" and a vision of a Latin American literature in which "dissimilar proposals and influences coexist," according to a McOndo writer, the Bolivian Edmundo Paz Soldán. The McOndo writers simply rejected the idea of a fixed Latin American identity, he said, and dealt instead "with the formation of more flexible identities . . . If today there is no explicit political commitment to a given ideology or social cause, this does not mean that we as writers are not interested in history or politics."[9]

Similarly, the Mexican Jorge Volpi claimed in 2009 that the new Latin American authors, particularly those affiliated with *Crack* and the McOndo movements, "are not waging a war against the idea of being Latin American, and their books do not have the declared object of escaping Latin America." Arguing that the new authors were indeed preoccupied with Latin America but without being obsessed by it (as were earlier generations of writers), Volpi declared:

> Let us be radical: Latin American literature does not exist anymore. Lovely: hundreds or thousands of Latin American writers exist, or better said, hundred of thousands of Chilean, Honduran, Dominican, Venezuelan (etcetera) writers exist, but a unique literary body endowed with recognizable characteristics, no. We have just seen it: the Spanish language is not a shared characteristic. And, if truth be told, there is nothing to lament.[10]

Volpi's judgment about the non-existence of a distinctly Latin American literature seemed to be contradicted by the appearance of a new genre, "narco-literature" or the literature of violence. Narco-literature was realism reborn, and its theme was the violence, corruption, kidnapping, and slaughter associated with drug-trafficking. The genre first appeared in Colombia with the publication of *La virgen de los sicarios* (1994) by Fernando Vallejo, translated into English as *Our Lady of the Assassins* (2001), a fictional account of the conversion of Medellín, the second-largest city of Colombia and hometown of the author, into a center of drug-driven violence and moral degradation. Hired killers or *sicarios* were the alienated protagonists of Vallejo's sordid world. In 1999, the Colombian Jorge Franco's *Rosario Tijeras*, a story centered on the life of a woman who overcame poverty by becoming the lover of drug lords, was published. But even Colombian authors who have no intention of addressing narco-trafficking in their novels end up incorporating it as a backdrop. This was the case of the renowned Laura Restrepo, whose novel *Delirio* (2004), a story of the troubled life of a young woman of the country's traditional oligarchy, could not escape the whirl of narco violence. Making reference to this fact, Restrepo told an interviewer:

> I think that [violence] marks all of us, even if that is not the intention. I will give you an example; with *Delirio* my purpose was to write an intimate story that took place within the four walls of a room, about a woman who becomes insane and about the attempt of her husband to help her to escape the dark waters of madness. Nothing in the story of national reality, nothing of denunciation, nothing of politics. Yet, the explosions of the bombs of Pablo Escobar [a Colombian drug-dealer] ended up imposing themselves as a backdrop.[11]

As drug-trafficking spread to other Latin American countries in proportions closer to those of Colombia, drug-dealers and violence became an important literary theme elsewhere. The Mexican Élmer Mendoza recreated the criminal environment of northern Mexican drug trafficking in such novels as *Un asesino solitario* (1999), *El amante de Janis Joplin* (2002), and *Balas de plata* (2008). Narco-violence informed the novels of other Mexicans, including Sergio Gonzáles Rodríguez, Mario Gonzáles Suárez and Yuri Herrera. Sergio Ramírez's *El cielo llora por mí* (2009) recreated the world of crime, corruption and abuse of power in the trafficking network that turned Nicaragua and other Central American countries into a bridge linking the drug-dealers of Colombia and Mexico after the 1980s.

For some critics, narco-literature is something to lament rather than to celebrate. "When it was thought that the distinctive features of Latin American literature had vanished – that McOndo had triumphed over the epigones of Macondo – *el narco* returned to supply Latin America with the violent and exotic character that one expects of it," Volpi declared.[12] Narco-literature, he added, "teaches no lessons, passes no moral judgments, and is barely an instrument of criticism."[13] He conceded, however, that a very few narco novels were "small literary jewels" in a "genre dominated by clichés."

One of them, many critics agreed, was 2666 (2004) by the Chilean Roberto Bolaño (1953–2003). This posthumously published novel gave Bolaño such a large international reputation that many critics spoke of him as the "new patriarch" of Latin American letters. His 2666 was a fictional reconstruction of the mysterious assassinations of more than 500 women since the early 1990s in Ciudad Juárez ("Santa Teresa"), Mexico. The darkness and chaos of the town – which in fact claimed the highest murder rate in the world – represented Latin America. But as the Spanish literary critic Ignacio Echeverría observed, Bolaño's writing "is neither magical realism, nor baroque nor localist, but an imaginary, extraterritorial mirror of Latin America, more a kind of state of mind than a specific place."[14] Unlike García Márquez's characters, who inhabit the exotically rural and sharply bounded "Macondo," the characters of Bolaño's fiction lived and traveled in the global village, even as Latin America remained an inescapable point of reference. This extraterritoriality was what made Bolaño an international or "post-national" writer, and explained in part his enormous success not only in Latin America but also in the United States and Europe. As a writer, Bolaño rejected any attempt to cage him in any aesthetic tradition or within the limits of any nation. "When I write the only thing that interests me is writing itself; that is, the form, the rhythm, the plot." Born and reared in Chile, Bolaño lived in Mexico, France and Spain. When asked whether he considered himself Chilean, Mexican or Spanish, he replied: "I am Latin American."[15]

The opening of the twenty-first century did not put an end to Latin American literature's obsession with history and identity, despite the intentions of many contemporary authors to distance themselves from that tradition. The words of Argentine literary critic César Fernández Moreno, uttered in 1972, have not lost their relevance: Latin American writers "have no choice but to express the world that surrounds them and imposes itself on them, surging and clamorous, a world of contradictions and upheavals, of contemplation and annihilation."[16]

Visual Arts

The preoccupation with history and identity in Latin American literature was a familiar aspect of the visual arts as well. The point can be demonstrated in the way that two major trends in avant-garde art – abstraction or formalism, on the one hand, and figuration or representation, on the other – interacted and competed throughout the twentieth century. Abstract art is self-contained;

its content depends on internal form rather than on external reality or pictorial representation. Figuration or representation, conversely, is centered in the outside world, not in the work of art itself.

The outstanding example of figuration until the 1950s was Mexican muralism, a movement in search of local meanings, identities and values driven by an overtly political commitment to social change emanating from the revolution of 1910. The muralists Diego Rivera (1886–1957), José Clemente Orozco (1883–1949), and David Alfaro Siqueiros (1896–1974) influenced the subsequent course of Latin American art more than any other artists, particularly in countries with sizeable indigenous populations.

Abstract art appeared first in Argentina in the 1920s and flourished there in the 1940s, when a group of abstractionists who called themselves the Grupo Madí (probably a made-up word) explicitly rejected meaning and representation in their art. In the 1950s, abstract art became the dominant trend in Latin America, displacing muralism. Young and talented artists everywhere took up abstractionism, developing it along a variety of innovative pathways, including the rigorously anti-figurative movement known as concretism, as well as neo-concretism, constructivism, kinetic and geometric art. If the artists of earlier decades had worked in isolation, those of the 1950s interacted frequently and learned to appreciate one another's work through exhibitions and competitions that embraced the whole region. The construction of new art museums and galleries, as well as a rising demand for international art publications (driven in part by escalating rates of economic growth and urbanization in the 1950s and 1960s), further stimulated artistic creativity and overall output.

This climate of change also brought forth a modernist architecture with a clear regional or nationalist flavor, very different from the dominant nineteenth-century "Europeanized" styles of the 1920s and 1930s. The construction between 1956 and 1960 of the city of Brasilia, the new capital of Brazil, stands as one of the most important architectural events in twentieth-century Latin America. Other giant architectural works included the building of the Universidad Nacional Autónoma de México in the early 1950s and Ciudad Universitaria of Caracas (1940s–1950s). These and other modernist construction projects sought to integrate the visual arts with architecture, adapting styles imported from outside Latin America to local and regional artistic tendencies.

The adhesion of Latin American artists to abstractionism was seen by some art critics to have stemmed from the promotion and support of abstract art by U.S corporations in Latin America during the Cold War. Because abstract art appeared to be politically neutral, it could theoretically counteract the influence of the figurative art nurtured by the school of "socialist realism," which highlighted the sufferings and struggles of the downtrodden classes. Regardless of the validity of this commentary, Latin America's abstract art was never monolithic, for it reflected the enduring regional tendency to readapt foreign aesthetic styles to local characteristics and needs. That in turn implied a direct or indirect interest in the extra-aesthetic reality of place and time. For example, in 1959 a group of Brazilians quit the concrete art movement to form neo-concretism, proclaiming as their goal the interaction of sensory and mental experiences, a reconnection of art with reality that they asserted had been blocked by concretism's excessive rationality.

The clearest illustration of the longing of Latin American artists to reconcile their art with the region's natural environment was the emergence in the early 1960s of neo-figuration (or neo-humanism, or expressionist figuration), a blend of the two great rival schools, abstractionism and figuration. Neo-figuration became an alternative to both socialist realism and pure abstraction-ism, and while its artists were found in most Latin American countries, the genre was cultivated most notably in Mexico among artists known as *Interioristas* (Interiorists) and practitioners of a *Nueva Presencia* (New Presence), and in Argentina, where they became known as members of the school of *Nueva Figuración* (New Figuration) or *Otra Figuración* (Other Figuration). For the neo-figurists, art was not a purely individual experience, as abstractionists averred. Rather, it was mediated by collective and historical experience.

Because of its hybrid character, neo-figuration could be used to condemn political dictatorship and social inequality, as in the work of the Venezuelan Jacobo Borges (1931–), who used expressionistic techniques to satirize violence and corruption through the deformed images of politicians, military officers and members of the upper class. A similarly satirical, expressionist approach to social and political themes was developed by the Colombian painter and sculptor Fernando Botero (1932–) through the use of grossly rotund human figures. Neo-figuration sometimes overlapped with surrealism in the 1960s and 1970s, making the fantastic and the surreal staple themes of art in Argentina, Chile, El Salvador and Peru. Benjamin Cañas (1933–1987) of El Salvador established himself as one of the most noted painters of the fantastic in Latin America.

An important art trend cultivated in the 1970s and the 1980s which expressed the enduring interaction between artistic and extra artistic concerns among Latin American artists was conceptualism. Conceptual art was also known as "non-conventional art" because it needn't result in either a painting or a sculpture, and was rooted in the mostly U.S. notion that the heart of any work of art was really an idea or a concept. "De-materialization" became a defining feature of conceptual art because in it the art object was deemphasized and even eliminated, while the concept was made explicit through a written message. The mainstream conceptual art of the United States and Europe was self-referential, given that the conceptual propositions embodied in it were the artists' perceptions of their own work. Latin American conceptual art became saturated with social and political content, turning external reality into its main point of reference. Without discarding the object entirely, Latin American conceptualist artists recovered it and made it a vehicle of their conceptual-ideological program. In 1970, for instance, the Brazilian Cildo Meireles (1948–) took returnable glass Coca-Cola bottles and printed political statements on them, including "Yankees Go Home." Because the message could hardly be read when the bottles were empty, the Coca-Cola factory refilled the bottle without noticing the subversive message. In a time of intensive political repression, when Brazilian art galleries were closed to any kind of overt political art, Meireles sought to undermine what he called the "imperialist ideology" carried in the Coca- Cola bottles.

Conceptualism emerged first in Brazil and Argentina, and moved on to Chile, Colombia, Mexico, Venezuela and other Latin American countries at a time when political upheavals and openness to experimentation defined art production in the region. Even when particular local or national themes were addressed, the conceptual movement had a Latin American perspective. In the words of one conceptual artist, the Uruguayan Luis Camnitzer (1937–), the movement transcended nationalism by sharing the "continental awareness, the idea about a political and economic Third World, and particularly the existence of the Cuban Revolution, which exemplified a political and economic alternative to the taken for granted or forcefully imposed U.S. capitalist model."[17]

If the art of the 1960s and 1970s functioned as an emissary of the impending glories of revolutionary political action, that of the 1980s and 1990s tended to evoke death, exile and hopelessness – the "memory of the defeat," as the Argentine critic Néstor García Canclini put it.[18] In Chile, for instance, as artists and intellectuals sought to recover from the trauma of the military coup of 11 September 1973, artistic work was marked by pessimism, anguish and a sense of guilt over the destruction of democracy. Political repression as well as the absence of a strong market for art forced Latin American artists to emigrate to New York, Paris and other major artistic centers. Yet cultural values and the reference to Latin America in work produced abroad were not lost. Luis Camnitzer moved to New York in 1964, arguing that a "unified" Latin American art (as opposed to a nationalistic art) was more likely to emerge in exile than in the region itself.[19]

This idea of Latin American art as a cultural product with a common core of beliefs and values, an ethos (rather than a mere geographic space), infused the work of the generation of Latin America artists who, whether working in the region or outside of it, associated themselves from the 1990s on with a diversity of "neo-isms" – neo-expressionism, neo-constructivism, neo-surrealism – or with postmodernism, or installation art. They claimed to be at once international and Latin American. Often conflictive and eclectic, the new trends and styles nevertheless retained, in different ways, the traditions that informed Latin American art since the beginning of the twentieth century, when the imagery of cultural change and socio-political strife native to the region began reshaping the dominant European-oriented artistic forms.

Notes

1   Sergio Ramírez, "Palabras al Recibir el Premio Alfaguara 1998," www.sergioramirez. org.ni/premio_alfaguara_1998.htm.

2   Quoted in Jean Franco, *Critical Passions. Selected Essays* (Durham, NC: Duke University Press, 1999), 260.

3   Nobel Prize Award Ceremony Speech, www.nobelprize.org/nobel_prizes/ literature/laureates/1982/presentation-speech.html.

4   Quoted in Ramón Xirau, "Crisis del realism," in *América Latina en su literatura*, ed. César Fernández Moreno (Mexico City: Siglo XX Editores, 1972), 185–203, here 198.

5   Quoted in Jorge Larrain, *Identity and Modernity in Latin America* (Oxford: Blackwell Publishing, 2000), 131.

6   Donald Leslie Shaw, *The Post-Boom in Spanish American Fiction* (Albany: State University of New York Press, 1998), 11.

7   "Manifiesto Crack," *Revista de Cultura Lateral* 70 (2000) www.circulolateral.com/ revista/tema/070manifiestocrack.htm.

8   Martin Solares, "Jorge Volpi," *BOMB* 86 (2004): 76–80.

9   Edmundo Paz Soldán, "From Macondo to McOndo: Latin American Fiction Today," Borders, 2004, www.bordersstores.com/features/feature.jsp?file=pazsoldan.

10   Jorge Volpi, "The Future of Latin American Fiction (Part II)," 2009. Three Percent, www.rochester.edu/College/translation/threepercent/index.php?id=2323.

11   *El País* (Madrid) 4 June 2010, Laura Restrepo, www.elpais.com/edigitales/ entrevista.html?encuentro=6779&k=Laura_Restrepo.

12   Jorge Volpi, "Cruzar la frontera," *Milenio* (Mexico City), 24 October 2009, http:// www.milenio.com/cdb/doc/impreso/8662190.

13   Jorge Volpi, "The Future of Latin American Fiction (Part IV)," 2009. Three Percent, www.rochester.edu/College/translation/threepercent.

14   Quoted in Larry Rohter, "A Writer Whose Posthumous Novel Crowns an Illustrious Career," *The New York Times*, 9 August 2005, 3.

15   Interview, Carmen Boullosa, "Roberto Bolaño," *BOMB* 78 (2002): 49–53; Roberto Bolaño, *Between Parentheses: Essays, Articles and Speeches, 1998–2003* (New York: New Directions, 2011), 357.

16   César Fernández Moreno, "Introducción," *America Latina en su literatura*, ed. César Fernández Moreno (Mexico City: Siglo XXI Editores, 1972), 5–18, here 13.

17   Luis Camnitzer, *Conceptualism in Latin American Art: Didactics of Liberation* (Austin: University of Texas Press, 2007), 4.

18   Néstor García Canclini, "Aesthetic Moments of Latin Americanism," *Radical History Review* 89 (2004), 13.

19   Camnitzer, *Conceptualism*, 225.

References

Bolaño, Roberto. *Between Parentheses: Essays, Articles and Speeches, 1998–2003* New York: New Directions, 2011.

Boullosa, Carmen. "Roberto Bolaño." *BOMB*, no. 78 (2002): 49–53.

Camnitzer, Luis. *Conceptualism in Latin American Art: Didactics of Liberation* Austin: University of Texas Press, 2007.

García Canclini, Néstor. "Aesthetic Moments of Latin Americanism." *Radical History Review*, no. 89 (2004): 13–24.

Fernández Moreno, César. "Introducción." In *América Latina en su literatura*, ed. César Fernández Moreno, 5–18. Mexico City: Siglo XX Editores, 1972.

Franco, Jean. *Critical Passions: Selected Essays*. Durham, NC: Duke University Press, 1999.

Larrain, Jorge. *Identity and Modernity in Latin America*. Oxford: Blackwell Publishing, 2000.

"Manifiesto Crack." *Revista de Cultura Lateral*, no. 70 (2000).

Paz Soldán, Edmundo. "From Macondo to Mcondo: Latin American Fiction Today," Borders, www.bordersstores.com/features/feature.jsp?file=pazsoldan.

Rohter, Larry. "A Writer Whose Posthumous Novel Crowns an Illustrious Career." *The New York Times*, 9 August 2005, 3.

Shaw, Donald Leslie. *The Post-Boom in Spanish American Fiction*. Albany: State University of New York Press, 1998.

Solares, Martín. "Jorge Volpi." *BOMB*, no. 86 (2004): 76–80.

Volpi, Jorge. "Cruzar la frontera," Milenio (Mexico City), 24 October (2009), http://www.milenio.com/cdb/doc/impreso/8662190.

Volpi, Jorge. "The Future of Latin American Fiction (Part IV)," (2009). Three Percent, www.rochester.edu/College/translation/threepercent.

Xirau, Ramón. "Crisis del realismo." In *América Latina en su literatura*, ed. César Fernández Moreno, 185–203. Mexico City: Siglo XX Editores, 1972.

Chapter 14

Cinema and Sports

Cinema

"Wherever filmmakers, of whatever age or background, place their cameras and their profession in the service of the great causes of our time, there is the spirit of Cinema Novo," said the Brazilian filmmaker Glauber Rocha in 1965, when the so-called New Latin American Cinema was at its peak.[1] Particularly strong in South America, the New Cinema arose in the late 1950s as part of the same trend in literature toward a more nationalistic and socially engaged art. The film industry in Latin America – strongest in Argentina, Brazil and Mexico – had reached its "golden age" in the 1940s, but the traditional Latin American cinematic fare of comedies and melodramas that drew their inspiration from Hollywood was condemned by the New Cinema movement for being "evasive" and "deforming," mere spectacle or entertainment, driven exclusively by the profit motive.

In opposition to the traditional genre, the film of the New Cinema sought to critically reveal the inequalities of Latin American society and promote their elimination by heightening the political consciousness of the viewer. As the Argentine filmmaker Fernando Solanas put it, the New Cinema was to be "involved ideologically and politically in and for the revolution."[2] The different names that the New Cinema movement adopted reflected its advocates' intention to revolutionize Latin American societies: Cinema Novo in Brazil, Cine Liberación in Argentina, Third World Cinema in Bolivia, New Cinema in Chile, Cine Popular in Colombia. In communist-ruled Cuba, it was "Imperfect Cinema," with aesthetic concerns subordinated to the movie's political aims.

Contemporary Latin America: 1970 to the Present, First Edition. Robert H. Holden and Rina Villars.
© 2013 Robert H. Holden and Rina Villars. Published 2013 by Blackwell Publishing Ltd.

In the seedbed of the social and political movements of the 1960s, the New Cinema matured in favor of "national liberation" and radical social change while explicitly challenging the products of Hollywood and of its imitators elsewhere in the world. In Argentina, anti-imperialist films such as *La Patagonia Rebelde* (*Rebellion in Patagonia*, 1974) were as successful as sentimental films such as *La tregua* (*The Truce*, 1973), which received an Oscar nomination. The military coup of 1976 and its consequent wave of terror and repression put an end to the notion of "revolutionary" film endorsed by the Cine Liberación movement, forcing many Argentine filmmakers into exile and leading to the "disappearance" of others. After the military government gave up power in 1984, the period of military rule became the subject of one of the most remarkable Argentine films of the era – *La Historia Oficial* ("The Official Story," 1985) a documentary-like accounting of the brutality and moral decadence of the dictatorship.

Chile's vigorous New Cinema suffered the same fate as that of Argentina when the military coup of 1973 led to the imprisonment, death or exile of numerous Chilean filmmakers. Political movies made before the coup were banned and films censored. One result was the creation of a Chilean cinema-in-exile by filmmakers living in Europe, Canada, the United States, the Soviet Union and many Latin American countries. Some of them were classified as a "Chilean cinema of the resistance" because they focused on the Chilean situation before and after the military coup as well as on the difficulties of exile and immigration. In 1985, five years before the fall of the Pinochet government, the exiled Chilean filmmaker Miguel Littín, posing as a businessman, returned clandestinely with a film crew. On his safe return to Spain after two months of filming, he produced the documentary film "Acta General de Chile" (1986). Littín's daring so impressed his friend García Márquez that the novelist interviewed Littín and wrote *La aventura de Miguel Littín* (1986).

If the 1970s witnessed destruction and stagnation in Argentina and Chile, Mexico of the 1970s was the scene of a cinematic renaissance. There, the golden age of the 1940s and 1950s was immediately followed by an era notable for commercially profitable but remarkably low-quality films. Then, during the left-of-center presidency of Luis Echeverría (1970–1976), the state took control of film production and began to encourage movies that did not shrink from social and political criticism. The industry languished again in the 1980s during Mexico's worst-ever economic crisis and the consequent reduction of state funding. Mexico was not alone. In Brazil, the industry collapsed when President Fernando Collor de Mello, following a neoliberal economic agenda, suspended all state support for the arts in 1990.

Not until the second half of the 1990s – in the midst of renewed economic growth, the expansion of international markets, and the globalization of electronic communications media – did an expanding corpus of profitable Argentine, Brazilian and Mexican films begin to be released. That revitalization, like those before it, again received the backing and encouragement of governments. The new films emerged from diverse aesthetic currents, aimed at a global audience, and dealt with a multiplicity of topics without much regard for politics or ideology. These characteristics became the basis for a dichotomy that some critics established between "cultural cinema" (e.g. the New Cinema) and "commercial cinema," i.e. the cinema developed since the late 1990s. While the first questioned social and economic injustice, the "commercial" cinema (some critics said) only sought to encourage conformity with the status quo.

An example of the tension between these two concepts of filmmaking can be seen in the way critics responded to *Diarios de motocicleta* ("The Motorcycle Diaries," 2004). A worldwide commercial success, the movie received more than thirty nominations and awards. It narrated a journey begun on motorcycles by the 23-year-old Argentine Ernesto (Che) Guevara and his friend Alberto Granado through South America in 1952. Guevara later joined Fidel Castro's revolutionary movement in Cuba and became a revolutionary icon after his execution in Bolivia in 1967. An international co-production, the movie was directed by the Brazilian Walter Salles and produced by Hollywood's Robert Redford. Filmed in Spanish with Mexican, Argentine, Peruvian and other South American actors, its overarching theme was the emergence of political consciousness in the young Guevara as a result of his journey, in which he encountered impoverished peasants, oppressed indigenous peoples, exploited miners, lepers and so on. With the stunning majesty of South America's Andean landscape as its background scenery, the movie took the viewer well beyond the superficial story of Che's political awakening by conveying, in an almost documentary style, a more subtle and affirmative message about the depth and beauty of the daily life of ordinary people and their ancestral heritage.

But *Diarios de motocicleta* was criticized for failing to consider Guevara's revolutionary attitudes, just as other commercially successful Latin American films dealing with the problem of urban violence – the Mexican *Amores perros* (2000), the Brazilian *Cidade de Deus* (*City of God*, 2002) – were denounced for not presenting violence from the perspective of class conflict. At the core of such criticism was a failure to understand that the Latin American film of the early twenty-first century could not resurrect the political idealism of the 1960s, if for no other reason than that it would not prosper commercially. Nevertheless, a certain continuity was not hard to detect between the political cinema of the 1960s and the post-2000 cinema in the persistent desire of Latin American filmmakers, in the words of Walter Salles, to portray Latin American reality "in an urgent and visceral manner."[3]

Sports

It was just before midnight on 13 October 2010. Millions of people around the world were watching the live video transmission of a Chilean miner being lifted to the surface in a specially designed rescue capsule from 700 meters below the earth. Florencio Avalos was the first of the thirty-three miners who had been trapped on 5 August after the collapse of the San José mine near Copiapó. Twenty hours later, all thirty-three miners had been rescued. On 25 October, the Chilean government honored the miners in a solemn ceremony at the presidential palace, and then organized a soccer match between Team Hope (the miners) and Team Rescue (the government) in Chile's National Stadium. President Sebastián Piñera, Mining Minister Laurence Golborne, and the engineer who headed the rescue operation, André Sougarret, were among the players for the Rescue team. The Rescuers won 3–2.

The choice of a soccer match to officially close the spellbinding drama of "Los Trienta y Tres" demonstrated the game's special place in Latin American culture. Known as *fútbol* in Spanish and *futebol* in Portuguese, soccer has been a powerful force for national solidarity since the early twentieth century in some countries of Latin America, and in nearly all of them since the mid-twentieth century. Thus it was natural for a soccer game to crown an event in Chile whose successful denouement had generated a torrent of national pride. "What emotion! What happiness! What pride to be Chilean! And what gratitude to God!" exclaimed President Piñera in an entry on his electronic social-networking page after the rescue. Identical sentiments would have been expressed had the Chilean national soccer team come close to winning the World Cup in South Africa in the summer of 2010 – an event that President Piñera himself attended in a show of support for his country's team in its first match against Honduras.

Introduced to Latin America by Englishmen in the nineteenth century, soccer began to manifest its special power to consolidate identities at various levels – local, regional and national – during the first decades of the twentieth century, about the time it mutated from an elite to a popular pastime. The first place this happened was in Uruguay, which not only served as the host of the first World Cup tournament in 1930, but went on to defeat twelve rival countries to win the first World Cup. Uruguay had already established itself as the dominant power in world soccer by winning the gold medal in the Olympics of 1924 (Paris) and 1928 (Amsterdam). Its subsequent victory in the first FIFA (Fédération Internationale de Football Association) sponsored World Cup tournament in 1930 happened to coincide with the commemoration of its first century of political independence. From that moment on, Uruguay's national soccer team and the Uruguayan nation were an indissoluble unity. In 1950, when Brazil served as the host of the World Cup tournament, Uruguay upset all expectations by defeating Brazil 2–1 to win its second World Cup. In the minds of Uruguayans, this was a heroic deed of mythic proportions, a milestone that highlighted the greatness of a little nation of just 2 million with the highest Gross Domestic Product per head in Latin America.

Paradoxically, however, that victory – known forever as the *Maracanazo* (a word composed of "Maracaná," the name of the stadium in Rio de Janeiro and the augmentative suffix -*azo*, meaning a blow) — marked the end of Uruguay's dominion in Latin American soccer and the birth of Brazil as a giant in world soccer. Uruguayans interpreted their country's fourth-place finish in the World Cup of 1954 as a humiliating defeat. But worse was to come in 1958, when Paraguay eliminated Uruguay 5–0 in the qualifying round for the 1958 World Cup. Yet even the shock of that defeat failed to tarnish the self-image of soccer superiority. Another fourth-place finish in the semi-finals of 1970 was seen as yet another humiliation. Not until 2010 was the country's next fourth-place finish (in South Africa) welcomed and celebrated.

As Uruguay declined as a soccer giant, Brazil ascended. While winning its first World Cup championship in 1958, Brazil fielded a team that included a 17-year-old who stunned the world by scoring six goals in six games. Edson Arantes Do Nascimiento, better known as Pelé, not only propelled Brazil to world-class status. His amazing ability ignited popular interest in soccer everywhere. Brazil captured the World Cup again in 1962, 1970, 1994 and 2002, finished second in 1998 and fourth in 1974 and 1978. Brazil also held the distinction of being the only country to have played in every World Cup tournament from 1930 to 2010. When Brazil was chosen as the site of the 2014 World Cup, FIFA president Joseph S. (Sepp) Blatter declared, "There is no country in the world that is identified more with football. In Brazil football is a religion. What other country in the world is as synonymous with this sport?"[4]

Apart from the varying fortunes of the region's national teams, throughout Latin America soccer has become more than a pastime, sport or entertainment event. It is a symbol of national identity. Everywhere, one hears the slogan, "Todos somos la selección" ("We are all the national soccer team"), a saying that reveals the way "the team" united all the members of the nation and represented it on the world stage. Costa Ricans, observed the sociologist Sergio Villena Fiengo, "not only know their team; they recognize themselves in it."[5]

The affinity between soccer and national identity facilitated the sport's politicization. Pelé, the most famous Brazilian in the country's history and the highest paid athlete in Latin America, made public statements that were widely interpreted as defending the military dictatorship that governed Brazil from 1964 to 1985. Appointed Brazil's minister of sport from 1995 to 1998 – a post created for him – he became the country's first black cabinet minister. Romário de Souza Faria, another soccer legend, was elected a federal deputy in 2010 shortly after joining the Socialist Party. His wide margin of victory was owing entirely to his immense popularity as a soccer figure rather than to his political credentials; having led Brazil to victory in the 1994 World Cup, it became known as "the Cup that Romário won for Brazil."

What was it about soccer that made it a symbol of a nation's destiny, and made its most talented players national heroes rather than mere athletes? The answer could be found in the interplay of two factors: the sport's enormous popularity, and the readiness of political leaders to exploit that popularity. Soccer was popular because its rules were easily understood and it required no specialized equipment to play except for a ball. It was therefore accessible to practically everyone, of all ages and all economic classes, as players or spectators. In addition, soccer neatly balanced the demand for both collective and individual effort, requiring the constant involvement of all the players even while giving the most talented individuals the freedom to stand out. The only sport played mainly with the feet, soccer was by nature a vigorous, free-flowing game in constant motion. As a result, the sport tended to give the spectator a sense of continuous involvement in an exciting and suspenseful spectacle.

To all these natural characteristics of the game one must add a distinguishing Latin American feature: most of the region's soccer players grew up in poverty. This is the case of both Pelé and the Argentine, Diego Armando Maradona, the two greatest soccer players in history. Men like Pelé and Maradona thus attracted to the game, as both fans and players, many who shared their humble origins and identified with the players in a special way. Nor did soccer in any way exclude the middle class or the wealthy, for one of its characteristics in Latin America was the way it brought together, in one place and for a few hours, people of the most diverse social, economic, racial and professional backgrounds. A sense of equality and solidarity pervaded the stadium as the fans identified with their local team (representing their home town, or *patria chica*) or with the national team, representing the *patria* or nation. "Few things happen in Latin America that do not have some direct or indirect relation with soccer," wrote the Uruguayan writer Eduardo Galeano in 2004. "Whether it's something we celebrate together or a disaster that sinks us all, soccer counts in Latin America, sometimes more than anything else, even if it is ignored by ideologues who love humanity but can't stand people."[6]

This integrating function of soccer can be exploited by political leaders but it can also facilitate reconciliation in times of turmoil. In 2009, in the midst of the country's worst political crisis in decades, Honduras qualified for the World Cup after a twenty-eight-year hiatus. President Manuel Zelaya had recently been replaced and forced to leave the country by the national legislature, which appointed Roberto Micheletti to replace Zelaya. With Honduras deeply divided between supporters and opponents of Zelaya, the new government suspended some individual liberties and declared martial law. Civil war seemed an imminent possibility, and the national soccer team's qualification for the World Cup seemed to be the only thing capable of unifying the people. Ricardo Martinez, one of the fans who filled the streets of the country's second city, San Pedro Sula, to celebrate on 14 October, the day the team qualified, told a reporter: "The right, the left, the rebels, the *Zelayistas* – today there are no rivalries; ¡*viva Honduras!*"[7] Micheletti quickly declared 14 October a national holiday and publicly thanked God for "this beautiful opportunity that has been given to us, the Hondurans." The next day, he invited the national team for lunch in the presidential palace and had his picture taken with the "new national heroes."

Another illustration of soccer's importance could be found in Ecuador's qualification for the World Cup in 2006 for the second time in its history. In Ecuador, soccer was as likely to stand for national differences as national unity, for it tended to reflect the historical, political and cultural divide that separated two antagonistic regions, the *sierra* ("the mountains") and the *costa* ("the coast"), represented respectively by the two biggest Ecuadorian cities, the capital of Quito and the port and trading center of Guayaquil. In the nineteenth century, the rivalry between these two cities was political and religious, as Quito advocated conservatism and the Catholic tradition, and Guayaquil, liberalism. But as the competitive spirit expanded to encompass other aspects of life, soccer games became the battlegrounds between the two city-regions. Even their respective soccer federations fought over control of the Federación Nacional Deportiva de Ecuador. Games between the regions' teams invariably provided settings for *Quiteños* and *Guyaquileños* to express their mutual hatred. In 1997, after living in Ecuador for a year, the coach of the Ecuadorian national team, the Colombian Francisco Maturana, observed that the two regions were "two countries in one," and that each transferred its enmity toward the other on the soccer field.[8] With the national team's qualification for the World Cup in 2006, however, and in the midst of a serious economic crisis, political leaders were able to appeal to Ecuardorans to unify as a nation to order to compete successfully in the global economy.

Soccer's role in national politics was also on display in a match in La Paz, Bolivia on 3 October 2010, between teams representing the staffs of President Evo Morales and the mayor of La Paz. A video camera caught President Morales kneeing a player in retaliation for a foul. The referee penalized his victim, Daniel Cartagena, a member of an opposing political party, but not the president. After the match, Cartagena went into hiding, fearful he would be arrested for attacking the president.

The most common expression of violence in soccer was not among the players but among spectators, typically in the form of rival crowds that rioted, assaulted one another, or committed vandalism. Latin America may claim the worst case of soccer violence in world history, during an Olympic qualifying match between Peru and Argentina in Lima's National Stadium on 24 May 1964. A total of 318 people, including children, were trampled and suffocated to death after a furious audience protested a referee's decision. In 1969, a soccer match between El Salvador and Honduras was popularly blamed for a war between the two countries. On 15 June, the national teams met in San Salvador to play the second match of a World Cup regional playoff. The night before the game, inflamed Salvadoran fans kept the Honduran players up all night, pelting their hotel windows with projectiles like dead rats and eggs. The next day, armored cars had to be used to drive the Honduran players to the stadium past hundreds of jeering Salvadorans, many of whom held up pictures of Amelia Bolaños, an 18-year-old Salvadoran woman who shot herself to death in despair over the country's previous week's loss to Honduras. If El Salvador's greatest soccer players were heroes of *la patria*, Bolaños was its martyr. Machine-gun wielding Salvadoran soldiers patrolled the stadium. After El Salvador won 3–0, the Honduran coach, Mario Griffin, seemed relieved: "We were lucky *not* to have won."[9]

In fact, politics had already penetrated and intensified the soccer rivalry. Only a month before, the Honduran government had begun to expel Salvadoran peasant families accused of illegally occupying the land they were farming. By 1 June, about 500 Salvadoran families had been stripped of all their possessions and sent back to El Salvador in the midst of a popular wave of anti-Salvadoran sentiment fanned by the Honduran press. The Salvadorans' hostility to the Honduran soccer team, and their violent attacks on Honduran fans, in turn provoked more violent reprisals against Salvadorans living in Honduras. As a result, some 20,000 Salvadorans fled back to their homeland in June and July, many of them having abandoned their property in Honduras. Border clashes were followed by El Salvador's invasion of Honduras on 14 July and Honduran bombing raids on El Salvador. A cease-fire ended hostilities on 18 July and the *status quo ante* was restored in August. What immediately became known as "the soccer war" was of course not a war over a soccer game, though the two matches in June undoubtedly aggravated a tense relationship. The third and final match was transferred to Mexico City, where El Salvador defeated Honduras 3–2 on 29 June.

Over time, the sporadic character of soccer-related violence gave way to new forms of violence that became customary in many Latin American countries, particularly in South America. There, *barras bravas* (in Spanish), or *torcidas organizadas* (in Portuguese-speaking Brazil) regularly threatened the peace. First formed in Argentina in the 1960s in imitation of the British prototype, the gangs spread throughout the region. While in Mexico and Central America they tended to adhere to their original status as support groups linked to particular teams, they evolved beyond that in other countries. Many Argentines considered the gangs to be a kind of mafia whose tentacles extended deep into the soccer teams and their respective clubs and organizations, as well as into political parties and other institutions. In Argentina alone, 144 persons were killed as a result of *barra brava* soccer violence from 1967 to 2008.

While soccer is the most popular sport in Latin America as a whole, it took second place to baseball in Cuba, Puerto Rico, the Dominican Republic, Venezuela, Nicaragua and Panama. Baseball also found a home in Colombia and parts of Mexico, and was played as a minor pastime in other Latin American countries such as Argentina, Honduras, Belize and El Salvador. Cubans were the first Latin Americans to welcome baseball into their country, where it was introduced by Cubans who had studied in the United States, and by U.S. sailors in the nineteenth century. Its popularity spread among Cubans with the U.S. military invasion of the Spanish colony in 1898 and the subsequent occupation of Cuba by U.S. military authorities after the defeat of Spain. Baseball became associated with the progress and modernity that many Cubans saw in U.S. culture generally, and the sport was seen as another way to separate culturally from Spain. After the Cuban revolution of 1959, an extensive sports bureaucracy converted Cuba into an international baseball power. "In Cuba, baseball is more than a sport," the Cuban baseball writer, Sigfredo Barros, told a U.S. reporter in 1997. "It is part of the culture. It is part of our national pride."[10]

The countries in Latin America where baseball reigned also became major recruiting markets for U.S. major league baseball teams, whose owners developed a "boatload mentality" toward Latin American players, Dick Balderson, the vice president of the Colorado Rockies, told an interviewer in 1996. "Instead of signing four [American] guys at $25,000 each, you sign 20 [Dominican] guys for $5,000 each."[11] By 2011, the share of Latin American players on U.S. major league teams had risen from 13% in 1987 to 28%, and by then, no Latin American country had supplied more players to the U.S. major league teams than the Dominican Republic (543), followed by Venezuela (270) and Mexico (112).

Conclusion

The classroom, the laboratory and the sports stadium, the Internet and the newspaper, TV and radio broadcasts, novels, paintings and movies – we have chosen to focus in Part IV on some of the most salient means by which modern societies *cultivate* their peoples and thus sustain a particular *culture*. Of course, no culture is an invariable monolith. Nevertheless, we have tried to convey, first in Chapter 2 and then in Chapters 11 to 14, the principal traits of a unique Latin American culture. We have seen how those traits vary from place to place and from time to time, even while preserving an essentially Hispanic character. In the same way, we have noted both region-wide consistencies and local variations in the diverse ways in which that culture has been conveyed over the last several decades. But this topic is practically inexhaustible, and a survey of Latin America's contemporary history can do little more than frame it conceptually, while highlighting its underlying unity and its manifold expressions.

Scholars of Latin America disagree about the ultimate significance of the core beliefs and values that define a culture. Some say they play a decisive role in every aspect of the region's history. Others emphasize the equal or superior influence of factors that can be defined as material rather than as habits of mind – such as economic inequality, the lure of political power, the intervention of nation-states from outside Latin America, and the interests of powerful business enterprises. In previous chapters we have tried to show how longstanding cultural dispositions interacted with political and economic interests, shaping policies and institutions. Whether in any given setting the influence of cultural dispositions was slight, or overwhelming, or moderate, and to what extent they themselves were influenced by material factors, are questions that continue to occupy a prominent place on the research agenda of Latin American historians.

Notes

1   Glauber Rocha, "An Esthetic of Hunger," in *New Latin American Cinema*, ed. Michael T. Martin (Detroit: Wayne State University Press, 1997), 1, 60–1.
2   Fernando Solanas and James Roy MacBean, "Fernando Solanas: An Interview," *Film Quarterly* 24 (1970) 1: 37–8.
3   Quoted in Luisela Alvaray, "National, Regional, and Global: New Waves of Latin American Cinema," *Cinema Journal* 47 (2008) 3: 48.
4   Quoted in Bruno Sassi, "Brazil's Turn," *FIFA World* (October 2010), 36.
5   Sergio Villena Fiengo, "Fútbol, mass media y nación en Costa Rica," *Cuadernos de Ciencias Sociales* (Costa Rica) 91 (1996): 11.
6   Eduardo Galeano, "Soccer: Opiate of the People?" *NACLA Report on the Americas* 37 (2004) 5: 42.
7   Martín del Palacio Langer, "Honduras' World Cup Success a Boon for the Country's Leaders," *World Soccer*, December 2009.
8   Jacques Paul Ramirez Gallegos, "Fútbol e identidad regional en Ecuador," in Pablo Alabarces, ed. *Futbologias: Fútbol, identidad y violencia en America Latina* (Buenos Aires: CLACSO, 2003), 114.
9   David Goldblatt, *The Ball Is Round: A Global History of Soccer* (New York: Riverhead Books, 2008), 533–4.
10 Tim Wendel, "Defections, Politics Diminish Proud Baseball Heritage," *USA Today*, 4 April 2001.

11 Marcos Bretón and José Luis Villegas, *Away Games: The Life and Times of a Latin Baseball Player* (New York: Simon & Schuster, 1999), 38.

References

Alvaray, Luisela. "National, Regional, and Global: New Waves of Latin American Cinema." *Cinema Journal* 47, no. 3 (2008): 48–65.

Bretón, Marcos, and José Luis Villegas. *Away Games: The Life and Times of a Latin Baseball Player*. New York: Simon & Schuster, 1999.

Del Palacio Langer, Martín. "Honduras' World Cup Success a Boon for the Country's Leaders." *World Soccer*, December 2009.

Galeano, Eduardo. "Soccer: Opiate of the People?" *NACLA Report on the Americas* 37, no. 5 (2004): 38–42.

Goldblatt, David. *The Ball Is Round: A Global History of Soccer*. New York: Riverhead Books, 2008.

Ramirez Gallegos, Jacques Paul. "Fútbol e identidad regional en Ecuador." In *Futbologías: Fútbol, identidad y violencia en America Latina*, ed. Pablo Alabarces, 101–21 (Buenos Aires: CLACSO, 2003).

Rocha, Glauber. "An Esthetic of Hunger." In *New Latin American Cinema*, ed. Michael T. Martin, 1, 59–61. Detroit: Wayne State University Press, 1997.

Sassi, Bruno. "Brazil's Turn." *FIFA World*, October 2010.

Solanas, Fernando, and James Roy MacBean. "Fernando Solanas: An Interview." *Film Quarterly* 24, no. 1 (1970): 37–43.

Villena Fiengo, Sergio. "Fútbol, mass media y nación en Costa Rica." *Cuadernos de Ciencias Sociales* 91 (1996): 9–20.

Wendel, Tim. "Defections, Politics Diminish Proud Baseball Heritage." *USA Today*, 4 April 2001.

Part V
Communities

Introduction

Our welfare and even our survival depend on the relationships we establish
and maintain, both individually and through associations or communities of
various kinds. The arena in which these relationships take shape and develop,
beyond the direct control of the state, is called "civil society." In the liberal
tradition of the West, a healthy civil society is one that guarantees the broadest
possible scope for the freedom of individuals and groups to express their beliefs
and act on their own interests. On this view, civil society precedes, and thus
generates, the state, whose function is to serve civil society.

Because of this tradition, the vigor and breadth of a country's civil society
are often considered a measure of its quality of life, and of its potential for
achieving and preserving stable, democratic rule with guarantees of individual
freedom. People in countries with weak or nonexistent civil societies typically
endure an authoritarian or even totalitarian state. In the history of contemporary Latin America, examples would include many of the military dictatorships
of the 1960s, 1970s and early 1980s, although the stringency of their attempts
to control the freedom of association varied considerably. In Cuba, the communist state's intolerance of free association has remained nearly absolute since
the 1960s. In most places today, people want the state to protect and nourish
civil society because they consider it to be indispensable to the common good,
including the goods of democracy and freedom.

Some social theorists assign to civil society activities related to economic
exchange and the market. As we have already seen, the patrimonial and corporatist character of the Latin American state established conditions that have
at times enabled it to act as a powerful economic regulator, developer and
proprietor, while encouraging groups and individuals to look to the state
for protection and for access to its revenue. That tradition was only partially
overcome by the market-oriented restructuring that began in earnest in the

Contemporary Latin America: 1970 to the Present, First Edition. Robert H. Holden and Rina Villars.
© 2013 Robert H. Holden and Rina Villars. Published 2013 by Blackwell Publishing Ltd.

1990s. And it was already roaring back in some places, like Venezuela and Bolivia, by the first decade of the twenty-first century. Beyond the economic realm, a less contentious category of civil-society activism is religion. Here, a Latin American tradition of state oversight of religious bodies and state-established religion has been on the wane for decades, as we noted in Chapter 6. The surge in Protestant evangelization and church-building during the last two decades, discussed in Chapter 2, is clear evidence of the enhanced vitality of civil society in respect to religious freedom.

In this chapter, we analyze the way various groups and movements have responded to the general relaxation of state-imposed constraints on civil society that has characterized the era of democratization. One result is a surge in the organization of groups formed for the purpose of advancing interests associated with collective identities such as ethnicity and sexuality. Before we turn to them, however, we need to examine the underlying demographic changes that have marked the societies of Latin America since the 1970s.

Population

On a global scale, the most dramatic demographic change of the last two centuries has been the breakdown of the high-mortality, high-fertility pattern of stable but very slow growth that prevailed for millennia. Starting in western Europe in the late eighteenth century, a much more dynamic period of rapid population growth, driven by constantly declining mortality rates, accelerated during the nineteenth and twentieth centuries and spread throughout the world. Having first reached the 1 billion mark in 1800, world population doubled by 1930, increased another billion by 1960, and added yet another by 1974. Five billion were counted in 1987, 6 billion in 1999, and the 7 billion mark was crossed in 2011. Accompanying this seven-fold rise in population over two centuries was a nine-fold increase in world income per capita. The very gains in healthcare and nutrition that set off the "population explosion" also contributed to the "prosperity explosion" of the twentieth century. (For data on world economic performance, see the introduction to Part III.)

Latin America's population growth rate (2.7%) was the highest of any world region in the 1950s and early 1960s. Its population doubled between 1950 and 1975. After 1965, the growth rate began to decline until it fell below Asia's in 2000–2005; from 1975 to 2000 the population only rose 60%. Figure V.1 illustrates the trends. After 2000, the only regions with lower rates of population increase than Latin America's were North America and Europe. The great, mid-century surge in Latin America's population growth reflected a death rate that was half or less than the rate of the 1930s – the result of

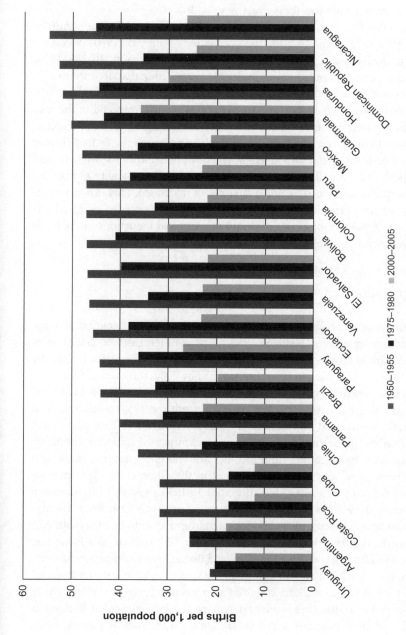

Figure V.1 Latin America: changes in crude birth rate, 1950–2005. Based on data from "World Population Prospects." United Nations, Dept. of Economic & Social Affairs, Population Division Homepage, The 2008 Revision Population Database, http://esa.un.org/wpp.

epochal improvements in health care. Life expectancy at birth rose from an average of 51 years in 1950–1955 to 70 by 1970–1975, though over the next quarter-century only two more years were added.

Birth rates, however, would not begin to decline in most countries until the mid-1960s, thus accounting for the population "bulge" of 1950–1975. One important effect was a vast increase in the proportion of youth. By 1965, 43% of Latin America's population was under 15, a proportion that declined to 32% in 2000 as a result of the shrinkage in fertility rates that started in the 1960s. Figure V.1 reveals substantial country variations in birth rate, and in the pace of decline. What accounts for lower fertility rates? In general, demographers attribute declines to a combination of both socio-economic factors (higher levels of education, and greater employment opportunities for women) and biological and cultural factors (such as the increased availability of artificial contraceptives and abortion, and a later age of marriage). That explanation is consistent with evidence we presented in previous chapters of rising educational attainment among both men and women, and reductions in the levels of poverty and economic inequality, since the 1970s.

Urbanization

As Latin America's population rose in the second half of the twentieth century, it became more urban. Already in 1950, four out of ten Latin Americans were living in urban areas – a rate more than three times that of Africa or Asia. By 1975, the ratio had risen to six out of ten, and by 2000, three out of four Latin Americans were living in urban areas, a proportion that even exceeded Europe's. The pace of urbanization in Latin America, from the 1950s to the 1970s, is practically unmatched in world history, and it was driven in large part by the deterioration of the rural economies that accompanied import-substitution industrialization. Declining rural incomes and job opportunities, along with the expansion of jobs and social services in the cities, encouraged massive migration from the countryside to the cities. In 1950, the only Latin American city among the world's ten biggest was Buenos Aires, with 5.1 million. Twenty-five years later, Mexico City had skyrocketed from sixteenth in 1950 (with 2.88 million) to the third largest in the world with 10.7 million. São Paulo had climbed to fifth place with 9.61 million, and Buenos Aires ranked seventh with 8.74 million. By 2000, Mexico City had grown to 18 million, placing it second behind Tokyo's 34.45 million while São Paulo was now fourth and Buenos Aires had slipped to ninth. One result was a sharp rise in substandard housing as millions of rural migrants seized vacant lands on the outskirts of big cities, building vast shantytowns.

We turn now to changes in the life of the family, the natural community that stands at the center of civil society.

Chapter 15

The Family, Women and Sexuality

The site of the first, most important and enduring personal relationships is the family, the community with the highest levels of personal interdependence. Because of its centrality, changes in the organization and life of the family powerfully affect individuals, groups and the larger society.

We define the family as a community of two or more persons associated by consanguinity or marriage. In the case of two adults, the relationship (whether they live together or not) may have been formalized by a marriage, a type of union sanctioned by the state and sometimes by a religious organization as well. In marrying one another, couples accept the customs and laws that govern marital unions and their offspring. Over time, marriage has taken on a diversity of forms, thus making it a preeminent expression of culture and a field of contention over its proper configuration and status, as we shall see. Couples may decline marriage and live in a "consensual union" or in a "cohabitation" arrangement, but even here, legal and customary restrictions can apply, particularly if they have children. In this section, our focus will be the family, the primary product of both marriage and consensual union, and therefore the core unit of community life.

One way to understand the role of the family in Latin American society is to analyze the values and beliefs associated with it. Many scholars argue that they are consistent enough across the Hispanic world to merit a particular name – "familism" or a belief in the centrality of the family. The key feature of familism has been its power to encourage Latin Americans to think of themselves first as members of the family, and secondarily as individuals. Thus, the family's needs and interests tend to take priority over those of the individual. In this way of thinking, the family is a kinship network that extends well beyond the nuclear family or the immediate relatives, and embraces grandparents, aunts and uncles, nephews and nieces, and even more distant ones.

Contemporary Latin America: 1970 to the Present, First Edition. Robert H. Holden and Rina Villars.
© 2013 Robert H. Holden and Rina Villars. Published 2013 by Blackwell Publishing Ltd.

Solidarity, loyalty and reciprocity are the virtues that all the members of the extended family are expected to live by. In what follows, we will try to capture the centrality of the family in both its private and public dimensions by examining two phenomena: family networks and international labor migration.

In Chapter 2, we identified family networks as a dimension of patrimonialism, a central feature of Latin American politics. A patrimonial system tends to *personalize* power and its attributes, such that the individual power-holder rather than the office itself or the political constitution emerges as the real authority. A reliable and cost-effective means for a *caudillo* or *patrón* to extend his personal authority has been to call on the solidarity and loyalty of family networks. We thus see, from a very early time, the emergence in Latin America of networks of family networks – associations of powerful, wealthy families – *familias acaudaladas* or *potentadas* – organized and developed through diverse types of alliances. The most secure form of alliance was marriage. But patrimonialism also relied on other relational modes such as godparenthood, patron-clientage, business partnerships, and so on. Through the nineteenth century, family networks had extended their power into government so far that they often controlled the destiny of a town, a city, a state, or an entire country.

By the middle of the twentieth century, family networks had lost much of the control they had enjoyed since colonial times. But their influence in politics and society remains potent even today. In fact, family networks operate at all socio-economic levels. Their presence can be seen, for example, in the management of commercial and industrial enterprises of all sizes and types, as well as in the allocation of jobs in private and public bureaucracies. Among the poor and the very poor, people depend on family networks to survive and to overcome poverty and deprivation, a pattern that can be seen in international labor migration, where family interests and values interact with the larger forces shaping migration discussed in Chapter 10. Some scholars even define international or transnational migration as a strategy for diversifying the family's livelihood.

The unprecedented surge of migration from Latin America to the United States since the 1960s, and more recently to Japan and Spain, was largely induced by inequality, poverty, and the lack of decent employment. As a survival strategy, migration's aim under such conditions was to benefit the family, not just the individual. The decision to migrate was thus more of a family choice rather than an individual one, and usually implied the collaboration of family networks in meeting the costs faced by the individual migrant, who in return, agreed to remit some share of the money that he or she earned back to the family in Latin America. Because relatives tended to follow relatives in the migration channels, family networks extended quickly across national borders. Relatives living in the destination country provided a temporary household for the newcomer, as well as cultural and economic support.

Migration thus became a collective act controlled by family networks in pursuit of a better standard of living for the entire family. A powerful sign of this instance of familism was the extraordinary volume of remittances, as discussed in Chapter 10. But behind the favorable macroeconomic impact on the household or the local economy lay the decisive cultural orientation of the typical Hispanic migrant: The profound sense of duty to *sacar adelante* or "lift up" the extended family continued to obligate the migrant long after she or he repaid the initial travel-related debts. Researchers have determined that emigrants send money back to their families whether or not the relatives collaborated in covering the costs of the trip. During the summer of 2002, the following exchange took place on a street in Honduras between one of the authors of this book and a Honduran migrant resident in Los Angeles since 1990 who had returned home for a brief visit.

Author:	What do you like the most about living in the United States?"
Honduran emigrant:	The fact that my work there allows me to send some money every single month to my parents and to my aunt Elena [an elderly widow].
Author:	But doesn't your wife resent the fact that you are still sending money back to your family in Honduras?
Honduran emigrant:	Not at all. She is Mexican-American, so she shares my values.

Of course, remittances can create an unhealthy dependence among relatives in the country of origin. Some scholars have identified a "migration syndrome" in which the initiative for self-sustained economic development becomes enfeebled among habitual recipients of remittances in the home country, a syndrome that could even extend to public opinion at large. Another harmful (and universal) aspect of migration, to be discussed below, was the way that the passage of time and the tyranny of distance undermined the very family ties that facilitated migration in the first place.

Recent Structural and Cultural Changes in the Family Household

A household is a group of individuals who live in the same residence and share resources and domestic functions. Although a given household may be composed entirely of individuals unrelated by blood or marriage, here we are concerned only with households in which at least some of the individuals are linked by familial ties.

Three basic types of family household could be found in Latin America by about 2010. Ideally constituted by two parents and their children, the *nuclear family household* accounted for about three out of five households. *Extended family households* included the members of the nuclear family (one or both parents, with or without children) and other relatives who lived in the same household. Extended households could bring together members of two or three generations, such as grandparents, husbands of sisters and wives of brothers, aunts, uncles, nieces and nephews. About one out of five households in Latin American were extended. Finally, *composite family households* included non-relatives (excluding live-in helpers), and they accounted for about 2% of all households. The prevalence of composite households was partly owing to the existence of *compadrazgo*, a practice discussed in Chapter 2.

Taken together, the three basic types of family household produced overlapping kinship networks, multidimensional in both scope and function, subject to cultural orientations as well as economic interests. *Compadrazgo* relationships stood to reshape the boundaries of any of the three household types. The move of a godchild to his or her godparents' household converted a nuclear family household into a composite one. The belief in maintaining strong family bonds gave rise to extended family households, most of which could be found among lower-income families, for whom they became a strategy for pooling resources when income was scarce. Migration created extended families because migrant parents, especially mothers, who left their children behind often placed them with close relatives, mainly grandparents. Spouses left behind by emigrants moved in with their own parents or their in-laws. These kinds of moves transformed nuclear households into extended ones. Outside the nuclear family, family heterogeneity became more common, as seen in a rising number of consensual unions and in the formation of one-person households, particularly those headed by women. Another trend was an overall reduction in household size across all types of family households.

We now turn to some of the demographic, cultural and economic shifts behind these changes in family household composition. The most prominent was undoubtedly the stunning increase in the female workforce. From the 1950s to the 1970s, the rate of participation of Latin American women in the labor force was among the lowest in the world. No more than a fifth of working-age women were economically active then. Women entered the labor market in force during the economic crisis of the1980s, and from 1990 to 2008, the share of women workers rose steadily, from 38% to 49%. By entering the labor force, women acquired more economic independence and social autonomy, thus facilitating separation or divorce in the case of an undesirable spouse or partner. The rise in female-headed households could also be attributed to migration, as the result of the decision, either by the emigrant (in the host country) or the spouse left behind in the home country, to form new families. On the other hand, as of 2004, two-parent nuclear families with children still remained by far the commonest type of Latin American urban household, accounting for 42% of all family households, though down from 46% in 1990. Mothers were working in more of them compared to 1990, and the share of one-person households as well as single-parent households (mostly headed by women) rose. But extended family households in urban areas held steady at 22–23% during the period 1990 to 2004.

A relatively high proportion of consensual or informal unions compared to other world regions has been a distinctive feature of Latin American society since colonial times. The assumption, by theorists of modernity, that such unions would gradually disappear, to be replaced by fully institutionalized marriages, has proved false. The standard explanation for Latin America's distinctiveness emphasizes the interaction of three conditions. The first, historical-cultural, refers to the overwhelmingly male character of the European conquerors; far from home, they quickly established informal unions with indigenous women. Among enslaved Africans, who were normally forbidden to marry, such unions were also common. Secondly, the short reach and instability of the political and ecclesiastical institutions required for the formalization of marriage fostered informality. To these two factors, one may add the cost of either a civil or a church wedding, which inhibited poor couples from marrying. The result was a culture with a high tolerance for extramarital partnerships that showed no sign of weakening in recent decades.

While the traditional pattern of cohabitation has always been most evident among the poor, mestizos and people of African descent, particularly in the Caribbean zone, it has lately been strengthened by a trend linked to an entirely different source – the rise of non-marital unions in North America and western Europe. These "new" consensual partnerships – typically among higher-educated urban couples – spring from distinctively modern preferences for personal autonomy, the avoidance of permanent commitment, and freedom from legal and bureaucratic entanglements. No longer considered a sign of deviance among the better-off, "living together" has become an acceptable alternative to marriage. The city of Buenos Aires, for example, saw the share of consensual unions rise from 1.5% of all partnerships in 1960 to 21% in 2001, while across Chile, they nearly tripled from 6% in 1982 to 16% in 2002.

Traditional consensual unions remained most common in the Central American isthmus and the Caribbean, where they still accounted for 40–60% of all partnerships. The proportion was somewhat lower in Colombia, Ecuador, Paraguay, Peru and Venezuela, where they ranged from 20% to 40%. They were least common (under 20%) in Argentina, Bolivia, Chile, Costa Rica, Mexico and Uruguay. Everywhere, they were more frequent among women in the 15–24 age group; in the Dominican Republic, 77% of all women in partnerships in that age group were in consensual unions. Neither poverty nor ethnicity by themselves should be taken as reliable indicators: Strongly indigenous Bolivia, one of the poorest countries in Latin America, was among the seven with the lowest percentage of consensual unions, and Argentina had more than Mexico though Argentina's standard of living was higher than Mexico's.

Everywhere, the proportion of informal unions was either stable or rising. Against the benefits of such arrangements – simplicity and lower initial costs – social science research pointed to some significant drawbacks. Besides the absence of the mutual obligations and rights that came with a legal marriage, informal unions were less durable than marriages, which often meant that upon its dissolution, the woman assumed the role of both breadwinner and mother. In addition, the children of such unions suffered higher rates of morbidity and mortality, saw more domestic violence, and performed less well in school. Because their parents were more likely than married couples to separate, the children of informal unions were more likely to be raised in a fatherless household. Not only did the children of fatherless families lose the material benefits of two working parents, they forfeited numerous other potential advantages. "Children are very conscious of the presence of their father, value his interest and guidance, and will experience emotional pain and may even bear a stigma as a result of not knowing, losing or feeling neglected or abused by him," according to a 2011 UN report on the rise of female-headed households and fatherless families. Children of resident fathers did better in school and reported higher levels of "socio-emotional development and adjustment."[1]

Instability and dissolution, with their negative effects on children, were not limited to informal unions. Divorces among married couples rose significantly. In 1985, divorce was still prohibited in Argentina, Bolivia, Brazil, Chile, Colombia, Nicaragua and Paraguay. Since then, all have adopted laws allowing divorce. Chile was the last to do so, in 2004. With legalization came a rise in the divorce rate. Nevertheless, as of the mid-1980s, in any Latin American country where divorce was legal, the rate of divorce was still considerably higher in the United States: it was two times higher than Cuba's, four times Uruguay's, seven times Paraguay's, and twelve to fourteen times higher than the rates in Ecuador, Honduras and Mexico.

In most Latin American countries, divorce rates rose from the 1970s to the early twenty-first century. Cuba, Costa Rica and Uruguay appear to record the highest divorce rate but only Uruguay's was comparable to the much higher level reported by the United States. Given the exceptionally high proportion of consensual unions in many Latin American countries, however, low divorce rates do not necessarily reflect the real rate of dissolutions, since a divorce can usually be granted only to a couple who are already married. In the case of Cuba, legislation adopted in 1975 gave judges the power to make exclusive and stable informal unions equivalent to formal legal marriages, thus subjecting them to legal divorce proceedings. So many Cubans continued to reject formal marriage that Jaime Ortega Alamino, the Roman Catholic archbishop of Havana, commented in 2003 that marriage in Cuba had become "almost irrelevant."

Women and the Movement for Women's Rights

"I do not know if it is a matter of nature, or if it is cultural, anthropological or biological, or related to the moment of history in which we find ourselves," President Michelle Bachelet of Chile told an interviewer in 2009.

> But I habitually see in the workplace . . . that in general women relate to power more from the perspective of service to others . . . It seems that in the case of men, one sees a kind of stronger, and fatal, attraction to power . . . We have to seek the best contribution of women and men, because apparently there are some features of leadership that can be different, and with complementary leadership, a society can do more things.[2]

From 2000 to 2002, before she was elected president, Bachelet – a pediatrician with postgraduate studies in military affairs – served as President Ricardo Lagos's health minister. In 2002, when Lagos appointed her Chile's first female minister of defense, she introduced herself to the military officials under her command by declaring: "I am a woman, a socialist, separated, and agnostic. I represent four capital sins, but we are going to work together." On 15 January 2006 she was elected president of Chile with 53.5 % of the vote, becoming the first woman to occupy the post. As her term of office expired four years later, the Chilean public still gave her approval ratings of nearly 90%. As president, Bachelet insisted that her leadership style was a "feminine" one in that it relied on dialogue and cooperation, attributes compatible with the service-oriented leadership that she associated with women in the interview quoted above.

"The Bachelet phenomenon" – the expression commonly used to refer to her successful performance, first as a presidential candidate and then as a president–represented both change and continuity in the history of women and politics in Latin America. In terms of change, Bachelet was the first woman president in Latin America to be elected entirely on her own merits, rather than as the result of an intimate connection with a male leader. After her presidential term expired, Bachelet's status as a leading feminist was confirmed by her appointment as the first executive director of UN Women, created by the UN General Assembly in 2010 to promote gender equity and female empowerment. Bachelet's very image as a woman – "socialist, separated and agnostic," as she put it – contradicted the conventional model of the virtuous woman – conservative, married and religious – that one might have expected to win the presidency in a profoundly Catholic country that prohibited divorce until 2004.

On the other hand, the ideas and attitudes of Bachelet concerning her roles as a woman, as a mother of three children, and as a female politician, comply with a tradition among politically active Latin American women that continues to separate them from their counterparts in North America and Europe. Whereas the latter are most likely to assert an absolute equivalence in the roles proper to men and women, Latin American women tend to stress complementarity – both between men and women as persons, and between the woman's private and public roles. In the first half of the twentieth century, when Latin American women agitated for political rights, they rejected the widespread argument that women were by nature unfit for citizenship. But they also argued that a distinctive female identity – and the experience of women as mothers and wives – not only endowed them with sufficient virtue to qualify as citizens, but also would make them better legislators than men because women were more sensitive and responsible. In her analysis of women's struggle for the right to vote in South America, the historian Asunción Lavrin noted: "Feminism oriented toward motherhood was more than a strategy to win favorable legislation, it was an essential component of their cultural heritage: a tune that feminists not only knew how to play but wished to play."[3]

Thus, when Michelle Bachelet observed that women in power behaved differently than men, and that "with complementary leadership, a society can do more things," she was sustaining a traditional Latin American feminism of complementarity. Chileans apparently saw things this way too, for both during and after her presidency, she was popularly known as "The Mother of Chile," an expression she never repudiated. It was not surprising, therefore, that motherhood remained among the most powerful images behind the development of the Latin American women's movement in the second half of the twentieth century. It was often *as* mothers and wives that thousands of women demonstrated publicly against economic hardship and political repression during the military dictatorships of the late twentieth century.

This pattern emerged clearly on the afternoon of Thursday, 30 April 1977 when fourteen women congregated in front of the Presidential Palace, at the Plaza de Mayo, the main square of Buenos Aires and the traditional site of political demonstrations. They wanted the military government that had seized power a year before to provide information about the whereabouts of their "disappeared" children. Their children were among the thousands of men and women who had been illegally detained, taken to clandestine detention centers, tortured and eventually killed, all without any public record or judicial procedure, hence the term "disappeared" (*desaparecido*). (For the state-sponsored terrorism of the Argentine "Dirty War," see Chapter 4.) The fourteen mothers were making the first public act of protest against the military junta, and they continued to congregate at the same place at 3:30 p.m. every Thursday to demand information about the fates of their "disappeared" children. Eventually numbering in the thousands, the women acted initially without any political motivation or program, and simply as mothers in pain, searching for their children, certain that the armed forces had taken them away. Two years later, the mothers organized the "Civil Association of the Mothers of the Plaza de Mayo," a name chosen to emphasize their apolitical intentions. "We are not moved by any political objective," they declared.[4]

Nevertheless, as their movement grew, it gradually reshaped itself into a platform of political resistance to military rule. The mothers began wearing white kerchiefs in order to recognize one another. Soon, the white kerchief became a popular symbol of opposition in many Latin American countries. In El Salvador, members of the Committee of Mothers of Political Prisoners, the Disappeared and the Assassinated donned white kerchiefs, which they also associated symbolically with the diapers that they once applied to their lost children. At the beginning of their protests, the women's emphasis on the maternal motivation of their struggle provided some safety. But as the Salvadoran movement became more politicized and more daring, some of the women were captured, tortured and disappeared. In Buenos Aires, a similar fate was in store for some of the mothers of the Plaza de Mayo. In December 1977, Azucena Villaflor, María Eugenia Bianco and Esther Careaga were arrested and – according to an investigation carried out by the mothers themselves – the three women were tortured and dropped into the sea from an airplane, a common practice of the military government. Some days after their disappearance, in fact, the bodies of the three women appeared on the shore at the town of Santa Teresita, on the mouth of the Río de la Plata. In 2005, their identities were confirmed by a team of forensic anthropologists.

In Argentina and elsewhere in Latin America, women's movements against state terror in the 1970s and 1980s often led to broader movements for demilitarization and democracy. The case of Liduvina Hernández of Honduras was typical. Between 1981 and 1984, roughly 150 people were "disappeared" by a secret unit, Batallón 3–16, of the Honduran army. One of its victims was the son of Liduvina, who made a living selling oranges in the public market of San Pedro Sula, the country's second-largest city. Although she scarcely knew how to write and read, in 1982 she helped to found the Committee of Relatives of the Disappeared of Honduras, whose members identified themselves as the mothers, sisters and wives of the victims. Hernández became a national voice for democracy, converting her loss as a mother into a lifelong commitment to political and social change.

A more recent illustration of the same phenomenon was the organization of Las Damas de Blanco (Ladies in White) in Cuba, a group of wives, mothers and other female relatives of the seventy-five individuals who were arrested and condemned to six to twenty-eight years of prison by the Cuban government in 2003 for allegedly collaborating with its foreign enemies. In response, the Damas de Blanco, wearing distinctive white dresses, began to ritually walk every Sunday from St. Rita's Church in Havana, where they attended Mass, to a nearby park. The courage required for this simple act of protest was recognized in 2005 when the European Parliament awarded the group the Sakharov Prize for Freedom of Thought. Weeks after dissident Orlando Zapata Tamayo, a 42-year-old construction worker condemned to 36 years in prison, died after an 85-day hunger strike on 23 February 2010, "las damas" began marching daily and chanting "libertad" (freedom). In doing so, they were following the example of the Argentine mothers in expanding their protest to demand democracy, in this case against the Communist Party's absolute control of the political process. Intermittently detained by the police and harassed by government-organized crowds, the women nevertheless succeeded in carrying out the first regular anti-government protests seen in Havana since the triumph of Castro's revolution in 1959.

Like political repression, poverty and economic inequality emerged as potent issues, from the 1970s onward, in the burgeoning women's movement. Economic hardship inspired many women in both rural and urban settings to organize or join a wide variety of self-help groups aimed above all at improving the quality of the lives of the poorest families. They planted curative herbs as an alternative to expensive, conventional pharmaceuticals, organized communal dining halls to reduce food costs, formed associations and cooperatives to produce kitchen utensils or clothing, and extended these self-help efforts into the political sphere by demanding schools for their children, access to cultivable land in the countryside, and urban services like running water. Such efforts comprised the core of the Latin American women's movement, with its focus on the survival and betterment of the family, or on some sector of the poor population.

In Latin America, the members of such economically oriented women's groups often dissociated themselves from feminism, the ideology that had become practically synonymous with the women's movement in North America and Europe. Feminists there and in Latin America were often viewed by the more economically-oriented women's groups as upper-class women preoccupied with less pressing questions of discrimination and inequality in gender relations. For example, at the October 1987 meeting of the Fourth Latin American and Caribbean Feminist Meeting in Taxco, Mexico, one of the authors of this book asked Rosa Dilia Rivera, a leader of one of Honduras' largest female peasant organizations, whether she was a feminist. "I am not a feminist," she replied. "How can I be a feminist, if for 17 years my only objective has been to take peasant women out of the kitchen so that they could fight like the men do for their rights, including the right to land?"

Her response illustrated the common perception among the female leaders of grassroots organizations that feminism was an imported ideology of limited relevance to the kinds of basic social changes they were seeking. But after the three-day Taxco meeting, many of the 150 Central American delegates from labor unions, political parties and various popular movements were finally persuaded that without realizing it, they were indeed feminists. Their feminism was "experiential" (*viviencial*), something they encountered in small ways every day as they tried to reconcile their traditional roles as mothers and wives with the struggle for survival and the defense of human rights.

The notion of *viviencial* feminism was not however welcomed by the leading feminists who since the 1970s had been trying to define a specifically Latin American feminist movement. Still known today as the veterans or the *históricas*, they had organized the previous three Latin American feminist meetings. The first, in Bogota in 1981, drew 200 mostly middle-class Latin American women who were principally concerned with debating the role of women's emancipation in the context of social revolution and Marxist ideology. At the second Latin American feminist meeting in 1983 in Lima, more than 600 women – including grass-roots activists, union organizers, university students and academics – discussed patriarchy and *machismo*, and the still-controversial distinction between the feminist movement and the women's movement. Feminists insisted that their goals also embraced the real interests of the grassroots women. But the latter and others associated with Marxist parties argued that a true feminist movement had to be engaged in the everyday economic and political struggles of women in the so-called "popular sectors" of society.

The tension between the opposing commitments of a feminist movement and a women's movement persisted at the third meeting in Bertioga, Brazil, in 1985, which drew 900 women. Nevertheless, it was clear that the traditional feminist movement was becoming more inclusive, a tendency that was even more evident by the end of the Taxco meeting in 1987, where a majority of the 1,500 participants represented "popular" groups. At one point, the Central American women – considered the least feminist at the meeting – chanted, "Todas somos feministas" (We all are feminists). Although this phrase was not in complete agreement with reality, it pointed to the fact that the two tendencies were complementary rather than contradictory. While the "women's movement" made the small and rather elitist feminist movement of the 1970s wider and more inclusive, feminism eventually inspired grass-roots women's organizations to consider gender relations as well as class relations. As a result, concern with gender discrimination spread to the leadership of trade unions, political parties, grassroots organizations of all kinds, and governmental agencies.

The rising interest in gender discrimination became a decisive force in one of the most remarkable social changes of the last three decades: the increasing participation of women in politics. In 1979, Elsa Chaney's seminal *Supermadre: Women in Politics in Latin America*, was published in the United States. Drawing on surveys of women in Peru and Chile who held political and administrative posts at the municipal level in the 1960s and 1970s, Chaney reported that women were extending their traditional roles and identities as wives and mothers into the political arena, rather than leaving them behind. This meant that their political focus was almost invariably on feminine issues: the family, children, food prices, inflation, peace and moral questions. In the political arena, in other words, women were *supermadres* or supermothers as they tended to the needs of their "big family in the larger *casa* of the municipality or even the nation."[5]

Since the publication of *Supermadre*, women's participation in politics has risen exponentially. Across all nineteen Latin American countries in 1979, of the 272 ministerial cabinet positions available, only twelve or about 4% were occupied by women. In the national legislatures, only sixty-two seats or about 0.9% of the 2,256 seats available were held by women. In 2010, an average of one out of every four cabinet ministers in the Latin America countries was a woman; in no country was the share of women less than 14% while in Bolivia, Costa Rica, Ecuador, Nicaragua and Peru the proportion exceeded 30%. In 2010, women made up no more than 8–9% of the national legislatures of Brazil, Colombia and Panama but in seven countries they held more than 25% of the seats: Argentina, Bolivia, Cuba, Costa Rica, Ecuador, Mexico and Peru. On the average, across Latin America in 2010, women held 21% of the seats in the national legislatures.

Nine women have served as president or head of state of one of the 19 Latin American countries since 1974, when the first, María Estela Martínez de Perón, the vice president of Argentina, succeeded to the office on the death of her husband, President Juan Domingo Perón. Five of the nine took office after 1998: Dilma Rousseff (Brazil, 2010–); Laura Chinchilla (Costa Rica, 2010–); Cristina Fernández de Kirchner (Argentina, 2007–); Michelle Bachelet (Chile, 2006–2010); and Mireya Moscoso (Panama, 1999–2004).

On the other hand, while in the 1970s female politicians focused mainly, if not exclusively, on traditional or domestic women's issues, by the twenty-first century they were also concerned with the feminist question of promoting women's political and social equality. Nevertheless, the figure of the "Supermadre" was still applied by researchers (especially those of North America and Europe) to refer to those Latin American female politicians who emphasized traditional women's concerns. A sort of distinction between the "super-mother" and the "non-super mother" politician was thus proposed. But such a distinction was questionable, if only because women politicians, whether they identified themselves as feminists or not, tended to give a higher priority to children and family issues than their male counterparts. In fact, that tendency was not limited to Latin American women but could also be found in North America, Europe and other world regions. The continuing use of the supermadre figure in scholarship on Latin American female politicians probably derived from a basic conflict in the two ways of seeing women's private and public roles. Whereas Latin American women tended to perceive them as complementary, European and North American feminist scholars usually saw them as antagonistic. So what for most Latin American female politicians counted as normal or expected behavior, for others amounted to a surrender to patriarchy.

Women's vastly expanded participation in politics over the period covered in this book matched a clear global trend in favor of women's equality. Both the UN Convention on the Elimination of all Forms of Discrimination against Women (1979) and the Fourth World Conference on Women (Beijing 1995) made the expansion of women's leadership in the political sphere a high priority. At the same time, scores of countries around the world began to adopt gender quota laws, particularly for legislative elections, in the 1980s. Most commonly, they required all political parties to nominate a certain percentage of women (typically 30–50%) for seats in the national legislature. Starting with Argentina in 1991, gender quota legislation swept Latin America, and by 2005 such laws were in force in Argentina, Bolivia, Brazil, Costa Rica, the Dominican Republic, Ecuador, Honduras, Mexico, Panama, Paraguay and Peru. While gender quota laws were widely credited with having contributed to an increase in women legislators, their impact varied considerably, depending on the strength of the laws, the level of enforcement, and the type of electoral system in use.

Contraception and Abortion

Few family-related public policy issues have generated more intense debate throughout the world in the last three decades than the movements to legalize two means of reducing family size: artificial birth control and induced abortion. For their advocates, they were essential elements of the emancipation of women, a status now widely said to include two new rights: those of "reproductive freedom" and "reproductive health." To the opponents of birth control and abortion, however, far from being human rights, they were grave affronts to human nature or divine law, or both.

In 1955, two U.S. scientists, Gregory Pincus and John Rock, chose the ex-Spanish colony of Puerto Rico, a U.S. dependency since 1898, as the site of the first large-scale human trials of a daily pill for women that appeared to inhibit hormonal ovulation. Legal obstacles and popular opposition to the new technology in the continental United States inspired their decision to choose Spanish-speaking Puerto Rico for the trials, for without experimental evidence, the U.S. Food and Drug Administration (FDA) would not permit the pill to be sold in the United States. Thousands of women in Puerto Rico and later Haiti participated in the studies, considered ethically dubious by later standards of research because the subjects were not told they were participating in an experiment. As a result of the studies, the FDA licensed "the Pill" for sale in the United States on 11 May 1960. At the same time, technical innovations in older techniques of contraception such as the diaphragm and the condom enhanced their popularity.

The great leap in birth control technology represented mainly by the work of Pincus and Rock coincided with a population surge in the developing world. Leading public figures in the United States and Europe by the early 1970s were issuing warnings of devastating social and economic effects of a global "population explosion" that could only be controlled by institutionalizing methods of "family planning" in countries throughout the developing world. Speaking at the twentieth-anniversary celebration of the founding of the United Nations on 25 June 1965, U.S. President Lyndon B. Johnson implored his audience to "act on the fact that less than five dollars invested in population control is worth a hundred dollars invested in economic growth."[6]

In what was widely interpreted as a rejoinder to the growing enthusiasm for antinatalist policies and the utilitarian spirit underlying it, on 4 October 1965 Pope Paul VI advised the United Nations General Assembly that "your task is to act in a way that makes bread abundant at the table of humanity and not to sponsor an artificial control of births, which would be irrational, aiming at reducing the number of guests at the banquet of life."[7] Three years later, Paul VI issued the encyclical letter "Humanae Vitae," closing a brief period of theological debate within the Catholic Church over the propriety of artificial birth control. The letter declared that "each and every marital act must of necessity retain its intrinsic relationship to the procreation of human life." The pope's restatement of traditional Christian teaching against artificial methods of birth control, sterilization and abortion made the Catholic Church the world's leading – and practically only – institutional obstacle to what was shaping up as a tidal wave of sentiment in favor of legalizing and promoting, first, artificial birth control and later, induced abortion, in both the developed and the developing countries.

In Latin America, still solidly Roman Catholic, international pressure on governments to promote access to birth control – now presented as an indispensable tool of economic development – intensified in the late 1960s and 1970s. The easiest way to enlarge Gross National Product, it was argued, was to reduce the number of poor people. Major U.S.-based non-governmental organizations and foundations, as well the World Bank and United Nations, added more resources and leverage to what was increasingly seen as a moral mandate to "defuse the population time bomb" in Latin America and other developing regions. In 1968, the UN's "Proclamation of Tehran" added family-planning services to the UN's 1948 Declaration of Human Rights, asserting that "parents have a basic human right to determine freely and responsibly the number and the spacing of their children." The feminist movement, a rising force both within and outside Latin America in the late 1960s and 1970s, argued that artificial birth control would emancipate women from the servi-tude of unwanted pregnancies, within marriage as well as outside it, and prevent the death of mothers who chose to undergo incompetently performed abortions.

By the 1990s, it was clear that the posited relationship between declining birth rates and rising per-capita income was in fact nonexistent. Nor did the population control programs do much to reduce fertility, for study after study disclosed that the most decisive determinant in changing fertility rates was the level of education of women. The higher their level of formal education, the fewer children they wanted. At the same time, feminists questioned the often coercive, male-dominated character of the population-control agenda, which tended to treat poor women as the problem while ignoring their indi-vidual right to make their own decisions about child-bearing. Feminists and other critics also argued that poverty and inequality would be more effectively ameliorated by macroeconomic policies designed to create jobs, and by more targeted spending on education, healthcare, housing and other priorities that would lead directly to higher standards of living and incidentally tend to moti-vate parents to voluntarily limit family size. The feminist critique consistently emphasized access to birth control as one element of an overall program of emancipation.

By the end of the 1990s, 72% of Latin America women who were married or in union were using some contraceptive method, and 63% were using "modern" methods only, i.e., not rhythm, withdrawal or other traditional techniques. This was the highest rate in the developing world, and even higher than that of Europe as a whole (68% any, 50% "modern") and close to that of North America (76% any, 71% modern).

While legal and cultural obstacles to artificial birth control were rapidly swept aside in Latin America, the same cannot be said of induced abortion. As of 2009, four Latin American countries – Chile, the Dominican Republic, El Salvador and Nicaragua – prohibited induced abortion under any circum-stances. Cuba alone allowed abortions on request. To save the life of the mother was the sole allowable reason for an abortion in Guatemala, Honduras, Paraguay, and Venezuela. In addition to saving the mother's life, abortions were permitted in Brazil and Mexico if the pregnancy was the result of rape or incest, though Mexico's federal district government made abortion legal in 2007 for any reason during the first twelve weeks of pregnancy. The rest of the Latin American countries allowed abortions only to preserve the physical or mental health of the mother or in cases of rape or incest.

The restrictive character of Latin America's abortion laws reflected weak public support for the full legalization of the procedure. In 2007, Latinobarómetro, the region's principal public opinion survey organization, interviewed 20,000 Latin Americans. One question invited respondents to tell whether abortion was always justifiable or never justifiable or somewhere in between, with "1" standing for "never justifiable" and "10" for "always justifiable." Uruguay reported the highest average approval rating – just 4.13. After Uruguay, Argentina (2.99) and Mexico (2.53) reported the highest levels of support, while the lowest were found in Venezuela (1.49), Paraguay (1.39) and Guatemala (1.31).

Even leftwing political leaders, who elsewhere ordinarily favored abortion rights, opposed full legalization. In 2008, President Tabaré Vázquez of Uruguay, a professed agnostic, member of the Socialist Party and an obstetrician, vetoed legislation that would have made abortion legal on request during the first three months of pregnancy. "The true level of a nation's civilization," Vázquez declared in his veto message, "is measured in how it protects the neediest." Physicians, he added, were obliged to act "in favor of life and its physical integrity." In 2007, Nicaragua's leftist government outlawed all abortions, repealing a law that had permitted it for therapeutic reasons. The repeal had been promised during the electoral campaign by the newly elected president, Daniel Ortega, leader of the Marxist-oriented Frente Sandinista de Liberación Nacional (FSLN). The Dominican Republic banned abortion entirely in 2009, after having allowed it to save the life of the mother. President Hugo Chávez of Venezuela, pledging to institute "twenty-first century socialism" in Venezuela, also opposed liberalizing the country's restrictive abortion law. In Argentina, President Cristina Fernández's support for the country's extremely restrictive abortion law effectively blocked efforts by legislators in 2011 to allow abortion on request during the first three months of pregnancy. Against the trend in favor of upholding restrictions, the high court of Colombia legalized abortion in 2006, overturning an absolute ban.

The Movement for Gay Rights

In November 2009, during the presidential campaign in Chile, the center-right candidate Sebastián Piñera amazed almost everyone when he appeared in a TV advertisement next to a hand-holding gay couple. Entitled "the voice of the voiceless," the ad depicted individuals who represented Indians, the poor, the elderly, the disabled, and homosexuals. Each whispered their concerns to Piñera and the candidate repeated each of them in turn, including the whispered plea of the gay couple: "Today people accept us; now we need a country that respects us." The commercial ended with one of the gay men exclaiming, "He [Piñera] will be our voice!"

The ad set off a contentious public debate. Piñera had already declared his support for governmental recognition of same-sex unions, a position that some interpreted as support for a kind of covert same-sex marriage and thus a threat to the institution of marriage and the family. Piñera responded to his critics by saying that he, like the immense majority of Chileans, defended the family and marriage as the union of one man and one woman. But, he added, to deny homosexual couples the same civil rights enjoyed by married heterosexual couples would be to unjustly discriminate against them.[8]

Piñera's daring move in favor of civil unions (but not marriage) for homosexuals attested to the extraordinary success of the movement for LGBT (for lesbian, gay, bisexual and transgendered) rights across much of Latin America during the period covered by this book. Beginning in the 1980s, every Latin American country that had penalized sodomy decriminalized it. The last to do so was Nicaragua in 2007. Besides decriminalization, the LGBT movement's political achievements included new laws prohibiting discrimination on the basis of sexual orientation (Bolivia, Chile, Ecuador, Mexico, Peru, Uruguay and Venezuela), and the legal recognition of same-sex unions and the granting of the same rights and obligations enjoyed by heterosexual de facto unions (Brazil, Colombia and Uruguay). Uruguay became the first Latin American country to allow homosexual couples to adopt children (2009). Argentina became the first Latin American country (and the tenth in the world) to legalize same-sex marriage in July 2010, a move already made by the federal district of Mexico (the capital city) in March. In other countries where national governments were slow to act, municipal and provincial authorities adopted legislation favored by the LGBT movement. For example, homosexual civil unions were recognized in at least two Brazilian states before the federal government of Brazil accepted them in 2011. Such unions were recognized by the city of Buenos Aires in 2003 and were accepted in the Mexican state of Coahuila in 2007.

Somewhat paradoxically, however, the remarkable political gains of the LGBT movement find only partial confirmation in public opinion polls. In a 2008 survey by researchers at Vanderbilt University of twenty-three countries in the western hemisphere, a sample of 40,567 persons were asked, "How strongly do you approve or disapprove of homosexuals being permitted to run for public office?" On a scale of one to ten (with one the lowest tolerance and ten the highest), the only Latin American countries where more than half the respondents replied with a least a seven were Argentina and Uruguay. Only

30% to 40% of the respondents in Chile, Colombia, Costa Rica, Mexico, Nicaragua and Venezuela gave at least a seven in response. The rate in favor of a seven or more fell to the 15–30% range in Bolivia, the Dominican Republic, Ecuador, El Salvador, Guatemala, Honduras, Panama, Paraguay and Peru. The poll revealed a strong positive correlation between education and high levels of tolerance; persons with only a primary education were less than half as likely as those with a university education to be highly tolerant of homosexuals running for public office. Another important determinant of attitudes toward homosexuals turned out to be religious preference. Non-Catholic Christians were significantly less tolerant than all others, including Catholics, non-Christian believers, and people with no religion. Age seemed to have little effect on tolerance, for people under 35 were not notably more tolerant than older people.

When considered along with the concrete political gains of the LGBT movement, the Vanderbilt poll suggested that, while tolerance of homosexuality was increasing, it was not unlimited. Other poll results confirmed the general rise in acceptance of homosexual conduct. The Corporación Latinobarómetro of Chile began polling Latin Americans about their views on the matter in 1998. Eleven years later, the company concluded that tolerance toward homosexuals rated as "perhaps one of the most significant value changes in Latin America during the last decade." While in 1998, 59% stated that they did not want to have a neighbor who was a homosexual, in 2009, the company's eighteen-country survey of 20,204 persons found only 29% who still agreed. On the other hand, the level of tolerance varied significantly by country, in roughly the same way that the Vanderbilt University researchers reported. The highest level of tolerance was found in Uruguay, where only 13% objected to a homosexual neighbor; Brazil followed with 14%, then Argentina (17%) and Mexico (21%). The highest rejection rates, and thus the lowest levels of tolerance, were found in the poorest countries with the lowest levels of formal education: Bolivia, Colombia, Ecuador, El Salvador, Guatemala, Honduras and Paraguay, all with a rejection rate of 33% to 39%. When the company asked the same question about other groups, substituting immigrants, indigenous peoples, illiterates and blacks for "homosexuals," it found that the rejection rate for homosexuals vastly exceeded that for the other groups, who were unwanted as neighbors by only 12% to 14% of those polled.

In grouping the questions and their responses in this way, however, Latinobarómetro evidently assumed that the reasoning of persons who objected to having immigrants or illiterates as neighbors would be no different from that of persons who objected to homosexuals as neighbors. In fact, anti-homosexuality reasoning typically relied on a judgment against the morality of homosexual conduct per se. A preference for literates over illiterates, or whites over blacks, was less a moral question than one of socio-economic status or class. Poll respondents who were black or indigenous or illiterate would probably not object to neighbors like themselves. Opposition to homosexuality usually stemmed from a belief that heterosexual relations were "natural" while homosexual ones were disordered because they were "unnatural' or (in religious terminology) "sinful." This distinction between a status-oriented motive and a moralistic one could explain why the rate of intolerance toward homosexuals as neighbors was twice the rate for the other classes of individuals in 2009, as well as the much higher levels of intolerance for homosexuals in public office, compared to having them as neighbors.

On the other hand, even though the opposition to homosexuality typically arose from a moral or religious commitment, Latinobarómetro's poll results did show that the tolerance level could change dramatically. In just a decade, the proportion of the Latin American population that would not want a homosexual neighbor fell by one-half, a change that was no doubt abetted by the increasing capacity of the LGBT movement to mobilize its members and to publicize its cause. Those successes depended in turn on an inventive organizing strategy. Instead of mobilizing "against" the status quo and the state, as social movements typically did, LGBT activists avoided direct confrontation and, in the words of a U.S. academic specialist, Javier Corrales, sought to "work the status quo, not destroy it." Rather than overturning institutions, they looked for loopholes or opportunities within existing ones.[9]

An example was the LGBT movement's decision to focus on the right of homosexual couples to marry, even though many homosexual activists initially rejected the idea because they considered monogamous marriage itself either irrelevant or an obstacle to human emancipation. Nevertheless, same-sex marriage became the defining gay-rights issue of the first decade of the twenty-first century, not only in Latin America but in the United States and Europe as well. Rather than attack marriage as an outmoded or discriminatory institution, activists claimed it for themselves. By asserting a right to marry, the gay rights movement sought to make homosexuality more socially acceptable by likening a homosexual couple to a heterosexual one, separated by nothing more than a sexual "preference." At the same time, the tactic was seen as a way to disarm the conservative opposition by adopting the essentially conservative position of favoring monogamy, a socially stabilizing institution, according to Corrales. The argument was intended to make conservatives who opposed gay marriage look like hypocrites, while undercutting the stereotype of gays as inherently promiscuous.

That strategy was unlikely to succeed wherever the opposition to homosexuality, and thus to same-sex marriage, arose from the belief that non-heterosexual relationships were "unnatural" and thus morally wrong. According to this view, marriage "by nature" can only bond a man and a woman. This was the position of the Catholic Church, the largest single religious denomination in Latin America. Still, many who took that position nevertheless accepted some kind of legal recognition of same-sex unions that fell short of marriage, as did Sebastián Piñera. The distinction between same-sex unions and same-sex marriage remained a fluid one, and thus some conservatives opposed the former on the grounds that they were a kind of covert marriage, or at least a step in that direction, and hence a blow to the traditional family. Many proponents of same-sex marriage, on the other hand, rejected the civil union as an inferior substitute for marriage.

Three countries took the lead in what seemed to be emerging as a conservative counter-trend: Protecting homosexuals against discrimination while stipulating that marriage was for men and women only. Bolivia defined marriage in its 2009 constitution as joining "a woman and a man," even as it prohibited discrimination on the basis of "sexual orientation" and "gender identity." Ecuador's 2008 constitution likewise banned discrimination on the basis of both "gender identity" and "sexual orientation," but decreed that "marriage is the union of man and woman." In neither country had any previous constitution defined marriage that way. In Honduras, the congress amended the constitution in 2004 to prohibit gay adoption and same-sex marriage.

The LGBT movement grew up in the 1970s in Latin America's biggest cities – notably Buenos Aires, Rio de Janeiro, São Paulo, Mexico City – under the influence and encouragement of the burgeoning gay-rights and feminist movements of western Europe and North America. LGBT activists also tended to share the outlook of the leftwing political groups dedicated to thoroughgoing social change that were sprouting all over Latin America in the 1960s and 1970s. All shared a commitment to radical emancipation from the prevailing orthodoxies, though as we shall see, they would eventually be divided by a subtle but eventually insurmountable difference. Groups dedicated to sweeping political and social change framed their discourse in terms of class or collective interests. Others, such as LGBT activists, motivated by a sense of injustice over questions of sexual identity or gender, presented their case in narrower, more individualistic terms oriented toward "rights" rather than comprehensive social change.

The first Latin American gay political organization – Grupo Nuestro Mundo (Our World Group) – was founded in 1969 in Buenos Aires. Most of its members were labor union activists. In 1971, Grupo Nuestro Mundo merged with other gay-rights groups to create the Frente de Liberación Homosexual (Homosexual Liberation Front), an underground organization that made common cause with other radical political groups. In a May 1972 manifesto, the FLH declared: "Homosexuals are socially, culturally, morally, and legally oppressed. They are ridiculed and marginalized, harshly suffering the absurdity of the brutality imposed upon them by monogamous heterosexual society." The FLH declared its solidarity with other causes championed by the Left, but it collapsed under the intense repression of the military junta that took power in 1976. The rebirth of the gay movement followed the return to electoral democracy in 1983. By the early 1990s numerous LGBT groups with diverse constituencies and aims had sprung up in Argentina, and organized the country's first Lesbian and Gay Pride March in 1992.

Movements similar to those of Argentina emerged in Mexico and Brazil in the 1970s and 1980s, almost always in close association with parties and groups linked to the revolutionary left and Marxist ideology. The LGBT groups, however, often encountered indifference or outright opposition from the leaders of the more traditional left, especially those of the communist parties. To them, homosexuality was a sign of bourgeois decadence, or a moral disorder bound to disappear under socialism. Fidel Castro's revolutionary government in Cuba, which prosecuted and imprisoned homosexuals through the 1970s, exemplified the left's anti-homosexual attitude. The Cuban government punished homosexuality with jail terms and forced-labor sentences, in what was unquestionably the most vigorous and thorough repression of homosexuality of any Latin American country in the history of the region. Explaining his antipathy to homosexuality to a U.S. interviewer in 1965, Castro declared that a homosexual could never "embody the conditions and requirements of conduct that would enable us to consider him a true revolutionary, a true communist militant. A deviation of that nature clashes with the concept we have of what a militant Communist should be . . . Homosexuals should not be allowed in positions where they are able to exert influence upon young people."[10] During the 1980s, communist Cuba's decade of crisis and abandonment by the Soviet Union, Castro underwent a gradual conversion. Sodomy was decriminalized in 1988 and the state's sex-education curriculum for schools began calling homosexuality a "variation" instead of a "deviation." In 2010 Castro publicly acknowledged that he had been the one "responsible" for the "great injustice" of prosecuting homosexuality, which he attributed to a "tradition" of discrimination.[11] By then the Cuban government was sponsoring national campaigns against homophobia, participating in the International Day Against Homophobia and paying for sex-change surgery for transsexuals. In 2006, the country's gay-rights groups welcomed what became the most-watched serial TV drama in Cuban history. "The Dark Side of the Moon" sympathetically portrayed the life of a married male construction worker who fell in love with a man and tested positive for HIV (human immunodeficiency virus).

Another sign of the astonishing gains in visibility and acceptance of the LGBT movement in Latin America was the rising popularity of such public expressions of solidarity as annual "Gay Pride" parades, in frank imitation of the model pioneered by LGBT activists in the United States in the early 1970s to commemorate New York City's "Stonewall Inn rebellion" of 28 June 1969.

That spontaneous two-hour protest by homosexuals angered by a police raid on a gay bar was said to have ignited the gay-rights movement in the United States, and was in turn recognized as a historic turning point by gay activists worldwide. The Brazilian city of São Paulo's annual gay pride parade (*Parada do Orgulho LGBT*), launched in 1997 before about 2,000 spectators, was the largest of its kind in the world by 2006. Held every June, it regularly attracted 3 million or more spectators and become an important source of revenue for the city as well as a platform for appearances by politicians. In Mexico City's twenty-third annual Gay Pride parade in 2001, about 5,000 people marched – some completely naked, and others proudly exposing surgically implanted breasts. In 2005, the Uruguayan capital of Montevideo unveiled what it announced was Latin America's first public monument to sexual diversity, a one-meter triangular monolith that carried a plaque engraved with the words, "Honrar la diversidad sexual es honrar la vida" (To honor sexual diversity is to honor life).

Thus, like so many other Latin American social movements, this one too both benefited from and fostered rising global action for LGBT rights. On a world scale, perhaps the most notable move was the first debate on homosexuality in the General Assembly of the United Nations on 18 December 2008. The delegates of sixty-six of the UN's 192 member countries endorsed a declaration favoring the decriminalization of homosexuality, while fifty-seven adopted an alternate statement opposing decriminalization, in some cases because they feared that decriminalization could eventually obligate them to accept same-sex marriage. Two years later, UN Secretary-General Ban Ki-moon pointed out that in seven countries homosexuality was still considered a crime. "This is not right," he declared.

At the same time, parallel moves were underway in the General Assembly of the Organization of American States. At its 2010 meeting in Lima, delegates voted to "encourage member states to consider ways to combat discrimination against persons because of their sexual orientation and gender identity" but did not call for a repeal of laws prohibiting homosexuality in the Americas. After Nicaragua repealed its anti-sodomy law in 2007, the only member countries of the OAS in which consensual same-sex acts remained a crime were eleven in the English-speaking Caribbean: Antigua & Barbuda, Belize, Barbados, Dominica, Grenada (men only), Guyana, Jamaica (for men), St. Kitts & Nevis (men only), St. Lucia (men only), St. Vincent & the Grenadines, and Trinidad & Tobago.

Notes

1   United Nations, Division for Social Policy and Development, *Men in Families and Family Policy in a Changing World* (New York: United Nations, 2011), 57, 59.

2   Quoted in John Carlin, "Los hombres sienten más una atracción fatal por el poder," interview with Michelle Bachelet, *El País* (Madrid), 1 November 2009, 6.
3   Asunción Lavrin, *Women, Feminism, and Social Change in Argentina, Chile, and Uruguay, 1890–1940* (Durham, NC: Duke University Press, 1991), 7.
4   Madres de la Plaza de Mayo, Línea Fundadora, "Declaración de principios, 1979," www.madresfundadoras.org.ar/pagina/declaracindeprincipiosao1979/24.
5   Elsa M. Chaney, *Supermadre: Women in Politics in Latin America* (Austin: University of Texas Press, 1979), 21.
6   Quoted in J. Mayone Stycos, "Politics and Population Control in Latin America," *World Politics* 20 (October, 1967) 1: 79.
7   Pope Paul VI, "Alocución a los representantes de los estados," 4 October 1965, www.vatican.va/holy_father/paul_vi/speeches/1965.
8   Quoted in Radio Cooperativa (Santiago de Chile) 21 November 2009, "Aparición de pareja gay en franja de Piñera generó molestia en la UDI," www.cooperativa.cl/aparicion-de-pareja-gay-en-franja-de-pinera-genero-molestia-en-la-udi/prontus_nots/2009-11-21/135453.html.
9   Javier Corrales, "Latin American Gays: The Post-Left Leftists," *Americas Quarterly* 19 March 2010, www.americasquarterly.org/gay-rights-Latin-America.
10   Quoted in Lee Lockwood, *Castro's Cuba, Cuba's Fidel*, rev. edn. (Boulder, CO: Westview Press, 1990), 107.
11   Quoted in Carmen Lira Saade, "Soy el responsable the la persecusión de homosexuals que hubo en Cuba: Fidel Castro," *La Jornada* (Mexico City), 31 August 2010, 26.

References

Carlin, John. "Los hombres sienten más una atracción fatal por el poder." *El País*, 1 November 2009, 6.
Chaney, Elsa. *Supermadre: Women in Politics in Latin America*. Austin: University of Texas Press, 1979.
Corrales, Javier. "Latin American Gays: The Post-Left Leftists." *Americas Quarterly* (2010). www.americasquarterly.org/gay-rights-Latin-America.
Lavrin, Asunción. *Women, Feminism, and Social Change in Argentina, Chile, and Uruguay, 1890–1940*. Lincoln, NE: University of Nebraska Press, 1995.
Lira Saade, Carmen. "Soy el responsable the la persecusión de homosexuals que hubo en Cuba: Fidel Castro." *La Jornada* (Mexico City), 31 August 2010, 26.
Lockwood, Lee. *Castro's Cuba, Cuba's Fidel*. Rev. edn. Boulder, CO: Westview Press, 1990.
Madres de la Plaza de Mayo, Línea Fundadora, "Declaración De Principios, 1979," www.madresfundadoras.org.ar/pagina/declaracindeprincipiosao1979/24.
Paul VI, Pope. "Alocución a los representantes de los estados" www.vatican.va/holy_father/paul_vi/speeches/1965.
Stycos, J. Mayone. "Politics and Population Control in Latin America." *World Politics* 20, no. 1 (1967): 66–82.
United Nations, Division for Social Policy and Development. *Men in Families and Family Policy in a Changing World*. New York: United Nations, 2011.

Chapter 16

Indigenous Peoples and Their Movements

The indigenous peoples are the majority of the Bolivian population ... We peoples have historically been marginalized, humiliated,
hated, scorned, condemned to extinction. That is our history. We have
never been recognized as human beings, although we are the absolute
owners of this noble land and of its natural resources ... Of those who
are enemies of the indigenous peoples, one still senses their presence. We
want to live on an equal footing with them, and that is why we are here,
to change our history. This native indigenous movement is not a conces-
sion from anyone; nobody has given it to us. It is the consciousness of
my people, of our people ...

President Evo Morales Ayma, 22 January 2006

On 18 December 2005, the voters of Bolivia made Evo Morales Ayma, the son
of Aymara Indians and the leader of Movimiento al Socialismo (Movement
toward Socialism, or MAS), the first fully indigenous president of Bolivia. He
won almost 54% of the vote.

Morales' victory capped a decades-long campaign for political representation among the 62% of Bolivians who identified themselves as Indians. But his
success resonated far beyond Bolivia. For Morales and his followers embodied
the amazing potential for radical social change that the indigenous-rights
movements had begun to unlock all over Latin America in the 1980s. The
epochal shifts of that extraordinary decade in favor of democracy, demilitarization and economic reform encompassed the takeoff of the greatest movement
for full equality by the indigenous peoples since the European conquest. Their
goal: the definitive reversal of a half-millennium of social and political exclu-

Contemporary Latin America: 1970 to the Present, First Edition. Robert H. Holden and Rina Villars.
© 2013 Robert H. Holden and Rina Villars. Published 2013 by Blackwell Publishing Ltd.

sion, economic exploitation and occasional extermination, often enforced by state-sponsored violence and driven by racially motivated contempt for them and their cultures.

Let us begin by first analyzing the numerical distribution of the people who identified themselves as indigenous, a task long hindered by two difficulties: The subjectivity inherent in arriving at a coherent and cross-national definition of "indigenous," and the practical and institutional obstacles to achieving an accurate count.

Defining "indigenous" will never be an exact science. Not only do somatic criteria (skin tone and other physical features) and the cultural criteria (language, religion, dress) vary from place to place and from time to time, but individual persons can be expected to apply them in idiosyncratic ways, in part because of the instability of the status implications conveyed by an "indigenous" identity. In some places, under certain conditions, to be "Indian" was and still is a stigma, and thus an identity to be avoided for reasons that will be discussed below. Moreover, the Spanish terms *indio* and *indígena* have at times referred more to social class than to ethnicity, so that to be an *indio* was to be poor, backward and uncivilized, regardless of one's actual ethnicity. In short, people could define themselves as Indian or non-Indian in ways that responded to the customs and expectations of a given social setting, time or place. Thus, identity should not be understood as an eternal category, nor one imposing an obligation of loyalty or solidarity. At the same time, government census takers and other officials imposed their own preferences and prejudices on the individuals they were responsible for counting.

These conceptual problems could be magnified by more practical challenges, such as state-directed data collection procedures that were inconsistent, poorly defined, underfinanced and weakly administered. They could be complicated still more by the geographical remoteness of many indigenous communities. Official census data were commonly subject to errors and undercounting, as well as to the influence of such factors as the level of the government's own commitment to accuracy, the public's confidence in the government, and political or ideological pressures aimed at favoring high counts or low counts of indigenous people. Underestimates could also occur because of civil conflict or war, common conditions in many of the most heavily indigenous countries during the period covered by this book.

The numerical estimates that follow were published in 2006 by two World Bank specialists, Heather Marie Layton and Harry Anthony Patrinos, who drew on a variety of official and non-official sources.[1] Technical and conceptual problems aside, there was no question that Bolivia had the greatest share of indigenous peoples in Latin America, followed by Guatemala and Peru. It also seemed likely that the Indian population of all three countries had tended to decline since the 1970s, though inconsistencies in the definition of indigenous complicated comparisons over time. In 2001, the Bolivian census reported that 52% of Bolivians over the age of 5 primarily spoke an indigenous language, but 62% of Bolivians over the age of 14 identified themselves as indigenous. In Guatemala, the census of 2000 reported that the indigenous population had risen to 41% from the 36% found in 1989, but that difference may well have been the result of an important procedural adjustment: In 1989, the government's interviewers decided the ethnicity of the respondents while in 2000, the government instructed census takers to ask the respondents to choose their ethnic identity. In Peru in 2001, 32% of the population claimed an indigenous language as their mother tongue, but 41% self-identified as indigenous.

While Bolivia, Guatemala and Peru stood out for the high proportions of their indigenous populations, other Latin American countries claimed substantial numbers. In absolute terms, Mexico's in 2000 outnumbered all other countries, with 6 million persons over the age of 4 who spoke an indigenous language. There, the number of Indians rose to 10.2 million (or about 9.5% of the population) when all family member were included in all the households in which at least one person spoke an indigenous language. Ecuador had for long reported the greatest range of estimates in its indigenous population, in part because many Ecuadorans who did not speak an Indian language nevertheless considered themselves to be indigenous, and because government statistics often failed to take full account of the country's ethnic diversity. Adjusting for these biases, Layton and Patrinos estimated Ecuador's indigenous population at 9.2% in 2001, the result of counting all Ecuadorans whose households included at least one person who either self-identified as indigenous or spoke an indigenous language (excluding domestic employees). While this stood as an unusually generous definition of "indigenous," the numerical result was considerably below the 32% proposed by the country's main indigenous organization, the Confederación de Nacionalidades Indígenas de Ecuador.

Paraguay was the rare case in which speaking an indigenous language was clearly *not* an index of indigenous identity. While about 80% of all Paraguayans spoke Guaraní, no more than 1–2% of the population were indigenous peoples. Thus, almost all Guaraní speakers were of European or mestizo descent. Most Paraguayans were bilingual in Spanish and in a version of Guaraní heavily influenced by Spanish. As a sign of national identity, and as the principal language of the home and the family, Guaraní has long been held in high regard, producing a substantial written literature in the form of poetry, theater, song and folk stories. In contrast to Bolivia and Peru, therefore, where we have seen how indigenous culture extended beyond the range of indigenous linguistic expression, the indigenous Guaraní culture of Paraguay has practically disappeared even as the Guaraní language thrived among non-Guaraní people.

Regardless of any country's relative share of people who identify as indigenous, almost everywhere in Latin America, the last three decades were marked by a surge in collective action by indigenous peoples. Its novelty and transformational potential cannot be appreciated without some awareness of the historical context of Indian-European relations. In Chapter 1, we noted the catastrophic impact of the European conquest on the native American populations. Within the territories claimed by the monarchies of Castile and Aragon (later "Spain"), a basic division in attitude toward the Indians had emerged as early as 1510. On the one hand, the Crown and above all some prominent Catholic clergymen and missionaries were horrified by the damage to the Indians carried out by the conquerors in the name of the monarchy and the Catholic religion. The monarchy responded with humanitarian legislation, and the Church with appeals to conscience, aimed at protecting the Indians from the abuse, exploitation and destruction they were suffering at the hands of the conquerors and their descendants. In their defense, the Spaniards claimed that exploitation – including forced labor – was necessary as compensation for the risks that they and their ancestors had undertaken on behalf of the Crown and religion. They pointed out that the Crown's own desire to exploit the region's stupendous mineral wealth could not be fulfilled without the use of forced labor and other forms of discipline directed against the Indians.

Some of the worst abuses faded during the sixteenth century. The Crown, aided by an elaborate bureaucratic apparatus of judges and administrators, continued to exercise a valuable protective function over Indian communities, providing them with land that was, at least theoretically, off-limits to the Spaniards, and a court system to which aggrieved Indians could successfully appeal for justice. The monarch's institutional ally, the Catholic Church, played a similarly protective role through its preaching as well as through the charitable, educational and spiritual works directed to the Indian communities. To be sure, this was a paternalistic kind of defense at best, aimed above all at preserving a kind of caste system that both separated Indian and Spaniard, while ensuring the former's subservience to the latter.

The post-independence republican governments eliminated colonial-era legal barriers to full civil and political rights for Indians, mestizos and other non-whites. But now, bereft of the juridical and corporatist devices the Crown had instituted for their own protection, the indigenous peoples were more vulnerable than ever. Typically led by men who considered indigenous peoples and their cultures to be their country's biggest obstacles to progress and civilization, the new republican governments ushered in a general decline in Indian welfare. Centuries-old Indian villages lost lands bequeathed to them "in perpetuity" by the Crown. New forms of forced labor were devised for the benefit of landowners. In places like Chile and Argentina, genocidal campaigns of extermination nearly succeeded in permanently solving the "Indian question." By the late nineteenth century, "scientific" racism – belief in the division of all humanity into a hierarchy of superior and inferior races, as propagated by intellectual and political leaders in the United States and Europe – governed the attitudes and policies of Latin America's ruling classes.

Anti-indigenous attitudes softened in the early twentieth century with the rise of the ideology of *indigenismo*. Its proponents romanticized Indian culture, denounced the historic exploitation and exclusion of the Indians, and in praising their resistance to European conquest glorified them as the true founders of the nation – a tendency especially marked in overwhelmingly mestizo countries such as Mexico. Nevertheless, the objective of *indigenismo* was emancipation through integration. The Indian would be assimilated – above all by means of the public education system – into a nation understood as necessarily and permanently singular in its culture and ethnicity. On this view, the once-noble Indian had degenerated into a passive and semi-conscious subject, incapable of self-direction, and in need of the paternalistic direction of the national state. This outlook corresponded well to the corporatism that still imbued Hispanic political culture, for *indigenismo*'s salvation-by-assimilation could be achieved by redefining Indians as members of a particular social grouping or class – *campesinos* or "country people." Organized into state-approved organizations under appropriate leadership, they were now available as the clients of political leaders who could reward them for their loyalty by facilitating access to land and other resources.

Before the 1980s, therefore, the indigenous peoples rarely participated in social and political movements as members of a distinct ethnic group with its own identity, grievances and agenda for change. Rather, their interests tended to be subsumed within larger movements or organizations – of peasants, or workers, or personalistic political parties. It was a process shaped not only by corporatism but also by the rise since the 1920s of Marxist ideology, an analytical current that advanced in power and influence with the radicalization of politics in the 1960s and the increasing appeal of social revolution as the cure for Latin America's political and economic backwardness. Marxism insisted on the priority of economic class (rich or poor, worker or capitalist, peasant or landowner) over every conceivable alternative type of identity. In this way of thinking, an ethnic identity would only divide Indians, mestizos, whites and blacks from one another, just as a sexual identity would divide women from men, undermining their supposedly revolutionary "class" identity.

Then came the economic collapse of the 1980s, which led rapidly to the abandonment of the statist model of development, with its traditionally corporatist controls, subsidies and regulations. Governments began to favor a neoliberal program of economic development, stressing personal freedom, responsibility and a new respect for the autonomy of civil society and the private sector of the economy. At the same time, direct military rule and other forms of authoritarian government gave way to civilian rule, competitive electoral politics, and incipient democratization. Increasingly, governments in the 1980s were being judged according to their respect for basic human rights, in both national and international political arenas. The 1980s also saw the decline and collapse of the socialist bloc of countries, purging the passion for social revolution that had blazed across Latin America for two decades, and discrediting its ideology, Marxism, and thus its rigidly class-oriented ways of categorizing people. Finally, the commemoration in 1992 of the five-hundredth anniversary of Christopher Columbus' first voyage to the Americas provided a golden opportunity to reflect on the impact of Europeanization. The anniversary inspired the creation of transnational networks of indigenous peoples intent on finding common ground in mobilizing for territorial rights, civil and political rights, and the protection of their language, religious traditions and other ways of life.

Overcoming the effects of decades of partial suppression of collective ethnic identities, indigenous peoples emphasized their separate status as members of communities with unique interests, united by blood and a non-Hispanic tradition. They began to insist, in short, on full citizenship – a status that would both ensure their membership in the nation as individuals with equal rights, and yet acknowledge their status as members of a distinct ethnic community with its own political, social and religious customs that merited protection, preservation and respect. Indians in effect challenged the longstanding policies of assimilation into the larger Hispanic culture, and in doing so, they launched one of the most conspicuous and far-reaching movements for social and political change in the period covered by this book.

Like many of the momentous social changes of our period, this one too could be understood as the regional expression of a global transformation in ideas about indigenous rights that was both nourished by, and in turn fostered, the changes underway in Latin America. In 1989, the UN's International Labor Organization adopted an Indigenous and Tribal Peoples Convention calling on governments to take "coordinated and systematic action to protect the rights of [indigenous or tribal] peoples and to guarantee respect for their integrity," including guarantees for "the full measure of human rights and fundamental freedoms without hindrance or discrimination." As of 2011, the convention had been ratified by twenty-two countries, including all of the Latin American countries except Cuba, the Dominican Republic, El Salvador, Panama and Uruguay. Of those, only El Salvador and Panama reported the presence of indigenous peoples in their territories – about 8% in both countries.

By ratifying the ILO agreement, states agreed to be permanently bound by its provisions. The convention's most remarkable feature was its specific repudiation of what it called the "assimilationist orientation" of the ILO's 1957 Convention on Indigenous and Tribal Populations, which repeatedly identified the ultimate objective of national policy as the social, economic and cultural "integration" of the indigenous peoples into the nations of the signatory states. For example, the 1957 convention mandated "a progressive transition from the mother tongue or the vernacular language to the national language or to one of the official languages of the country." The 1989 convention, however, only mandated that indigenous peoples receive the "opportunity" to attain fluency in the national language, while directing that measures be taken "to preserve and promote the development and practice of the indigenous languages." The 1989 agreement also established self-identification as "a fundamental criterion" for defining indigenous; the word "identity" does not even appear in the 1957 document. Like the 1989 covenant, the overwhelming majority of the countries that ratified the 1957 convention were Latin American (thirteen out of seventeen, compared to fourteen out of twenty-two for the 1989 convention, by 2011).

Even the titles of the two conventions – the first referring to "populations" and the second to "peoples" – revealed a change in attitude over the intervening thirty-two years. In 1957, it was thought that indigenous "populations" would eventually disappear under the pressure of "modernization." But by referring to them as "peoples," the signatories of 1989 revealed a new awareness of the intrinsic dignity of the indigenous peoples along with their customs and languages, and therefore their right to survive and flourish as distinctive members of the human family.

Among the most far-reaching provisions of the 1989 convention were those aimed at ensuring the freedom of indigenous peoples to participate "at all levels of decision-making in elective institutions and administrative and other bodies responsible for policies and programs which concern them," while also establishing the "means for the full development of these peoples' own institutions and initiatives, and in appropriate cases to provide the resources necessary for this purpose." Furthermore, the indigenous should be allowed to "exercise control" over their institutions and ways of life "within the framework of the States in which they live." Today, language reflecting these mandates can be found in most of the constitutions of Latin America, and in some cases had been added even before 1989.

As indigenous peoples in Latin America and elsewhere gained new levels of protection against discrimination, and legislation favoring their rights to preserve their cultural heritage, a new question arose: To what extent should indigenous communities be allowed to "exercise control" over their institutions and ways of life? Should they, for example, be allowed to adopt their own laws and judicial institutions? Govern themselves according to their traditional political institutions? The ILO's 1989 covenant omitted any reference to "autonomy" and "self-determination" but these very ideas would move to the center of indigenous demands by the 1990s.

After more than two decades of debate and negotiation, the United Nations General Assembly adopted the Declaration on the Rights of Indigenous People in 2007. The non-binding text was approved by a vote of 143–4 (Australia, Canada, New Zealand and United States) with eleven abstentions, including that of Colombia, the only Latin America country not voting in favor. A central concern of the countries that abstained or voted against the Declaration was precisely its strong support for self-determination in three separate articles, as well as a much firmer statement of land rights than that of the ILO convention (see all four articles in the accompanying sidebar.) On the land question, the ILO had merely called on governments to "respect the special importance for the cultures and spiritual values of the peoples concerned of their relationship with the lands or territories, or both as applicable, which they occupy or otherwise use" while the UN Declaration referred to a "right" to lands that indigenous peoples may no longer even occupy. The UN Declaration introduced a loophole, or at least a note of ambiguity, in the application of these four articles by asserting (in Article 46) that nothing in the Declaration was meant to imply the right of anyone to "dismember or impair" the territorial integrity or political unity of any sovereign state.

UN Declaration on the Rights of Indigenous Peoples (2007)

Article 3. Indigenous peoples have the right to self-determination. By virtue of that right they freely determine their political status and freely pursue their economic, social and cultural development.

Article 4. Indigenous peoples, in exercising their right to self-determination, have the right to autonomy or self-government in matters relating to their internal and local affairs, as well as ways and means for financing their autonomous functions.

Article 5. Indigenous peoples have the right to maintain and strengthen their distinct political, legal, economic, social and cultural institutions, while retaining their right to participate fully, if they so choose, in the political, economic, social and cultural life of the State . . .

Article 26.
1. Indigenous peoples have the right to the lands, territories and resources which they have traditionally owned, occupied or otherwise used or acquired.

(Continued)

2. Indigenous peoples have the right to own, use, develop and control the lands, territories and resources that they possess by reason of traditional ownership or other traditional occupation or use, as well as those which they have otherwise acquired.

3. States shall give legal recognition and protection to these lands, territories and resources. Such recognition shall be conducted with due respect to the customs, traditions and land tenure systems of the indigenous peoples concerned.

By the end of 2010, all four of the countries that had voted against the Declaration in 2007 reversed their positions and sanctioned it, though Canada heavily qualified its endorsement of the land-claims rights in Article 26. At the same time, defenders of autonomy and self-determination in Latin America dismissed the possibility of indigenous secession movements on the grounds that the region's indigenous peoples only sought "internal" autonomy within the confines of the national state, rather than any "external" right to determine their international status. As one Mayan activist in Guatemala put it: "We want a role in the states from which we have been so long excluded; we want their reform, not their overthrow."[2]

More than any other Latin American country, Bolivia moved farthest in satisfying indigenous-rights claims. It was no coincidence that Bolivia was also the country with the strongest and most successful indigenous political movements, with an impressive record of electoral victories since the 1990s. This was not surprising considering that no Latin American country claimed a higher percentage of indigenous peoples – well over half Bolivia's population. Bolivia's Indians were thus well-positioned to win elections and change government policy as long as the movement could maintain political unity and a high level of voter turnout. And this they did, achieving major breakthroughs by uniting behind the successful candidacy of Evo Morales in the presidential election of 2005, and then behind his campaign for a new constitution aimed at guaranteeing indigenous rights and identity. Morales' victory was itself the culmination of a decades-long political mobilization whose initial victory was the election in 1993 of Víctor Hugo Cárdenas Conde, an Aymara Indian, as vice-president of Bolivia.

Born in 1959 into a poor farming family, Morales grew up in a one-room adobe house with a straw roof. As a child, he shepherded the family's llama herd and joined his father as a migrant worker on trips to Argentina to harvest sugar cane. After his family turned to coca farming, Morales became an advocate for coca farmers whose livelihoods were threatened by U.S.-financed campaigns sponsored by the Bolivian government to eradicate or greatly limit the cultivation of coca, the source of cocaine. But coca leaves had been chewed as a mild stimulant by the indigenous peoples of the Andes for centuries, and Morales vowed to defend the Indians' right to continue to grow coca – a potent symbol not only of Indian culture, but also national sovereignty (against both the international drug cartels and U.S. anti-drug policies) and economic opportunity for the rural poor.

Building on his growing popularity as a leader of Bolivia's poor farmers, Morales won 70% of the vote in his first run for public office in 1997, when he was elected to the national Congress. There, he continued his campaign for the full legalization of coca cultivation against the government's stepped-up eradication efforts. In the 2002 presidential election, Morales stunned the country by finishing second, losing by just 1.5% of the votes. Over the next three years, Morales and his party, Movimiento al Socialismo, took the lead in numerous public demonstrations against coca eradication, tax rises and government privatizations, and in favor of action to help the country's landless population.

In 2005, Morales became the first presidential candidate to win an outright majority since the end of military rule in 1982. His MAS party took a commanding seventy-two-seat majority in the lower house of the national Congress. Among the new Congress' first acts was to authorize a constitutional convention. Over the bitter and at times violent opposition of voters in the largely non-Indian eastern lowlands, the new constitution was approved by a 63% margin in a popular referendum on 25 January 2009 and hailed by President Morales as terminating "five-hundred years of colonial subordination and more than twenty years of neoliberalism." Article I established Bolivia as a "Social unitary state of plurinational communitarian law – free, independent, sovereign, democratic, intercultural, decentralized and with autonomous units. Bolivia is founded on plurality and on political, economic, juridical, cultural and linguistic pluralism, within the country's integrating process." The constitution created a Plurinational Legislative Assembly, and mandated new legal rights for thirty-six different indigenous groups while conveying to them a measure of political and judicial autonomy. It also set aside assembly seats for indigenous delegates, gave the state more control over natural resources, and placed a ceiling of 5,000 hectares on individual land holdings. Morales' government immediately began to divide large, privately owned landholdings and redistribute them to indigenous groups.

Xavier Albó, a scholar and linguist, compared the enactment of the constitution to Spain's final Reconquest of the Iberian peninsula from the Moors in 1492, except that the Bolivian event took place democratically, without excluding or subjugating anyone. Opponents of the constitution rejected the claim of inclusiveness, arguing that the document excluded the "the other vision of the country" (the non-indigenous one) and sought to break with Western economic, cultural and political norms and practices in part by replacing the liberal state with an "ethnicist" state. Others claimed that the constitution fused liberal, plurinational and communitarian modes of government called for by the very composition of Bolivian society, in which two traditions, one Western and the other indigenous, continued to thrive. In terms of the principle of majority rule, at any rate, the legitimacy of the new order could hardly be doubted; twelve months after its adoption, Morales won re-election with an unheard-of 64% of the vote, while his MAS earned two-thirds of the seats in both houses of the new assembly.

In contrast to Bolivia, Guatemala's indigenous candidates for the presidency and the congress have had little success, in part because of consistently low turnouts by indigenous voters at election time. Consequently, the impressive oratorical commitments to major improvements in the status of the country's indigenous peoples by one Guatemalan government after another since the 1980s remained largely unfulfilled. Those commitments began with the 1985 constitution's implicit rejection of assimilation. The 1965 constitution had directed the President to ensure "the integration of the indigenous population into the national culture." The 1985 version (see accompanying text) included an entire section affirming the dignity and value of Guatemala's indigenous peoples, while pledging the state's "special protection" of indigenous land. It also provided guarantees for migrant workers, a response to the century-old custom by which Indians migrated – often under coercive conditions sometimes enforced by the state – from the highlands to the principal coffee-growing areas along the Pacific piedmont at harvest time.

Guatemala Constitution of 1985

Third Section: Indigenous Communities

Article 66. Protection of ethnic groups. Guatemala is made up of various ethnic groups, among those that comprise the indigenous groups of Mayan descent. The State recognizes, respects and promotes their ways of life, customs, traditions, forms of social organization, the use of indigenous dress by men and women, languages and dialects.

Article 67. Protection of the lands and indigenous agricultural cooperatives. The lands of the cooperatives, indigenous communities or any other form of communal or collective agricultural property tenure, as well as family estates and popular housing, will enjoy the special protection of the State, preferential credit and technical assistance, guaranteeing their possession and development for the purpose of assuring all the inhabitants a better quality of life.

The indigenous communities and others holding lands that historically belong to them and which they have traditionally administered in a special way, will maintain that system.

Article 68. Lands for indigenous communities. By means of special programs and adequate legislation, the State will provide state land to indigenous communities that need them for their development.

Article 69. Transfer of workers and their protection. Labor activities that imply the transfer of workers outside of their communities will be subject to protection and legislation to assure adequate conditions of health, security and social security for the payment of wages in accord with the law and to avoid the disintegration of those communities and in general all discriminatory treatment.

Guatemala extended its commitment to indigenous rights well beyond the skeletal language of the 1985 constitution in 1995, when it signed an extraordinary, 6,400-word indigenous-rights accord with the insurgent Unidad Revolucionaria Nacional Guatemalteca. It was one of ten agreements hammered out from 1994 to 1996 between the revolutionaries and the government that ended the thirty-four-year civil war discussed in Chapter 3. The 1995 treaty on "identity and rights of the indigenous peoples" acknowledged that Guatemala's indigenous peoples "have been particularly subject to levels of de facto discrimination, exploitation and injustice owing to their origin, culture and language, and that, like many other sectors of the national collectivity, suffer from unequal and unjust treatment and condition." It obligated the government to undertake a series of specific and far-reaching measures to correct both de facto and de jure discrimination; to promote indigenous culture (including language, religion and dress); and to extend a host of civil, political, social and economic rights (including rights to land) to the indigenous peoples by means of constitutional amendments and appropriate legislation.

Nevertheless, by 2010, Guatemala had made little progress in achieving these goals. To be sure, the indigenous question had attained more prominence than ever in national political debates. Government-funded agencies carried out publicity campaigns to promote inclusiveness, and several laws had been passed aimed at implementing the accords. But required legislative action remained "notoriously limited" and still faced enormous political obstacles, the government's own human rights office observed in 2011. The government ministry in charge of carrying out the peace accords noted in 2009 that of the ten 1994–1996 peace accords, the one on indigenous identity and rights was still among the least addressed, particularly in its commitments to improving political representation and access to the country's justice system. Almost nothing had been done to carry out the accord's promise of such "collective rights" as religious freedom and access to land and mass communication facilities. The election of Alvaro Colom, a mestizo, to the presidency on 4 November 2007 raised hopes for faster change, especially after Colom promised "a social-democratic country but with a Mayan face" to "pay back the historic debt to the indigenous peoples." But little real action followed, and Colom's administration was widely criticized for illegally granting mining concessions in 2010 to foreign companies on lands claimed by indigenous peoples, who almost unanimously opposed the concessions.

Elsewhere in Latin America, as in Guatemala, impressively pro-indigenous commitments, pledged in constitutions and various international accords, have been considerably less fruitful in comparison to Bolivia's recent experience. After a national debate on indigenous rights, Brazil's 1988 constitution turned away from the country's longstanding policy of assimilation, for the first time adding a section called "The Indians" that recognized their right to maintain their "social organization, customs, languages, creeds and traditions," as well as "their original rights to the lands they traditionally occupy." Such lands were "inalienable," and thus remained in the "permanent possession" of the Indians, for their "exclusive use." The state was obligated to delimit the lands, protect them "and ensure respect for all of their property," as well as to consult the indigenous peoples regarding the use of their lands and natural resources.

Nevertheless, two decades after the passage of the constitution, and five years after Brazil signed the 1989 ILO accord, little had been done to implement them, according to the country's principal indigenous organization, *Abril indígena*. Land invasions by settlers, illegal exploitation of indigenous lands, and the murder and enslavement of Indians were still common. Although many more indigenous peoples were winning election to municipal offices, they were unlikely to play a significant role given the fact that they constituted no more than 0.4% of the population, and were divided into 227 different ethnic groups, of which half counted fewer than 500 individuals. Despite the constitutional language – or perhaps just because of its extraordinary guarantees of land rights – many Brazilians still viewed the indigenous peoples as obstacles to progress.

In Paraguay, where 2% of the population identified themselves as indigenous, a wide range of indigenous rights, including rights to land, was acknowledged in the 1992 constitution and in statutory law. But by 2010 Paraguay was the Latin American country with the largest number of complaints in the Inter-American Court of Human Rights concerning the violation of indigenous land rights. Racial discrimination against Indian peoples, continuing legal efforts by developers to block indigenous use of their ancestral lands, lack of enforcement by the state, and extreme poverty posed serious obstacles to implementing Paraguay's commitments to indigenous rights. Nevertheless, as demonstrated by the rise in litigation over land claims, Paraguay's legislation at least provided the Indian peoples with a new and potentially effective instrument to advance their cause. Precisely for that reason, proposals for sweeping legislation in favor of indigenous rights often encountered strong opposition, particularly in the case of indigenous claims for autonomy and self-determination.

Mexico's recent experience illustrated the point. On a national scale relative to its population, Mexico's indigenous peoples made up a relatively small (10–11%) share of its citizens. On the other hand, 80% were concentrated in eleven southern states; in Oaxaca, 35% of the population over 4 years of age spoke an indigenous language; in Yucatán, 33%; Chiapas, 26%. In many municipalities, the proportions were much higher. In 1991, Mexico became the first Latin American country to ratify the 1989 ILO covenant and in 1992 a constitutional amendment declared that "The Mexican nation has a pluricultural composition based originally on its indigenous peoples."

In the heavily indigenous state of Chiapas, the rural poor began seizing land in the 1980s. As government repression of activist Indians increased, a guerrilla army of largely Indian peasants, the Ejército Zapatista de Liberación Nacional or EZLN, began to form, and on 1 January 1994 the EZLN announced its revolutionary program with attacks on government installations in Chiapas. At the time of the uprising, the demands of the EZLN had focused almost exclusively on the class-based economic and social-welfare grievances typical of movements of the rural poor. But as the violent phase of the protest gave way to negotiations with the Mexican government, the EZLN leadership sought political support beyond Chiapas. As a result, autonomy for Mexico's indigenous peoples displaced the living conditions of the peasantry as the center of the EZLN's agenda for social change.

On 16 February 1996, representatives of the Mexican government and the EZLN signed an accord in the Chiapas town of San Andrés Larráinzar committing the Mexican government to a remarkable exception in the country's longstanding constitutional norms. "The State," the Accord declared,

> must promote the recognition, as a constitutional guarantee, of the right to self-determination of the indigenous peoples . . . The right to self-determination will be exercised in a constitutional framework of autonomy, maintaining national unity. They will be able, as a result, to

decide their form of internal government and how they organize themselves politically, socially, economically and culturally.

Despite the fact that its own representatives had accepted this language, the
government of President Ernesto Zedillo rejected the pact out of fear that
implementing the autonomy provision of the Accord would balkanize Mexico
by promoting and legitimizing separate and potentially rival "nations." The
EZLN terminated negotiations and continued to agitate for indigenous autonomy. In 2000, Mexicans elected the first president since the 1920s who was not
a candidate of the official Partido Revolucionario Institucional (PRI). President
Vicente Fox of the conservative opposition party, Partido Acción Nacional
(PAN), had famously pledged during the campaign to resolve the problem of
Chiapas and the EZLN "in fifteen minutes." Within days of his swearing-in,
Fox submitted the EZLN-backed version of the constitutional changes to the
national Congress. But Congress, still fearful of its implications for national
unity, revised the proposal in ways that restricted the level of autonomy sought
by the EZLN and its allies. In 2003 the EZLN, in defiance of the law, established
autonomous governing units in areas under its control in Chiapas.

In Ecuador, political action in favor of the country's indigenous minority
appeared to gain new ground in 1996, when the country's main Indian-rights
organization, the Confederation of Indigenous Nationalities of Ecuador
(CONAIE), joined non-indigenous organizations in launching a political party,
the MUPP (Movimiento Unidad Plurinacional Pachakutik), or Pachakutik
Movement for Plurinational Unity. In the Indian language Quechua, spoken
across the Andes region, the word *pachakutik* suggests rebirth or transformation in reference to both time and the land. The party participated in the 1996
election, gaining several seats in the national Congress, as well as a significant
number in local posts. Its sponsored presidential candidate –a non-indigenous
television commentator – finished third among nine candidates.

By that year, Ecuador had already established itself as the Latin American
country with the most unified and aggressive indigenous movement, and its
leaders were eager to translate a series of recent, attention-getting demonstrations into political power. The watershed event was the CONAIE-organized
levantamiento indígena de Inti Raymi, the "indigenous uprising" of 4 June 1990,
about two weeks before the celebration of an Incan religious rite marking the
summer solstice. Looking ahead to the 1992 quincentenary of Columbus' first
voyage, CONAIE proclaimed that the history of Ecuador was "the history of
500 years of indigenous resistance" and issued a sixteen-point platform for
change that encompassed respect for Indian culture, economic development
assistance, and political reform. As the *levantamiento* unfolded, two key
demands emerged: that Ecuador's constitution acknowledge the country's
plurinational character, and the confiscation of Ecuador's large land holdings

and the redistribution of the land to the poor and the country's indigenous communities. Two hundred persons occupied Quito's Santo Domingo cathedral. Across the country, protesters blockaded roads and occupied haciendas, disrupting commerce and preventing supplies from reaching the cities. The army and police moved in to clear the roads, and the rebels responded by taking military hostages.

After three days, the government agreed to negotiate; the hostages were released and the demonstrations ended. The most extraordinary facet of the uprising was the impressive level of popular support it drew in such a brief period of time. Overnight, the *levantamiento* turned the indigenous movement into an important political force, and emboldened its leadership to intensify pressure for radical change, including territorial autonomy and self-determination. A series of dramatic marches, strikes and other public demonstrations in support of these demands followed in the early 1990s as CONAIE kept up the pressure for a "New Multinational Nation" in which a democratic government would take decisive action in favor of land redistribution, improved health and education, and against discrimination and unemployment. Perhaps the key underlying development was CONAIE's rejection of the government's official "pluricultural" or "multicultural" policy because it "merely" promoted respect for indigenous cultures and life ways, in the context of a more or less unified mestizo nation-state. Against it, the indigenous movement proposed its "plurinational" or "multinational" model of change. Here, indigenous communities would be recognized as among so many "nationalities" with their own cultures and thus their own special rights that included economic and political control over their ancestral territories and life ways.

In their first opportunity to carry out this goal, the MUPP won seats in a constitutional convention elected in 1997. But, forced to compromise, the party accepted a new constitution that recognized Ecuador's "pluricultural and multiethnic" character, a partial victory that nevertheless also included the statement that "Indigenous peoples, who self-define as nationalities of ancestral races, and Negro or Afro-Ecuadorian peoples, form part of a united and indivisible Ecuadorian state." Similar language had already been inserted into the constitutions of Colombia (1991), Peru (1993) and Bolivia (1994). MUPP continued to participate, but with little success, in congressional and presidential elections. In 2006, its first presidential nominee, Luis Macas, earned only slightly more than 2% of the vote. By then, the indigenous movement was badly divided by internal disputes, including opposition by some activists to direct participation in a system of electoral politics notorious for its corruption and clientelism. Ironically, given the movement's lack of success in the electoral arena, it finally gained recognition of Ecuador's "plurinationality" in a constitutional revision in 2008 that also conveyed various "collective rights" to the country's "indigenous communes, communities, peoples and nationalities."

Perhaps the most innovative element of the revised constitution was its acknowledgement of the "rights of nature or Pacha Mama," (the "mother earth" celebrated in the religion of the Inca).

Conclusion

The indigenous peoples of the region had gained at least one great victory since the 1970s. Constitutions and statute books were rewritten to bestow a lavish and diverse array of collective and individual rights on the descendants of their countries' pre-conquest inhabitants. As a result, public sensitivity to the grim history of indigenous peoples' status, and their claims for redress, was never higher. The indigenous peoples successfully organized across ethnic, regional and national boundaries, and they made themselves heard. But the effort to correct ancient injustices through legislation collided with another ancient tradition: disregard for the rule of law. The actual application and enforcement of pro-indigenous legislation remained a highly selective, if not forgotten, part of the governing process. Only Bolivia – the sole Latin American country with a majority of indigenous peoples, and the only one to elect a fully indigenous president with a long record of rights activism – appeared to be implementing the rights it proclaimed. On the other hand, while scholars and activists repeatedly identified Ecuador as the country with the strongest and most unified indigenous rights movement, by 2011 it had few practical results to show. Paradoxically, the decision to engage in electoral politics seemed to be yielding diminishing returns.

Notes

1   Heather Marie Layton and Harry Anthony Patrinos, "Estimating the Number of Indigenous Peoples in Latin America," in *Indigenous Peoples, Poverty and Human Development in Latin America*, ed. Gillette Hall and Harry Anthony Patrinos (Basingstoke: Palgrave Macmillan, 2006).
2   Phillip Wearne, "Indigenous Peoples in Latin America in the 21st Century," in *South America, Central America and the Caribbean 2003*, ed. Jacqueline West (London: Europa Publications, 2003), 46.

References

Layton, Heather Marie, and Harry Anthony Patrinos. "Estimating the Number of Indigenous Peoples in Latin America." In *Indigenous Peoples, Poverty and Human*

Development in Latin America, ed. Gillette Hall and Harry Anthony Patrinos, 25–39. Basingstoke: Palgrave Macmillan, 2006.

Wearne, Phillip. "Indigenous Peoples in Latin America in the 21st Century." In *South America, Central America and the Caribbean 2003,* ed. Jacqueline West, 44–8. London: Europa Publications, 2003.

Chapter 17

Toward a Latin American Community of Nations?

With the approach of the bicentennial of Latin American independence during the first decade of the twenty-first century, the governments of the region acted to revive a notion as old as the republics themselves. In 1824, Simón Bolívar invited the heads of state of the newly independent republics to "form a confederation" aimed at resolving conflicts and acting together against common dangers. At that time, however, settling conflicts *within* the incipient nation often seemed well beyond the reach of the republics' new leaders. And few of them saw any advantage in yielding up what little power they had to a supranational authority.

The dream of regional unity persisted nevertheless. Between 1847 and 1883, decades marked by political instability and the incapacity to forge coherent national identities, Latin American leaders tried and failed to establish a Hispanic-American confederation at least four more times. Ironically, but understandably in view of the region's internal turmoil, it would fall to a non-Latin American power, the United States, to initiate Latin America's first and most enduring regional organization of states. In 1889, James G. Blaine, the U.S. Secretary of State, presided over the first in a series of international "Conferences of American States" whose principal objectives were defined by Washington as the encouragement of free trade and the establishment of a mechanism for peacefully settling disputes. At Blaine's invitation, every country but the Dominican Republic sent delegates. Three more conferences led to the creation in 1910 of the Pan American Union, headquartered in Washington DC, with the U.S. Secretary of State as its permanent chairman.

Pan Americanism had defeated Hispano-Americanism. The new association of Latin American states not only found itself headquartered far from Latin America. But it was now directed by a non-Latin American power that, despite

Contemporary Latin America: 1970 to the Present, First Edition. Robert H. Holden and Rina Villars.
© 2013 Robert H. Holden and Rina Villars. Published 2013 by Blackwell Publishing Ltd.

its initial aim of seeking the peaceful settlement of disputes in the Hispanic world, had already declared a Latin American policy in 1904 whose defining operational technique consisted of unilateral intervention. Military occupation, or the threat of occupation, became Washington's principal means of imposing political stability, particularly in the Caribbean Basin, and the opinions of the member nations of the Pan American Union were practically irrelevant. The foundational motive for U.S. intervention was to prevent non-hemispheric imperial powers – above all Germany, Great Britain and Japan – from exploiting the chronic political disorder of the Latin American republics in order to establish colonies or protectorates in the region. In this respect, the United States could claim that it was doing nothing more than implementing the Monroe Doctrine's traditional warning against territorial acquisition by non-hemispheric powers. On the other hand, a good deal of U.S.-government meddling and direct intervention also aimed at advancing U.S. economic interests.

As a result, distrust of the United States became the predominant attitude in much of Latin America, and the periodic international conferences held under the auspices of the Pan American Union saw concerted efforts by the Latin American delegates to force the United States to respect their sovereignty and endorse the principle of non-intervention. In 1933, Washington finally complied unequivocally when President Franklin D. Roosevelt implemented what he called his "good neighbor" policy toward Latin America, pledging to respect the equal sovereignty of every American republic, while encouraging free trade and the peaceful settlement of disputes. After joining with the United States in defeating the Axis powers during World War II (1939–1945), the Latin American republics along with the United States met in Bogotá from March to May of 1948 to replace the Pan American Union with the Organization of American States (OAS). Based in Washington like its predecessor, the OAS defined its mission in terms congruent with U.S. interests, now identified above all with preventing the spread of communism from Europe and Asia to Latin America. Meeting in Brazil the previous year, all the republics and the United States had already negotiated the hemisphere's first mutual security pact, the Inter-American Treaty of Reciprocal Assistance, better known as the Rio Treaty. It committed the signers to defend any member state subjected to armed attack by either a hemispheric or a non-hemispheric power, and established mechanisms for joint action against the aggressor.

Washington's towering military, political and industrial superiority meant that, until the 1970s, the United States tended to determine when and under what conditions the treaty would be activated. By 1979, it had been invoked eighteen times, mostly among the countries of the Caribbean Basin in response to accusations of infringements of territorial sovereignty or communist subversion, usually involving Cuba. But after 1979 the Rio Treaty was almost entirely neglected, even during the Central American civil wars of the 1980s, despite their notably transnational character. It was invoked in 1981 to douse a flare-up in a perennial border dispute between Ecuador and Peru, and in 1982 in the war between Argentina and Great Britain over the Falkland Islands. In that war, the United States shocked the Latin Americans by siding with Britain, which went on to win the war – a doubly ironic outcome, considering that it was the first time the treaty had ever been invoked against a non-hemispheric power, the very contingency that had led the United States to propose the treaty in 1947. Thoroughly discredited by its eternal association with U.S. foreign policy objectives, the Treaty by the 1990s was seen as little more than a relic of the Cold War.

A similar fate appeared to be awaiting the OAS, for its prestige had dwindled considerably since the 1970s, and for reasons much like those that had undermined the Rio Treaty. Unlike the treaty, however, the OAS recovered by creating a new mission as an enforcer of democratic norms. Although the genesis of the organization's makeover was not recognized as such at the time, in retrospect it might be dated to 23 June 1979, the day the OAS General Assembly voted to condemn the human rights record of Anastasio Somoza's government in Nicaragua and to recommend its removal. In doing so, the OAS not only laid aside its traditional commitment to non-intervention. But it effectively endorsed the guerrilla war against Somoza led by the Frente Sandinista de la Liberación Nacional (FSLN), which succeeded in seizing power twenty-six days later.

The vote against Somoza inaugurated a series of moves over the next two decades that would turn the OAS into a kind of multilateral court, self-endowed with the authority to assess the legitimacy of any given Latin American government. In 1985, as democratization and demilitarization swept Latin America, the OAS charter was amended to add as an "essential obligation" the duty to "promote and consolidate representative democracy, with due respect for the principle of nonintervention." In 1991, the OAS General Assembly went still further, mandating OAS action within ten days in the case of a breakdown in democracy in any member country. In 1997, the General Assembly assumed the authority to suspend a member state whose democratic government had been overthrown.

By now, little if anything was left of the principle of non-intervention, forced to yield to the higher good of democratic rule. The remaking of the OAS culminated in the General Assembly's adoption of the Inter-American Democratic Charter on 11 September 2001. The Charter further enhanced the OAS's monitoring and enforcement powers and defined democracy as

"respect for human rights and fundamental freedoms,
"access to and the exercise of power in accordance with the rule of law,

"the holding of periodic, free, and fair elections based on secret balloting and universal suffrage as an expression of the sovereignty of the people,

"the pluralistic system of political parties and organizations, and

"the separation of powers and independence of the branches of government."

However, outside of the United States and Canada (which joined the OAS in 1990), very few members of the OAS could themselves be said to have institutionalized all of these traits. And some member states were clearly backing away from the little progress they had made since the 1980s, particularly in regard to the rule of law and the separation of powers. Nevertheless, as the OAS responded to the coup attempts and temporary breakdowns that dotted the 1990s and the first decade of the new century (see Chapter 5), it managed to carve out for itself a new and possibly influential role as a genuinely Latin American authority, despite the continued presence of the United States and Canada. The mere threat of OAS disapproval of interruptions of constitutional order would, it was hoped, deter the enemies of democratic consolidation.

For some Latin American leaders, however, no regional organization that not only seated the United States and Canada, but operated out of Washington could possibly retain its credibility, particularly in light of the long history of U.S. domination of the OAS, and of U.S. intervention in Latin America. "Why do we have to go to Washington to discuss our problems?" demanded the president of Ecuador, Rafael Correa, in 2011. Of course, there was nothing new about that affirmation. In 1829, five years after the collapse of Bolívar's plan to join the Latin American republics in a single great confederation, the Liberator himself commented in a letter to a British diplomat that the United States already "seemed destined by providence to plague America with torments in the name of freedom." In subsequent decades, no argument for continental unity ever found greater favor than the supposed protection from the political, military, economic and cultural domination of the United States that a truly Latin America union would furnish.

Except for the Organization of Central American States (ODECA), formed in 1951 by the five countries of Central America to encourage cooperation on a variety of fronts, the first exclusively Latin American regional organizations were trade-oriented and aimed at economic coordination and integration. Emerging in the 1960s, they proliferated from the 1990s onward, as we saw in Chapter 8. Earnest efforts by the United States to convince the Latin Americans to join it in establishing a hemisphere-wide free-trade zone in the 1990s were for the most part greeted with suspicion, as yet another scheme to enrich the United States at the expense of Latin America. Then, as the new century

Table 17.1 Principal Latin American regional organizations by 2011. Source: author.

Name	Purpose	Members (2011)	Headquarters	History
Unión de Naciones Suramericanas (UNASUR). (Union of South American Nations).	Political social, cultural, economic, financial, environmental and infrastructural integration.	All the republics of South America including Guyana and Surinam.	Quito, Ecuador.	Founded 8 December 2004 at Third Meeting of Presidents of South America, Cuzco, Peru as Comunidad Sudamericana de Naciones; name changed to UNASUR in 2007.
Grupo de Río (G-Rio). The Rio Group.	Encourage political and diplomatic cooperation and regional integration.	All nineteen Latin American countries plus Belize, Guyana, Haiti, and Suriname.	Rotates annually.	In 1983, Colombia, Mexico, Panama and Venezuela met on the island of Contadora (Panama) to discuss ways to resolve the armed conflicts in Central America; in 1985, Argentina, Brazil, Peru and Uruguay joined them. Formally constituted as the Rio Group on 18 December 1986.

Cumbre de América Latina y el Caribe sobre Integración y Desarrollo (CALC). Latin American and Caribbean Summit on Integration and Development.	Encourage political, economic, social and cultural integration of Latin America, including the Caribbean region as a necessary condition of economic development.	All thirty-three republics of Latin America and the Caribbean.	Founded 16–17 December 2008, at Salvador de Bahía, Brazil. At its third summit, set for July 2011 in Caracas, CALC was to be renamed the Comunidad de Estados Latinoamericanos y Caribeños (CELAC), Community of Latin American and Caribbean States. The meeting was postponed by the Venezuelan government.
Alianza Bolivariana para los Pueblos de Nuestra América (ALBA). Bolivarian Alliance for the Peoples of Our America.	The political unification of Latin America.	Antigua & Barbuda, Bolivia, Cuba, Dominica, Ecuador, Honduras (until 2009), Nicaragua, St. Vincent & the Grenadines, Venezuela.	Caracas. Founded by governments of Venezuela and Cuba on 14 December 2004 in Havana.

opened, a revival of the Bolivarian passion for something more than regional economic integration, as well as for something exclusively Latin American, seized the region's governments. The newest initiatives claimed to be laying the groundwork, not only for economic union, but for political, cultural, military and diplomatic integration as well. They would aim at coordinating foreign policies and security measures, fix mechanisms for settling territorial disputes, punish governments that strayed from democratic, constitutional norms, and set up forums to debate action on all matters of common interest. The most-cited reason given for their formation was the need to draw the Latin American countries out of the shadow of the United States and the OAS. In doing so, the region would at last achieve the capacity to shape and coordinate policies independently of U.S. interests and in consonance with interests defined exclusively by Latin Americans. Acting as members of an overarching community of nations, the Latin American countries also stood a better chance of influencing events beyond the hemisphere. In this respect, they might overcome the historic disproportion between the region's immense size and population, on the one hand, and its powerlessness on the world stage, on the other – a situation owing partly to the tendency elsewhere in the world to "see" Latin America through the lens of the United States.

Table 17.1 presents the main regional organizations as of 2011. Only one of them embraced all thirty-three republics to the south of the United States and thus stood as a possible rival of the OAS. The Latin American and Caribbean Summit on Integration and Development (CALC – Cumbre de América Latina y el Caribe sobre Integración y Desarrollo) was founded in 2008 – exactly two centuries, it was widely noted, after the breakdown of the Spanish and Portuguese monarchies had unleashed the independence process. By excluding the United States and Canada from membership, and including Cuba (which still refused to participate in the OAS even after its 1962 suspension was lifted in 2009), the CALC stood as the highest expression, so far, of the Bolivarian ideal of unity. At CALC's second meeting in 2010 the members pledged to deepen integration still more, and accordingly renamed itself the Community of Latin American and Caribbean States (CELAC – Comunidad de Estados Latino-americanos y Caribeños). "Only united will Latin Americans be completely independent," President Hugo Chávez of Venezuela told the assembly delegates. More than any other leader, Chávez, true to his often-avowed loyalty to the ideas of Bolívar, had agitated over the previous decade for an exclusively Latin American regional organization. At the Community's founding meeting in Caracas on 2–3 December 2011, all thirty-three heads of state pledged to concentrate on the "political, economic, social and cultural cooperation and integration" of the region.

Even as they began moving away from their historic dependence on the United States, the Latin American countries embraced an opportunity to solidify cultural and linguistic ties with two even older but more venerable over-lords: Spain and Portugal. Spain, "la madre patria" – roughly, "the mother land" – made the first move in the 1980s, when Spain as well as Latin America was moving away from authoritarian rule. It was thus a good time to revive memories of ethnic familyhood, or *hispanidad*. Madrid's democratic government saw the chance to promote human rights, economic development and democracy in America, while building its own trade balance and its American investment portfolio. In their bumpy transition to democracy, the American governments could in turn, it was thought, learn from the Spanish model of peaceful, democratic change through carefully negotiated pacts. At the same time, Spain and Portugal could present themselves to Latin Americans and Europeans alike as a gateway to closer ties between the two regions.

The result was an annual "summit" of heads of state and government that began in 1991 in Mexico, and was anchored in a permanent secretariat in Madrid. The only requirement for admission to these family reunions was that the official language of the country be Spanish or Portuguese, a rule eased somewhat in 2004 with the admission of Andorra (whose official language is Catalan, though Spanish is widely spoken) as the third European member. Unlike other regional groups, the purpose of what was at first called the "Comunidad Iberoamericana" and then later the "Conferencia Iberoamericana" (CI) was not political or economic integration but simply dialogue and common action. Against the background of a formal acknowledgment of their Iberian roots, the members cooperated in a range of programs that extended well beyond cultural affairs, including health services, environmental protection, the transfer of technology, education and security matters.

Among the participants, their Iberian identity was often compared to that of a family, but in this case, "family" was more than a metaphor. Millions of Spaniards and Portuguese had emigrated to America long after the independence wars, and millions of Spanish-Americans had themselves emigrated from one Latin American country to another. Spain even allowed émigrés to Latin America to hold dual citizenship for several generations – more than 1 million of Spain's residents in 2004 were born in Latin America. The Hispanic world was thus crisscrossed by familial ties, and for this reason no institution seemed better suited to symbolize the Iberoamerican family of peoples than the Spanish monarchy. Beginning in 1996, Felipe, the Prince of Asturias, the heir to the Spanish throne, was welcomed at the inaugural ceremony of every elected president of Latin America, with the exception of Honduran President Porfirio Lobo's in 2009, for reasons explained in Chapter 5. Like the taken-for-granted presence of such common cultural resources as language, literature and religion, the regular attendance of Spain's future king at presidential inaugurations stood to fortify the vital Hispanic strand of Latin American identity.

Conclusions

Any challenge to the status of the OAS as the region's primary instrument of collective action would have to overcome a number of obstacles. The first was the sheer number of new multilateral organizations. Beset by overlapping, ambitious and vaguely defined agendas, regional groupings proliferated so rapidly that the movement for integration seemed to be on the verge of a self-defeating fragmentation and instability, as governments withdrew from one group, joined another, or collaborated in the creation of still another. Moreover, significant cultural, linguistic and historical differences persisted across national borders. All of the organizations listed in Table 17.1 included a varying number of non-Hispanic, Caribbean-basin countries that had acquired their independence after the 1950s and shared little historically or culturally with the overwhelmingly dominant Hispanic bloc of countries. Personal and ideological discord posed another obstacle to common action, beyond the signing of high-sounding declarations of intent. For example, all thirty-three members of the Community of Latin American and Caribbean States declared their allegiance to the "protection and promotion of all human rights and democracy." But Communist-ruled Cuba, as well as the left-leaning governments of Bolivia, Ecuador, Nicaragua and Venezuela, defined democracy and human rights in ways clearly not shared by others.

Perhaps the most enduring obstacle was the Latin American governments' historic lack of dexterity in building stable, effective and accountable state institutions capable of matching the liberal constitutional discourse that created them. For example, the founding documents of the December 2011 meeting of the Community of Latin American and Caribbean States repeatedly proclaimed the member nations' commitments to the rule of law, democracy and human rights. Inexplicably, however, they omitted any reference to the onslaught of lawless violence, impunity and official corruption that had been eviscerating their societies for well over a decade. Nor did those same commitments accord with the undiminished ability of some popularly elected presidents to accumulate exceptional power for themselves as they sought to check their opponents and indefinitely defer their departure from office, in bold defiance of constitutional and statutory limitations. In some respects, it seemed, authoritarianism had merely been purged of its longstanding association with direct military rule. Would the task of institutionalization, which had long proved to be so troubling at the national level, not present even greater difficulties on the multilateral plane?

On the other hand, the last three decades produced some momentous departures from longstanding norms that stood to enhance regional solidarity. They included the longest uninterrupted period of constitutional rule and electoral democracy in the history of Latin America, the definitive acceptance of civilian rule by the armed forces almost everywhere, and a newly embedded discourse of human and civil rights. Leading advocates of democratic procedure and human rights could count on wide popular support. On two other fronts, the results of the previous decades seemed promising but somewhat less certain. The first was the pursuit of stable national identities, capable of resolving a congeries of longstanding ethnic, racial, regional, national and class differences. The second was the search for economic justice and the abatement of the region's immense inequalities in material welfare. As we have tried to show throughout this book, neither the sources nor the reach of the momentous changes in these and other arenas over the past three to four decades can be understood apart from the historical continuities that define Latin American civilization.

Sources Consulted

Part I

Balmori, Diana, Stuart F. Voss, and Miles L Wortman. *Notable Family Networks in Latin America*. Chicago: University of Chicago Press, 1984.

Bastien, Joseph W. "South American Indians: Indians of the Modern Andes." In *Encyclopedia of Religion*, ed. Lindsay Jones, 8614–21. Detroit: Thomson Gale, 2005.

Céspedes del Castillo, Guillermo. *América Hispánica (1492–1898)*. Barcelona: Editorial Labor, 1983.

Collier, George Allen. *Basta!: Land and the Zapatista Rebellion in Chiapas*. Oakland: Food First Book, The Institute for Food and Development Policy, 2005.

Ferreira, Francisco, David De Ferranti, Guillermo E. Perry and Michael Walton. *Inequality in Latin America and the Caribbean: Breaking with History?* Washington DC: World Bank, 2004.

Gillin, John. "Ethos Components in Modern Latin American Culture." *American Anthropologist* 57, no. 3 (1955/6): 488–500.

Inglehart, Ronald. *Modernization and Postmodernization: Cultural, Economic, and Political Change in 43 Societies*. Princeton: Princeton University Press, 1997.

Inglehart, Ronald, and Christian Welzel. *Modernization, Cultural Change, and Democracy: The Human Development Sequence*. Cambridge: Cambridge University Press, 2005.

Larrain, Jorge. *Identity and Modernity in Latin America*. Oxford: Blackwell, 2000.

Mecham, J. Lloyd. *Church and State in Latin America: A History of Politico-Ecclesiastical Relations*. Chapel Hill: University of North Carolina Press, 1966 (rev. edn.).

Religions of the World: A Comprehensive Encyclopedia of Beliefs and Practices. Santa Barbara: ABC-CLIO, 2010.

Scholte, Jan Aart. *International Relations of Social Change*. Buckingham: Open University Press, 1993.

Contemporary Latin America: 1970 to the Present, First Edition. Robert H. Holden and Rina Villars.
© 2013 Robert H. Holden and Rina Villars. Published 2013 by Blackwell Publishing Ltd.

Simpson, George. "Caribbean Religions: Afro-Caribbean Religions." In *Encyclopedia of Religion*, ed. Lindsay Jones, 1432–40. Detroit: Thomson Gale, 2005.

Smith, Brian H. *Religious Politics in Latin America, Pentecostal vs. Catholic*. Notre Dame, IN: University of Notre Dame Press, 1998.

Smith, Christian. *Moral, Believing Animals: Human Personhood and Culture*. New York: Oxford University Press, 2003.

South America, Central America, and the Caribbean 2000–: Regional Surveys of the World. London: Europa Publications, 1985–.

United Nations Development Programme. *Human Development Report 2006: Beyond Scarcity: Power, Poverty and the Global Water Crisis*. New York: United Nations Development Programme, 2006.

Part II

Arias, Enrique Desmond. "The Dynamics of Criminal Governance: Networks and Social Order in Rio De Janeiro." *Journal of Latin American Studies*, no. 38 (2006): 293–325.

Bonachea, Ramón L., and Marta San Martín. *The Cuban Insurrection, 1952–1959*. New Brunswick, NJ: Transaction Publishers, 1995.

Eisenstadt, Todd A. "Measuring Electoral Court Failure in Democratizing Mexico." *International Political Science Review / Revue internationale de science politique* 23, no. 1 (2002): 47–68.

Fajnzylber, Pablo, Daniel Lederman and Norman Loayza. *Determinants of Crime Rates in Latin America and the World: An Empirical Assessment*. Washington, DC: World Bank, 1998.

Feitlowitz, Marguerite. *A Lexicon of Terror: Argentina and the Legacies of Torture*. Rev. edn. New York: Oxford University Press, 2011.

Gualdoni, Fernando. "En los últimos meses Lula ha actuado más con el corazón que con la cabeza." *El País*, 15 June 2010.

Gutiérrez Sanín, Francisco. "Criminal Rebels? A Discussion of Civil War and Criminality from the Colombian Experience." *Politics & Society* 32, no. 2 (2004): 257–85.

Gutiérrez Sanín, Francisco. "Telling the Difference: Guerrillas and Paramilitaries in the Colombian War." *Politics & Society* 36, no. 1 (2008): 3–34.

Hammond, John L. "Land Occupations, Violence, and the Politics of Agrarian Reform in Brazil." *Latin American Perspectives* 36, no. 4 (2009): 156–77.

Homicide Trends in the U.S.: Trends in Justifiable Homicide by Police and Citizens. United States, Department of Justice, Bureau of Justice Statistics. http://bjs.ojp.usdoj.gov/content/homicide/tables/justifytab.cfm.

Human Rights Watch. *Lethal Force: Police Violence and Public Security in Rio de Janeiro and São Paulo*. New York: Human Rights Watch, 2009.

International Statistics on Crime and Justice. Helsinki and Vienna: European Institute for Crime Prevention and Control and United Nations Office on Drugs and Crime, 2010.

Llanos, Mariana, and Leiv Marsteintredet, eds. *Presidential Breakdowns in Latin America: Causes and Outcomes of Executive Instability in Developing Democracies*. New York: Palgrave Macmillan, 2010.

Mecham, J. Lloyd. *Church and State in Latin America: A History of Politico-Ecclesiastical Relations*. Rev. edn. Chapel Hill, NC: University of North Carolina Press, 1966.

Mejía Acosta, Andrés, and John Polga-Hecimovich. "Parliamentary Solutions to Presidential Crises in Ecuador." In *Presidential Breakdowns in Latin America: Causes and Outcomes of Executive Instability in Developing Democracies*, ed. Mariana Llanos and Leiv Marsteintredet, 73–90. New York: Palgrave Macmillan, 2010.

The New Authoritarianism in Latin America. Ed. David Collier and Fernando Henrique Cardoso. Princeton, NJ: Princeton University Press, 1979.

Palacios, Marco. *Between Legitimacy and Violence: A History of Colombia, 1875–2002*. Durham, NC: Duke University Press, 2006.

Palmer, David Scott. "Collectively Defending Democracy in the Western Hemisphere." In *Beyond Sovereignty: Collectively Defending Democracy in the Americas*, ed. Tom Farer, 257–76. Baltimore, MD: Johns Hopkins University Press, 1996.

Pérez, Orlando J. "Crime and Support for Coups in Latin America." *Americas Barometer Insights*, no. 32 (2009).

Pérez-Liñán, Aníbal, and Scott Mainwaring. "Latin American Democratization since 1978: Democratic Transitions, Breakdowns, and Erosions." In *The Third Wave of Democratization in Latin America: Advances and Setback*, ed. Scott Mainwaring and Frances Hagopian, 14–62. Cambridge: Cambridge University Press, 2005.

Pinheiro, Paulo Sérgio. "Democratic Governance, Violence, and the (Un)Rule of Law." *Daedalus* 129, no. 2 (2000): 119–44.

Rios, Viridiana, and David A. Shirk. *Drug Violence in Mexico: Data and Analysis through 2010*. San Diego, CA: Trans-Border Institute, Joan B. Kroc School of Peace Studies, University of San Diego, 2011.

Robben, Antonius C. G. M. *Political Violence and Trauma in Argentina*. Philadelphia, PA: University of Pennsylvania Press, 2005.

Rodgers, Dennis, Robert Muggah, and Chris Stevenson. *Gangs of Central America: Causes, Costs, and Interventions*. Geneva: Small Arms Survey, Graduate Institute of International and Development Studies, 2009.

Safford, Frank, and Marco Palacios. *Colombia: Fragmented Land, Divided Society*. New York: Oxford University Press, 2002.

Saranyana, Josep Ignasi. *Cien años de teología en América Latina (1899–2001)*. San José, Costa Rica: Ediciones Promesa, 2004.

Simmons, Cynthia S. "The Political Economy of Land Conflict in the Eastern Brazilian Amazon." *Annals of the Association of American Geographers* 94, no. 1 (2004): 183–206.

Thoumi, Francisco E. "From Drug Lords to Warlords: Illegal Drugs and the 'Unintended' Consequences of Drug Policies in Colombia." In *Government of the Shadows: Parapolitics and Criminal Sovereignty*, ed. Eric Wilson, 205–25. London: Pluto Press, 2009.

Homicide Statistics, Criminal Justice and Public Health Sources – Trends (2003–2008). UNODC crime and criminal justice statistics. United Nations Office on Drugs and Crime. www.unodc.org/unodc/en/data-and-analysis/crimedata.html.

United Nations Office for Drug Control and Crime Prevention. *Global Illicit Drug Trends 2000*. Vienna: United Nations International Drug Control Programme, 2000.

United States, Department of State, "2005 Report on International Religious Freedom." www.state.gov/j/drl/rls/irf/2005.

Wiarda, Howard J., and Harvey F. Kline, eds. *Latin American Politics and Development*. Boulder, CO: Westview Press, 2011.

Wickham-Crowley, Timothy P. *Guerrillas and Revolution in Latin America: A Comparative Study of Insurgents and Regimes since 1956*. Princeton, NJ: Princeton University Press, 1993.

World Bank. *Crime and Violence in Central America*. Washington, DC: World Bank, 2010.

Zimmermann, Matilde. *Sandinista: Carlos Fonseca and the Nicaraguan Revolution*. Durham, NC: Duke University Press, 2000.

Part III

Aja Díaz, Antonio. "La migración desde Cuba." *Aldea Mundo* 11, no. 22 (2006/2007): 7–16.

Alianza Boliviariana para los Pueblos de la Nuestra América/Tratado de Comercio de los, "¿Qué es el alba?" www.alianzabolivariana.org/modules.php?name=Content&pa=showpage&pid=2080.

Brinsek, Jorge Carlos. "Nobel más que merecido." *Diario El Siglo* (Tucumán, Argentina), 13 October 2004.

Bulmer-Thomas, Victor. *The Economic History of Latin America since Independence*. Cambridge; New York: Cambridge University Press, 1994.

Bulmer-Thomas, Victor. "Globalization and the New Economic Model in Latin America." In *The Cambridge Economic History of Latin America: The Long Twentieth Century*, ed. Victor Bulmer-Thomas, John H. Coatsworth and Roberto Cortes Conde, 2, 135–66. Cambridge: Cambridge University Press, 2006.

Close, David. "Undoing Democracy in Nicaragua." In *Undoing Democracy: The Politics of Electoral Caudillismo*, ed. David Close and Kalowatie Deonandan, 1–16. Lanham, MD: Lexington Books, 2004.

Eckstein, Susan. "Remittances and Their Unintended Consequences in Cuba." *World Development* 38, no. 7 (2010): 1047–55.

Economic Commission on Latin America and the Caribbean. *International Migration, Human Rights and Development in Latin America and the Caribbean: Summary and Conclusions*. Santiago, Chile: United Nations, ECLAC, 2006.

Estevadeordal, Antoni, Matthew Shearer and Kati Suominen. "Multilateralizing RTAs in the Americas: State of Play and Ways Forward." Paper given at the Conference on Multilateralising Regionalism; Sponsored and organized by WTO – HEI, coorganized by the Centre for Economic Policy Research (CEPR). Geneva, Switzerland, 2007.

Ferreira, Francisco, David de Ferranti, Guillermo E. Perry and Michael Walton. *Inequality in Latin America and the Caribbean: Breaking with History?* Washington, DC: World Bank, 2004.

Fitzgerald, E. V. K., and Rosemary Thorp. "Introduction: The Acceptance of Economic Doctrine in Latin America." In *Economic Doctrines in Latin America: Origins,*

Embedding and Evolution, ed. Valpy FitzGerald and Rosemary Thorp, 1–22. Basingstoke; New York: Palgrave Macmillan in association with St. Antony's College, Oxford, 2005.

Granados, Jaime, and Rafael Cornejo. "Convergence in the Americas: Some Lessons from the DR-CAFTA Process." *The World Economy* 29, no. 7 (2006): 857–91.

Haber, Stephen. "The Political Economy of Industrialization." In *Cambridge Economic History of Latin America: The Long Twentieth Century*, 537–4, ed. Victor Bulmer-Thomas, John H. Coatsworth and Roberto Cortes Conde, 2. Cambridge: Cambridge University Press, 2006.

Hojman, David E. "Economic Policy and Latin American Culture: Is a Virtuous Circle Possible?" *Journal of Latin American Studies* 31, no. 1 (1999): 167–90.

Huang, Xiaoming. *The Rise and Fall of the East Asian Growth System, 1951–2000: Institutional Competitiveness and Rapid Economic Growth*. London; New York: RoutledgeCurzon, 2005.

International Fund for Agricultural Development. *Sending Money Home: Worldwide Remittance Flows to Developing Countries*. Rome: IFAD, 2007.

International Organization for Migration, and United Nations. *World Migration 2008: Managing Labour Mobility in the Evolving Global Economy*. Geneva: International Organization for Migration: United Nations, 2008, 1561–5502.

Jaramillo, Laura, and Cemile Sancak. "Why Has the Grass Been Greener on One Side of Hispaniola? A Comparative Growth Analysis of the Dominican Republic and Haiti." *IMF Staff Papers* 56, no. 2 (2009): 323–49.

Maddison, Angus. *Growth and Interaction in the World Economy: The Roots of Modernity*. Washington, DC: American Enterprise Institute, 2005.

Martínez Pizarro, Jorge, and Miguel Villa. *International Migration in Latin America and the Caribbean: A Summary View of Trends and Patterns*. New York: United Nations, 2005.

Mesa-Lago, Carmelo. *Market, Socialist, and Mixed Economies: Comparative Policy and Performance: Chile, Cuba, and Costa Rica*. Baltimore: Johns Hopkins University Press, 2000.

Mesa-Lago, Carmelo. "Social and Economic Problems in Cuba during the Crisis and Subsequent Recovery." *CEPAL Review*, no. 86 (2005): 177–99.

Nassar, André Meloni. "Brazil as an Agricultural and Agroenergy Superpower." In *Brazil as an Economic Superpower?: Understanding Brazil's Changing Role in the Global Economy*, ed. Lael Brainard and Leonardo Martinez-Diaz, 55–80. Washington, DC: Brookings Institution Press, 2009.

Orlando Melo, Jorge. "The Drug Trade, Politics and the Economy: The Colombian Experience." In *Latin America and the Multinational Drug Trade*, ed. Elizabeth Joyce and Carlos Malamud, 63–96. Basingstoke: Macmillan, 1998.

Pang, Eul-Soo. *The International Political Economy of Transformation in Argentina, Brazil, and Chile since 1960*. Basingstoke; New York: Palgrave Macmillan, 2002.

Pedraza, Silvia. *Political Disaffection in Cuba's Revolution and Exodus*. New York: Cambridge University Press, 2007.

Pérez, Louis A. *To Die in Cuba: Suicide and Society*. Chapel Hill: University of North Carolina Press, 2005.

Rios-Morales, Ruth. "Structural Weakness in Nicaragua: Hindrances to Economic Growth and Poverty Reduction." In *IIIS Discussion Paper*. Dublin: Institute of International Integration Studies, School of Business Studies, 2006.

Schmidt-Hebbel, Klaus. "Chile's Economic Growth." *Cuadernos de Economía* 43, no. 127 (2006): 5–48.

Solimano, Andrés, and Raimundo Soto. "Economic Growth in Latin America in the Late Twentieth Century: Evidence and Interpretation." In *Vanishing Growth in Latin America: The Late Twentieth Century Experience*, ed. Andrés Solimano, 11–45. Cheltenham: Edward Elgar, 2006.

Thompson, Frank W. "Cuban Economic Performance in Retrospect." *Review of Radical Political Economics*, no. 37 (2005): 311–19.

United Nations Development Programme. *Informe regional sobre desarrollo humano para América Latina y el Caribe 2010*. San José, Costa Rica: Editorama, 2010.

United Nations Economic Commission for Latin America. *Time for Equality: Closing Gaps, Opening Trails*. Santiago, Chile: United Nations ECLAC, 2010. www.eclac.cl.

United States, Department of Justice, National Drug Intelligence Center. *Domestic Cannabis Cultivation Assessment 2009*. Washington, DC, 2009.

United States, Department of Justice, National Drug Intelligence Center. *National Drug Threat Assessment*. Washington, DC, 2010.

Wynia, Gary W. *Argentina: Illusions and Realities*. 2nd edn. New York: Holmes & Meier, 1992.

Zúñiga Herrera, Elena. "International Migration in Latin America and the Caribbean: Contributions from Mexican Meeting." Paper presented at the International Symposium on International Migration and Development. Turin, 2006.

Part IV

Bonilla, Marcelo, and Gilles Cliche. "Creating Synergy between Research on the Social Impact of ICTs and Political Action for Equitable Development." In *Internet and Society in Latin America and the Caribbean*, ed. Marcelo Bonilla and Gilles Cliche, 431–5. Penang, Malaysia: International Development Research Centre, 2004.

Comisión Interamericana de Derechos Humanos. *Democracia y derechos humanos en Venezuela*. Washington, DC: Organización de los Estados Americanos, 2009.

Drori, Gili S., John W. Meyer, Francisco O. Ramirez and Evan Schofer. *Science in the Modern World Polity: Institutionalization and Globalization*. Stanford, CA: Stanford University Press, 2003.

"Estadísticas sobre muertes en el fútbol Argentino." Salvemos al fútbol. www.salvemosalfutbol.com/numerosmuertes.htm.

Favell, Adrian, Miriam Feldblum and Michael Peter Smith. "The Human Face of Global Mobility: A Research Agenda." In *The Human Face of Global Mobility: International Highly Skilled Migration in Europe, North America and the Asia-Pacific*, ed. Michael Peter Smith and Adrian Favell, 1–28. New Brunswick, NJ: Transaction Publishers, 2006.

Figueiredo-Cowen, Maria de. "Latin American Universities, Academic Freedom and Autonomy: A Long-Term Myth?" *Comparative Education* 38, no. 4 (2002): 471–84.

Fox, Elizabeth, and Silvio R. Waisbord. "Latin Politics, Global Media." In *Latin Politics, Global Media*, ed. Elizabeth Fox and Silvio R. Waisbord, 1–21. Austin: University of Texas Press, 2002.

Glick, Thomas F. "Science and Society in Twentieth-Century Latin America." In *The Cambridge History of Latin America: Latin America since 1930; Economy, Society and Politics; Part I: Economy and Society*, ed. Leslie Bethell, 6, 463–536. Cambridge, UK: Cambridge University Press, 1994.

Hill, Derek L. "Latin America Shows Rapid Rise in S&E Articles." *InfoBrief: Science Resources Statistics* 2004/8.

Holm-Nielsen, Lauritz B., Kristian Thorn, José Joaquín Brunner and Jorge Balán. "Regional and International Challenges to Higher Education in Latin America." In *Higher Education in Latin America: The International Dimension*, ed. Hans De Wit, Isabel Christina Jaramillo, Jocelyne Gacel-Ávila and Jane Knight, 39–69. Washington, DC: World Bank, 2005.

Hudson, Rex A., ed. *Brazil: A Country Study*. Washington: U.S. Library of Congress, 1998.

Hughes, Sallie, and Chappell Lawson. "The Barriers to Media Opening in Latin America." *Political Communication*, no. 22 (2005): 9–25.

Inter-American Development Bank. *The Politics of Policies: Economic and Social Progress in Latin America; 2006 Report*. Washington, DC: Inter-American Development Bank, 2005.

International Telecommunication Union. *World Telecommunication/ICT Indicators Database*. Geneva: International Telecommunication Union, 2010.

Jackson, William Vernon. "Libraries in Latin American Society." In *The Library in Society*, ed. A. Robert Rogers and Kathryn McChesney, 200–13. Littleton, CO: Libraries Unlimited, 1984.

Johnson, Randal. "Chilean Cinema in Revolution and Exile." In *Latin American Cinema: Essays on Modernity, Gender and National Identity*, ed. Lisa Shaw and Stephanie Dennison, 397–419. Jefferson, NC: McFarland & Co., 1997.

King, John. "Chilean Cinema in Revolution and Exile." In *Latin American Cinema: Essays on Modernity, Gender and National Identity*, ed. Lisa Shaw and Stephanie Dennison, 397–419. Jefferson, NC: McFarland & Co., 1997.

"Laura Restrepo." *El País* (Madrid), 4 June 2010.

López, Luis Enrique, and Küper Wolfgang. *Intercultural Bilingual Education in Latin America: Balance and Perspectives* Education Report. Np: Deutsche Gesellschaft für Technische Zusammenarbeit, 2002.

Marrero, Adriana, and Ricardo Piñeyrúa. "Fútbol, mística e identidad nacional en el Uruguay moderno." *Bitácora, Suplemento del diario La República* (Montevideo), no. 31 (22 March 2007).

Merquior, G. J. "The Brazilian and the Spanish American Literary Traditions: A Contrastive View." In *Brazilian Literature; Bibliographies*, ed. Roberto González Echevarría and Enrique Pupo-Walker, 3, 363–82. Cambridge: Cambridge University Press, 1996.

Miniwatts Marketing Group. "Internet World Stats." www.internetworldstats.com/am/us.htm.

Organisation for Economic Cooperation and Development. *Literacy Skills for the World of Tomorrow: Further Results from Pisa 2000*. Paris: OECD Publications, 2003.

Pierce, Robert N. *Keeping the Flame: Media and Government in Latin America*. New York: Hastings House, 1979.

Ramírez, Sergio. "I premio internacional de novela alfaguara 1998." www.sergioramirez.org.ni/premio_alfaguara_1998.htm.

Ramírez Gallegos, Jacques Paul. "Fútbol e identidad regional en Ecuador." In *Futbologias: Futbol, identidad y violencia en America Latina*, ed. Pablo Alabarces, 101–21. Buenos Aires: CLACSO, 2003.

Rockwell, Rick. "Status of Media in Mexico." In *Encyclopedia of International Media and Communications*, ed. Donald H. Johnston, 143–8. San Diego: Academic Press, 2003.

Rodríguez, Adolfo, and Suelí Angelica do Amaral. "The Role of University Libraries in Latin America in the Promotion of Democracy and Diversity." In *International Federation of Library Associations General Conference*. Np: Glasgow, 2002.

Ruddle, Kenneth, and Philip Gillette, ed. *Latin American Political Statistics; Supplement to the Statistical Abstract of Latin America*. Los Angeles: Latin American Center, University of California, 1972.

Shapiro, Joseph. "Guatemala." In *Indigenous Peoples, Poverty and Human Development in Latin America*, ed. Gillette Hall and Harry Anthony Patrinos, 106–49. Basingstoke: Palgrave Macmillan, 2006.

Sinclair, John. *Latin American Television: A Global View*. New York: Oxford University Press, 1999.

Subcommittee on the Western Hemisphere, Committee on Foreign Affairs, House of Representatives, U.S. Congress. *Press Freedom in the Americas*. Washington, DC: U.S. Government Printing Office, 2010.

UNESCO. *EFA Global Monitoring Report 2005: Regional Overview, Latin America and the Caribbean*. New York: UNESCO, 2005.

UNESCO. *EFA Global Monitoring Report 2007: Regional Overview, Latin America and the Caribbean*. New York: UNESCO, 2007.

UNESCO. *Science & Technology in Latin America and the Caribbean: Cooperation for Development*. Paris: UNESCO, 1996.

UNESCO. *Statistical Yearbook/Annuaire Statistique 1968*. Paris: UNESCO, 1969.

UNESCO, Regional Office of Education for Latin America and the Caribbean. *Overview of the 20 Years of the Major Project of Education in Latin America and the Caribbean*. Santiago, Chile: UNESCO, 2001.

United Nations. *UN Global E-Government Readiness Report 2005: From E-Government to E-Inclusion*. New York: United Nations Department of Economic and Social Affairs, 2005.

United Nations Development Programme. *Human Development Report 2000: Human Rights and Human Development*. New York: Oxford University Press, 2000.

United Nations Development Programme. *Human Development Report 2006: Beyond Scarcity: Power, Poverty and the Global Water Crisis*. New York: United Nations Development Programme, 2006.

United Nations, Economic Commission for Latin America. *Road Maps toward an Information Society in Latin America and the Caribbean*. Np: United Nations, Economic Commission for Latin America, 2003.

Viatori, Maximilian. "Soccer Nationalism: Ecuador and the World Cup." *City & Society* 20, no. 2 (2008): 275–81.

Volpi, Jorge. "Cruzar la frontera." *Milenio* (Mexico City), 24 October 2009.

Volpi, Jorge. "The Future of Latin American Fiction (Parts II and IV)." *Three Percent* (2009). www.rochester.edu/College/translation/threepercent/index.php?id=2323.

Part V

"Aparición de pareja gay en franja de Piñera generó molestia en la UDI." *Radio Cooperativa* (Santiago de Chile), 21 November 2009.

Arriagada, Irma, ed. *Familias y políticas públicas en América Latina: una historia de desencuentros.* Santiago, Chile: Comisión Económica Para América Latina, 2007.

Aviel, JoAnn Fagot. "Political Participation of Women in Latin America." *Western Political Quarterly* 34, no. 1 (1981): 156–73.

Brown, Stephen. "Democracy and Sexual Difference: The Lesbian and Gay Movement in Argentina." In *The Global Emergence of Gay and Lesbian Politics: National Imprints of a Worldwide Movement*, ed. Barry D. Adam, Jan Willem Duyvendak and André Krouwel, 110–32. Philadelphia: Temple University Press, 1998.

Carlos, Manuel L., and Lois Sellers. "Family, Kinship Structure, and Modernization in Latin America." *Latin American Research Review* 7, no. 2 (1972): 95–124.

Castro Martin, Teresa. "Consensual Unions in Latin America: Persistence of a Dual Nuptiality System." *Journal of Comparative Family Studies* 33, no. 1 (2002): 35–55.

Cooper, Andrew F., and Thomas Legler. "The OAS Democratic Solidarity Paradigm: Questions of Collective and National Leadership." *Latin American Politics and Society* 43, no. 1 (2001): 103–26.

Corrales, Javier. "Gays in Latin America: Is the Closet Half Empty?" *Foreign Policy* (2011). www.foreignpolicy.com/articles/2009/02/17/gays_in_latin_america_is_the_closet_half_empty.

Dabène, Olivier. *The Politics of Regional Integration in Latin America: Theoretical and Comparative Explorations.* New York: Palgrave Macmillan, 2009.

Economic Commission on Latin America and the Caribbean. *Cambios en el perfil de la familia: la experiencia regional.* Santiago, Chile: CEPAL, 1993.

Economic Commission on Latin America and the Caribbean. *Economic Survey of Latin America and the Caribbean.* New York: United Nations, 2004.

Economic Commission on Latin America and the Caribbean. *Economic Survey of Latin America and the Caribbean.* New York: United Nations, 2009.

Economic Commission on Latin America and the Caribbean. *Social Panorama of Latin America*: ECLAC, 2006.

Elizaga, Juan C. "The Participation of Women in the Labor Force of Latin America: Fertility and Other Factors." *International Labour Review* 109, no. 5/6 (1974): 519–38.

Ellis, Frank. "The Determinants of Rural Livelihood Diversification in Developing Countries." *Journal of Agricultural Economics* 51, no. 2 (2000): 289–302.

Jelin, Elizabeth. "Las familias latinoamericanas en el marco de las transformaciones globales." In *Familias y políticas públicas en América Latina: una historia de desencuentros*, ed. Irma Arriagada, 93–124. Santiago, Chile: CEPAL, 2007.

Jelin, Elizabeth, and Ana Rita Díaz-Muñoz. *Major Trends Affecting Families: South America in Perspective*. New York: United Nations, 2003.

John, Robert, Rosalva Resendiz and Linda W. de Vargas. "Beyond Familism?: Familism as Explicit Motive for Eldercare among Mexican American Caregivers." *Journal of Cross-Cultural Gerontology* 12, no. 2 (1997): 145–62.

Jones, M. P. "Gender Quotas, Electoral Laws, and the Election of Women: Evidence from the Latin American Vanguard." *Comparative Political Studies* 42, no. 1 (2008): 56–81.

Jütte, Robert. *Contraception: A History*. Cambridge, UK; Malden, MA: Polity Press, 2008.

Latinobarómetro. *Informe 2009*. Santiago, Chile: Latinobarómetro, 2009.

Levitt, Barry S. "A Desultory Defense of Democracy: OAS Resolution 1080 and the Inter-American Democratic Charter." *Latin American Politics and Society* 48, no. 3 (2006): 93–123.

Observatory: Gender Equality Observatory for Latin America and the Caribbean. Economic Commission on Latin America and the Caribbean. www.eclac.org/oig/adecisiones/default.asp?idioma=IN.

Psacharopoulos, George, and Carolyn Winter. "Women's Employment and Pay in Latin America." *Finance & Development* 29, no. 4 (1992): 14–15.

Rodríguez Vignoli, Jorge. *Unión y cohabitación en América Latina: ¿modernidad, exclusión, diversidad?* Santiago, Chile: CEPAL, 2005.

Rossi, Máximo, and Patricia Triunfo. *Opinión ciudadana sobre el aborto: Uruguay y América Latina*. Montevideo: Universidad de la República, 2010.

Seligson, Mitchell, and Daniel E. Moreno Morales. "Gay in the Americas." *The Americas Quarterly* (2010). www.americasquarterly.org/node/1316#1301.

United Nations. "World Abortion Policies 2007." New York: United Nations, Department of Economic and Social Affairs, Population Division, 2007.

United Nations. "World Abortion Policies 2011." New York: United Nations, Department of Economic and Social Affairs, Population Division, 2011.

Waddington, Hugh, and Rachel Sabates-Wheeler. "How Does Poverty Affect Migration Choice? A Review of Literature." Brighton, UK: University of Sussex, Development Research Centre on Migration, Globalisation and Poverty, 2003.

Index